ALISTAIR MOFFAT was born in Kelso, Scotland.
He is an award-winning writer and historian, and was Director
of the Edinburgh Festival Fringe and is former Rector of the University
of St Andrews. He is founder of Borders Book Festival and
Co-Chairman of The Great Tapestry of Scotland. His many books
include *The Highland Clans* and *Scotland's Forgotten Past*
(also published by Thames & Hudson).

Fai

North Ronaldsay

Rousay

Skara Brae · Isbister
Ring of Brodgar · Maes Howe
Stones of Stenness

ORKNEY

South
Ronaldsay

Shurto

SHETLAND

Mous
Broch

Lewis

Fair Isle

Harris

Hilton of Cadboll

Moray Firth

Beauly Firth

Burghead

Skye

Inverness

Pitglassie

Bennachie

East Aquhorthies

Rum
Eigg

The
Mounth

Balbridie

Muck

Tiree

Coll

Aberlemno

Iona

Mull

Oban

Rannoch
Moor

Loch Tay

Inchtuthil

Cleaven Dyke

Loch Awe

Fendoch

Firth of Tay

The Gask Ridge

Perth

Colonsay

Kilmartin

Callander

Clash Farm

Ochil Hills

Oronsay

Dunadd

Loch
Lomond

Stirling

Marshill

Balfarg

Loch Fyne

Dumbarton Rock

Antonine Wall

Firth of Forth

Jura

Firth of Clyde

Cramond

Coldingham

Islay

Cairnpapple Hill

Lammermuir
Hills

Edin's Hall Broch

Lindisfa

Arran

Upper Clydesdale

Peebles

Newstead

Kelso

Whitmuirhaugh

Crawford

Lintshie
Gutter

Yarrow Valley

Jedburgh

Yeavering

River Aln

H
H

Eskdalemuir

River Cocquet

Hoddom

Burnswark

Hadrian's Wall

Dere Street

0 5 10 15 20 25 kilometres

Dunragit

Carlisle · Stanwix

Whithorn

Solway Firth

ALISTAIR MOFFAT

Before Scotland

A PREHISTORY

With 23 illustrations

For John Goodall

Frontispiece by Jim Lewis

First published in the United Kingdom in 2005 in hardback
under the title *Before Scotland: The Story of Scotland Before History*
by Thames & Hudson Ltd, 181A High Holborn,
London WC1V 7QX

First published in the United States of America in 2005 in hardcover
under the title *Before Scotland: The Story of Scotland Before History*
by Thames & Hudson Inc., 500 Fifth Avenue,
New York, New York 10110

This paperback edition published in 2023

Before Scotland: A Prehistory © 2005, 2009 and 2023
Thames & Hudson Ltd, London
Text © 2005 Alistair Moffat

Cover illustration by Sarah Kirby

British Library Cataloguing-in-Publication Data
A catalogue record for this book is available from the British Library

Library of Congress Control Number 2023932918

ISBN 978-0-500-29725-4

Printed and bound in the UK by CPI (UK) Ltd

MIX
Paper | Supporting
responsible forestry
FSC® C171272

Be the first to know about our new releases,
exclusive content and author events by visiting
thamesandhudson.com
thamesandhudsonusa.com
thamesandhudson.com.au

Contents

Preface

History ought to be a personal matter, something people can feel and intuit as well as read or listen to. We are all part of it, every one of us, even those who believe that only élites make it or feel its hand on their shoulder while being interviewed on television. History is not only something written down in books or taught in drowsy double periods on a Friday afternoon. It is the story of our lives and the only really worthwhile context against which we can see our short time here. Striving to understand it is more than laudable – it is essential. But those who see history as something written by winners, by successful minorities in apparent positions of power, might be forgiven for believing that it has little to do with them, something they can only observe: a procession of kings, queens, laws, wars and battles. These moments of change are not unimportant but they have too long been seen as a framework, the way in which we should order our history. However, a recital of the successive kings of England or Scotland, or both, is a narrow prism through which to observe the past. If a much wider view is taken, their actions and decisions fade into the background, where most of them belong.

If on the other hand we look at our landscape (and townscape) and try to imagine it as a deposit of our history, the role of the mass of ordinary people becomes absolutely central. Continuity becomes as insistent a theme as change. The uncounted generations who worked the land over many millennia made it the shape it is now; and when society became urbanized, the people who built the tenements and laid out the streets undoubtedly had a motive hand in making history. That altered view is an attractive aspect of early history, the time before the names and doings of so-called great people came to be recorded and premiated. Perforce, early history *is* the history of ordinary people in Britain, of the ancestors of almost all of us (as will be shown) and how they made Scotland.

This long period of time, our early history, is the principal focus of this book. In so far as it is possible the story will rewind to the point that any and every sort of record allows, back to the last Ice Age, and to its retreat between 10,000 and 8000 BC. It will end at a much more precise moment in our past, around AD 900, when the name *Alba*, Gaelic for Scotland, began to come into currency.

Over nearly 9,000 years, an immense sweep, the greatest changes in our history took place; a post-glacial landscape was peopled and exploited by hunter-gatherer-fishers, farming transformed the landscape, metal-working was introduced and recognizable versions of Celtic languages were first spoken and sung. And yet this long period is often dismissed under the heading of 'prehistory'. Even though the span of our 8,000 years BC on this island is easily the overwhelming majority of all of our history, it barely seems to qualify as such and is often tucked away out of sustained attention as *pre*-history, not quite the real thing. Because no records, written or otherwise, of datable events exist, or of named individuals, we think of these eight millennia BC as a preliminary, a time shrouded in the subjunctive, hedged about by qualified ignorance and, most dismaying of all, populated by primitives who have little to do with us, the sophisticated, post-imperial, progressive British. Too often we fail to appreciate that the people who made this landscape were in many ways not much different from us. For reasons to be explored below we sometimes see them as unrelated, not as pioneers possessed of tremendous courage, ingenuity and vision, but rather as a race of – at best – child-like innocents constantly raising their bushy eyebrows in surprise.

The Romans were more like it. As we once did, they had an empire to run, and when the Emperor Claudius arrived in Britain in AD 43 to switch on the lights and to civilize the gormless natives out of their woad and tattoos, proper history began. The Romans brought legality, Latin, literacy and a sense of the order of history which began the comforting jingle of dates, events, people, coins, roads, towns, drainage, central heating, all adding up to a fitting prelude to the dignified procession of real history across this sceptred isle, something a lot more suitable than grunting savages scurrying from cave to cave in ragged animal-skins.

When the Romans left in AD 410, they inconsiderately switched off the lights and plunged Britain into the Dark Ages. This was, nonetheless, the period when much of the enduring political shape of Britain was formed, its languages developed and settled, and the Christian church established itself – enormously important processes, but all of them achieved in the shadows of sub-history and supposition.

Surely this is unsatisfactory, a situation in need of a radical shake-up, or at least a change of attitude? But then much of our prehistory is also unsatisfactory. So much will never be known, no matter how enlightened any new approach might be. Because there are no named people, events or dates, it lacks the basic stuff of history – it has no stories to tell, or at least none that we would recognize. That is the central problem which leaves the early history of Britain, and more especially Scotland, so sparse: a scatter of stones and bones. Often the only sign archaeologists can find of the remains of a hunter-gatherer-fisher camp is a discoloration of the subsoil where fires were once lit. Sometimes a ploughman will notice that he has turned up a few flakes of flint to reveal the gossamer trace of another camp.

However, ignorance is no excuse for a collection of attitudes that persist in condemning our prehistoric past as another country, peopled by fleeting shadows whose lives bore no relation, in any sense, to ours. Despite heroic revisionism by historians such as Fernand Braudel, Barry Cunliffe and Norman Davies, our habits of thought about our distant ancestors are still securely coupled to the Victorian locomotive of 'The Idea of Historical Progress'. In the 19th century our history was – and continues to be – seen as the story of man's progress from prehistoric savagery to modern sophistication. To call someone Neanderthal is an insult, and the Americans who threatened to bomb the Taliban of Afghanistan 'back to the Stone Age where they belong' supplied an even more vivid and recent example of an old attitude. The term 'caveman' seems infinitely elastic, consigning thousands of years of our history to a few grunts and the shake of a wooden club at a bare-breasted cavegirl of his choice. And the tattooed, woad-painted hordes of savages who hollered and hurled themselves at the drilled ranks of sober Roman legionaries in AD 43 were only a generation or so removed from the hairy bone-gnawers of popular imagination. Amongst many ironies, there is no doubt that our ancestors revered – even worshipped – the dead and were somehow comforted by the physical presence of their remains. And yet it appears that we now despise these forebears.

Such attitudes are deeply ingrained. We find it very difficult to believe that 10,000 years ago people who looked very like us lived on this island, hunted and gathered their food, had families that they cared for, talked about ideas, about the mundane, gossiped, told funny stories, told lies, sat on a summer riverbank and threw stones into the water, believed in gods and were often worried about the future. And yet all the evidence shows that they were indeed like us, and, further, that they were in fact our direct ancestors. And as such they deserve a history and nothing less.

But how is it possible to overcome these prejudices and convert prehistory into history? How can we make intelligible the aridity of those long stretches of time before history was recorded and written down? How can some of the pungency and detail be traced in the 400 generations who lived here before the Roman historian Tacitus named Calgacus as the first identifiable figure in our history? We might make a start by not disconnecting those early millennia from the latest two, by seeing and accepting continuities, by understanding connections over 500 generations, and particularly by understanding something of the lives and thoughts of those who have lived in the same places for much of that long time. Occasionally this approach will necessitate a link between events and processes separated by millennia, perhaps stretching credibility near to breaking-point. But the recorded experiences of – for example – the 21st-century guga hunters of the isle of Lewis and the life-cycle of the St Kildans seem to have much to say about the unrecorded experiences of hunter-gatherer-fisher bands operating in the same sorts of places eight millennia before.

In a sketchy fashion the opening discussion of the names of Britain and Scotland reveals a continuity of sorts and the shadows of some ideas. Some of our prehistory is still with us, still part of the way we see the world and respond to it. Like Calgacus we live in the north of an island called Britain; like him, some of us speak a Celtic language which still calls this island Alba. Some of us are his descendants, just as he was descended from many generations before – because the historical reality is that he is remote from us only in time.

1

The Painted Islands

Names tell stories. Often they are the oldest words we use and inside them sound the faint echoes of a long and distant past. The names of places sometimes remember who we were and how we used to see the world. They can also chart changes and come to represent the cultural deposit of forgotten victories, political decisions based on the exercise of an ancient power by groups which were dominant at various periods in our history. Scotland, England and Wales all came about in that way. After the accession of Kenneth macAlpin in AD 841, celebrated in school classrooms as the first king of Picts and Scots, and the less renowned consolidations of his grandson, Constantine II, 'Scotland' began slowly to emerge as the name of the country. The victors in the long war for the north were the Scots, and what their kings claimed became Scotland.

In the south, Germanic invaders began a transfer of power in the 4th century AD which culminated in the naming of the country after one particular group, even though many new arrivals were successfully asserting themselves. England is so called after the Angles, who came originally from Angeln, an area of southern Denmark, and the name gained wide currency after 731 with the publication of *The Ecclesiastical History of the English People* by the monkish historian Bede of Jarrow. He dedicated the book 'To the Most Glorious King, Ceolwulf', the ruler of the Anglian kingdom of Northumbria, and called all of the Germanic peoples of the south 'the English'.

Wales is an English word. It means the 'Land of the Foreigners', or more precisely the 'Land of the Romanized Foreigners', and as the frontiers of the English rolled westwards the Welsh found their sense of themselves and their immense past compressed and misnamed. They were the natives, not the foreigners, and they resisted the label of Welsh and Wales for a long time. As late as the 12th century they knew themselves as the *Brythoniaid*, the British.

This is an old name, much older than either England or Scotland, but, like Wales, it was conferred by outsiders. *British* was most probably a description coined by those who lived on the northern coast of what is now France, and how that name made its way through history into contemporary use is both instructive and determinant.

The 'Father of History', the great Greek historian Herodotus, lived and worked a long way from Britain, but he had heard whispers of its existence. Writing in the mid-5th century BC, he noted a place called the 'Tin Islands' which probably lay somewhere in the Northern Sea, if there was one. Ever cautious and scrupulous, Herodotus refused to go further; 'I cannot speak with any certainty,' he said, and left it at that. Tin was vital to the economy of the Greeks and their neighbours, for it was an essential component in the alloy known as bronze, but the Mediterranean area had very few deposits immediately to hand. Along with amber and gold, tin was imported from the far north, probably passing through several pairs of mercantile hands before it reached the forges of southern smiths. As often, the impulse to go beyond existing knowledge and discover more about the world and the extent, as the Greeks saw it, of its farther reaches was driven by commerce, the wish to get rich, the chance to exploit new resources, buy them cheap and sell them dear, and, it must be added, by simple curiosity.

In the 6th and 5th centuries BC Greek merchants and their political backers had gradually expanded westwards, colonizing Sicily, southern Italy and the coasts of Mediterranean France and northern Spain. One of their most successful foundations was Massalia (Massilia), the great port now known as Marseilles. Perched on niches in the façade of the stock exchange in Marseilles are statues of the city's founding fathers: two Greek sailors and merchants, Pytheas and Euthymenes. The latter may have sailed south through the Straits of Gibraltar in search of trade and riches, eventually reaching the coasts of modern Senegal and Ghana. Pytheas was said to have sailed north to the shadowy Northern Sea and the Tin Islands so briefly mentioned by Herodotus. Some time around 320 BC, when safely back home in Massalia, Pytheas sat down to record what he had seen and where he had been. *On the Ocean* is now lost; no copy of the manuscript has come down to us, but the text was widely quoted by both Greek and Roman geographers and historians, and by other more recent writers.

It seems likely that Pytheas began his journey northwards by travelling overland. From the port of Narbo (Narbonne) he may have sailed up the River Aude as far as it would take the draught of a boat, walked or ridden over the watershed to the source of the Garonne and again taken a boat down to what is now Bordeaux. This route may have been well known to Pytheas as the overland stretch of the long journey made by British tin to the Mediterranean in the 4th century BC. From the mouth of the Garonne he could have bought a passage up the coast of the Bay of Biscay and around the great headland of what is now Brittany. Within less than 30 days the Massaliot Greek could have found himself on the south side of the Channel talking to people who had been to Britain.

Because that is what they called it. Like their neighbours across the Channel, the people who lived along that coast spoke a Celtic language, which historians call Gaulish. (Modern Breton is thought to be a survival of Gaulish much strengthened by numerous incoming Britons in the 4th and 5th centuries AD, whose arrival is the reason why the Roman province of Armorica became known as Brittany, or Little Britain.) Since they are now mostly extinct, the Celtic languages of mainland Europe are often forgotten, but it is likely that those living on both sides of the Channel could understand each other reasonably well. It is certainly true that 19th-century Cornish and Breton speakers had little difficulty in being mutually intelligible. And Pytheas obviously had some grasp of Gaulish because he asked a question: 'What are these people called, those who live across the narrow sea to the north?' *Pretannikai* was how he wrote down the reply, 'they are the Pretannikai, and the island is called

Pretannike'. Over the following three centuries this word changed only slightly, to be noted by Julius Caesar as *Britannia*. When the Romans finally organized an invasion in AD 43 and colonized Britannia, the name stuck through nearly 400 years of occupation, and it has stuck in various forms ever since.

'Britain' is so much part of the way we think about the world that we rarely consider that it might mean something, literally. And it might even have something important to say about the beginnings of our own history, about who we were and what we were like. When the Gaulish sailors and merchants who spoke to Pytheas pointed across the sea to Pretannike, they were using a descriptive term. The Celtic-language version is *Pretani* and it means 'the People of the Designs', 'the Painted People', or, much more precisely, 'the People of the Tattoos'. The widespread cultural habit of tattooing the skin with coloured designs and pictures was noted by the Gauls (presumably because it was worthy of comment, being less common amongst themselves) and became a handy label to attach to their neighbours. The great historian of place-names W.J. Watson has coined the more mellifluous 'the Figured Folk', which carries fewer negative overtones. In 55 and 54 BC, when Julius Caesar skirmished in Britain, he saw that the southern tribesmen painted themselves with a blue plant dye known to generations of schoolboys as woad. The southern Pretani may have put on warpaint to confront Caesar's legions but their name is undoubtedly derived from the application of permanent pigment, in tattoos. As with modern designs, blue may indeed have been the predominant colour, and there are many native British plants such as woad itself, bilberries, elderberries and sloes, which can be processed to produce it. Woad was also practical since its chemical properties aided blood coagulation in the event of the wearer's being wounded. It eased the process of being tattooed, for the same reason.

The evidence for the practice of tattooing rather than painting is linguistic and comes from an examination of the word *Pretani*. Celtic languages divide into two groups: modern Welsh, Cornish, Breton and ancient Gaulish are P-Celtic, while modern Irish, Scots and Manx Gaelic are Q-Celtic. The distinction comes mainly from consonant changes. The Welsh talk of *pen* and the Gaels use *ceann* for 'head', *pedwar* and *ceithir* respectively for 'four', *map* for 'son of' compared with *mac*. And it is *Cruthen*, the Q-Celtic version of *Pretani*, which reveals the origins of the description most clearly. The word comes from the root *qrt*, 'to cut'. And since tattooing involves exactly that, piercing the skin and often drawing blood in the process, it seems very likely that this ancient meaning refines the derivation of *Pretani*. Perhaps the Gauls who spoke to Pytheas knew of compatriots who sometimes painted their bodies, but few who went so far as the Pretani and had permanent designs incised by bone or metal needles.

The Roman version, *Britannia*, lasted a long time, and carried the aura of grandeur with it, memories of the might of the Empire. When the Germanic tribes who labelled the Welsh as the 'Romanized Foreigners' came to rule over much of the old territory of the Pretani, their kings aspired to the semi-imperial title of *Bretwalda* or 'Britain-Ruler'. And when in the 12th century Geoffrey of Monmouth gilded the old Celtic tales into the clanking armour of Arthurian fantasy, he called his hero 'the King of the British' and his bestselling book *The History of the Kings of Britain*. In 1586 the antiquarian William Camden even revived the term 'Britannia' and a century later Frances Stuart, Duchess of Richmond and Lennox, was clutching a trident, wearing a Roman helmet and holding a shield, modelling for the emblematic and contradictory figure of Britannia which was to be stamped on copper coinage and which still appears on the 50p piece. There are no tattoos, at least none on display.

Changes in the use of words are seldom events, and while the Welsh refused that name and continued to call themselves the *Brythoniaid*, they also developed an alternative, parallel identity. *Cymru* is the Welsh word for Wales and it comes from *Combrogi*, which means 'fellow country-men'. As early as AD 633, it was used not only for the inhabitants of what is now modern Wales but also included those in southern Scotland and Cumbria who still spoke P-Celtic or early Welsh. These *Cymry* formed what was called *Yr Hen Ogledd*, the Old North, and their contributions to poetry and history were never forgotten in Wales. This use of *Cymry* to incorporate those in southern Scotland sets up a telling distinction. Even though vigorous, notoriously warlike and successful peoples lived to the north of the northern Cymry, they were not included in that community, not seen as fellow countrymen. Like the southern Cymry they resisted the advance of the Germanic invaders who took over much of England and, like the western Cymry, they were successful in halting that advance.

The people known as the Picts are perhaps the greatest mystery of British history, but a strong sense of their separation from the other native peoples of Britain can be found in the attachment of names. The Cymry called the Picts the *Prydyn*, a name derived from *Brython* but with closer similarities to the early form *Pretani*. It may be that the Welsh, the 'fellow countrymen', saw the Picts as more primitive, old-fashioned, a people who had not been exposed to the refining influence of the Roman Empire. Their language was part of the P-Celtic group of Welsh, Cornish and Breton, but it remains obscure, and in the 560s when the Gaelic-speaking St Columba visited the court of the Pictish King Bridei, probably at Castle Urquhart on Loch Ness, he needed an interpreter. Amongst the early peoples of Britain this was an unusual requirement, sufficiently out of the ordinary to be noted by St Adomnan, Columba's biographer. By contrast the Gaelic-speaking monks of Iona appear to have had no difficulty in communicating with the northern Cymry, the people of what became the kingdom of Strathclyde. But they were their near neighbours and contact must have been regular. The Picts were much more distant, dwelling on the eastern coasts, living on the other side of what Adomnan called the *montes dorsi Britannici*, the mountains of the ridge of Britain, the range now known by the Gaelic name of Drumalban. Remote, unfamiliar and pagan, the Picts seemed to be a race apart, even to their contemporaries.

These wisps of difference are clearer in the way that the Irish, the Q-Celts, saw the Picts. In Gaelic *Breatainn* and *Breatainnach* are used for 'Britain' and 'British', a form which dates the absorption of these terms in the period after P- and Q-Celtic diverged, since they appear to be borrowings based on the Roman name of the province of Britannia. But the Gaelic-speaking peoples who lived in Argyll, in their settlement of Dalriada, in the 4th and 5th centuries applied these names only to the early Welsh-speaking kingdoms of the Old North, Strathclyde, Rheged, Gododdin and Manau. The boundary between Dalriada and Strathclyde lay at the head of Loch Lomond and it was known as *Clach nam Breatainn*, the Stone of the Britons, and the great fortress on the Clyde was *Dun Breatainn*, or Dumbarton. To the Irish the Picts were different from the British, and the old labels of *Cruthen* for Pict and *Cruthenech* for Pictish were applied with the consonant change in place. This may recognize that not only were the Picts never part of the Empire but that they also continued to colour their bodies by cutting, tattooing in the old style, the cultural habit noticed by Pytheas' contacts in Gaul, by Caesar and other classical authors.

In AD 297 an anonymous Roman panegyric confirmed the old-fashioned practice when it spoke of *Picti et Hiberni* or 'the Tattooed People and the Irish'. And then in AD 310 another source records 'the Caledonians and other Picts'. As late as about AD 600 the historian Isidore of Seville wrote that the Picts were so called because they tattooed their bodies with needles. The repeated use of this term *Picti* is intended to make a clear distinction between the inhabitants of the northern part of the island known as Britannia and the rest, those who did not, or no longer, tattooed their bodies. The panegyric writer and the others were, it appears, unaware of *Pretani* and the origins of the name of Britannia, but in creating the tautology of 'the Picts of Britannia' they supply useful information. Alongside the fact that the Picts continued to decorate their bodies when others had ceased the practice sits their greatest legacy, their decorative art. What has survived on symbol-stones and elsewhere may tell us something about what their tattoos looked like and what their function might have been. Many different animals appear in Pictish art and they seem to carry great significance.

Early Mediterranean geographers and historians recorded the names of tribes in Britain and particularly in Scotland, several of which were derived directly from the names of animals; the Epidii of Kintyre were the Horse People, the Caereni of Sutherland were the Sheep Folk, and their neighbours, the Lugi, the Raven People (see page 132). These animals may be seen as tribal totems and, while their appearance on Pictish symbol-stones is later and offers no direct correlation, it is possible to make some general points. Even the abstract designs of Z-rods, discs and crescents look like modern tattoos, but the likely habit amongst the Painted People, and what marked them out to observers, was the use of body decoration as a means of showing identity, the marks of belonging – both to a tribe and perhaps to a society or faction within that tribe. Most of the North American Indian tribes developed tattooing and body paint to a high degree of sophistication to convey all manner of messages about their connections and status, and it is likely that the early British and their conservative cousins, the Picts, did something very similar.

Earlier European history offers corroboration. When the Romans first drew up battle lines in their wars with Celtic kings in Europe they were surprised to see some warriors strip off all of their clothes so that they could fight completely naked. Two of the most famous classical sculptures of Celtic warriors show them as nudes – not as an artistic conceit but rather as a documentary reality. *The Dying Gaul* wears nothing but a torc around his neck, and the small bronze figurine of a spearman now in the Staatliche Museen in Berlin has only a helmet, a torc and a leather belt to protect his body. In the 3rd century AD Herodian noted that the north British went about for the most part naked and that they were in the habit of tattooing their bodies with designs and representations of animals.

Many Roman commentators found the practice of nudity in battle inexplicable. Most soldiers wore as much protection as they could without restricting movement, but here were men who, according to Polybius, exhibited 'a proud confidence in themselves'. Modern historians have interpreted this ritual nudity as evidence of an absolute belief in the Celtic Otherworld, a certain destination for a warrior who died in the glory and cleansing gore of the battlefield. But that is to assume the worst, and it sounds like a rationalization from the Roman ranks. There is another explanation. Celtic warriors almost certainly stripped off their tunics and leggings so that their gods, their enemies and their comrades could see their tattooed bodies – because the tattoos were powerful, magical weapons in themselves, what a modern tattooist has described as 'psychic armour'. Not only would the abstract designs, the totem animals and other figures mentioned by Herodian shield a warrior from the blows of his enemies, they would also show the gods who he was, how to direct him in battle, where he came from, and would perhaps reveal some idea of his lineage.

When the Romans were routed by Hannibal at the battle of Cannae in 216 BC, bands of Celtic warriors from northern Italy fought as mercenaries for the Carthaginians. Like the American Indians of the 19th century they were formed into soldiers' societies, one of whose most important links was warpaint, or, in the case of the Celts at Cannae, tattoos of symbols or animals. The Carthaginians were more than surprised to see their allies remove their clothing and charge at the legions with only spear, sword and shield. But the magic worked, for a crushing defeat was inflicted on Rome.

The wider identification of whole peoples in early Britain with animals was a persistent tradition, and it is very likely that their role was protective. The great Pictish symbol-stones of northern and eastern Scotland echo that ancient purpose. Standing proud in the landscape, conspicuous and impressive, they announced the borders of the Raven People, the Sheep Folk or the Horse People. And it may be that when they roared their war-cries and charged into battle, the Picts still showed on their bodies who they were and what power protected them.

After the name was first recorded in AD 297, the far north of Britannia came to be called *Pictavia* or Pictland, a name now out of modern currency but which resonated for most of the first millennium of our era. Just as importantly, these labels attached to them by the Gauls, the Gaels, the Welsh and the Romans also tell us that in many ways the Picts were the last of the British, the *Pretani*, the last to be absorbed and assimilated by incoming historical cultural changes; and that their art and their history are central to any understanding of what Scotland was like before it came to be called Scotland.

Other, earlier names for Scotland are scattered through the pages of the historical record, and there may have been more which were never written down. Some of these ancient names are still to be found in the landscape, and several more in the mouths of Gaelic and Welsh speakers. Writing in the 1st century AD, the Roman historian Pliny the Elder is refreshingly clear about what is perhaps the oldest of all the names:

> Across from this location Britannia Island, famed in Greek and in our own records, lies off to the north-west, separated from Germany, Gaul, Spain and the greatest portion of Europe by a large interval. Albion was its own name when all were called the Britannias.

Not conferred by outsiders but recognized as native to Britain (presumably because Pytheas or another visitor asked the question), *Albion* was a British name for Britain, and one which distinguished it from the other large island in the Britannias, Ireland. In the 2nd century AD the great geographer Ptolemy produced the first surviving map of Britain, noting on it the names of many tribes, towns, rivers, estuaries and headlands, and he confirmed that the larger island was known as Albion and the smaller as Ivernia, a version of *Hibernia*. Much later, Bede of Jarrow made it clear that the old name was passing out of use when he opened his *Ecclesiastical History of the English People* with a sentence owing a little to the Elder Pliny:

> Britain, formerly known as Albion, is an island in the ocean, lying towards the north-west at a considerable distance from the coasts of Germany, Gaul and Spain, which together form the greater part of Europe.

While 'Britain' was beginning to eclipse 'Albion' in the English-speaking world, the Celts of the west developed a double meaning, a usage which reflected political complexities. Irish kings of the early 10th century continued to think of Britain as *Alba* and their bards sang that the Saxons lived there 'as far as the Sea of Icht', meaning the Isle of Wight and the Channel. However, the growing ambitions of the Gaelic-speakers of Argyll presented confusions. In the remarkable 6th/7th-century document known as the *Senchus Fer nAlban*, or 'The Traditions of the Men of Alba', the meaning is absolutely specific, referring to the Gaelic-speaking peoples as the Albans. As a military and naval muster-roll, it listed the number and service owed by all of the houses of the kindreds living in Alba, but the geographical frame was strictly limited to the south-west, to Argyll, Cowal and some of the southern Hebrides. A century later Gaelic kings and their warbands were foraying far from Argyll and one, Aedan macGabrain, fought a losing battle at the head of Lauderdale in the Borders, at a place called Degsastan. Despite his defeat by Aethelfrith, King of Northumbria, Aedan persisted in arrogating to himself the title of *Righ Alban*, King of Alba, by which he appears to mean more than Argyll, but not all of what is now Scotland.

By the time King Kenneth macAlpin had converted Aedan's aspirations into solid reality and made himself King of Picts and Scots the name of Alba was coming to be applied to his new combined kingdom, and its use to describe the whole of Britain was slipping into desuetude, a matter of footnotes and antiquarian curiosity. But as *Alba* itself began to give way to *Scotia* and *Skotland* in the 10th and 11th centuries, the name remained in the Gaelic and Welsh lexicons. The modern equivalents, *Alba* and *Yr Alban*, show no change from their long past.

Some interesting remnants of the old usages persisted in odd corners of the English-speaking world. When in 1579 Sir Francis Drake attempted to colonize what is now California he called it 'New Albion', and he certainly did not have Scotland in mind. The phrase 'Perfidious Albion' was applied to the whole island when Napoleon's recruiting sergeants attempted to whip up anti-British sentiment in 1809, and it now forms part of the vocabulary of suspicion occasionally employed on both shores of the Channel. Later in the 19th century the surge in the popularity of mass participant and spectator sports prompted a casting around for romantic and patriotic names such as West Bromwich Albion, Brighton and Hove Albion in England and Albion Rovers in Scotland.

'Alba' was more than a name to the early peoples of the place others called Britain. Like *Pretani*, it meant something, but the meaning is now difficult to parse. It may simply have stood for 'the Land', in the sense of being the only large land-mass its inhabitants knew. Of course stories about the nature of Alba circulated, were told and retold, and it is likely that there was widespread awareness that Britain was an island; the sense of 'the Land' gains from the notion that its limits were clear, finite and singular.

However, toponymists argue persuasively that *Alba* is closely related to the root word *alb*, 'white', and can be read in names like the Alps. But what were the geographical characteristics that persuaded the natives to regard their island as 'White-Land'? Snow, for one thing – most of the early peoples who travelled any distance did so by boat, and particularly around the busy coasts of the Irish Sea and the North Channel there was snow to be seen in most seasons of the year. Seamarks used for pilotage were often headlands and, from further out to sea, mountains. And in the south-western Highlands, Cumbria and Snowdonia in North Wales there are plenty of snow-covered peaks to be seen and marked by sailors. There are no mountains in what is now southern England, but from South Foreland in Kent to the Isle of Wight there are chalk cliffs which might have struck mariners in a similar way, just as the pale, rocky headlands of the Isle of Purbeck and Lyme Regis further west may have done. And it is important to note that on the shortest crossing of the Channel, between what are now Calais and Dover, the white cliffs appear first, looming out of the sea-mists, so prominent that they at first seem like the shores of a peninsula projecting into the sea, and it is some time before the duller colours of the coastline to the east and west can be made out at all. To the many sailors who plied the European seaboard but never made landfall in Britain, it may indeed have been all they saw of Alba.

The name is inherently comparative, a White-Land as opposed to other sorts, and comparisons were readily available in the shape of low-lying green Ireland to the west and the rolling coastline of northern France to the south. And 'White-Land' appears more plausible alongside modern names for places seen from the sea, such as 'the Land of the Long White Cloud', a translation of the Maori name for New Zealand, or, closer to home, 'the Green Isle' for Ireland or 'the Dark Island' for Benbecula in the Hebrides.

In contrast to these uncertainties, Roman historians had a very specific name for northern Britannia. Lucan, Pliny the Elder, Tacitus and Ptolemy all wrote of *Caledonia*, and the name has shown considerable staying power. Not only has it survived in place-names like Dunkeld, the nearby mountain of Schiehallion and elsewhere, it is also frequently used in the brands of commercial companies as a pungent and meaningful alternative to 'Scotland' or 'Scottish'. And its poetic atmosphere is often found in popular music and poetry. Exiles appear to be homesick more readily for Caledonia.

Caledonia was a very early synonym for what became *Pictavia* or Pictland, or parts of it. In some of the military contexts described by the Romans the Caledonians were the southern Picts centred on Strathmore and the Angus glens, with occasional shifts (mainly by a stroke of Ptolemy's pen) into the Highland massif to the east of the Great Glen. Supplying a little confusion, Tacitus asserts in his account of Agricola's northern campaigns of AD 79 to 83 that Caledonia is the whole of the area beyond the Forth and Clyde isthmus. There was also a Caledonian Forest, known to Pliny, and this played a part in Tacitus' narrative. Each time the Caledonians emerged to skirmish or fight a battle against the legions, they melted away back into the forest, much as the Germans did in the same era of imperial expansion. The Caledonian Forest persisted in the history of the north for a long time. Welsh poetry of the 6th century sends the bard Myrddin fleeing into the Forest of Cellydon to seek refuge and solitude. Myrddin later transmogrified into the wizard Merlin.

Caled appears to be the basis of the name *Caledonia* and its meaning is clear, even if its application is not. It meant 'hard' in P-Celtic or early Welsh, and since the first recorded use was in *Caledonii*, the tribe, it may be that it referred to them, 'the Hard Men'. However banal or ironic this may sound as a name for a group of aggressive Scotsmen, it is by no means unlikely. To the north Ptolemy notes the tribal name *Smertae*, which comes from the same root as the English word 'smeared', and it described either a religious or military (or both) practice of smearing the body with blood. This was done possibly for religious purposes, possibly before battle, possibly both. The *Smertae* might have made the Hard Men appear tame.

Alternatively the name of Caledonia might have derived from the land inhabited by the Hard Men. The Highland mountains, corries and high glens are often bare, rocky and bleak, and *caled* might have been the root word of something like 'Rock-Land', rather in the same way that part of Knoydart is known as 'the Rough Bounds'.

All of these names are important to the beginnings of our history. Often they are all we have to supply a sense of how the early peoples of Scotland and Britain saw themselves and the places where they passed their lives. The Tattooed People of the White-Land became the Fellow Countrymen who refused to call themselves the Romanized Foreigners. Some who lived in Rock-Land continued to be seen as the Figured Folk and they wore their allegiances on their bodies. In some ways the assimilation and gradual surrender of these colourful names to the more prosaic *Scotland* is to be mourned. But their existence, and that of many more like them, and their persistence add up to a point at which to begin, the frame of a story, the story of Scotland before Scotland.

2

The Ice Domes

Time and its measurement govern our lives. We save it and spend it, but our ability to grasp its range of meanings is very limited. Tiny fractions of time happen beyond our ability to conceive or imagine them. Even though scientists and engineers have developed the technology to measure a nanosecond, none of us has any real sense of the passing of a thousand-millionth of a second. It is simply inconceivable. And it may well be that our universe was created in just such an instant.

We also have great difficulties with very long periods of time. Using what is called radiometric dating (a technique that emerged from research into the behaviour of radioactivity), geologists now estimate that the nanosecond of creation took place about four and a half billion years ago. Expressed in numerals, that makes the Earth 4,500,000,000 years old – a length of time that passeth all understanding.

Over the span of this immense period, life began, flourished for millions of years, was almost extinguished, sometimes left fossil traces embedded in the earth's crust, and then, millions of years after the extinction event, flourished again in some form or other. Only the dinosaurs have left a mark on the popular consciousness, and even then few people could take even a wild guess at what points in our unimaginable past they roamed the earth. Comic strips, films and cartoons have synthesized some of this distant history and persuaded many of us that human beings co-existed with the *Tyrannosaurus rex* and the Pterodactyl, living fragile lives of constant terror as volcanoes spewed out molten lava and monsters prowled outside the cave. The reality is of course different and less dramatic, a story of processes rather than events. Evidence found in 2002 in Chad, in central Africa, suggests that humans, or hominids with a large brain which could walk upright, first appeared around seven million years ago. This latest ancestor has been given the usual Latin tag and is known as *Sahelanthropus tchadensis*. Archaeologists have uncovered many subsequent mutations and developments, but there is general agreement that *Homo sapiens*, people who resembled us, were living in southern and eastern Africa 100,000 years ago. The earliest evidence for the presence of *Homo sapiens* in Britain was found in Kent's Cavern in Devon and the dates of occupation begin to approach our understanding. People like us were living in the cavern around 29,000 BC. Other finds of roughly the same date in South Wales confirm a marginal presence at around the same time, one which was all but erased in the ensuing millennia.

Cataclysm

Of all the extinction events to punctuate the long history of the earth, the end of the Permian period, about 251 million years ago, appears to have been the most cataclysmic, a near total wipe-out of all life on the planet. Some commentators have called it 'the Great Dying'. According to Professor Michael Benton (author of *When Life Nearly Died*) the fossil record was almost stopped dead in its tracks. Coral reefs decayed, plants became extinct and 90 per cent of all the earth's species were wiped out. What happened? A meteorite? A shift in the planet's orbit around the sun? Professor Benton believes that a series of immense volcanic eruptions in Siberia brought about the abrupt end of the Permian age. The eruptions were so violent and sustained that they warmed up the atmosphere of the earth by 6°C. Apparently this was sufficient to bring about a state of near-sterility. It is salutary to note that 6°C is the upper limit estimated by the United Nations for the extent of global warming by the year AD 2100.

More recently, scientists have discovered a very large crater in the Pacific Ocean, off the north-west coast of Australia. While drilling in search of oil, a commercial company brought to the surface a series of cores which were found to contain meteorite fragments, shocked quartz and other evidence of a huge impact. Similar samples, probably related to what has become known as the Bedout Crater, have been picked up over an immense area, from India to Antarctica, and scattered across Australia itself. Luann Becker of the University of California at Santa Barbara has analysed the cores from the Bedout Crater and believes that the Great Dying may have been the immediate consequence of a deadly combination of factors – widespread volcanic activity in Siberia and a massive meteor impact in the Pacific.

The more hospitable periods in the long history of the earth were interrupted by episodes that repeatedly wiped out entire ecosystems, erasing them from the surface of much of the planet. Ice ages, which had this effect, have taken place throughout the 4.5 billion years of our history, and at least 20 occurred in the last 2.5 million years, comfortably within the continuum of human experience.

Some time around 24,000 BC, the weather was once again deteriorating as another glacial episode gathered momentum. The mean annual temperature in Britain began to fall, winter snow persisted all year round on high ground, vegetation was gradually reduced and the animals that depended on it retreated southwards. They were followed by the people who in turn depended on them.

The weather was growing colder because the earth had begun to wobble. As it orbits on its own axis on its yearly journey around the sun, the planet can wobble like a child's spinning top slowing down. Over a long period this process alters the angle of the earth's tilt and radically affects the amount and intensity of sunlight striking the northern hemisphere. And this initiates a vicious cycle. As lower temperatures allow more and more snow to accumulate over the North Pole and on high ground, the snow both reflects the sun's rays back into space and insulates the ice it covers, encouraging it to thicken and spread further south. The more snow and ice there is on the earth's surface the more the area covered expands.

Rock of ages

James Ussher, Archbishop of Armagh in Ireland until 1656, took a direct, no-nonsense approach to the important question of the age of the earth. It all started at 'the sensible hour of 9 am' on 23 October 4004 BC. Using a combination of scriptural authority and a fossil he believed to be an ear of corn (it was probably part of a starfish or a sea-urchin), Ussher did a simple calculation and came up with a date sufficiently far back for most learned people to accept. By the middle of the 18th century estimates had stretched out to 75,000 years. In late-19th-century Glasgow, William Thomson, later Lord Kelvin, came up with something altogether more expansive – a date around 98 million years ago, but allowing plenty of elbow room for error with a lower limit of 20 million and an upper of 400 million. Charles Darwin was anxious that these elastic timescales prove long enough to allow the process of natural selection to be played out. In 1896 the discovery of radioactivity tore up all the earlier calculations. By measuring the rate at which certain elements decayed, it became possible to be more precise. And the immense number of 4.5 billion was accepted, although no time of day has yet been put forward.

This vicious cycle is accentuated, may even be initiated, by variations in the shape of the earth's orbit around the sun. When this is approximately circular the seasons fall into a regular pattern recognizable to us today. But when the orbit becomes more elliptical, the earth spins a little further from the sun at the extreme ends of the ellipse, and, sustained by lower mean temperatures over a long period, the ice begins to form, and does not retreat in the summertime.

Volcanic activity may also have played a role in the coming of the ice ages. Some 73,500 years ago Mount Toba in Sumatra blew itself apart in an enormous eruption, ejecting a mass of dust and debris which had the immediate effect of screening out the sun's rays for two or three years. Average summer temperatures cooled by about 12 °C. Such a huge eruption also sent up enough sulphur to create a vast aerosol of sulphuric acid in the outer atmosphere, scattering the sun's rays and bringing down temperatures even further.

Time lords

No one is absolutely certain what time it is. Since 1967, when atomic clocks took over from the motion of the earth as the most accurate way of keeping time (they count the steady shaking of atoms), things have become very confusing. Three other systems for measuring time have been adopted. In addition to what is known as Co-ordinated Universal Time (based on the atomic clock), there is also International Atomic Time (used for scientific experiments), Satellite Global Positioning System or GPS (used for navigation) and Greenwich Mean Time (enshrined in legislation and the basis of the world's time zones). All of these systems show slightly different times. At present (whenever that is) the differences are measured only in seconds, but if there is no rationalization, these could stretch into minutes and hours.

At its height, around 16,000 BC, the last Ice Age engulfed all of what is now Scotland, reaching as far south as Wales and the English Midlands. And on its way the ice erased all traces of a human presence before that date. Drought also drove people southwards. When much of the earth's water is tied up in ice-sheets, there can be little precipitation and consequently too little rain to sustain life.

But the last Ice Age also brought the beginnings of our history within the range of comprehension. Because we have detailed knowledge of it and can sometimes see the physical remains of our activities over the last two millennia and even before, it is possible, just, to imagine the span of time since the ice began to retreat some time around 11,000 BC. It may be little more than a nanosecond in the immense life of the earth but it is a period which encompasses as much history as most of us can cope with. And it supplies this narrative with a place and a time to begin.

~~~

Everyone talks about the weather, every day. It is part of our discourse, a subject embedded in politenesses such as 'Grand day!' or 'Lovely morning!' and so on. Because the weather in Britain appears to be particularly changeable (any period of consistency is in itself something to be remarked upon), we are perhaps more given to extended discussions of its trends. Many people are able to count back over recent summers and winters to produce a reasonably reliable appraisal of the previous ten or even twenty years. There is no reason to believe that these habits of memory are new, and there are many reasons to persuade us of their very great antiquity. In 24,000 BC the people who lived in Britain would have had as much, if not even more, to say to each other about the sort of morning it was.

But unlike our general, highly partial and romantic view that the summers of childhood and youth were always sunny and warm, the longer-term memories and detailed appreciation of generations of prehistoric peoples must have been a great deal more reliable. They had to be. The weather was much more important to them than it is to us. Their daily lives directly depended on it. In 24,000 BC the weather was most certainly worsening – and over a relatively short period, probably within the cumulative memory of several generations. For people who hunted animals, gathered wild plants and fished in the seas and rivers, sensitivity to the vicissitudes of climate was undoubtedly sharper than ours. Over only a handful of years the domino effect of changes in the weather on vegetation, the birds and animals which depended on it and the people whose livelihoods in turn depended on exploiting the entire ecosystem would have been observable and a matter for more than polite exchange 26,000 years ago. From one winter to the next, ice was spreading quickly. As the weather grew colder, the summer sun did not melt the ice and the mountain-tops stayed white all year. The grip of the ice tightened; frozen rivers formed and ground their way out of corries and down into the high valleys. There was less rain, snow and sleet, and chill and constant winds began to blow. Plant cover shrank back to lower altitudes, birds and animals failed to follow their ancient migratory journeys and many were no longer seen so far north. And the ice began to creep southwards, chasing people before it.

BC/AD

To make the sequence of events as clear as possible in his *Ecclesiastical History of the English People*, the Venerable Bede adopted the AD system of dating, some time in AD 731. It was invented by Dionysius Exiguus (died AD 550) who worked out AD 1 as the year in which Christ was both conceived and born. There is nothing to show that he was correct in his workings, and some evidence that he got it wrong. According to the gospel writers, Christ may have been born in the last year of the reign of King Herod the Great, that is, 4 BC; or in the year of the first Roman census of Judaea, which was AD 6 to 7. It may be that we are all living in the wrong year. Bede wrote *On the Reckoning of Time* in AD 725 to establish the AD system, to work out a table of dates for Easter up to 1063, and to sort out a chronology of world history up to the reign of his contemporary, Leo the Isaurian, Emperor of Rome in the East at Constantinople.

AD implies BC, and aside from the need to count backwards, it is a method of dating which is well understood and widely accepted. New methods of reckoning generally only serve to complicate a simple picture. Those who wished to replace Bede's AD and BC with BP, meaning 'Before the Present', quickly realized that the dates of events in the past would constantly have to change as the dates of the present advanced. And so the end of the Present Era was fixed at 1950, making it the 'Present Era', but a while ago. And those non-Christians who refuse to accept the existence of a 'dominus' often prefer BCE or Before the Common Era – just to add further complication.

In prehistoriography there often appears to be much confusion about dating. Where this is due to the uncertain nature of the evidence, it is easily understandable and of course acceptable. Where confusion arises because of the use of BCE instead of BC, for example, it verges on the self-inflicted.

Much more recent historical experience offers some notion of how these ancient changes impacted, and perhaps recalls the effects of the encroaching ice. During one of the more severe periods of the Little Ice Age (from approximately AD 1350 to 1900) the Norse settlements in eastern and western Greenland were abandoned because of worsening weather. The mean annual temperature quickly dropped by 2°C and the increasing severity of winter storms and the proliferation of sea-ice made navigation and fishing very much more difficult. When archaeologists came upon Norse cemeteries in Greenland and exhumed burials dug before 1350, they found bodies showing normal signs of decay, with tree roots piercing their clothing. But after that date, bodies were discovered in much better states of preservation because of the relatively sudden arrival of permafrost. In the Alps, on the slopes of the highest mountain, Mont Blanc, glaciers were advancing rapidly, on both the French and Italian sides, and threatening the town of Chamonix. By 1653 the ice had edged much closer, and in desperation the local people carried the statue of their patron saint out of the parish church and up the mountainside. With the blessings of the priest and the prayers of his congregation, it was placed at the foot of the glacier, facing the great river of ice. And it worked. St Ignatius stopped the glacial juggernaut in its grinding tracks, and by his intercession Chamonix was saved.

As the temperatures dropped in the centuries around 24,000 BC, earlier Europeans no doubt used what magic they had to hand to halt the creep of the ice. But unlike the townspeople of Chamonix, they were forced to retreat if they could. Huge ice-domes were forming in the far north. Hemispherical and symmetrical in shape, and often building up around land mountains like Mont Blanc, the domes could be several kilometres thick. As the high focal points in the ice-sheets, they attracted most of the precipitation, be it rain, sleet or snow. And they gave rise to constant, severe winds resulting from the extremely cold air that swirled at the rounded summits of the domes and flowed downwards to create areas of low pressure on the fringes of the ice-sheets, the sort of bad weather that drove the Norse settlers out of Greenland. Up on the domes it could be very different. The downward flow of wind produced long periods of anti-cyclone and the clear, sunny skies accompanying it.

When the skies darkened and there was precipitation, ice formed on the dome summits. As it solidified, it flowed radially downwards, forming the symmetrical dome-shape and developing into slow-moving frozen rivers or glaciers. Modern equivalents in Antarctica have been measured up to 2 km/1 mile thick, 30 km/20 miles wide and moving at a speed of 1 km/½ mile a year. Gravity caused the ice to move, the tremendous accumulating weight of the domes pushing the glaciers downhill and ultimately towards the edges of the massive ice-sheets. Invisible under the frozen rivers was a narrow slick of meltwater where the ice met the land, and it acted as a lubricant, allowing the seemingly solid mass to inch forward and downward. The ice itself was not simply a body of frozen water, like an ice-cube from the freezer. It often carried a great deal of debris locked inside: boulders, gravel, silt, plant matter, even artefacts, and, famously, people like Ötzi, the prehistoric hunter dating from around 3300 BC, found in a melting glacier in the Alps in 1991.

The ice-sheet may have been a sterile landscape, but it was not featureless. Valleys, plateaux and ranges of hills gave definition and variety, and there is some evidence that at one stage during the ice age Scotland's highest mountains poked up through the frozen crust.

As the winds roared around the greatest European ice-dome, which had formed over what is now Sweden (on an area north of Stockholm), the last Ice Age reached its maximum extent around 16,000 BC. Average annual temperatures had cooled by 5 to 10°C and more than one third of the surface of the planet was frozen, most of it in the northern hemisphere. Sea levels had dropped dramatically all over the earth, in places by as much as 120 m/400 ft. Not only had the ice-winds created long periods of clear weather, but the ice had also taken a great deal of water out of the cycle of evaporation and precipitation.

The tremendous weight of the ice-sheets affected all of the earth's crust in a surprising fashion. Where the domes were thickest, it depressed the land to the greatest extent – but it also pushed up those areas which remained ice-free, like a large man sitting on one half of a long cushion. Parts of northern Sweden were 800 m/875 yds lower than at present, and are still rebounding since the ice disappeared; areas of what is now the North Sea were much higher and have fallen since the weight was lifted off Scandinavia. This seesaw effect continued long after the retreat of the ice. For example, Dunbar in East Lothian is still rising at a rate of 55 mm/2 ins a year.

If the variations in the earth's tilt and orbit around the sun stimulated the beginnings of the ice, their return into kilter probably brought about its retreat. The drama began at the edges. As temperatures rose, the sea slowly filled and what is known as the thermohaline effect strengthened. In the North Atlantic, cold, salty water flowed southwards at the bottom of the ocean, causing warmer and less dense water from the south to flow northwards near the surface. The Gulf Stream is part of this phenomenon. As the weather improved after 16,000 BC, the thermohaline effect made the edges of the northern ice-sheet very unstable, breaking off huge icebergs and gradually melting them as they drifted south.

On the land the movement of retreating (and advancing) glaciers and the torrents of meltwater from the shrinking ice-sheets scoured out Scotland's landscape and gave it much of its character. In the far north, especially noticeable on the islands of Lewis, Harris and the Uists, is an ice-effect known by its Gaelic name of *Cnocan agus Lochain*, or hillocks and small lochs. Perhaps thousands of large rock pools, filled with brown, peaty water, pattern the islands' landscape, and are mirrored by a scatter of small hills that look as though they were scooped out of the lochans. Further south, in English-speaking Scotland, the pools are called *pots*. Both lochans and pots were made by relatively fast-moving glaciers sliding on a film of warmer water.

On the mainland there are extensive areas of high ridges and U-shaped trough formations, almost all of them in the Highlands. Between high and sometimes jagged strings of mountains, which probably jutted above the ice-sheets, glaciers scraped through the glens and scooped out these corries. In the Midland Valley, stretching from the

Mounth area, south of Aberdeen, down to Glasgow, with its southern boundary running from Girvan to Eyemouth on the Berwickshire coast, the effects of glaciation were less spectacular. Softer sedimentary rocks were further ground down, but from Dumbarton Rock to Edinburgh Castle, the Bass Rock and North Berwick Law beyond it, several singular plugs of igneous rock were left to stand out in the landscape.

The glaciers and the meltwater torrents did more than scour; they distributed deposits of silt, sand and clay, which have developed over millennia into some of the richest farmland in Britain. In the Southern Uplands the ice left a series of ranges of folded, rolling hills and the broad and fertile river valleys of the Tweed, Teviot, Nith, Annan and Clyde. Not so dramatic as the precipitous mountains and glens of the Highlands or as low-lying as much of the Midland Valley, the Southern Uplands nevertheless follow the same north-east to south-west orientation of all Scotland's major geographical features.

The ice made Scotland the shape it is, and that shape moulded all of our history. Glaciers carved routes through the western ranges at Glencoe and Glen Shiel; the Clyde, Forth and Tay estuaries allowed deep penetration into the Midland Valley; the great rivers flowing out of the Southern Uplands watered the landscape and encouraged access deep into the interior. But too often in Scotland our gaze is directed to the landward. Until the 19th century the easiest and fastest way to travel around these islands was by water, and Scotland's rivers and coastal seaways, especially in the west where the Atlantic shore is deeply incised, were the key to understanding the movement of people and ideas. Once the ice retreated, it is very likely that the first pioneers to venture north came in boats.

But that is to anticipate events, and by some distance. Once Scotland was ice-free, by about 11,000 BC, the most important pioneer was vegetation. As the ice shrank back northwards in the cold and arid conditions prevailing between 12,500 and 11,000 BC, it was followed by tundra, areas of underlying permafrost which greened over in the warmer temperatures of short summers. As happens now on the edges of the Arctic, animals such as the caribou and reindeer moved north to enjoy the fresh summer grazing. These are flight and herd animals which feel safe in wide open spaces where predators can be seen at a distance. Prehistoric reindeer bones have been found in caves in the north of Scotland, and their presence recalls the time of the tundra. Herds of grazing animals brought the seeds of gradual change inside them. Their droppings distributed those seeds and nurtured them into shoots where they fell. The wind blew spores northwards and floated them down on to the warming grasslands. A green frontier slowly edged its way up Scotland, sometimes advancing quickly, at other times patchily, inhibited by the terrain.

As the climate warmed up rapidly after 11,500 BC, trees followed the retreat of the permafrost. Dwarf willow was first, in sheltered, damp places, then came aspen, birch, pine, hazel, elm, oak and finally lime. As they grew, and the leaves of a thousand autumns fell and enriched the soil, Scotland became a vast, green wildwood whose canopy reached far up the slopes of the highest mountains. Deciduous trees grew as high as 750 m/2,500 ft above sea level, and only in the Highland ranges would the forest fail to carpet the whole landscape.

In this period Britain experienced the Climatic Optimum. Until about 3200 BC average temperatures were two to three degrees warmer than they are now, and this encouraged the rapid spread and growth of very tall trees in places we now think of as bleak and barren. Dense woodland covered the Western Isles, Rannoch Moor and the Southern Uplands from the highest hills right down to the riverbank and seashore. It was like a temperate rain forest, a place without tracks, filled with dense undergrowth where the canopy permitted. Much of this wildwood would have been dark and shaded at ground level, like modern jungle. Under the thick layers of Scotland's peat bogs, the remains of this ancient forest can be found. Local people digging their peats for fuel have come across the huge, bleached tree-stumps of the wildwood preserved in the acidic, anaerobic ground. Scientists have dated these and found that many are millennia old. Few areas of open grassland interrupted the forest, and these mostly occurred at its margins, at estuaries, river flood-plains and rocky sites of various sorts.

The wildwood forced the extinction of the plains animals, the reindeer, the giant Irish deer and the arctic fox. With the trees came animals which nested, burrowed and browsed in their shade, living off a richness of insects, seeds, leaves, grasses, roots and shoots. The aurochs, wild cattle with huge hornspreads, thrashed through the undergrowth; red and roe deer, wild boar and elk flitted amongst its shadows. Smaller animals – the marten, polecat and squirrel – may have arrived first, while the rivers and streams sheltered fish, waterfowl, otters and beavers. As ever, they were closely followed by their predators, wolves, lynxes and bears, and, principal amongst them, the first human beings to arrive in Scotland since the ice-sheets began to grip the land 12,000 years before.

Mammoth molecules

'Jurassic Park meets Dolly the Sheep' sounds like a pitch to a movie studio, but it is in fact a serious scientific proposition from a group of Japanese geneticists. Having procured samples of bone marrow, muscle and skin from the frozen remains of a woolly mammoth recently dug out of the Siberian permafrost, they intend to use an egg from an elephant to clone the extinct species back into existence. If successful, the experiment would recreate an animal not seen since the period immediately following the last Ice Age. But perhaps the most important question of all has less to do with helices of DNA and more with the fate of such a creature in a rapidly warming world. Where could it live?

In the late summer of 1993 a party of archaeology students were field-walking at the village of Bridgend on the island of Islay, near the Bowmore Distillery. Systematically quartering a newly ploughed field, they were looking for flints and other artefacts. In the best conditions – after rain and under a bright (but not dazzling) sky – a practised eye can often spot these small items glinting on the surface. One of the students stopped suddenly, picked up a flint arrowhead and put it in a bag with the other finds. When these were closely examined a few days later, a fascinating discovery came to light. The arrowhead turned out to be datable to about 10,800 BC, at least two millennia earlier than the earliest evidence of a human presence in Scotland after the end of the last Ice Age.

Detailed interpretation of the local geology suggests that the westernmost point of modern Islay, known as the Rinns, was free of ice much earlier than the rest of the island or neighbouring Jura and the mainland beyond. In fact the Rinns may have escaped glaciation entirely. And it is likely that as the land thawed, a sea journey would have been possible up the western coastline to an area where plant and animal regeneration was more advanced. The arrowhead found at Bridgend was probably dropped by a member of a summer expedition of pioneers from the south, a band who beached their canoes on the shores of the sea-loch Indaal and went inland to explore. Other arrowheads of a similar sort have been found in nearby Tiree and Jura, and in Orkney. These, however, were damaged, badly recorded and more difficult to date. But they do represent the first faint traces of the return of men and women to the deserted landscapes of the north, locked for so long in the sterile grip of the ice.

By 10,000 BC annual temperatures had risen close to modern norms, and it is likely that more parties of pioneers penetrated post-glacial Scotland, edging their way up the coastline, probing the mouths of rivers, living in temporary shelters and moving on after only a few days. But it proved to be a false summer. Around 9400 BC the weather once again began to worsen, storms blew and the cold crept back over the face of the land. What geographers have labelled 'the Loch Lomond Stadial', and historians call 'the Cold Snap', was beginning. Within only a few centuries the ice had reclaimed much of the western Highlands of Scotland, covering the ranges of what St Adomnan called 'the Mountains of the Back of Britain' and the Gaels know as *Drumalban*. The great jagged peaks along the spine of Britain may again have jutted through the ice-crust and the sea have frozen once more around the Firth of Lorne, Loch Fyne and parts of the Clyde estuary. Small valley glaciers were to be found as far south as Broad Law, Hart Fell and White Coomb in the Southern Uplands.

The Cold Snap was sufficiently severe to bring pioneering settlement to an end and chase almost all evidence of it out of Scotland. The new ice-dome was centred over Rannoch Moor and the north of Loch Lomond, and once again the ice was thickest where it was highest. Around 8000 BC the ice-sheets groaned and cracked when a rapid thaw began, and the land underneath rebounded, in some places by as much as 12–14 m/39–46 ft. Debris was distributed over a wide area. Glacial moraines were bulldozed and dumped by the frozen rivers and a landscape of humped, rocky little knobs would make future cultivation in the low-lying areas of Drumalban impossible, leaving ground suited only for rough grazing and hunting. The Scotland which emerged from under the ice of the Cold Snap and its meltwater torrents was beginning to take its modern shape – but not before more buffeting from the weather and the earth's volatile crust.

In a simple exchange the sea level rose as the ice on the western ranges melted, but the land also rose with it, rebounding as it was relieved of the tremendous weight of the dome. Around Scotland's coastline, especially near Oban, close to the centre of the ice-sheet, there are raised beaches and cliffs which remember an ancient shoreline. And elsewhere undersea shelves exist which were once dry land. The pattern of change was not uniform and in some places offers a picture of dazzling complexity. At first the land rebounded faster than sea levels rose, creating the raised shorelines. And then, by about 5500 BC, the relative position was reversed. The Firths of Forth and Tay reached so far inland that northern Scotland remained only just connected to Britain. The sea lapped a coast near modern Aberfoyle, now nearly 65 km/40 miles from a beach, the Tay estuary inundated Strathearn as far as Crieff and the Clyde broke through to Loch Lomond. The land-bridge shrank to a slim waist of only 12 km/8 miles in width. And the long fingers of the firths were deep. Ancient whalebones have been dug out of the clay soils of landlocked places such as Stirling and Gartmore, south of Aberfoyle. But as the sea fell back to its present levels, it left a valuable legacy, laying down deposits of rich, silty soil to create the farmlands of Strathearn and the country up towards Callander. In several places other reminders of a maritime past were found buried in sediment: the dugout canoes of people who had once fished over the fertile fields.

Beneath the earth's crust more change was rumbling. Between 9000 BC and as late as AD 10, old fault-lines running under Scotland were reawakening and produced many major earthquakes. Some measured 6.5 to 7 on the Richter scale (the most severe earthquake ever recorded reached 9.5 in Chile in 1960). Combined with the rebounding land, this level of seismic activity often had dramatic effects: from large rockfalls to landslips, particularly in the Highland ranges, and even the collapse of a mountain ridge. Such apocalyptic moments must have affected human settlement patterns and developed a body of important knowledge about where was safe to live and where was dangerous.

But no one heard or saw one of the most destructive earthquakes Scotland suffered after the end of the last Ice Age. It happened underwater, some time around 5840 BC. What is known as the second Storrega Slide took place on the edge of the continental slope, about halfway between Norway's west coast and Iceland. When unquantifiable cubic yards of rock slipped, they created a momentary gap into which the sea rushed. Modern observers have witnessed what would have happened next. When a submarine landslip takes place, the sea recedes extremely rapidly, sounding like a monstrous vacuum cleaner, revealing great expanses of the sea-bed. A faint rumble is heard far in the distance. Seabirds shriek and take to the air, and the rumble becomes a roar as the first gigantic wave races towards the shore. Tidal waves, or tsunamis, can travel at incredible speed, up to 480 km/300 miles per hour. And when the first and biggest wave crashes down, it rains boulders and gravel before roaring inland, snapping trees and sweeping all before it.

Sailing uphill

What appears to be a universal principle of plumbing – that water always finds the same level – does not apply to the largest bodies of water, the world's oceans. They do not all have the same surface level. In places the Indian Ocean is in fact 180 m/590 ft lower than the seas around Indonesia. This happens because of variations in the strength of the earth's gravitational pull and the shape of the ocean floor. It is possible, therefore, to sail uphill.

The evidence for the great tsunami which hit the eastern coast of Scotland in 5840 BC was found by accident. When the houses at 13–24 Castle Street in Inverness were demolished in the 1980s, archaeologists expected to find the remains of part of the medieval town. This they duly did, but under that stratum was something entirely unexpected. Prehistoric material began to appear. In addition to the tell-tale flint scatter of a hunter-gatherer-fisher camp of the 6th millennium BC, the diggers came upon a thick layer of white marine sand, the sort found on the ocean bed, and mixed with it were many stones and pebbles. Further investigation told the story of the immense 8-m/26-ft-high tsunami which had roared in from the North Sea nearly 8,000 years before. It lifted up approximately 17,000 cu. km of marine sand and debris and brought it crashing down on to the eastern coasts of Scotland. Traces of its impact have even been detected on the western shores of continental Europe as far south as Amsterdam.

Many people would have died, unable to get out of the way in time, unaware of the scale of what was happening – perhaps living some distance inland, or dragged into the sea by the ferocious undertow that followed the waves. But nowhere suffered more lasting damage than a lost land, a huge prehistoric hunting ground, probably the most productive in Europe, a place which has passed out of all but the most specialist knowledge and has now completely disappeared.

A hundred kilometres/60 miles east of the Northumberland coast lies the Dogger Bank. Sometimes only six or seven fathoms (10 to 12 m) below the surface, these extensive shallows are named after the Dutch word for a trawler. The description is entirely apt because the Dogger Bank used to be one of the richest fishing grounds in the world and many doggers have cast their nets there over the centuries. Marine charts show that the bank is in fact a range of undersea hills rather than a continuous feature like a shoal or sandbank. There are rolling valleys and rounded summits stretching for many nautical miles to the east. But few who fish there realize that they are sailing over what used to be dry land, and that the undersea hills used to be hunting grounds of a different kind. Deer, wild boar, wild cattle, smaller animals and all sorts of birds were trapped or shot in the Dogger Hills because, until some time after 4000 BC, they formed a focal part of a huge land-mass which linked the east of Britain with the Low Countries and Denmark. Doggerland occupied most of the area of the North Sea south of the Dogger Bank and its geography encouraged an abundance and diversity of animals, birds and fish, enough to support a substantial population of hunters and trappers. In fact, some researchers believe that Doggerland was the cradle of hunter-gatherer-fisher culture in northern Europe.

The coastline of the land-mass was ragged, deeply indented by wide estuaries fed by the Elbe in the east and the Humber and the rivers flowing into the Wash in the west. The Dogger Hills were its northern bulwark against the sea, and to the south the long finger of the Channel reached far enough to allow the Thames and the Rhine to drain into it.

The first traces of this prehistoric Atlantis were discovered by accident in 1931. Night fishing in the shallow waters of the North Sea, about 40 km/25 miles off the East Anglian coast, the skipper of the *Colinda* ordered his crew to wind in their nets. In the half-light Captain Lockwood noticed a lump of peat come up and, setting it down on the deck, he split it open with a shovel. Inside was something that had no business being there, an antler point with barbs carved along its length, like a small harpoon. It could not have been dropped in the sea by whatever unlikely accident, especially not so far from shore. It was embedded in peat, a sediment laid down millennia before on what eventually became the sea-bed. The implications were perplexing.

Himalayan prawns

Everest, the world's highest mountain, just keeps getting higher. Because the tectonic plates which first pushed up the Himalayas are still pushing, the mountain adds approximately an inch to its height every year. Surprisingly, Everest is not constantly covered in snow and ice, and rock formations can be made out by climbers. The 'Yellow Band' is just that, a stratum of yellowish rock near the surface, and at the summit those conquerors with a geological interest have detected sedimentary rock containing a variety of marine fossils, including prawn-like creatures. What goes down must come up, it seems.

Following this remarkable discovery, botanists from Cambridge University dredged up samples of peat from the sea-bed off Norfolk, near where the *Colinda* had been fishing. Laboratory analysis revealed that the antler point was no freak find, and that dense oak woodland had once grown there in the period after the last Ice Age. The remains of prehistoric trees found under the North Sea closely matched examples from England, Denmark and northern Germany. Since this early research was completed, oyster dredgers have brought up more peat samples, and the process of improving the mapping of the North Sea bed (since oil was discovered) has produced more artefacts. An antler or bone tool from the Dogger Bank has been carbon-dated to 6050 BC.

The most recent archaeological finds were also made by accident. In the summer of 2003, a team from Newcastle University's archaeology department were learning to scuba-dive in the North Sea, about half a mile offshore, near the mouth of the River Tyne. Dr Penny Spikins spotted a cluster of flints lying on the sea-bed and immediately realized what they were. An arrowhead and some cutting tools were brought to the surface, seeing the light of day after being lost for millennia. Traces of two hunter-gatherer-fisher settlements were found, one dating to between 6500 and 3000 BC and the other even earlier at between 8000 and 6500 BC. The older site is further out to sea and the locations of both appear to show how the coastline of the western estuary of Doggerland shrank over time. These recent discoveries are very significant in that they have supplied the first hard evidence of undersea settlements. Much more awaits discovery.

Dancing girls

At Creswell Crags in Nottinghamshire the archaeologists who discovered a remarkable series of cave paintings at first thought that they were looking at depictions of long-necked birds, perhaps swans. A more worldly reinterpretation confirmed that they were nothing of the kind. The 'birds' were in fact naked women painted in profile, dancing with raised arms and their backsides thrust out. The cave art at Creswell has been dated to 11,000 BC and its discovery has radically altered thinking on ice-age history. It seems that the artists who painted the dancing girls were part of a group of pioneers who penetrated as far north as Nottinghamshire while the ice still covered Scotland. They may have pursued herds of reindeer as they moved north to graze the brief summer pasture on the tundra plains of what is now midland England. Even more surprising than the dancing girls is a painting of an ibex, a species of European goat now found only in the Pyrenees. No traces of prehistoric ibex have yet been found in Britain. And it seems likely that the hunting band who sheltered at Creswell travelled over Doggerland from what is now Belgium and Germany. Near-contemporary ibex remains have been found there. The cave-paintings themselves also show stylistic similarities with the more famous art found at Lascaux in France and Altamira in Spain. And they add powerfully to the impression of a pan-European prehistoric culture which moved over long distances to find good hunting in summer.

Now, the undoubted existence (and persistence over a long period) of Doggerland has important implications for the repopulation of Britain after the last glaciation. A land-bridge of this scale and richness was not only that. In fact if the combination of estuaries, woodland and good fishing grounds was as productive as some researchers believe, then Doggerland may have been a destination rather than a bridge. No contemporary could have anticipated its ultimate fate. But equally, the presence of a continuous coastline linking Denmark and the Baltic with England allowed regular and sustained contact, much of it by boat.

Recent excavation of a site on the slopes of Ben Lawers, above Loch Tay, has uncovered one of the very earliest settlements yet found in Scotland. Dated at around 7000 BC, it has produced a number of artefacts, flints and tools which are almost identical to items found in western Norway in the same period. The existence of Doggerland, with its navigable coastline and narrow, easily crossed estuaries, makes the idea of such long-range contact and exchange much more readily conceivable. And it allows the rich prehistoric legacy of Denmark and the Baltic to adumbrate the sparser picture we currently have of our past.

As the sea level rose and the land which had borne the weight of the ice rebounded, Doggerland slowly sank and was finally completely inundated. The tsunami of 5840 BC hastened a process which had already begun and had been accelerated by other, earlier, but equally dramatic events. Around 6400 BC the ice-dams of northern Canada broke. Almost overnight between 70,000 and 150,000 cubic kilometres of fresh water poured out of the huge lakes known as Agassiz and Ojibway, surging through the Hudson Straits and out into the North Atlantic. Within only two days the world's sea level rose by 20–40 cm/8–16 ins. And huge floating ice-islands appeared in the ocean, drifting southwards, displacing even more water. The effect of this on the lower-lying areas of Doggerland must have been immediately devastating, sending communities fleeing into the northern hills, abandoning their coastal camps in a matter of hours. By 4000 BC the European land-bridge had been flooded, leaving Britain isolated and Doggerland as an island as large as Denmark. It almost certainly survived for several centuries beyond the time when the North Sea linked with the Atlantic through the Channel. No indication of an approximate date for the final drowning of this remarkable place has been found so far and, more surprisingly, its existence appears to have passed out of all memory.

Undammed

When the freshwater lakes of northern Canada broke down their ice-dams, the effects were felt worldwide. More localized cataclysms were no less spectacular. Around 9600 BC the Baltic Sea was held back behind a 25-m/80-ft ice-dam. When it melted, the sea drained into the North Sea, leaving boulders, gravel and silt as it rushed through the Kattegat. Over a period of some months the sea level dropped by 25 m/80 ft, exposing dry land in what is now northern Germany, Poland and the Baltic States. But it turned out to be only a temporary reclamation for, as Scandinavia rebounded after the ice-melt, it pushed the sea further south, inundating the recently dry areas. About 3,000 years later the Mediterranean burst into the lower-lying Black Sea, at that time a huge freshwater lake. Evidently the roar could be heard 100 km/60 miles away. Most of eastern Scotland's gravel plains were formed by much smaller ice-dammed lakes which eventually broke down.

The discovery of Doggerland is salutary. It invites us to think radically about the prehistory of Britain, to use such scant evidence as exists to imagine a world very different from ours, one inhabited by people who were like us, but whose environment was much more volatile. Despite earthquakes, tsunamis and the uncertainties of living off the land, it would be a mistake, however, to think of that world as necessarily devoid of pleasure or beauty. Prehistoric life was almost certainly not 'nasty, brutish and short', as the philosopher Thomas Hobbes had it.

Our ancestors, the Old Peoples who may have walked across the North Sea to come to Britain, lived a life which is distant from us in time and style. But rather than stoop to make value-comparisons between now and 8000 BC, we would do better to use our experience and our technology to understand as much of it as we are able to. These people were not aliens, they were our first mothers and fathers.

3

The Wildwood

Mist worried the oarsmen more than anything. It could blot out the sun so completely as to make navigation in the open sea very chancy until nightfall, when it often lifted and the homing stars shone. When the greyness did come down, the old pilots in the bow immediately shushed all conversation and called for the oars to be shipped. They needed to listen to the run of the sea, try to make out the call of the seabirds or the boom of whales or the splash of seals, and, most important of all, sift out the sound of the wash of breakers on a rocky shore before it was too late. The old men took only short shifts at the oars but their knowledge of the moods of the ocean could turn aside a drifting death and keep men alive.

The appointed day had dawned bright and clear with no sign of sea-mist or storm. They would need good weather, for the voyage to the north-west, from the Butt to the Gannet Rock, was across open sea. Once they had rowed out of sight of the home bay and its sheltering cliffs, there was nothing before them, no seamarks for guidance, nothing to help, except knowledge. The Gannet Rock was small, only half a mile long, and easy to miss even if it was not misty or no storm was blowing. But its cliffs were steep, rising sheer out of the water like the tip of an undersea mountain.

Having stowed enough food, water and firewood for four days, the crew shoved the boat down the beach through the tidemark and into the Atlantic waves. On the shore the whole village stood to wave and wish them good luck. There was never much of a choice about this voyage. It had to be made at the same time each year, when the summer ended and the autumn began. Any later and the young birds would have fledged their flight feathers and flown their nests on the ledges and cracks on the sheer cliff-faces of the Rock.

Once they had rowed through the tidewash and secured the empty boat behind, the crew settled on to the thwarts to begin their work. No one had to speak or beat time. The six oarsmen fell immediately into a rhythm, the stern-man occasionally looking over his shoulder and up at the sky. If the course needed correction, nothing was said. He just pulled harder for a few strokes to bring the prow round to the direction he wanted. Sitting on top of the sea like a gull, the boat moved easily forward, the splash of the oars and the sway of the crew almost hypnotic. Measuring distance by the length of shifts at the oars, the stern-man knew that they were making good time.

The old pilots saw it first. They looked at each other. Ever watchful of the far horizon, they saw a thin sliver of grey, then blue-black cloud beginning to thicken, rolling in from the south-west, with a strong wind behind. There were no patches of clear sky at its edges; this was a storm approaching and it would not pass over without at least soaking the boat. Bailing buckets were readied and the men pulled oilskins on.

When the storm hit, the winds were ferocious, whipping spindrift off the top of huge waves. The stern-man struggled to keep the boat from turning broadside on to the walls of water as they washed down. To avoid swamping he kept the bow always to windward, slicing into the waves and falling into the troughs on the other side. As the sky grew darker, the pilots roared that they could see something off the starboard side. Looming out of the gathering storm came the black sea-cliffs of the Gannet Rock. The oarsmen pulled hard to keep from smashing against them. There was no good landing place to aim for, no bay or cove, just an inlet dominated by a great white rock.

Shouting to the men behind them, the pilots passed it down to the stern that they should make for Seal Island, a short distance to the north-east. There was a beach where they might make safe landfall without much damage to either boat. After an hour's blistering pull on the oars, the pale strip of sand could be seen through the half-dark. Exhausted, soaked, their hands bleeding, the crew felt the comforting thud of the keel meeting the soft sand and jumped into the sea to haul the boats as far up the beach as possible. After unshipping every precious item of stores, they turned the boats upside down and took grateful shelter underneath.

When the storm broke over the village back at the Butt, prayers begged that it was not so severe out at sea, that the fiercest weather was breaking over their houses and pasture, that the seamen had somehow fared better on the other side of all that fury. But as the wind howled on through the night, even the most optimistic grew as dark as the weather, and over the cooking fires little was said.

By noon of the next day, the sky had cleared and a second expedition set off for the Gannet Rock. If there had been a wreck, perhaps there were survivors. If not, then all could return together with room for more birds than usual. But despite an easy passage and a thorough search of the Rock, nothing could be found. With no idea that the crew was safe on the nearby island, the rescuers rowed back to the Butt with their news.

Meanwhile all was made ready on the beach of Seal Island. Unaware of the rescue attempt, the crew set about reaching their original destination. Gannet Rock was a difficult anchorage. Once they had rowed into the inlet where the white rock jutted into the sea, there were two possibilities. Either part of the crew stayed in the boat to keep it from damage, or they hauled it 20 m/60 ft up the cliff face to a broad shelf where it could be lashed safe. Since much time had been lost to the storm, the old pilots advised the former course of action. It meant fewer hunters for the birds but it ensured that they would get home safely with what catch they could make.

Young gannets are quite tame, fatally trusting. It was easy for the hunters to kill them with a sharp blow to the head, since they did not flee the nest at the approach of humans. The adults were another matter, wheeling, diving, shrieking at the men as they climbed around the cliffs and killed their young. Some of the hunters were roped to each other so that they could lean far out on the more dangerous ledges. Some used a long pole with a looped piece of cord at the end to lift and strangle the birds. They were easy prey and good eating.

Once the spare boat was full, the pilots guided the oarsmen's strokes carefully until they were clear of the cliffs and their reefs. Pushed on by a northerly breeze, they made good time. And when the home bay and the cliffs began to rise ever larger on the horizon, the crew could make out their families on the tops. Word had quickly spread, and the people watched in joyful relief as the men brought the kill home.

~~~

When Donald Campbell and his men came back from the dead in September 1912, they unloaded their boats and laid out their catch of young gannets on the pier at Port of Ness. A photograph survives. Like many groups of hunters they stood proudly behind the rows of their bag, ten men who had risked their lives to feed their families and their community. In Gaelic the birds are known as *guga* and the island they come from lies 48 km/30 miles to the north-west of the Butt of Lewis, the northernmost island of the Outer Hebrides. Sulasgeir, 'Gannet Rock', is near North Rona, 'Seal Island'.

The guga hunt was dangerous and the men often failed to return home when expected. In 1912 a tremendous storm forced Donald Campbell to abandon any thought of landing on Sulasgeir and drove him to seek refuge on North Rona. Prolonged bad weather kept his crew there for some weeks while a rescue expedition searched Sulasgeir and presumed them all dead. Apparently Campbell brought back one of the richest harvests of guga ever seen at Port of Ness.

The annual voyage to Sulasgeir still goes on and the oily, fishy flesh of the guga is greatly prized on Lewis as a delicacy. Animal rights activists have begun a campaign to have the guga hunt banned, claiming that it is barbaric and unnecessary. Two hundred years ago the Lairds of Lewis, the MacKenzies, attempted to force the men of Ness to pay a tithe of birds and feathers or the equivalent in cash. They refused, saying that they had never had to ask anyone's permission to hunt the guga on Sulasgeir. Furthermore, the island belonged to no one. It was an ancient right and they would not desist from it.

And nor have they. The guga hunt is that rare thing, one of the last survivals of an ancient way of life, an example of what the great French historian Fernand Braudel called the *longue durée*. In similar geographical, social and economic circumstances, groups of people maintain habits of life and mind over immense periods. When challenged by whatever authority, the people of Ness claim that the guga hunt goes back to the 15th century and that it is theirs by right and custom. But the overwhelming likelihood is that it goes much further back, all the way to the arrival of the early pioneers after the retreat of the last Ice Age. There is of course no scientific trail of proof to follow, only common sense and instinct. But all the characteristics of ancient practice are there.

Sulasgeir has no source of fresh water and no soil to sustain any but the most primitive plant life. To a hungry community its only value is the guga, for its nourishing flesh and comforting feathers. The hunt is seasonal and depends on a clear understanding of animal behaviour, and it is only undertaken when the birds are young enough to be killed without much of a struggle. Easy prey is the only sort wanted by those clinging to high sea-cliffs. Technologically it requires no more than a prehistoric tool-kit to achieve: a heavy club, ropes and cords, long poles, containers, sound knowledge and boats. Plank-built rowing boats represent the only major change. Since Lewis lost its forests, the probability is that prehistoric voyages to Sulasgeir were made in curraghs, the seagoing hide boats still made in Cork and the south-west of Ireland. Until recently the men who rowed to the Gannet Rock did not use a compass, depending on passed-on sea lore to make the trip safely and accurately. When the expeditions return the birds are plucked by groups of women before being salted in brine to preserve them. But in the past fewer were taken and the need for preservation might have been less, or met by smoking or drying. And as late as the last century harvests of guga were shared amongst the whole community as an annual natural bounty. The outrage of the men of Ness is palpable at a distance of two centuries since the MacKenzies attempted to tax an ancient right.

In 1954 the Protection of Birds Act had a special clause inserted to protect the guga hunt, limiting the kill to 2,000 birds a year. The hunters still share the catch amongst themselves; each house in Ness is given one and the remainder is sold, at high prices. If animal rights activists succeed in having the guga hunt banned it is likely that the men of Ness will ignore the ban, just as they ignored the MacKenzies' taxmen and carried on doing what they have done on Sulasgeir for thousands of years.

The guga hunters of Ness return to their ancient past only once a year, but far out to the west, buffeted by the waves of the mighty Atlantic, there is an abandoned island where the natives hunted all year round to sustain life. Until the main island of Hirta was evacuated in 1930, the islanders of St Kilda spent the best part of nine months every year hunting the seabirds which nested on the cliffs and seastacks of their tiny, windswept archipelago. In the spring they collected the eggs by the thousand, sometimes eating them fresh or boiled, sometimes keeping them for weeks 'to improve the flavour'. In the late summer and autumn, they went out after the birds themselves. Although it has long ceased to exist and almost outrun living memory, the ancient way of life on St Kilda fascinated the Victorians, and several observers wrote down what they saw. Surprisingly, their tone is often neutral, lacking the usual condescension. John Ross, a schoolmaster, had been sent from the mainland, and one day in the mid-19th century he found himself in a boat at the foot of the high cliffs on the north-east coast of Hirta.

The first thing to attract our notice was one of the men and his little boy on a rugged but fairly level piece of ground rather down near the sea. One end of the rope was tied around the father's waist while the other was tied around the boy's waist, most probably lest he, being young, rash and inexperienced, might slip into the sea. There they were, all alone then, killing away at a terrible rate, for the boy was collecting while the father kept shaking and twisting.

The man removing himself from the rope shouldered a burden of dead fulmars, made for a cutting in the rock, too narrow one would think for a dog, and too slippery for a goat. Along this he crawled on hands and knees. A single slip in the middle would have hurled him at least 80 feet sheer down into the sea. But he landed his burden safely and returned to the boy. The rope was tied as before, but only about a yard was left between them this time and that brave little fellow of only ten summers fearlessly followed his father and reached safety without a hitch. This is how St Kildans train their young to the rocks and what a dangerous life it is.

The islanders climbed the cliffs in bare feet, and over time their ankles and toes had modified. In order to stay securely on the surface of the rock, often while doing something else, the St Kildans' toes had evolved to become more widely spaced than those of any mainlander or Hebridean. And they could spread out their toes and grip a foothold just as most people can spread their fingers and hold on to a handrail or an edge. The hunters' ankles had developed tremendous strength, and were half as thick again as most people's.

It was not an indiscriminate slaughter. The islanders' main quarry, the fulmar, laid only one egg a year and these were never collected. And to prevent sheep or dogs approaching the nests, fences were built on the clifftops. Each morning, except the Sabbath, the men of St Kilda met to discuss the day's work, standing in the open air on either side of the village street. Probably because hunting was so dangerous, and certainly because all the gear needed for it was owned in common, agreement on what was required was desirable. In such a small and fragile community, everyone depended on everyone else. Before an expedition set off, ropes were brought out and tested for safety. In full view of the morning meeting, four men tied each rope to a boulder and pulled hard to check that it would hold. The weather was often a determining factor in any discussion of hunting, and the collective experience of the group was called up to predict what the day's conditions were likely to be. The morning meeting appears to have had no leader or leading clique. Even though it was inevitable that strong personalities will have asserted themselves, all decisions were arrived at through consensus. Perhaps centuries, even millennia of experience routinely doing dangerous work had taught the island community the merits of co-operation.

It was less hazardous to go after puffins, because they dig burrows rather than build nests. The women and girls of St Kilda followed a curious and cruel custom in the Victorian period. They laid a set of horsehair snares on the grass or rock near the burrows, and would then catch one puffin. Carefully keeping it alive, the women plucked the bird's body on the spot, leaving the feathers on its wings and tail, and let it go. Curiosity killed its neighbours. As the other puffins approached the plucked bird, interested to see exactly what it was, their clumsy, waddling feet quickly became entangled in the snares.

The St Kildans also hunted the guga, but they did it at night, when the birds were roosting and more could be caught. Of course, this was extremely dangerous and undertaken only in bright moonlight. On the gannetry out on Boreray, a rocky islet to the north-east of Hirta, the first and most vital task was to find the sentry bird and kill it before it could wake the others. How the gannets had evolved this method of protection remains a mystery, but it was something that uncounted generations of St Kildans had come to understand well. Once the sentry bird had been quietly stalked and despatched, the men clubbed hundreds of gannets to death, and left them where they lay on the nests. In 1886 George Murray described what happened next:

After working for an hour or two, we rested and three of us sat down on the bare rocks with the ropes about our middles, the cloudless sky our canopy, the moon our lamp, and had family worship. The scene to me was very impressive, the ocean still and quiet far below, and we offered praise and prayer to Him who was able to preserve us in such dangerous work.

When dawn crept over the eastern horizon, the hunters on Boreray went to pick up their night's kill and threw the birds down into the sea for their boat to collect.

The most important hunt took place in August when the men went out after the fulmar. This bird provided many of their daily needs. In addition to its nutritious flesh, it gave oil for their lamps, feathers for pillows, mattresses and quilting (fulmar feathers and down had the added virtue of not attracting lice) and a stomach secretion that had medicinal properties. Surpluses from the fulmar kill were substantial and the St Kildans used them to pay rent in kind to the MacLeod landlords; they also traded what they did not need.

As with the young guga, fulmars were killed before they could fly from their cliff-edge nests. Men let down on ropes clubbed the young birds and wrung their necks to make sure that the precious stomach secretion was not lost. Like countless generations of fowlers and hunters, they tucked the heads under their belts. This habit is probably the origin of the phrase 'getting something under one's belt'.

The whole kill of fulmars was divided equally amongst the island community of about a hundred people, even though the fulmar cliffs had been apportioned to different families who had, inevitably, taken varying numbers of birds. Although they had taken no part in the hunt the elderly and infirm received their share, just as in their day they had given it to their elders. Once the birds had been gutted and plucked, the carcasses were taken up to the *cleitean*, small turf and stone huts, to be dried and preserved. These were loosely built and allowed the perpetual wind to whistle through and dry the fulmar flesh so that it would last into the winter.

St Kilda was evacuated in 1930 and the islanders were re-settled on the mainland. But some could not settle, and for years men returned to climb down the cliffs and go after the fulmar so that they could bring a few birds away for themselves. Ultimately the islands were bought by the Earl of Dumfries, a keen ornithologist.

~~~

The guga hunt on Sulasgeir has outlasted the way of life on St Kilda, perhaps because of the eternal interplay of geography, geology and people. The soil of the Western Isles is not fertile, and farming was able to provide only a proportion of their food needs, so hunting of various sorts persisted as a vital part of the local economy. The guga hunt may now be a relic, undertaken by people who are not starving and do not depend on it in the way that the St Kildans did, but it is profitable and does not threaten the gannet population. Fishing also remains important. It has supplemented farming for millennia and the same maritime skills needed to reach and land on Sulasgeir are used to pull fish and shellfish out of the seas around the Hebrides. Traditions appear to die hard in communities which still hunt, perhaps because of the role luck has always played. And the precise language used by these communities can be an insight into a past forgotten over the rest of Scotland. For more than 2,500 years, Gaelic, with its specialized way of thinking about the world, has understood and described these very old habits of mind and marked them out as singular from our English-language culture. Possibly most important of all, the remoteness of the islands has preserved prehistoric remains in much greater quantity and antiquity than on the mainland. And so, remembering the power of Braudel's *longue durée*, it should perhaps come as no surprise that the story of Scotland's first peoples, the Old Peoples who came here after the ice, should begin on its wild western margins.

The story begins in the west because that is where archaeologists have found it, painstakingly piecing together a few tiny fragments of history into an incomplete mosaic. Most of the pieces will never be retrieved; the picture will always be patchy and in places unrecognizable. But in recent years scientists have been looking in new places, showing how much of our prehistory is carried inside us today. Passed down through thousands of generations are the genes of our ancestors, a DNA map charting a way back into the immense darkness of our long past. The sensational discoveries recently made by Professor Bryan Sykes and his team of researchers have produced something no amount of more conventional historical scholarship could have unearthed: nothing less than a prelude to the story of Britain and Scotland, and answers to some fundamental questions.

Man bites man

The first pioneers to reach Britain after the end of the Last Ice Age may have had to endure harsh winters and been driven to desperate measures. Around 12,700 BC cannibals were sheltering in Gough's Cave in south-west England. Human bones discovered on the floor of the cave show the marks of stone-cutting tools, incontrovertible evidence that four adults and one adolescent had been systematically butchered. Burn marks on some of the bones show that they were roasted. And if they were roasted, then they would certainly have been eaten.

Who were the first pioneers to enter Britain after the retreat of the ice and make the long journey to leave their traces in the western islands of Scotland? And where did they come from?

In 1995 Bryan Sykes wrote up his research and showed something stunningly simple – that we are who we were. Far from being a distillate of successive immigrations to these islands, waves of invasions and bouts of bloody genocide or a string of mysterious disappearances, 80 per cent of us in Britain are the direct descendants of the hunter-gatherer-fishers who came north after the last Ice Age; 80 per cent of us can trace an unbroken lineage to the people who hunted in the wildwood, who gathered roots and berries in its glades and who fished our rivers and seas. We are not a mongrel race, a unique mixture of many arrivals over our long history. We are who we were, a very long time ago. Bryan Sykes has shown that the population of Britain has remained stable, with only small admixtures of very influential élites, and that we are the undoubted descendants of those whom too many believe to have been bone-gnawing, shaggy, grunting cavemen.

Split genes

At the Edinburgh Science Festival of 2004, Professor Stephen Oppenheimer confirmed that recent DNA mapping had revealed a British population overwhelmingly descended from the first pioneer hunter-gatherer-fishers to settle after the last Ice Age. However, he added an interesting gloss which appears to show an ancient divide between western Celts and eastern English. Broadly, Oppenheimer's research has discovered strong genetic links between the peoples of the Atlantic seaboard. Over 8,000 years of prehistory evolved in such a way that the Celts of Ireland, western Scotland, Man, Wales and Cornwall had much in common with the Basques, in particular, while the English were close relatives to the Anglo-Saxons who lived in north-western Europe. When the early existence of Doggerland is remembered, these shades of affinity are perhaps not surprising. In any case research work tracing the inheritance of the Y-chromosome, passed on from fathers to sons, as well as Bryan Sykes' work on mitochondrial DNA, confirms the influential underlay of a common hunter-gatherer-fisher gene pool stretching right across Britain and Ireland.

What Sykes did was to sample DNA sequences from the modern population and look at the number of mutations which had taken place in those sequences. The latter analysis allowed the sequences to be dated, and most went back at least 10,000 years, to or before the date of the first arrivals in Scotland. He then compared his modern samples with what could be retrieved of prehistoric DNA.

Like many epoch-making discoveries, this line of research came about while Sykes was looking at something else. In attempting to discover the causes of genetic diseases in Polynesia, he noticed that the DNA sequences he was recording had no parallels in the Americas. They were completely different. Being interested in history and remembering Thor Heyerdahl's epic voyage across the Pacific Ocean on *Kon-Tiki*, a balsa-wood raft made in South America, Sykes realized that his conclusions about the populating of Polynesia were wrong. The people who settled on Easter Island and elsewhere could not have come from South America. If Heyerdahl had been correct in his belief that the ancestors of modern Polynesians came from the east, there would have been DNA links to support him. But there were none, not even tenuous ones. It turned out that the Pacific islands had been populated from the west, from China, Taiwan and south-east Asia.

In his early research Bryan Sykes had compared sequences of what is called mitochondrial DNA, that is, a genetic inheritance passed on only through matrilinear descent. Although only women carry this, it reveals much about the origins and movement of prehistoric populations. *Mitos* is the Greek word for thread, and that is what it is, a thread leading us back through the labyrinth of our past. When British and European patterns of mitochondrial DNA were examined in sufficiently large samples (whole schools took part), it was discovered that we in Britain are overwhelmingly the descendants of hunter-gatherer-fishers: not Romans, Vikings, Normans or other, more famous invaders, but the prehistoric peoples who came quietly, threading their way unannounced up our rivers and into the dark interior of the wildwood.

For incontestable corroboration of these remarkable findings, Sykes felt he needed to persuade the Natural History Museum in London to allow him to take DNA from the bones of an ancient skeleton. Cheddar Man was discovered in Gough's Cave in the Cheddar Gorge in Somerset in 1903. After much nervous negotiation, Sykes was allowed to drill into the teeth of the skeleton (he took the jawbone back to Oxford on the bus) in an attempt to extract some viable DNA. The result was astounding. The ancient DNA was a close match with samples taken from people living in Cheddar in 1996, so close that a local history teacher was shown to be undoubtedly a direct descendant of Cheddar Man, the hunter who had died in Gough's Cave some time around 7000 BC.

Wider sampling and more intensive analysis allowed Sykes to replace supposition with facts. It became clear that all Europeans are the descendants of *Homo sapiens*, and not the mutation known as Neanderthal Man. Our ancestors reached Europe between 40,000 and 50,000 years ago and penetrated every corner of the continent. Moreover, the mitochondrial DNA samples appeared to arrange themselves into distinct clusters. There turned out to be seven strands in Europe, traceable back to seven women, what Sykes calls 'Clan mothers'. These women had different geographical origins and their DNA answered another fundamental question. Where did the pioneer hunters come from?

Low foreheads

The *Missing Link* between what Benjamin Disraeli described as 'the apes and the angels' (memorably placing himself 'on the side of the angels') was thought to have been discovered in a grotto in the ravine of the Neander River near Düsseldorf in 1856. Found at the height of the evolution controversy, Neanderthal Man seemed to confirm the basic notion that human beings were indeed the descendants of the higher primates. The bones were thick and short, reconstructing into stocky skeletons topped by skulls showing massive brow-ridges, low foreheads and large flat noses. The latter were a necessary protection against the cold. When very cold air is inhaled it can be damaging, and Neanderthal noses were large enough to warm it slightly before it was taken into the lungs. Their stocky physique and powerful musculature made these people hardy and well adapted to extreme climate fluctuation as well as periods of food scarcity. Close examination of Neanderthal skeletons also shows a tough and sometimes bruising way of life as they hunted down the woolly mammoth and the reindeer. Healed fractures of the arms and shoulders indicate brutal encounters with their prey. Neanderthals concentrated in Europe and, in the warmer periods between ice ages, probably populated Scotland. Recent research indicates that for a time they may have co-existed with *Homo sapiens* for a few millennia before the last Ice Age. And some geneticists have claimed that the unique gene producing fair or red-haired Europeans (all other continents have dark-haired populations) came about during that overlap period when these two different sorts of human beings mixed.

Six of the seven clusters dated to more than 10,000 years ago, which placed them in Europe well before the advent of farming. The seventh originated in modern Iraq, on the banks of the River Euphrates, and its movement into Europe represented the spread of new ideas and techniques. This Middle Eastern cluster of farmers makes up only 20 per cent of the modern European population, while the other six form the balance.

The clusters of mitochondrial DNA can be located to the regions of prehistoric Europe lying south of the furthest extent of the ice. It appears that most of the immigrants to post-glacial Britain came from what is now south-western France, northern Italy and Greece; 47 per cent of all Europeans originate from hunter-gatherer bands based in the valley of the Dordogne.

To test and investigate these extraordinarily precise findings, a group of Italian, eastern European and American geneticists began to work on DNA which was passed down through the male line. It may have been true to say that mitochondrial DNA could set up these ancient links, but perhaps the picture would be greatly complicated when patrilinear patterns were explored. A total of 1,007 men had their Y-chromosomes fingerprinted and dated by an analysis of the number of mutations in the sequences. The dating agreed with Sykes' conclusions. It was true: 80 per cent of all Europeans, traced through both the male and female lines, are indeed direct descendants of the original hunter-gatherer-fisher population. We are undoubtedly who we were. And the men of Ness who hunt the guga each year are only doing what their ancestors did – for millennia.

~~~

The story of Scotland's prehistory properly has its prologue in England. (It should always be borne in mind that these modern national labels are anachronisms and used only because they are handy.) More accurately, the story of the repopulation of the north after the end of the Cold Snap begins on the west coast of the North Sea, on the shores of the wide estuary of western Doggerland.

By the end of the 20th century the seascape and landscape of north Northumberland had changed a great deal. (There is anecdotal evidence that before the First World War cricket was played at low tide on the Dogger Bank for a few days at midsummer.) Those looking out to the east could no longer make out the shape of the Dogger Hills in the far distance, and the existing coastline had shrunk back from its prehistoric margins. Some of these radical changes must have been in the back of an observant local's mind when he walked his dog along the cliff path overlooking Howick Haven, a shallow bay not far from the town of Alnwick (see plate 11). Where the path had eroded the turf, he noticed several sharp flints, some of them still embedded in the sand. Having the awareness and presence of mind not to disturb the area, but to alert an archaeologist, he set in train a sequence of events which was to alter the conventional wisdom about early hunter-gatherer-fisher society in Britain.

When a dig was organized and archaeologists lifted the turf by the sand-cliff at Howick, they came across something entirely unexpected. At first all they could discern was 'a big smear of material', no more than a large stain on the sand. But since the site was very fragile, perched on the edge of a cliff which might crumble away at any moment, it was decided to conduct a full excavation. And in case human clumsiness destroyed any of the faint traces of prehistoric use, the diggers had to remove their boots and work in bare feet.

Tipis

Two North American Indian women could erect a tipi in an hour and ensure that it could withstand the severest weather. First, three long poles were tied with rawhide at one end and set up as a tripod before other poles with loops of rawhide fixed on the ends were added. Then a cord attached to the apex was tied to a peg and hammered into the ground to make the frame secure and rigid. The tipi was not built as a true cone but slightly off-centre, with the more slanting side facing the prevailing wind. This arrangement also ventilated the smoke-hole better. Then a heavy, buffalo-hide cover was laid on with a strong lifting pole, the bottom edges pegged down and weighted with stones, if available, and the seam tied with wooden pins. Smoke-flaps could be adjusted with two attached poles or closed against rain or snow. Tipis were pitched in a circle with door flaps facing the east and the morning sun. Often the women built separate arbours out of brush and branches so that they could cook in the daylight outside the dark tipi and sit out of the sun and rain.

Their delicate probing produced an extraordinary result. Overlooking Howick Haven was the oldest intact settlement ever found in Britain. Using radiocarbon dating, the archaeologists could be certain about the period of occupation of the settlement. People lived at Howick for about a hundred years, between 7700 and 7600 BC, and then moved away. But even more remarkable than the age of the site was its nature. Traces of early hunter-gatherer-fishers had always been thought of as slight, when they could be found at all – no more than temporary camps of tent-like structures made of pliable poles and twigs with hides sewn together for a roof, shelters rather than buildings. Such transience left only faint wisps of evidence: burn marks where hearths had blazed or flint chips scattered where stone tools had been made.

At Howick the archaeologists unearthed something quite other, the remains of a large roundhouse built out of thick tree-trunk posts and topped with a conical roof constructed on straight poles and probably thatched with dried wild grasses. This was no temporary tent but a permanent house, built to last and to accommodate a large family. Its construction had involved long-term planning (waiting for straight coppiced poles to grow in the nearby woodland), co-operation and a great deal of skill. But despite the co-ordination of all these resources, the Howick house was occupied for only about a hundred years, the span of perhaps four or five generations. Supplies of firewood may have run out or needed to be carried for longer and longer distances, or perhaps the house timbers had begun to rot in the damp sand. Even nowadays it is often easier to construct new buildings than to restore or repair old ones.

Carbon time

All organic material contains a type of carbon known as C-14, which begins to decay at a steady rate from the moment the living matter dies, be it wood, bone or shell. Increasingly sophisticated techniques for measuring that rate have enabled an amazing range of data to be established. Accelerator Mass Spectrometry can now date items that died 100,000 years ago. Every archaeological dig hopes to uncover organic material which will reveal its age through the use of these techniques. Unfortunately the most common survival in Scotland's acidic soil is stone, which contains no carbon.

When the Howick people moved about, they may not have travelled very far. The original choice of location was carefully considered, and turned out to be a good one. Digging down through their hearths, the archaeologists came across the bones of the animals the Howick hunters caught and ate. From the thickly wooded hinterland they certainly took wild boar, fox (valued also for its fur) and bear. It is likely that deer and other, smaller animals formed part of their staple. Over 10,000 years little has survived of the hunters' diet of fruits, roots and nuts. But one find was absolutely priceless. Hazelnuts appear to have been abundant in prehistoric Britain, and what convinced archaeologists that Howick was used as a permanent settlement was evidence that the nuts had been roasted. This simple process preserves the hazelnuts as a winter food when all other vegetation has died back. Added to this observation was another crucial characteristic of the nut harvest. When they were roasted, many empty shells were discarded. Since these grew and were picked within one year, they supplied perfect raw material for accurate carbon dating.

Aveline's Hole

In Somerset's Mendip Hills, 18th-century antiquaries came across a cave containing the bones of between 70 and 100 people who appeared to have been buried there. Until modern methods allowed accurate analysis, it was not realized just how old these bones were. Recent research has produced a startling conclusion. The cave, known as 'Aveline's Hole', turns out to be a unique site: the first and, as yet, only hunter-gatherer-fisher cemetery ever to be found. Over a 200-year period, some time around 8000 BC, a community of early people brought their dead and laid them out in Aveline's Hole. It must have been seen as a powerfully sacred place of some sort, perhaps a very early example of a claim or the assertion of rights over a piece of land by the interment of ancestors inside it, or at least inside a cave in that territory. Testing has shown that the dead were local to the Mendip Hills. The remains of 21 individuals have been examined and their bones indicate people with a slight build, an average height of around 1.52 m/5 ft, one of them suffering from arthritis, and a life expectancy of little more than the late twenties.

On the eastern, seaward side of Howick lay the other excellent reason for the location of a permanent settlement. Fish, seals, seabirds and shellfish (such as limpets and mussels, which are available all year round) could all be caught along the coast, and in the estuary of western Doggerland there may have been extensive marshland, reedbeds and wetland containing further bounty. The hunters at Howick would have known the seasonal habits of migratory birds and would have been waiting with traps and nets for the flocks to arrive.

In the autumn of 2002 a group of archaeologists began digging in a field near the farm of East Barns, on the coast of East Lothian, not far from Dunbar. An unremarkable field, with no distinguishing features other than some gentle undulations, it was investigated because a limestone quarry was about to eat into it and there was a history of prehistoric finds nearby. The archaeologists made sensational discoveries. Dating to the centuries around 8000 BC, the remains of a permanent house built by a band of hunter-gatherer-fishers were uncovered. Very like the building at Howick and perhaps even a little older, the East Barns house could accommodate a family of seven or eight. It was laid out in an oval shape with 30 sturdy posts supporting a roughly conical roof and the sides were filled in with turf or timber walling, which was later burned. Like Howick, the house stood near the seashore, where two shallow bays either side of Barns Ness would have provided a year-round source of fish and shellfish.

Now that archaeologists know what to look for and where to look for it, it seems highly likely that more large houses like this wait to be discovered. And as they are, the lives of our hunter-gatherer-fisher ancestors will continue to emerge from the shadows.

In the Severn Estuary, far to the south-west and close to the Mendip Hills, there is poignant evidence of wetland hunting at approximately the same period as the East Barns and Howick houses. At low tide the remains of a prehistoric forest are revealed. Fallen trees and stumps have been preserved in the mud of what was a salt marsh of the sort found in the Doggerland estuaries. Archaeologists have stumbled across a slightly eerie discovery, the fossilized footprints of bands of hunters stalking through the willows and reeds in search of deer or birds. Right and left feet, placed carefully at a slow pace, can be clearly made out, and in one place the hoofprints of deer have been found on the same track. Elsewhere in the ancient salt marsh is evidence of who went hunting: from precise measurements it has been ascertained that women accompanied their men. It had been assumed that, like modern hunter-gatherer societies – including the guga hunters of Ness – men did the hunting and women processed the kill.

The footprints of children have also been found. It may be that they accompanied adults, to learn by observation and imitation. But the risks of a mis-step or an inadvertent shriek might have been too great, and the tracks may be of children sent out into the reedbeds in springtime to gather birds' eggs.

Gathering

When archaeology begins to discover details of diet in the early historic period, around the 1st century AD, the time of the Roman occupation of southern Scotland, it turns out that it was mostly vegetarian. Porridge flavoured with seasonal berries such as juniper, raspberry and wild strawberry, or sometimes with beechnuts or hazelnuts, was popular, the sort of thing we would be happy to eat as part of a modern, healthy diet. But there is a great deal in nature's vegetable and fruit larder which has been forgotten. A good example of an item in yesterday's menu is silverweed, an innocuous-looking green herb now found in hedgerows and meadows. Far from being a weed, it helped to sustain life, probably in prehistoric times and certainly as recently as the 19th century. The roots are tasty (a bit like parsnip) and nutritious, and when dried could be stored over winter and pounded into a meal from which porridge could be made. It was such an important dietary element that the Gaels called it *an seachdamh aran*, the seventh bread. The collector of folk poetry and music Alexander Carmichael (1832–1912) recorded this celebration of silverweed's year-round versatility:

Honey under ground,
Silverweed of spring.
Honey and condiment
Whisked whey of summer.
Honey and fruitage
Carrot of autumn.
Honey and crunching
Nuts of winter.

Three differing ecologies were immediately available to the Howick people – the woodland, the seashore and the estuary. From the work done at low tide on the Severn, evidence has been found that hunters in the 8th millennium BC not only exploited what they found but also managed it. We often think of these people as being at one with nature, part of the eco-system, not dominating it as we do now, but more like the animals they hunted. That now seems overly romantic. The hunters burned the woodland deliberately. No doubt this provided the benefit of driving terrified game animals before the roaring fire towards a place where they could not avoid the hunters waiting to kill or net them, or perhaps to a natural feature like a precipice from whose foot their bodies could be retrieved.

The woodland was also fired to make hunting easier by creating clearings. These were intended to offer browsing or grazing places for animals such as deer or the giant cattle known as aurochs, where hunters could lie in wait for them or set traps along the tracks. Often clearings were made near water. It was much easier to shoot a deer when its head was down grazing or drinking. This required less energy and was preferable to tracking animals through the woodland. In Denmark an aurochs skeleton was found with dozens of flint arrowheads around it, and it looks as though the beast had set off a trap, placed on a path, which fired many arrows at it in some sort of whiplash mechanism.

The discovery and recent recognition of Doggerland as a region in its own right as well as a link between Denmark, north-western Europe and Britain begs a number of important questions. If there was a common prehistoric culture across this area, how did its members communicate? The ancient geography of estuaries, river systems and lakes insists that boats must have been the primary mode of travel, certainly over any distance. Overland, through dense woodland and stretches of wet and boggy ground, walking must have been very difficult, chancy and slow. And in the absence of pack-animals (still to be domesticated), everything had to be carried. In the period following the end of the last Ice Age, the weather had improved greatly, with fewer storms and a generally higher mean temperature than nowadays. That meant a safer passage for smaller craft. At Friarton, near Perth, a dugout canoe was discovered which may date back to the hunter-gatherer-fisher period. The earliest boats yet found in Europe come from Pesse, a town in the Netherlands which lies inland, but not far from the ancient estuary of eastern Doggerland, the long outfall of what are now the estuaries of the Ems, Weser and Elbe. These were also dugouts or log boats, and they begin a tradition of wooden craft well attested by later finds in eastern Britain.

Log boats took a lot of making. Once a thick-trunked tree had been found, felled and brashed, it took much effort and skill with flint axes and adzes to hollow it out. Controlled fire was also used, but the amount of work was nevertheless substantial. An alternative technology existed and is likely to have been much used, but by its nature, it has left little prehistoric trace. Early rock carvings found in Scandinavia show what appear to be boats made from hides or skins. They were certainly sufficiently common in the 1st millennium BC to be noted as a novelty by early Mediterranean writers. A fragment of a lost navigational guide compiled in the 6th century BC reappeared in a manuscript of the 4th century AD, and it talks of northern sailors in 'skiffs of skin', while a historian of the 3rd century BC mentions 'boats of osier [willow] covered with stitched skins'. Surprisingly, a model of what a hide boat looked like was made out of gold in the 1st century BC in Ireland. It shows a large craft with a mast and a yard to hold a sail, a steering oar at the stern, an anchor, and nine seats or thwarts with oars at each threaded through grommets. This is a replica of a large and sophisticated boat, late in the evolution of such craft.

The hide boats that sailed along the coastline of Doggerland were what are known in Ireland as *curraghs*, and the Irish still make them on the same principles and sail them in the same way. In West Kerry skilled and patient enthusiasts have learned the ancient ways of curragh building, and are passing them on to younger people. By the River Lee, opposite the Beamish Brewery in the city of Cork, is the Michel Mara boatyard. It is like no other. Instead of stacks of seasoned planking, swirls of sawdust, the whine of electric saws and planes and the thud of hammering, there is quiet. What appear to be bundles of twigs and limbs of young trees are stacked under the corrugated iron roof of a lean-to, and the workshop seems to have few tools in it, only some dusty old boats slung from its rafters. An old, somewhat neglected Georgian house stands between these, closing off the yard, and inside are stored a great number of inexplicable items, the sort of thing that just might come in handy, whatever it is. Padraic O'Duinnin works outside in the yard, and as he begins to think about building a new boat, he rummages around the lean-to in what seems like a random manner. Picking up countless lengths of green wood, some with brittle leaves still attached, he examines each one carefully, sometimes flexing it, mostly throwing it back on the stack. When at last Padraic has found two long and slightly curved poles of the right thickness, he lays them on the ground. And then he spends some time looking at them.

After more silences, headshaking and some cigarettes, the curved poles are arranged into a narrow oval shape with the ends laid one over the other. Tiny adjustments are made. And then in a flurry of action, Padraic takes some twine and lashes the poles together, putting some tension on each so that the oval widens. Beginning to work quickly now, he bores a dozen small holes along the length of each pole but stops short of piercing through. With the help of his young assistant Michael, he drags a sheaf of hazel rods out of the back of the lean-to. 'Magic wood', he mutters to himself. When the thicker ends of the rods have been whittled to the correct diameter (best if they are left a wee bit too fat), Padraic gently works each one, screwing them back and forth, into the holes made in the oval, the poles which are quickly becoming the gunwales of a curragh. As all 24 hazel rods are fitted, 12 on each side, placed exactly opposite, they are bent over in pairs to meet each other. This is the most technically difficult phase, which takes all of Padraic's practised eye and skill to get right. As each pair of rods is bent together, he and Michael lash them with twine, but leave the ends untrimmed. This slow process shapes the boat, making it sleek or sluggish on the waves, and it needs to be done carefully. As they approach the bow and stern, the pairs of rods get shorter, and Padraic spends much time squatting on his haunches, sighting along the curved spine of tied hazel branches, one eye closed, his hands constantly moving. He walks around the emerging curragh again and again, running a hand over what will become its ribs and belly. All the while he mutters comments (and expletives) in Irish Gaelic, a language the boat understands.

Often he bends a rod a little more, fussing, sometimes he fiddles for several minutes with the poles at the gunwales, his eyes never moving off the curragh. '*OK mata!*' he suddenly exclaims. '*OK a bhalaich!*', straightening his back. It's done. He and Michael quickly trim off the rods, the gunwale poles and the lashings. Then lathes are tied lengthwise, from bow to stern, and the shape of the skeletal boat is complete. To check the tension generated by the bent green wood – very important in a hide boat – Padraic lifts it up with one hand and weighs it for a moment. Then he smiles.

Hide is too expensive to be used now, and for more than a century past the West Kerry men have put black, toughened canvas on their curraghs. Michael and Padraic stretch it tight, like a thick membrane, and begin to lash it to the gunwales. Once that is done they flip over the boat and force in light wooden benches to act as thwarts and keep the frame taut and rigid. Although there is work to be done on waterproofing the canvas as well as bits and pieces of tidying up, the curragh has taken no more than a morning to make.

But they did not have long lives, like some wooden boats. No remains of prehistoric curraghs have yet been found. Partly this is because they are constructed out of organic materials, which quickly decay – and even if preserved by some outrageous chance, what is there to be found? The skeleton of a curragh might resemble no more than a bunch of whittled sticks, twigs of magic wood.

Birthing

The customs surrounding the birth of North American Indian babies offer some sense of how early societies saw the turning points in their lives. Expectant mothers always went walking in the morning because it was believed that babies grew in the womb in the hours around dawn and that walking helped them grow better and bigger. Delivery took place kneeling on a straw-covered robe, firmly grasping an upright pole planted in front. The afterbirth was not buried, since it was believed that such a form of disposal might lead to the death of the baby, and to encourage long life the umbilical cord was dried and hung around the newborn's neck. Grandparents, not parents, conferred names, and they usually chose from a range of totem animals, adding an adjective or phrase and sometimes an indication of gender. The babies were always carried upright in a papoose so that they could see the world they had entered and begin to understand it.

There can, however, be little doubt that they were widely used in prehistoric times. Along with their smaller cousins, the round craft of rivers and lakes called coracles, curraghs are well suited to travel by sea, land and river in north-western Europe. Because they are so light, their draught is measured in inches rather than feet, allowing them to be rowed, paddled or sailed in very shallow water. Even if they are holed by some underwater obstruction, they can be repaired while still afloat – unlike a wooden boat. And when passage becomes difficult through a rocky river-bed, rapids or a waterfall, portage is easy. One man can carry a coracle, two men can manage all but the largest curragh. Even away from the shelter of the coast, the hide boats were capable of long voyages and could survive bad storms. Padraic O'Duinnin has sailed far out into the Atlantic more than once:

> When the sea is big, you must have faith, must not panic or move around. At times like that I imagine a seagull sitting quiet on the waves, letting the swell carry it up and down. The curragh is so light that it sits like a bird on top of the water.

In most circumstances sailing is better and faster than walking, but there were some compelling ancient advantages which we forget all too easily. Hunters moved around a good deal in search of seasonal game and new harvests, and when they moved they took gear with them, and hoped to bring back food after an expedition. Much more can be stowed in even a small curragh than can be carried on the broadest back. And when very small children formed part of the luggage, the boat could act as a welcome prehistoric pram.

If a difficult journey was in prospect, involving very long portages, then it is likely that only the hides needed to make a boat would have been taken. Given the wide availability of the wood required and the speed with which a frame could be put together, it made sense not to bother with an unnecessary burden. Hides were also always useful to make tipis, bender tents or any other form of temporary shelter. There is some late evidence that the kit to make curraghs was routinely taken on journeys. When the Irish monk St Brendan set out on his voyage to the North Atlantic some time in the 6th century AD, his prudent brethren stowed enough spare hide to make two extra curraghs, just in case. On shorter journeys overland, between stretches of water, it might have made sense to carry a boat intact. Turned upside down, it made a grand shelter.

Through the dense woodland of the interior, travel by water was much easier for another, obvious reason. It was difficult to get lost. Small rivers usually maintained the same course, joined bigger ones and eventually flowed into the sea. In contrast with these relative certainties, it was easy to lose a sense of direction in the dense woodland where the canopy was thick and shaded, and anyone who came to realize that they were lost had to climb up above the tree cover to regain their bearings.

Because they were less energy-sapping, boats could take people long distances. Archaeologists digging in Scotland have found the remains of deep-sea fish consumed by hunters who must have been sufficiently skilled and experienced to sail their curraghs far out into the ocean to catch them. And even what appear at first to have been long-range overland contacts between prehistoric peoples were probably achieved at least partly by boat. Shells discovered in cave dwellings in southern Belgium can only have come from strata found in the Paris region, 150 km/95 miles to the south. But it is probable that they were carried in a boat which sailed down to the mouth of the Seine, up the coastline as far as the Channel Estuary would allow and then inland on the south Doggerland river system to their destination. In the same caves shells from the Loire Valley have also been found, an overland distance of 350 km/220 miles, much longer by river and sea – but much easier. Sceptics should recall that until the middle of the 19th century the fastest route between New York and San Francisco was via Tierra del Fuego.

Curraghs, coracles and log boats linked the peoples of north-western Europe together into a coherent culture because their geography encouraged and enabled it. Doggerland should perhaps be thought of less as a land-bridge and more as a water-bridge, with the land acting as a sort of handrail. The people who came to Howick Haven almost certainly rowed up the great western estuary of Doggerland. The recent finds off Tynemouth certainly support that supposition. Stories played an important part in these journeys. Even if they were pioneers, the Howick hunters are highly unlikely to have ventured into a land about which they knew nothing. Stories of the lands in the north may have endured and been repeated throughout the thousand years of the Cold Snap and encouraged a return when the weather improved. Pioneers may also have mounted summer hunting parties to the north, each one a recce as well as an expedition in search of food.

Navigation

Prehistoric sailors had no magnetic compass, but their sea lore must have been rich and usually reliable. Most made passage by pilotage, by sighting seamarks on land and using them for guidance. When crossing a stretch of water, it was important to 'aim off', that is, to take account of the strength of the tides and wind and to aim to the right or left of a seamark so that the boat finally came at it exactly. Distance could also be measured by shifts at the oars, and speed by dropping a log into the water and estimating how quickly the boat passed it. The ship's log was attached to a piece of knotted cord, so that the speed in knots could be worked out. To find the sun in foggy conditions, and take a bearing from it, a piece of feldspar was used, known by the Vikings as a sunstone.

However it came about, the establishment of the permanent settlement at Howick has altered our understanding of the early hunter-gatherer-fisher communities. Until recently we saw their impact on the landscape as slight, fleeting and transient – they moved, we believed, like wraiths through the wildwood and along the seashore rather than living on it, without making anything resembling a home, spending almost the whole of their lives in the open air. While this impression of the lives of our early ancestors may still be the conventional wisdom, the atmosphere at Howick is different, and demands a revision of long-held views.

First and most obviously, the building of a permanent house implies settlement and not transience. And in turn settlement means ownership in some form or other. The Howick hunters had a territory which they thought of as theirs. For a hundred years they gathered nuts and berries in their woods, harvested mussels, oysters and limpets from their stretch of seashore, took fresh water from their stream and were, it must be assumed, prepared to assert ownership of that territory and protect it from encroachment. The Howick land may have been extensive, down to the estuaries of the Aln and Cocquet, on into the interior penetrated by these meandering rivers, and to the north, up to the singular crags of Bamburgh and Lindisfarne and the Farne Islands (where seals could be hunted). It is impossible to be sure. Only one house, after all, has survived the erosion of the sand-cliff at Howick and, if there were indeed more, no sense of the size of the whole settlement is now available.

No substantial houses from the 8th millennium BC have been unearthed in eastern Doggerland, in what is now Denmark, but a strong sense of how ownership of territory was established has come to light. At Vedbaek in north-eastern Denmark finds have been made which reveal a great deal about the culture of early hunter-gatherer-fisher societies. Archaeologists came across the gossamer remains of an encampment, a series of soil marks left by hide-covered tents made out of bent-over sticks rammed into the earth. What seemed significant was that, despite its flimsy nature, this settlement was well established, used again and again. And within the ground area of some of the tents, the archaeologists found burials. Mostly they were parts of bodies, but one was complete and it offered a powerful, almost magical symbolism. A child had been laid in the earth with a small piece of local stone placed in its mouth. The stone had been shaped like a tongue. It was a remarkable find, full of meaning, difficult to grasp. The Danes interpreted the grave as a clear example of territory marking, a claim staked by burial, expressing the notion of continuity of ownership by the interment of ancestors in the ground upon which they had once walked their lives. Perhaps the connection is too clumsy and lumbering, but the tongue-shaped stone in the mouth of the dead child may represent a magical manifestation of a practical principle – the centrality of territory to existence, the way that the bounty of the land filled the mouths of its people.

Near the Vedback settlement there is a cemetery, several burials which give a further and poignant sense of the spiritual life of the people of north-western Europe. We do not understand the details of meaning in their symbolism, but it does reach across the millennia between us to touch something deep and shared. In some graves the dead were laid to rest with head and feet on deer antlers. In another is a woman adorned in all her finery, with around her neck a string made from the teeth of 43 different stags. Either she herself or someone who loved her had been a hunter of great prowess. Beside her lies an image of tenderness and mystery. The body of her baby is buried nestled in a white swan's wing. And for reasons we can only guess at, the family had laid a small flint knife at the baby's waist. This burial is beautiful, powerful and with much to say about how the hunters understood death, hinting at a belief in an afterlife, perhaps even the migration of souls, but we do not know the language and cannot read the messages in the graves at Vedbaek.

One at a time

Mobility was important to hunter-gatherer-fisher bands and this could have been critically impaired if mothers had been forced to carry more than one baby or toddler. Evolution coped with this practical difficulty by ensuring that while women still lactated they remained unable to conceive another child. Breast-feeding probably went on as late as possible (there being no substitute source of milk), up to the point where a four- or five-year-old could both chew and become a useful member of the band.

Aboriginal Australians were ruthless with unwanted pregnancies. Abortions were induced with herbs, and if that was unsuccessful, the woman's belly would be pummelled. If that didn't work the baby was killed at birth. And if a mother did not survive childbirth but her child did, it was routinely killed because there was no one to suckle it.

The prehistoric peoples of northern Europe wanted to be close to their dead. Clearly their remains were thought to have power which could be enlisted both to protect and to claim precious territory. Nowadays we corral our ancestors into cemeteries kept separate from the living, often hidden behind high walls on the edges of towns and villages, and the thought of burying them under the floors of our houses belongs only in the macabre world of insane serial killers such as Frederick West. But the hunters appear to have been comforted by the presence of their dead, and there is strong evidence that this sense of comfort and reverence lasted a long time in Scotland.

In 2003 excavations on the Hebridean island of South Uist uncovered a house dating to 1000 BC at Cladh Hallan, on the Atlantic coast. Under the floor the archaeologists made an astonishing find. The remains of two mummified bodies emerged from the soil. And they turned out to be 500 and 300 years respectively older than the house. At some point around 1500 BC (and probably long before) people who lived near Cladh Hallan had discovered that peat could be used as a preservative. Immediately after death they took the body of what must have been an important ancestor and placed it in a peat bog for a period of between six and 18 months. When they exhumed the body, they found that all the processes of decay had been pre-empted. The bodies probably resembled brown leather, but with all of their features recognizable to the people who had known them. Bog-bodies have been found in Cheshire and in Denmark, and the mummies from Cladh Hallan may have looked like them. Once the exhumation had taken place and the mummification seen to be successful (the 1500 BC body was a man and the 1300 BC body a woman), although it is not clear what happened next the mummies do not appear to have been buried. Perhaps they were kept for display in a special building, perhaps they lay after death in the houses of their descendants, perhaps they were kept safe in some sort of sarcophagus like Egyptian mummies. However unlikely it may sound, these bodies were seen as part of a community and their families probably communicated with them regularly.

Some time around 1000 BC, the mummies were buried under the floor of the house at Cladh Hallan. Each body was interred intact, with no bones missing or disturbed, presumably because the skin and sinew preserved through mummification were enough to bind them in place. Perhaps the inhabitants at Cladh Hallan finally buried the man and the woman 500 and 300 years after death because most of the flesh and sinew had perished and there was a danger that the skeletons would disarticulate.

Over time much personal knowledge of these people – what they looked and sounded like, for example – would also have withered, and knowledge of who they were would have become much less vivid than whatever it was they represented. In this way the lives of ancestors entered into a mythology and were revered for whatever it was they had done or enabled; perhaps they were even worshipped or propitiated. If an ancestor had, say, discovered a new hunting ground, or developed a new technique of tool-making, the reality of that may have become bound up with their spirit, literally embodied in the mummified remains.

Çatalhöyük

Early urban cultures also liked to be close to their dead. In the remarkable town of Çatalhöyük in southern Turkey, founded around 7000 BC, the mud-brick houses were packed together in dense clusters, with no streets or lanes between. There were no front doors either and access to each house was gained by climbing a wooden ladder to the roof and entering through a door in a small tower.

Before burial, bodies were exposed on platforms so that vultures and insects could remove the flesh. The skeletons were then buried under the beds of their relatives. Sometimes several generations were packed in below a sleeping bench.

Excavations in South Uist have found seven conical-roofed round-houses, similar to the much earlier building at Howick, but as yet there is no clue as to why the mummies were kept above ground, almost certainly on display in some way. It may have much to do with the proving of title to a particular territory, and the selection and preservation of the man and the woman may have been related to important incidents in the past which lent weight to such claims. Perhaps they were heroes who became gods or totems. It is impossible to know very much past the obvious – that prehistoric people were comfortable in the physical, tangible presence of their dead, that they needed them, went to considerable lengths to preserve their remains, gave them valuable grave goods, had some sense of a life after death and believed that in their corpses lay tremendous spiritual power.

Indigenous Australians of the present day appear to share similar beliefs and in particular to understand their land in similar ways. All of their history and spirituality, their *dreaming* as it is known, is bound up with the territory on which they walk their lives. They do not see it as property in the sense that we do, as something that can be exchanged for another piece of land or for money. All of its particular features, its rivers, trees, mountains and grasslands, are an intimate part of how they experience their world. Much more intense than the sentiment we might feel for the place where we were born, their attachment to their land is umbilical. Their ancestors are planted in it and make it fertile, across its face their lives are played out and on its air their spirits fly. They have no sense of owning it – it simply *is* them, and they are it.

The remnants of this intensity can sometimes be observed in the Celtic communities of western Britain and Ireland. Until the 19th century this was an overwhelmingly rural society with no large towns and a people who had worked the land, often the same piece of land, for uncounted generations. When the forced emigrations began, many Welsh, Scots and Irish Celts suffered badly, often physically, from what commentators miscalled 'homesickness'. It was nothing of the kind, or rather only very distantly related to the hearthside cosiness implied in the term. In Welsh it is called *hiraeth*, in Gaelic *ionndrain*, and both express the sense of loss, longing or even something irretrievably missing. These emotions relate less to the warmth of a family kitchen and more to the landscape, to the territory holding the bodies of their ancestors, over which all their past happened, and from which they have been ripped away.

It is inadequate to assert that the prehistoric peoples of Scotland loved their land. Like Aboriginal Australians, their relationship to it was more complex. They were buried inside it and it was inside them, indivisible.

~~~

People danced in imitation of the animals which shared the land, perhaps to show affinity or reverence, perhaps mastery. At one of the earliest hunter-gatherer-fisher sites yet found in Britain, 20 sets of deer antlers have been discovered. Dating to about 9000 BC, immediately after the end of the Cold Snap, the antlers were found at Star Carr in North Yorkshire. What convinced archaeologists that these were masks and not trophies was something very obvious and practical: holes had been drilled through the skull-bone at the base of each set. This enabled a dancer or a shaman-priest to tie the horns on to his head. And because they were solid bone and heavy, the antlers had been shaved down to make them lighter.

The finds at Star Carr are very early and very significant. There are links with the remnants of Doggerland culture. Some analysts believe that the site was an inland camp, perhaps a summertime out-station for a coastal settlement. The skeleton of a young dog found nearby, at Seamer Carr, showed a predominantly marine diet, suggesting that it had been brought inland to the place where it died. Whatever the pup's origins, other Doggerland links add to what the find of the deer-masks suggests. In the National Museum in Copenhagen, some of the earliest surviving art made in northern Europe is on show. Carved in low relief on bone are images of a deer hunt, a depiction which historians have interpreted as magical, more than a celebration, perhaps an invocation of the spirits of the chase. Beautiful amber amulets of bears have also been discovered. These were probably worn around the neck as a way of co-opting the spirit of the bear as a protector and possibly an enabler. Bears were the largest and most ferocious carnivores to hunt in the wildwood, and when they stood on their hind legs they looked almost human, as no other animal could – giant, immensely powerful versions of men. They hunted like men, could swipe salmon out of the rivers, climb trees, take honey from wild bees. If a bear charged, its target was slashed to ribbons with the claws on hand-like paws, ripped apart by razor-sharp teeth.

The men – and perhaps the women – who tied on the deer masks at Star Carr aimed to represent the deer they stalked in the woods and by the lakeside where they lived. There can be no doubt about that. But what were they doing when they imitated the movements of the animals, and why did they go to such lengths to do it?

In Staffordshire, in the heart of England, at the village of Abbot's Bromley, the deer-men still dance. On the Monday following the first Sunday after 4 September, they are up at dawn to dance for a day around the farms surrounding the village. In what is called 'the deer running' six men each carry a set of huge 12-pointer reindeer antlers fixed to a wooden mask. Carbon dating has shown that the antlers are at least a thousand years old and originated in Scandinavia. Three sets are painted white and three black. Accompanying the deer-runners are four other characters: the Fool, Maid Marion (also known as the 'Man-Woman'), the Hobby Horse and the Bowman.

Bogs

Scotland has two sorts of bogs. Raised bogs began to develop about 5500 BC and are shaped like upturned soup-plates. Sphagnum moss grows abundantly on raised bogs such as Moss of Cree in Wigtownshire or Bankhead Moss in Fife. Blanket bogs are more widespread in the north, and they can be very large indeed, such as Rannoch Moor. Peat is the decomposing deposit of all the plants that grew in the area of a bog and its spread appears to have accompanied a change in the earth's climate. Between 12,000 and 6000 BC the earth's tilt altered, bringing colder winters and warmer summers, and there was what geologists are fond of calling 'a major shift in pluviality': it started to rain more. It will come as no surprise at all to the inhabitants of the Highlands and Islands that the prime cause of peat growth and spread was wetness. Other factors, such as volcanic eruptions in Iceland which blocked out sunshine for a few years, or compacted soil and poor drainage caused by human land use, may have contributed, but high rainfall and low evaporation appear to have created the bogs. Peat now covers areas which were cultivated in the past. It contains ancient tree stumps which lie well above the modern treeline, and perhaps a good deal of well-preserved, as yet undiscovered evidence for the lives of the hunter-gatherer-fishers who lived in sunny Scotland before the last major shift in pluviality.

After the deer-men have danced to the music of a melodeon, with the Hobby Horse snapping his jaws and the Bowman twanging his bow-string to keep time, they separate into two groups. Black antlers face white and a ritual fight begins. Because the antlers are so heavy, the deer-men have to rest them on their shoulders before lowering their heads for a dignified, slow-motion charge. The oldest part of the ritual is thought to be the moment when the Bowman begins to stalk the herd of deer-runners, firing imaginary arrows at them. As the small tableau makes its way down the main street of Abbot's Bromley, the ghosts of a long past hover behind. Some touch the edges of recorded history. It cannot be a coincidence that the village lies in the heart of the territory of the Cornovii, an ancient Celtic tribe noted on Ptolemy's map of Britain. *Cornovii* means 'The Horned People'.

Over ten centuries the dance of the deer-runners has no doubt been much corrupted. Maid Marion and the Fool are obvious late-medieval additions, and there is a strong local tradition that this version of the dance was brought over the North Sea to England by the Angles who came from southern Denmark between AD 400 and 550. But that does not make it an alien intrusion or irrelevant. Ideas and people had come to Britain from that direction for millennia. And although the running of the deer-men at Abbot's Bromley is dressed up as a quaint bit of 'heritage', it is nevertheless clearly very old, and informative, telling us something about what went on at Star Carr in 9000 BC.

The hunters who first wore the ancient deer masks were doing what is whispered by the rituals of the modern deer-runners. They were engaged in asserting their power and knowledge, making their luck with good magic and encouraging each other, especially the less experienced. Well-documented hunting societies of the recent past had similar ceremonies. Before going out after the buffalo, the Oglala Sioux Indians of North America danced. Around the silhouette of a speared buffalo painted in the grass they circled, singing, chanting and ululating, praising the spirit of the animal. Since it was central to their lives, providing almost all their wants, from glue to hide for their tipis, the Sioux worshipped the buffalo as a sacred animal, and revered it for its bravery and strength. It was part of their world, and they were part of the world it inhabited. The buffalo had virtues admired by the Indians – they did not see it as a victim or a dumb animal to be exploited. It could be heroic. There exists an Indian report which marvelled at the courage of a wounded bull attacked by wolves. Despite having its eyes, nose and tongue torn out and its hind legs shredded, it fought on, tossing its attackers with its horns.

The hunters of Star Carr, Howick and the north did not depend on a single species in the same way. But such archaeology as has come to light suggests that they did revere the deer and the bear, perhaps even worshipped them. And in order to trap or kill them, they certainly had to understand and be able to outwit the animals they hunted. Perhaps enough of them escaped or fought back to engender respect and reverence.

Cavemen

There is no doubt that early hunters used handy caves, particularly by the seashore, as places to live, even if they sometimes had to compete with animals for tenancy. However, it is in caves that the stereotype of grunting prehistoric savages is most effectively dismissed. Great and vivid art was made by these so-called savages, and much of it was painted on the walls of caves. In the south-west of France and the north of Spain there are extraordinary depictions of animals and people. At Altamira, near Santander in Spain, there exists a dazzling menagerie of animals painted in a long labyrinth of underground chambers. They are very beautiful, created with a startling economy of line and pigment, suggesting vivid movement and showing real character. It is thought that the act of painting an animal was closely related to hunting it. If it was possible to capture its spirit in paint, it might be possible to capture it in body. As flickering torchlight played on the cave walls at Altamira, it may have seemed to contemporaries that the animals came alive. But it is the business of painting itself which seems to be more important than looking at it. Many scenes were painted in inaccessible places, not visible without great effort, certainly not for the casual observer or the ignorant. And often earlier work was painted over several times. Perhaps the sense of being underground was important to the cave painters, the booming resonances of sound, the echoes and the silences, the atmosphere.

It may be that prehistoric peoples depicted much more than is suggested by surviving cave painting. Art may have existed out of doors in the wildwood, in places where it could have been weathered into invisibility or washed away after a heavy shower of rain. If the act of making it was what mattered, then its impermanence may have been unimportant. But they could paint, these people, and when considering the hunter-gatherer-fisher bands of Britain, we should remember that they were directly descended from the extraordinary artists of Altamira.

When the weather warmed after the Cold Snap and the wildwood began to carpet the plains and hills, men were forced to adapt their hunting techniques. In the open, herds of reindeer or wild horses could often be intercepted on their migratory routes at a vulnerable place, a river crossing or a narrow defile that restricted their ability to flee, a place where hunters could get close. When the encroaching wildwood drove the herds further north, or to extinction, different animals occupied the natural vacuum. Deer, both roe and red, wild boar, the aurochs and a host of smaller fauna liked the dense forest, acquiring camouflage, learning to move quietly and unobtrusively, emerging to browse in the half-dark of dawn or evening.

The smaller prey, such as badger, otter or pine marten made identifiable tracks on the floor of the wildwood, habitually tunnelling through the same clumps of cover and leaving droppings. A hunter who observed these daily movements or signs knew where to set snares. Larger prey also had regular habits that proved fatal. Pits were dug on pathways and stakes set at the bottom to skewer aurochs, deer and boar. Both these methods of trapping required more forethought than energy, and certainly no bravery. But they probably supplied a reliable source of food and pelts, depending on the time of year. Much less certain was hunting by stalking. Animals such as deer possess keenly honed senses of smell, sight and hearing, and while there is no doubt that a stalk ending with a kill is very exciting, it often failed. Perhaps that is precisely why this method of hunting figures so prominently in the archaeological record – excitement would have been just as attractive to prehistoric people as to most of us. And the sense of man and his wits pitted against an animal and its senses and speed was just as dramatic. There was more glory and a better story in stalking and bringing down a stag with an expertly aimed arrow or spear than in finding it impaled on stakes at the bottom of a pit that took hours of sweat to dig out. Grave goods often underline the prestige of this method of hunting.

More often than not hunters who stalked their prey missed with one shot, and were unable to get off another quickly enough to kill. When a deer or an aurochs escaped with a wound, it lost blood, and blood could be tracked through the wildwood. Found near Blackpool in Lancashire is a grisly example of how long that process could take. In the mud at High Furlong the skeleton of an elk and some artefacts found beside it show that around 10,000 BC it was attacked by hunters wielding spears or arrows and a chopping weapon of some kind. Although the terrified animal was badly wounded, it escaped. But some time later, its pursuers attacked again with spears, and again the animal managed to get away, only to die as it made its way through the boggy lake where it was found 12,000 years later.

Early in the era of the hunter-gatherer-fishers, dogs were domesticated to help do a better job than the Blackpool hunters. From around 6000 BC they trotted at the heels of their masters as they entered the forest. Good hunting dogs were much prized, and in Denmark and northern Germany their burials have been discovered. Resembling Alsatians or German Shepherds (scarcely surprising, since they were domesticated wolves), some were interred with rich grave goods, flint blades and antlers. And as if to add further honour, the dead dogs were laid out in the same attitudes as humans. In fact some seem to have been killed so that they could be buried with their masters, in a clear implication of great intimacy and a singular relationship. The modern notion of dogs is of course as pets, but it is likely that these animals were less than cuddly, probably ferocious when need be, and responsive to the commands of only one person. The modern notion of hunting dogs is limited to foxhounds, the panting mass of brown, black and white which sniffs around the feet of horses ridden by people in pink or black. But in the distant past, and particularly in Scotland, there were several sorts. Scent hounds were known as *rauchs* and were trained to work on a leash and never to bark, even when excited. Once a deer or an aurochs had been hit by an arrow or lance from its master, a rauch could follow a blood trail until it caught up with the exhausted animal and finished it off.

Best friends

Both chihuahuas and bull mastiffs are descended from wolves, although it requires a great stretch of the imagination to see much of a connection. Recent research conducted by Dr Deborah Lynch of the Canine

Studies Institute in Ohio has identified ten progenitor breeds for all dogs, and her belief is that distinctions were first made in prehistoric times. The different progenitor classifications are: sight and scent hounds, working and guard dogs, toy/companion, flushing spaniels, water retrievers, pointers, terriers and herding dogs. Various ongoing DNA sequencing projects, not unlike that conducted by Professor Bryan Sykes, aim to determine how old these progenitor types are and possibly where they originated. Geoff Sampson, the canine genetics co-ordinator of the Kennel Club UK, commented: 'We are literally [!] sitting on our seat edges waiting for the publication of this.'

The landscape of Scotland and its place-names tell a much less glorious and more practical tale, the story of the hunt by drive and sett. Straddling the western end of the border between England and Scotland lies one of the largest man-made woods in Europe, the Eskdalemuir-Craik Forest. Almost buried by the eastern edges of the huge wood is a series of place-names recalling the deer-hunts of the past. The Eildrig Burn trickles off Eildrig Hill, flowing by Eilrig [*sic*] Cottage and the Eild Rig, before tipping into the Borthwick Water. It is a quiet place now, but many generations ago it would have echoed to frantic shouts and screams and the grass would have been soaked with blood. This dense concentration of names, and the particular configuration of the landscape, betrays one of the hunting grounds of the hunter-gatherer-fishers. Eildrig is from *eileirg*, a defile – natural or artificial. And it was the destination of a deer drive. Beaters strung out in a line attempted to push as many animals as possible towards the wide mouth of a geographical funnel (often others were mixed up in the mad rush – wild boar, aurochs, foxes, all sorts of small creatures). Once in, they were driven to a narrow point where groups of hunters stood, probably hidden from view, waiting for the kill. The most important hunter was given a place of honour, generally where he was most likely to make a kill. This was known as a *sete, sett* or *seat*. Near Eildrig is Kingside Loch, a name that remembers a forgotten king who enjoyed the killing sete of honour.

If natural features such as cliffs were not available, a narrow valley of the right shape could be adapted. At Eildrig it looks as though the course of the steep-sided burn was suitable. Before the drive began, the hunting party would have prepared the ground. A high fence was built at the top of a slope, and since adult deer can jump prodigious heights when badly frightened, it had to be at least 2 m/7 ft tall. Living trees were often used, with long stakes driven into any open ground between them. *Palus* is the Latin for stake, and it is the origin of 'pale', the precise English term for a deer fence. Branches were woven between the stakes and the trees to present as formidable a barrier as possible; if necessary, a ditch was dug directly in front of the pale.

But it was important to give the fleeing animals the impression that the passage was open at the narrow end, so that they kept on coming and did not wheel away. And as they passed through, the hunters emerged from cover and used arrows and spears to slaughter as many as possible. Any that escaped might be tripped and caught by nets laid on the grass. Hunting was usually a necessity, and needed to be well organized to be productive.

How many?

The population of hunter-gatherer-fishers was probably small, at least in the millennia immediately following the retreat of the ice. Estimates for the number of people living in Scotland vary wildly – from 150 to several thousand. The only safe assumption is that the number was small and that bands ranged over wide areas. If that is so, meetings with other bands are unlikely to have been accidental, especially if young men and women were looking for marriage partners. The overwhelming probability is that meetings were matters of tradition, both in time and place. The solstices are a good and widely understood way of keeping ancient time, and somewhere easily accessible by boat would have made a good meeting place.

The finding of marriage partners was probably not the sole purpose of such meetings. Perhaps trade went on as well. Surpluses could have been bartered to fill shortages. Information might also have been exchanged and new items or techniques passed on. All of this implies good communication skills, perhaps even a commonly understood language. When Native Americans met, those with different languages used a lexicon of signs, made mainly with the hands, and it may be that hunter bands in early Scotland did the same.

The tone of these meetings is difficult to guess at, but they may well have been friendly if marriages were to be made. Provided there was no competition for land or resources, everyone had much to gain by being neighbourly.

Archaeologists have calculated that pioneer hunter-gatherer-fishers edged northwards at a rate of about 1 km/½ mile a year after the ice had retreated. It seems likely that bands first ventured out into little-known territory on summer hunting expeditions. From Howick the simplest way to travel was by sea, coasting up to the estuary of the River Tweed and on to the Firth of Forth, using these waterways to penetrate inland. At some point summer camps became base camps, occupied all year round. What prompted pioneers to become settlers can never be known for sure, but motives probably changed little over millennia. As family groups expanded and marriage took people out of their original settings, new territory would have been needed and even preferred. As the prehistoric population expanded, slowly, more room was required. It has been estimated that one hunter's territory extended to 10 sq. km./4 sq. miles. In the north there was virgin ground available, where fruits, roots and nuts were harvested only by the animals, game and fish were abundant and there was no human competition for any of it. And then, of course, there was simple curiosity. What was the land under the northern stars like?

Traces of a very early hunter-gatherer-fisher site have been found at Cramond, on the Firth of Forth near Edinburgh. Some time in the 9th millennium BC people came ashore here at the mouth of the River Almond, where landward, seashore and estuarine environments could supply a year-round means to live. It was almost certainly colonized from the south, by people coasting in curraghs or log boats, perhaps from Howick or East Barns, perhaps the ancestors of the hunters who built the roundhouse there in 7700 BC. Evidence of a slightly earlier settlement has been found at Daer, in the Lowther Hills, near the watershed of the rivers Clyde and Tweed.

The earliest, most fully documented hunter-gatherer-fisher site in Scotland was certainly colonized by sea, because even in the period immediately following the Cold Snap it was an island. And it was also an integral part of a busy seaway. Rhum is nestled between the southern wings of Skye and faces the deeply indented coastline at Morar, where sea-lochs penetrate far into the interior; it has Canna at its back, and Eigg and Muck to the south-east. Rhum may be an island but it was not isolated. And when it is remembered that sea travel was for millennia preferred to any other method, its location comes to be seen as prime, neither cut off nor remote.

The origins of the pioneers who came to Rhum after the Cold Snap are a matter for speculation. If they sailed up from the south, their voyage would have been well signposted by distinctive seamarks of all sorts – mountains, islands, sea-lochs. But they could have approached from the north, having coasted up eastern Doggerland, made passage between Shetland and Orkney (the latter then joined to the mainland) and sailed down to the Hebrides.

Shaped like a nick chopped out of the body of the island, Loch Scresort is the only substantial sea-loch to penetrate any distance into Rhum. It is an attractive landing, facing east towards the mainland, sheltered from the wilder Atlantic weather. At Kinloch, a Gaelic name meaning 'head of the loch', the remains of Scotland's earliest recorded settlers have been found. Bender tents or tipis were set up there regularly, possibly over many centuries after 7000 BC, as hunters made repeated use of a classic seashore site. One of the attractions of Rhum must have been the presence of bloodstone. Scotland is not rich in flint deposits and places with good alternatives, such as the igneous rocks of bloodstone and pitchstone, were worth exploiting. Thousands of microliths (small worked pieces of stone) have been found at Kinloch, most of them bloodstone, some agates.

When shelters were erected, the space inside them would have been strictly organized. Discipline was needed around hearths where fires burned for warmth and cooking, particularly when roofing was made from plant material. Dividers may have marked off areas for women, single men, older people, children, perhaps even sacred objects or gods. The status of the site at Kinloch is not clear. Unlikely to have been a base camp – there is no evidence of anything as substantial as the earlier house at Howick – it may only have been occupied by summer hunting parties. If an entire band visited Rhum over a long period, it is likely that they stored wooden building materials for a planned return the following year, perhaps taking away only the hide covering for a tipi or a bender in their boats. With such benign sailing conditions, clear sea-marks and routeways in constant sight of land, and the advantages of living at coastal locations, it is impossible to imagine the Kinloch band travelling long distances in any other way. There is compelling evidence that the settlers on Rhum sustained themselves with whisky, what is sometimes called 'heather ale'. Traces of pollen found on potsherds have been analysed as the possible residue of a sort of alcohol resembling whisky. Of particular note were the spores of the royal fern, often used as a painkiller by herbalists. The archaeobotanist Dr Brian Moffat believes that the presence of the spores was not medicinal in this case, but practical. Evidently royal fern can be used as a chemical agent to halt the fermentation process.

Ochre

Red ochre is made by heating a yellow clay containing iron oxide. It was the first coloured paint, and ochre mines dating to 38,000 BC have been found in southern Africa. In the classical period the best sort came from the Black Sea, from the city of Sinope, and sinoper or sinopia became synonymous with the colour red. Much later, native North Americans were called 'Red Indians' because they wore it as a protection against evil. Perhaps the red ochre in prehistoric burials had a similar purpose. Because of its association with blood, red has come to stand for danger in our society. It is only a small imaginative leap to associate it with death. An alternative interpretation is that red ochre was daubed on the cheeks of the pallid faces of the dead to make them seem alive as they moved from one world to another.

Because of their modern remoteness and the strong possibility that prehistoric remains lie untouched by the plough or have been covered over and protected by peat, archaeologists in search of the beginnings of the repopulation of Scotland have paid special attention to the Hebrides. On the island of Jura three stone hearths were found lying side by side. They were dated to the 7th millennium BC and may be the first hint of more substantial dwellings. Traces of red ochre were found, maybe relating to burial practice. In northern Europe ochre was used when interment took place and may have been intended to mark out sacred ground in some way.

Weired

Fish-traps could be complex structures but they were usually based on the use of a weir. Like the Indigenous peoples of north-western Canada, whose culture was founded on an abundance of salmon, the hunter-gatherers who fished in Scotland's rivers and streams were skilled at building a weir across a river. This resembled a close-knit wicker fence and was staked at intervals with heavier posts. It was very important not to make a dam, creating a head of pressure which could bring down a weir, but rather to allow the current to flow through with a minimum of obstruction. Equally, if the fence was too gappy, the salmon could swim through it and make their way upstream. In the pools behind the weir, where the trapped fish milled around, they could be speared at ease and according to need by a *leister*, a three-pronged spear. Or the fish could be funnelled into small traps where they could be taken even more readily. Some of Scotland's rivers still retain the ghost of these and later traps in their place-names. Yair on the Tweed near Selkirk is one such. It means 'fish-trap'.

Digs on the island of Islay discovered more stone artefacts and located groups of hunters who were there around 6500 BC. But no human or animal bones survived the acidic nature of the peat cover. Tiny charcoal deposits recovered from cores sunk into the bogs hint that the hunters may have burned the woodland to create pasture around Loch Gorm, to encourage game. At Bolsay, more than 250,000 flints were found, an immense quantity that persuaded archaeologists that they had come across a base camp rather than a set of temporary shelters. But the finds yielded little more than dates, offering a limited sense of the texture and detail of the lives of early settlers.

On Colonsay, 20 km/12 miles to the north-west of Islay, something extraordinary did emerge. At Staosnaig, on the old raised beach, a pit had been scooped out to reduce the need for a high-pitched roof for a shelter. When the location was abandoned, the hunters filled in the pit with something surprising. Hundreds of thousands of charred hazelnut shells had been dumped in it, too many to count. Carbon dating showed that this huge number had all been harvested in the same year, around 6700 BC. Near the main rubbish pit, other smaller pits had been dug and it appears that these were used to roast the hazelnuts. The method of processing was straightforward: a pit was filled with nuts and a fire lit on top. As was noted at Howick, not only does roasting nuts often improve their flavour, it also preserves them. And so that the sheer volume did not prove too great a logistical difficulty, it is likely that the nuts were mashed into a paste.

Big ochre dough

The longest continuous tradition of painting is Australian. For more than 40,000 years Aboriginal Australians have used natural colours to create art and, recently, to do so very profitably. A picture painted with ochre and gum entitled *All That Big Rain Coming From Topside* by Rover Thomas was auctioned by Sotheby's in Melbourne. It fetched the astonishing price of 786,625 Australian dollars (about £340,000) and was bought by the National Gallery of Australia to prevent it from falling into foreign hands and leaving the country.

Hazelnuts had been found on hunter-gatherer-fisher sites before, but in nothing like these quantities. Because of its distance from the mainland, Colonsay had no squirrels to compete with humans for the nuts. This ecological oddity probably encouraged the growth of many trees, but the sheer weight of the harvest implies a degree of management, of cultivation. To encourage growth, pruning must have gone on over a period of some years before the great harvest. Many people were involved and the planning and social organization needed to complete such a large-scale enterprise must have been considerable. Given all of that, it is surprising to note that the harvest appears to have been very destructive. Pollen samples taken on Colonsay show that the hunters cut down the hazel trees as well as stripping them of nuts. Perhaps that was simply a brutal way of collecting them. In any case they would have understood what they were doing, and cannot have expected or intended to return for some time, if ever. Alternative sources of nuts and other winter staples must have existed in abundance at other handy locations. It may be that the destruction of the trees was a religious act of some kind, returning the island to the gods of uncultivated nature. It is impossible to be sure, or even more than vague.

Rubbish is often eloquent. On the tiny Hebridean island of Oronsay, linked to Colonsay at low tide, large amounts of prehistoric rubbish were piled up in five middens at various points near the shoreline. Nearly 1,500 years after the hazelnuts were gathered hunters began to throw away great quantities of seashells. Hundreds of thousands of mussel, clam, oyster, limpet, razor and scallop shells were deposited between 5300 and 4300 BC. Mixed in with these were fish-bones, bits of antler, even human remains, as well as much else.

The shell middens of Oronsay are strange, the deposit of an unknowable decision. Analysis of the human bones shows an exclusively marine diet of fish, seabirds, shellfish and seals. Oronsay is small and unremarkable, and it seems that during the period when the middens were made all of the other nearby islands were uninhabited. Colonsay, Islay, Jura, Rhum and others all have traces of hunter-gatherer-fisher occupation both before the earliest and after the latest date of the Oronsay middens. But between 5300 and 4300 BC, they appear to have been deserted. The unanswerable question is why.

This surprising information strongly suggests that Oronsay was permanently settled, with a band living on the island throughout the winter. A brilliant analysis of some of the fish-bones found in the middens has demonstrated that each one was filled at a different time of the year. The band that occupied Oronsay may have moved around for some reason, perhaps following the seasonal appearance of fish, birds or seals in different places; perhaps the wind direction or the weather prompted mobility. Given that Oronsay is a small island, the uprooting of well-established shelters to move them only 3–5 km/2–3 miles seems unlikely – even more so when it is recalled that the hunters who lived there were skilled inshore seamen able to reach any coastal location quickly. Alternatively, it may be that the different middens represent seasonal visits by five or so different bands who enjoyed fishing rights off the island.

When archaeologists found human fingers deliberately placed on seal flippers and buried in one of the Oronsay middens, the image struck a note of recognition. Like the baby nestling in the swan's wing at the Vedbaek grave in Denmark, there was an unmistakable sense of ancient symbolism. Perhaps the soul of a baby was thought to fly in the evening sky with the great white birds, while on Oronsay there was a sense that souls swam with the seals in the deeps of the world.

Less speculative is the notion that the dead, or parts of their corpses, were buried in the shell middens of Oronsay, and in other places on the long Atlantic shoreline, to mark ownership of the land and the fishing in the waters off it.

I PREVIOUS PAGE The Kilmartin Valley in Argyll, a good example of glaciated landscape and also the site of the great linear cemetery of *c.* 1500 BC.

II OPPOSITE, ABOVE Howick Haven, the site of the earliest hunter-fisher-gatherer settlement in Britain, dating from 7800 BC.

III OPPOSITE, BELOW Cairnpapple Hill. Surrounded by the remains of its henge and cist and Christian graves, the cairn has been rebuilt and fitted with a metal hatch to protect the burial at its centre.

IV ABOVE Skara Brae, Orkney, the remains of the oldest village yet discovered in Europe. Dug into the midden, the houses were snug, dark and beautifully built – some time around 3100 BC.

V AND VI ABOVE AND OPPOSITE The Ring of Brodgar in Orkney (V) is enormous. Originally 60 stones were erected in a circle more than 100 m/328 ft across. It was linked to the nearby Stones of Stenness (VI) by a ceremonial way leading across the isthmus between Lochs Harray and Stenness.

VII OPPOSITE One of the
Stones of Stenness, Orkney.

VIII ABOVE Calanais
(Callanish) stone circle on the
Isle of Lewis, Western Isles.

IX RIGHT The
recumbent stone circle
at East Aquhorthies in
Aberdeenshire, with the
singular peak of Bennachie
in the background.

X OVERLEAF Cup-and-ring
carvings at Baluachraig in
Strathclyde. These enigmatic
markings are often found
near sacred sites and almost
certainly had a spiritual use.

What is clear from Oronsay, and other sites, is that life was not relentlessly devoted to food-gathering. The remains of antlers and antler tools found in the middens are witness to other activities. Colonsay and Oronsay had no indigenous deer population and the antlers were probably brought from Jura (in Gaelic the name *Diura* means 'Deer Island') or one of the other large islands, or the mainland. What prompted these imports was time, enough spare time to find a quiet spot and settle down to make tools such as harpoons. Bevel-ended tools have also been found and it is likely that they were made for leather-working. Along with the antlers, hide was probably brought to Oronsay to make clothes. Some of these outfits were elaborate and well tailored. It is misleading to think of prehistoric hunters dressed in rough pelts, and much more likely that their clothes were close-fitting for warmth and comfort. Hide flexes to fit a shape and the sinew used to sew it together is also elastic. Shells, beads, animal teeth, feathers and other decorations were added and colour used to dye or pattern tunics and cloaks. It made every sort of sense for hunter-gatherer-fishers to take a pride in their appearance, to keep hair and teeth clean, and to enjoy the results of such care just as we do now.

It may be only coincidental that the names of the Hebridean islands are often very old, to judge from the sound of them – perhaps even as old as the archaeology found there. *Arran*, *Tiree*, *Islay*, *Rhum*, *Uist* and *Lewis* are all pre-Celtic words, that is, probably dating to before the 1st millennium BC. Perhaps this scatter of ancient names gives us the oldest words in common use in Scotland; perhaps they were the names used by the fishermen who piled up the shell middens.

While any impression of the quality of life of the early hunters who settled in Scotland can only be sparse, perhaps informed by little more than intuition, one point does come across clearly. These people appear to have lived amid relative abundance, to have had time to talk and rest – they were not engaged in ceaseless and desperate toil, hunting to feed starving mouths, fearful of every new day and changing season. Of course there were hard winters, accidents, difficulties and shortages, but we should not assume that, when new ideas about settlement and cultivation began to spread, the hunters eagerly embraced them and quickly became farmers. Why should they have? As the distinguished historian Norman Davies has commented:

> The big question about the hunter-gatherers, therefore, does not seem to be 'How did they progress towards the higher level of an agricultural and politicized society?' but 'What persuaded them to abandon the secure, well-provided and psychologically liberating advantages of their primordial life-style?'

4

The Kindred Ground

At the beginning of the 4th millennium BC the peoples of the north began to create mysteries. Tombs, banks and ditches, barrows, stockaded enclosures and stone circles were built by communities all over what became Scotland. Their unifying theme appears to have been a grim one; death caused the great monuments to be raised and their function appears to have been closely related to the burial and commemoration of the dead. But past that general observation, little more is immediately evident. What exactly took place at the standing stones of Calanais (Callanish) on the Isle of Lewis is a mystery. No one knows. And most attempts at reconstruction are bound for the mists of vagueness, the deserts of banality or the swamps of wackiness. As one historian pointedly put it, working out the nature of the ceremonial that took place at the Ring of Brodgar on Orkney or the enclosure at Balfarg in Fife is like trying to piece together the details of Christian worship by looking only at the ruins of the Border abbeys. And to heap up further confusion, it may be that the exclusive association of these great monuments with death is itself mistaken or at least incomplete. Perhaps important births or the renewal of the seasons or the bringing in of the harvest were also celebrated inside the stone circles.

We have not been alone in our bafflement. Long after these monuments were made in the 4th and 3rd millennia BC, those who gazed upon them have despaired of discovering meaning; they have been forced to remain mystified, and sometimes driven to something worse. In the *Orkneyinga Saga*, the doings of the Viking Earls of Orkney were recorded by an Icelandic scribe some time around AD 1200. Earl Harald made a winter journey across Mainland, from Stromness to Firth, when his party was caught in a bitter snowstorm. Nearby loomed the ancient mound known to the Vikings as *Orkahaugr*, and to history as Maes Howe, a tomb of the 3rd millennium BC – perhaps the most impressive prehistoric tomb to survive in Britain. In their desperation to find refuge from the foul weather, the Earl's men broke into the tomb, but, said the matter-of-fact saga writer, 'they took shelter in Orkahaugr and there two of them went insane, which slowed them down badly, so that by the time they reached Firth it was night-time'. Some time around AD 1150 more Vikings had crawled into Maes Howe and they left clear and unambiguous evidence of their reaction to the tomb. Several runic inscriptions were cut on the walls of the chamber and some witness the insatiable Viking appetite for gold and silver: 'It is long ago that a great treasure was hidden here', or 'It is certain and true as I say that the treasure has been moved from here. The treasure was taken three nights before they broke into this mound.' This interpretation of Maes Howe may not have been fanciful. Radiocarbon sampling from part of the mound which covers the chamber has shown that it was rebuilt in the 9th century AD when the Vikings first came to the Orkneys. Perhaps there really had been a glittering treasure, and tales of its magnificence had survived into the 12th century. The name is, in any case, witness to a long tradition of understanding. Orcadians have always known that the tomb was there, for *Maes Howe* means 'Mound Field'.

Whoever dug into the tomb, or any other, had to face down millennia of discouragement, and to have stronger nerves than two of Earl Harald's men. From the Viking era, and probably long before, Orcadians believed that the mounds of prehistoric tombs retained their ancient power and were protected by a spirit known as a *hogboon*, Norse for 'mound dweller'. These traditions were strong and reached into the 20th century. In 1911 it was reported that a farmer had begun to dig into a prehistoric mound, only to be interrupted by 'an old, grey-whiskered man dressed in an old, grey, tattered suit of clothes', who whispered dread consequences if he did not desist:

Thou are working thy own ruin, believe me, fellow, for if thou does any more work, thou will regret it when it is too late. Take my word, fellow, drop working in my house, for if thou does not, mark my word, fellow, if thou takes another shovelful, mark my word, thou will have six of thy cattle dying in thy corn-yard at one time. And if thou goes on doing any more work, fellow – mark my word, fellow, thou will then have six funerals from the house, fellow; does thou mark my words; good-day, fellow.

Orcadians understood that the tombs under the mounds were very old, and some believed them to have been the houses of the 'peedie people', the little people. Perhaps the very low entrances to the tomb chambers encouraged this notion. And because it was also understood that they were built before the Vikings colonized Orkney, they were also called 'Picts' hooses', after those who had lost power to the new élite from Scandinavia.

It is perhaps surprising that so many monuments have survived on Orkney. The curses of the hogboons and the peedie folk may have deterred some fainthearts, but it is much more likely that local people inherited a respect for these places of ancient sanctity. Even if there was some damage over the centuries – tombs have certainly been destroyed and standing stones cast down – the density and volume of relatively undisturbed prehistoric monuments on the islands is a witness to their continuing power and mystery.

They are also the deposits of radical cultural change. Before 4000 BC the hunter-gatherer-fishers who ranged over Scotland left little more than their footprints across the wild landscape. By 3000 BC their descendants had built massive timber halls 24 m/80 ft long, they had erected awe-inspiring stone circles, and they had begun to whisper something of the way they lived their distant lives. In less than a thousand years the most profound shift in world history took place, but its mechanics are far more difficult to detect and understand than its concrete results. Many of the great prehistoric structures of Scotland, and Britain, had been created by 3000 BC, but the processes, the thinking and the beliefs that placed them in the landscape remain obscure.

In essence what happened was simple. The old peoples who came to Britain after the retreat of the ice began to learn how to farm. Planned cultivation of sown crops and the domestication of animals combined with hunting, gathering and fishing to shape a new way of living. The changes, particularly in Scotland, were not absolute and were certainly very gradual. Much of the north and west is ill-suited to the cultivation of crops, and the peoples who lived on the coasts had access to a rich repertoire of natural resources. There is evidence to support a hesitation in north-western Europe, perhaps even a resistance to the new methods of food production. Some of the innovative aspects of farming may have been adopted for a time and then dropped as hunter bands returned to the old way of living off the wild. But despite periods and patches of diffidence, there is no doubt that over the span of the 4th millennium BC immense change eventually took hold over most of Scotland.

Food historians have produced a set of fascinating statistics which show clearly how profound that cultural change was and how influential it remains. Throughout the world there are 148 species of large animals, with individuals weighing in at 45 kg/100 lb or more. And yet only 14 of these have been domesticated as farm animals, husbanded for food, milk or wool, or used for draught. Of 200,000 higher plant species, only 100 or so have been successfully cultivated for fodder or food. Almost all of these animals and crops were first farmed in the 4th millennium BC in Europe. Despite sustained efforts by modern research scientists, well funded by the agricultural industries, few new plants and no domesticated animals have been added to this historical larder in the last 6,000 years. Since that period farming methods have changed a great deal, but what we eat and cultivate has changed hardly at all.

The archaeological record shows that farming spread across Europe from the south-east, originating in Mesopotamia before fanning out to what is now Turkey, Greece and the Balkans. The ideas, methods, animals and seeds travelled in boats and overland as people colonized the eastern Mediterranean. At Çatalhöyük in Anatolia wheat, barley, peas and lentils were grown, while herds of cattle were kept for meat, milk and hides. By 5000 BC farmers were building large timber longhouses on the fertile terraces of the north-western European river valleys, the Rhine and the Weser. These people made pots decorated with linear motifs – *Bandkeramik*. Sometimes farming was adopted only when a key element in the hunter-gatherer-fisher economy failed or was threatened. The final inundation of Doggerland some time after 5000 BC and the rise in the level of the North Sea probably contributed to the disappearance of the oyster crop around the shores of Denmark. This was an important resource because it had been available year-round. Farming was adopted by the hunters of eastern Doggerland soon after this disaster.

Yam yam

Hunter-gatherer-fishers were rarely just that. They understood how to manage the resources they depended on. In north-west Australia Indigenous peoples who dug up yams always cut off a piece and replanted it in the ground so that they could return for a repeat harvest the following year. In North America, the Shoshone enhanced their wild harvests of bulbs and seed-bearing plants by creating irrigation systems. They dammed streams and dug small canals to take water to the natural stands of these plants, and thereby greatly enhanced the crop. In general, hunters avoided killing pregnant female or young animals, tending to concentrate on old or mature males. Trapping was of course indiscriminate. In Britain a harvest of a different sort was widely practised. Trees were coppiced regularly to produce valuable wood. When a tree is cut down to a stump, instead of dying it usually grows young shoots from the old wood. These are generally straight and very useful for making tools, baskets and fencing.

Prehistorians used to believe that the introduction of farming to Europe was effected by large-scale immigrations from the east, perhaps even military invasion. But the research of Bryan Sykes and his team (see pages 57–62), and the recent revisionism of some archaeologists and historians, have called for a radical modification of this view. Farming is only a set of ideas, and it is much more likely that they spread by word of mouth than by invasion and the coercion that that implies. However, Sykes' findings do not dismiss the older view out of hand. The seventh cluster of DNA sequences that he uncovered was judged to be, crucially, originally located outside Europe, on the banks of the Euphrates in Mesopotamia, where farming methods were first adopted. Some time after 7000 BC people with this distinctive DNA sequence began to move westwards out of the Middle East into Europe. It seems that, once on the move, they followed two routes of migration. Some went north-west, from the Balkans to the Baltic and overland across the Northern European Plain. Others made a series of coastal voyages to Greece, Italy, Spain, Portugal and across the Bay of Biscay to western Britain and Ireland, making landfall in Cornwall, Wales, Man, Galloway and the Hebrides. In all of these places the distinctive DNA sequence can be found amongst the modern population.

Taking the myth

The unlikely source for the Atlantis myth was the great philosopher Plato. In the *Timaeus*, he recounted the tale as it was told by his teacher, Socrates, at a dinner party. Evidently Socrates believed that Solon, the law-giving founder of the fabric of Athenian democracy, had heard of the lost continent on a visit to Egypt in the 6th century BC. Larger than the then known extents of either Europe or Asia, and dominated by a great city built in concentric circles, Atlantis lay beyond the Pillars of Hercules (the Straits of Gibraltar), somewhere out in the ocean. The Egyptian priests, said Socrates, were certain that the huge island sank overnight, inundated by a tidal wave caused by an earthquake. The story of Atlantis sank for many centuries, little remarked upon until Christopher Columbus began planning his expedition in 1492. In addition to finding a westward route to India Columbus hoped to come across Anthilea, a remnant of the lost continent. Instead he made landfall on a string

> of Caribbean islands which he immediately named, after the sunken
> continent, the Antilles. But perhaps Columbus should have sailed into
> the North Sea. Under the waves there really is a lost world, one which
> was definitely inundated, as we have seen, possibly by a tidal wave
> following an undersea earthquake – Doggerland.

This new DNA cluster makes up a large proportion, 20 per cent, of all Europeans. And very significantly, the routes they took 7,000 to 8,000 years ago are the routes tracked by archaeologists as they traced the spread of farming. It seems that there was indeed immigration, that new ideas were brought to Europe by new people. No doubt they brought seeds and animals with them, and even where they penetrated little or at all, the new ideas could be transferred by word of mouth, by example and by shared experience.

The old Celtic cultures of Ireland and the west of Britain appear to have retained in their fabric an echo of immigration, of the arrival of new people with new ideas. *An Lebor Gabala Erenn*, the 'Book of Invasions', was transcribed by monastic copyists in the 11th century and tells the ancient foundation story of the Irish people. A central part of the narrative concerns a migration from Spain to Ireland at some point in the long-distant past. In 1320 some elements of the *Lebor Gabala* were appropriated by the brilliant Scots cleric Bernard de Linton. In the face of sustained English aggression, and with a new king in the doughty shape of Robert de Bruce, he was anxious to compile as much proof of national legitimacy as he could lay his hands on. The Declaration of Arbroath was addressed to the Pope, as an international arbiter, soliciting his support for continued Scottish independence. It contains much stirring, beautifully written stuff, often quoted by misty-eyed nationalists, but it also carried a version of a foundation story for Scotland which owed a great deal to the *Lebor Gabala*. When it is remembered that Scotland was invented by the Gaelic-speaking kings of Argyll, whose kinsmen lived on the other side of the North Channel, this is scarcely surprising. The relevant passage reads:

The which Scottish nation, journeying from Greater Scythia by the Tyrrhene Sea and the Pillars of Hercules, could not in any place or time or manner be overcome by the barbarians, though long dwelling in Spain among the fiercest of them. Coming thence, 1,200 years after the transit of Israel, with many victories and many toils they won that habitation in the West, which though the Britons have been driven out, the Picts effaced, and the Norwegians, Danes and English have often assailed it, they hold now, in freedom from all vassalage; and as the old historians bear witness, have ever so held it. In this kingdom have reigned 113 kings of their own Blood Royal, and no man foreign has been among them.

Greater Scythia is usually located on the shores of the Black Sea, and the Declaration of Arbroath may just whisper the outline of a very old story, the movement of the first farmers through the Mediterranean and up the Atlantic coast of Europe. It is intriguing to note that in the Dark Ages, the area of eastern Doggerland around the mouth of the Elbe in north-western Germany was also known as Scythia.

When people and ideas move, languages often move with them, and some prehistorians have contended that the spread of farming out of Mesopotamia distributed the Indo-European family of languages across Europe and as far east as the Bay of Bengal. A British judge serving in Calcutta, Sir William Jones, had a brilliant *aperçu*. Writing in 1786, he was the first to recognize that the major Indian languages are very like the major European languages in both structure and vocabulary. This revelation may have been prompted by a bilingual background. Jones' parents hailed originally from Llanfihangel on Anglesey and almost certainly spoke Welsh in their London home. Perhaps the connections seemed obvious; some of them are, for example *agnis*, Sanskrit for *fire*, *ignis* in Latin, producing *ignite* in English. As might be expected from a devout and literal Christian, Jones understood the close links between European and Indian languages and their currency from the Highlands of Scotland to the foothills of the Himalayas as a historical consequence of the grounding of Noah's Ark on Mount Ararat, somewhere halfway between these outer limits. Despite this, much of Sir William's basic thesis holds good.

In Europe there are linguistic exceptions which may be earlier survivals or later arrivals; neither Basque nor Hungarian, Estonian, Finno-Ugrian nor Caucasian appear to be part of the Indo-European family, but all of the remaining languages do. The Romance, Celtic, Baltic, Germanic and Slavonic groups are like each other and are inter-related. Interestingly, many words associated with close family relationships seem to be similar in all these groups. The Greek *frathr* (transcribed in Latin as *frater*) and the Gaelic *brathair* are clearly the same word as *brother*, *bruder* and most versions in between. There are other examples: *mater, mother, mutter, mathr* and so on.

These are basic words, language which must have been in use across Europe long before farming and farmers first entered hunter-gatherer-fisher society in the 7th millennium BC. Would a new proto-Indo-European language have supplanted such everyday usage? Hunters had mothers and brothers just as farmers did. But it is not impossible. The figure of 20 per cent is a large proportion, and if these new people brought influential new ideas the specialized language used to describe cultivation, animal husbandry and much else may very well have been adopted wholesale. Radical language shifts have after all taken place in Scotland within the space of only two or three generations without any large-scale immigration to stimulate them. In living memory English has entirely replaced Gaelic in most parts of the Highlands. There is no one today who speaks the native dialect of Perthshire Gaelic, and while in 1971 there were 477 monoglot Gaelic speakers who figured in the census, there are none now. It may very well be that in the 4th millennium BC the gradual spread of new methods of food production brought with it a new way of describing the world.

MacCaesar

Considering the length of time they co-existed on the same small island, it should come as no surprise that the Welsh language borrowed a great deal from Latin. There are at least 600 loan-words in everyday use and, perhaps more surprisingly, a number of proper names which recall the time of Britannia and the Empire. *Iestyn* is Welsh for *Justinus*, *Emrys* for *Ambrosius*, and *Tegid* for *Tacitus*. The similarities between Gaelic and Latin are also close, but for quite different reasons. Ireland was never dragged into the Empire and the colonization of Scotland by the Irish post-dated the fall of Britannia. Yet the connections are there, in heavy disguise, showing the languages to be part of the same Indo-European family. Words common to both often drop an initial consonant or are aspirated. For example, *athair* (father) is *pater* without the 'p', and *lan* (full) is *plenus*, also without the 'p'.

While philologists find it extremely difficult to reconstruct what a prehistoric proto-Indo-European language might have sounded like, there are intriguing clues to be found in the landscape. River names are thought to be very ancient. *Tweed* appears to come from a root-word which exists in Sanskrit, a language used 8,000 km/5,000 miles to the east of Berwick-upon-Tweed. It is *tavas* and means 'the surger', and this affinity to Sanskrit may attest great antiquity. Across Europe other river names are clearly connected with a particular group in the Indo-European family, what became known as the Celtic languages. Water words such as *afon*, *dwr*, *uisge*, *rhe* and *don* are all to be found in various versions – from the several Avons and Esks in Britain to the Danube, Rhone, Adige, Douro, Dordogne, Oder and many others.

In the 1st millennium BC Celtic languages were spoken over much of western Europe before being obliterated by French, Italian and Spanish. Gaulish, Lepontic and Celtiberian are obviously all older than their successors, and as such a little more closely related to the speech of the first farmers. In so far as these things can be understood over such broad expanses of time, it appears that in the course of the

1st millennium BC Celtic culture spread out over Europe from the centre, from what is now Bavaria, Austria and Switzerland. Artefacts track this spread, principally items of beautifully wrought metalwork. But was this cultural transmission accompanied by a new language, what became known as the Celtic language group, or did it travel along pathways already cleared by early versions of these intimately related languages? It is impossible to know and foolish to take any discussion beyond speculation.

What can be useful, however, is analogy, and how that device might offer not a lexicon but rather a pungent flavour of the language spoken by the first farmers. One of the central difficulties of writing about prehistory is the lack of texture, the fact that the lives of the early peoples are so elusive, only a rickle of stones and bones or sometimes merely a stain on the soil. More imaginative historians close their ears to the routine academic accusations of being ahistorical when they look for analogy, or for examples of Fernand Braudel's *longue durée*; they do this not out of a desperate search for a story to tell but in pursuit of clearer understanding. One of these analogies turns out to be very attractive as well as thought-provoking. There exist, it is suggested, very helpful similarities between the lives and concerns of the first farmers and the crofting communities of the west of Britain and Ireland.

The most initially striking comparison is one of appearance. Where an old black house survives (*black house* was the common term for a crofter's house up until the early 20th century, and it refers not to the exterior but to the fact that it is very dark inside) and the arrangement of dyked infield and farther pasture is still discernible, the resemblance between it and the excavated remains of farmsteads of the 4th millennium BC is close. Black houses have few, if any, windows, are drystone-built and usually situated hunkering down into the landscape behind banks and ridges, seeking shelter from the wind and rain. Their roofs were heather-thatched and weighted down by ropes attached to heavy boulders. At prehistoric sites these boulders have occasionally been uncovered. The only major observable difference in roofing materials over several millennia was the widespread adoption of corrugated iron in the 19th century.

On a croft everything is small-scale, designed to be worked by a family and to support that family, surpluses generally being created only in good years. Often crofters supplemented what they grew and reared with a cash income from knitting and weaving, particularly on islands such as Harris and Shetland, where their products acquired a reputation for high quality.

In Scotland the crofting economy depended on a mixture of resources for its livelihood. Not only were some crops cultivated, but there were elements of hunting, gathering and especially fishing. Much depended on local geography and geology. Shetlanders were sometimes described as fishermen with crofts, while Orcadians were crofters with boats. This mixed approach naturally required a broad range of skills and bred an attractive attitude of self-reliance and self-sufficiency, much of it a concomitant of remoteness and a lack of complicated technology. Until the appearance of the affordable Ferguson tractor, the 'Wee Grey Fergie', after the Second World War, almost everything on a croft was managed by hand or with the pulling power of horses. And hoes, foot-ploughs, shovels and hayrakes are much easier for a crofter to maintain and repair than a tractor, even a Fergie.

The analogies to be drawn between the lives of the first farmers and modern crofters will come increasingly into play when the archaeology of the 4th and 5th millennia BC is considered, but, for now, one simple observation on the matter of language is apposite. The Celtic languages of Europe are not only members of the Indo-European family, they are amongst its older relatives. And Scots and Irish Gaelic are the languages of crofting. If some notion of the homesteads of the first farmers can be gleaned from Highland, Island and Irish crofts, then some sense of what they talked about and how they expressed it can be heard if modern crofters are closely listened to.

The first and most sustained impression is one of detail. The great illustrated Gaelic dictionary compiled between 1902 and 1911 by the

Englishman Edward Dwelly lists a wealth of words clustering around agricultural and food-gathering activities. The parts of horse harness needed for a draught animal are so many and so specialized that Dwelly struggled hard to find English equivalents which made sense. Usually he was forced to resort to compounds or phrases such as 'strap across the nose' for *sronein* or 'strap below the jaws' for *smeachan*. When the parts of a rowing boat are described in Gaelic terms, the complexity is mind-numbing. Diagrams everywhere attempt to plug linguistic leaks, and essays are sometimes required to unpick the meaning of a single Gaelic word. *Sgiathan* are evidently 'flat pieces put on each side under water to keep the boat steady and from rolling. They are much shorter and broader than the bilge-piece, and are used for "crank" boats', while *achlaisean* are 'beam-knees, used to fix the thwarts to the side or planks of the boat, as the *cinn-tobhta* fix them to the gunwale. The *achlasan* lies horizontally in the angle which the thwart makes with the side, but the *ceann-tobhta* is upright.'

The importance of this sort of precision on both sea and land can be read on many of the pages of Dwelly's dictionary. On page 908 *stuadhach* means 'billowy, surgy, having huge waves'. The point of this example is an everyday one. The condition of the sea influenced routine decisions and it had to say more than simply *stormy* or *calm*. On the landward side, detailed directions were also important, and on the same page as *stuadhach* there is entered *stuc* and its meaning of 'little hill jutting out from a greater, steep on one side and rounded on the other'.

Agriculture and its terminology in Gaelic might have made a dictionary by itself. The range of tools, some of them very primitive such as the *cas-chrom* or foot plough, outruns anything to be found on a modern farm, and some defy definition completely. Once more precision is the most striking characteristic. For example *aitheornach* is 'land ploughed for a second crop'. Under *bo* ten different descriptions of a cow appear; the adjectival range available to characterize the look of any one cow is broad and subtle at the same time, and far beyond the colour spectrum to be found in English. The Gaels have a dozen shades of pale.

What this whirlwind excursion around Dwelly's dictionary shows is something obvious and fascinating. In contrast to the urbanization of English and most other European languages, Gaelic remains rooted in the land. But that does not make it hayseed-simple. In fact the effect is the reverse. In order to cope with the diversity of nature, the weather, geography, agriculture, fishing and much else, Gaelic had to develop a huge vocabulary and demand a lexical skill and facilities of recall which would stretch a speaker of standard English to breaking point. When it came to matters of ownership – of cattle, for example – or considerations of the weather – if sea travel was being proposed – then it was extremely important, sometimes a matter of life and death, to be precise. Clearly it is impossible to know what the first farmers said to each other, the actual words and phrases, but Gaelic offers a pungent flavour of the sorts of things they talked about and how they put it. And it is very likely that they spoke a language of greater richness, complexity and detail than we use now.

What it sounded like is obviously unknowable, but once again analogy is suggestive. Theirs was an oral culture, dependent on memory just as Gaelic was until well into the modern era and dictionaries like Edward Dwelly's. Duncan Ban MacIntyre was one of the greatest poets in the language. He lived at the end of the 18th century and all of his magnificent work was composed in his head and retained there. MacIntyre was illiterate and what he created has survived only because it was transcribed by an amanuensis. Oral traditions require conventions to act as aids to memory, and also mouth-filling vocabulary to supply music as it is spoken or sung. Gaelic has these attributes in glorious abundance and they reach back across hundreds of generations to show an unbroken link between poetry and the natural world. The most beautiful poems in the language never lift their gaze from landscape or seascape. And their atmosphere is ancient, the swirl of the words echoing back to a deep past. Perhaps this medieval transcription of a very ancient poem gives some sense of how the hunter-gatherer-fisher-farmers looked upon Glen Etive in Argyllshire.

Glen of cuckoos and thrushes and blackbirds, precious is its cover to every fox; glen of wild garlic and watercress, of woods, of shamrock and flowers, leafy and twisting-crested.

Sweet are the cries of the brown-backed dappled deer under the oakwood below the bare hilltops, gentle hinds that are timid lying hidden in the great-treed glen.

Glen of the rowans with scarlet berries, with fruit fit for every flock of birds; a slumbrous paradise for the badgers in their quiet burrows with their young.

Glen of the blue-eyed vigorous hawks, glen abounding in every harvest, glen of the ridged and pointed peaks, glen of blackberries and sloes and apples.

This poetry loses much of its alliteration, onomatopoeia and metre in translation, but the ideas inside it and the images are clear enough. And its links with the relatively modern work of Duncan Ban MacIntyre are similarly clear. In his love poetry, he turns readily to the natural world of the old life on the land to sharpen his imagery.

White the swan and white the seagull, white the snow as it falls in February, white the cotton-grass over the heather, whiter than that my love's skin.

And MacIntyre's observation of the deer on Ben Dorain, the mountain at the centre of perhaps his greatest poem, is both precise and timelessly beautiful. This is from a translation made by Iain Crichton Smith.

Pleasant to me rising
at morning
to see them the horizon
adorning.
Seeing them so clear,
my simple-headed deer
modestly appear
in their joyousness.

They freely exercise
their sweet and level cries.
From bodies trim and terse,
hear their bellowing.

A badger of a hind
wallows in a pond.
Her capricious mind
has such vagaries!

How they fill the parish
with their chorus
sweeter than fine Irish
tunes glorious.

More tuneful than all art
the music of the hart
eloquent, alert,

on Ben Dorain.
The stag with his own call
struck from his breast wall –
you'll hear him mile on mile
at his scale-making.

The sweet harmonious hind –
with her calf behind –
elaborates the wind
with her music.

Palpitant bright eye
without squint in it.
Lash below the brow,
guide and regulant.
Walker quick and grave,
so elegant to move
ahead of that great drove
when accelerant.

There's no flaw in your step,
there's all law in your leap,
there's no rust or sleep
in your motion there.

Lengthening your stride,
intent on what's ahead,
who of live or dead
could outrace you?

~~~

On the eastern fringes of the Highland massif, more than 240 km/150 miles from Ben Dorain, a remarkable light was shed on the lives of the new farming communities. What amazed the excavators at Balbridie, in Aberdeenshire, was how different their discovery was from anything else previously known, and its sheer scale. They had come across a huge building. First noticed as a set of cropmarks on an aerial survey, the remains of the structure on the banks of the River Dee measured out an area 26 m/85 ft long by 13 m/43 ft wide – a hall rather than a house.

It was radiocarbon-dated significantly earlier than any previously discovered domestic building in Scotland, to between 3900 and 3700 BC. The great hall may have been much more than merely domestic. Its scale suggests religious possibilities, a place designed to inspire awe, perhaps even worship of some unknowable sort.

When the turf was removed and rows of post-holes identified, measurements of their depth suggested a structure with a roof pitch more than 10 m/30 ft high and enough floor space to accommodate between 30 and 50 people with ease. To a casual observer (and indeed to the excavators, who believed they were digging a Dark Age site), unaware of its great antiquity, the building at Balbridie looks more reminiscent of the great halls of the Anglo-Saxons, the sort lovingly described in the poem *Beowulf*. When archaeologists dug at Yeavering in north Northumberland, they came upon the royal hall of the Anglian kings of Bernicia, and hailed it as a major discovery – which indeed it was – but at 24 by 12 m/80 by 40 ft marginally smaller than the hall at Balbridie, a building just as technically complex but 4,500 years older.

It is unlikely that a warrior-king like Hrothgar of the Shieldings feasted and drank with his warriors at Balbridie. The builders of the hall were farmers. In the excavated post-holes, grains of wheat grown for bread-making and also some barley were found. Stock may have been penned and fed at a handy distance to supply milk, meat and hides. Nearby, the River Dee could be fished or traps set for salmon, trout and other species. Fencing, made from willow withies or some other wands of pliable wood, probably sectioned off fields for cultivation and made pens for animals, care being taken to keep the two apart. Because hundreds of years of ploughing have effaced the floor surface at Balbridie, no trace of a hearth has been found and the only indications of how the enormous space was organized came from the fact that the distribution of cereal grains concentrated at the west end. It was probably a storage area. Loft space might have been a sensible way to keep valuable produce out of the way of all but rats or mice, and the scale of the structure could certainly have supported upper-storey flooring.

The earliest farming site yet discovered in Scotland, Balbridie is remarkable. It is as though American society moved directly from tipis to skyscrapers. Where did the builders of this huge hall come from? It is unlikely that the hunter-gatherer-fishers of north-east Scotland made such an amazing cultural leap. There appear to be no intermediate stages, nothing part-way between. Perhaps the closest ancestor of Balbridie is the substantial house built on the east coast at Howick, 320 km/200 miles to the south. But even that relationship is highly tenuous, since the Howick building is dated to 4,000 years before.

Cropmarks

These are usually detected from aerial surveys and, as in the case of the halls at Balbridie and elsewhere, can reveal the existence of very important new sites. Cropmarks have two causes. Holes in the ground, such as the post-holes which held the timbers of the great halls or ditches around a henge, fill with topsoil and when a cereal crop is planted over them, the stalks grow taller and stay greener for longer because more moisture has been retained. In the opposite effect, if corn is planted over the foundations of a wall it has less soil and therefore less moisture in which to flourish; consequently it grows short and yellows or even fails completely.

When the excavators analysed the cereal grains found in the post-holes they came to the conclusion that they did not originate in Aberdeenshire. What they had found was much closer to European types. And while no buildings comparable to the scale and style of the great hall have been found in England, something very similar had been erected in north-western Europe for at least a millennium before 3900 BC. The remains of substantial timber longhouses have been uncovered in southern Poland, in the German river valleys and southern Holland. It seems very likely that Balbridie was built by people new to Scotland, perhaps the ancestors of the DNA cluster which now makes up 20 per cent of the population, those who originally moved out of the Middle East and slowly fanned out across Europe, the first farmers.

Most of the European timber longhouses are to be found on river terraces, where the soil is fertile and light enough to be worked with the tools at the disposal of the new people. When the builders of Balbridie hall prospected for a suitable site, they settled on a fertile terrace of the River Dee. They were not working in isolation. Aerial photography has identified the remains of at least two other large timber halls in eastern Scotland. The right sort of cropmarks tell of a similar structure near Kelso, on a terrace of the River Tweed at the farm of Whitmuirhaugh, and at Claish Farm near the River Teith (a tributary of the River Forth) another hall has recently been excavated. The layouts were found to be almost exactly the same as at Balbridie and the date of 3800 BC contemporary. Inside the building at Claish there appear to have been internal divisions, lateral features connecting the long walls, which may have been used as storage areas or compartments for sleeping or even for privacy. The ends of the hall were more rounded than at Balbridie and the concentration of pottery finds at one end seems to suggest that different activities were organized in specific places.

The nature of these impressive halls is mysterious. It is unlikely that they were used as very large integrated houses and byres. The excavators have specifically rejected the notion that animals overwintered in them, because access arrangements do not allow it. These are complex buildings made with consummate skill by people who took the trouble to replicate the same architectural features even though the three examples so far found lie at considerable distances from each other.

What the three halls at Claish, Balbridie and Kelso also have in common is size, structure and type of location. All are on the eastern side of Scotland, adjacent to navigable rivers which led their builders easily into the interior. Perhaps good land for immigrants was simply not to be had in the sort of coastal areas which were favoured and already being worked by native hunter-gatherer-fisher groups. All of the sites are placed within rapid reach of necessary resources: rich and mature woodland, areas of fertile, light soil and nearby upland pasture for summer grazing. Such evidence as presents itself suggests strongly that these remarkable buildings were raised by people who came to Scotland from north-western Europe some time at the beginning of the 4th millennium BC.

What prompted the hall-builders to sail westwards and up the mouths of Scottish rivers? Perhaps they were refugees. It is impossible to move beyond general speculation on their origins, but it may be that the final or imminent inundation of Doggerland persuaded people with new ideas, skills and resources to look urgently for new homes in eastern Scotland.

Some time around 3200 BC the great halls at Balbridie and Claish burned down. Carelessness, aggression or a conscious decision to move on – any of these might have sparked the destruction of these impressive buildings. The reasons or motives are unknowable. But it is possible that the settlement came to the end of its life through the onset of sickness. One of the most profound difficulties to beset the first farmers was the beginning of epidemic disease and the way in which it tore through small communities. They caught these diseases from the animals they lived so close to. Tuberculosis, measles and smallpox jumped the species barrier between cattle and human beings. If the farmers at Claish and Balbridie kept dairy cows, it was a fatally simple matter to ingest the pathogens by drinking their milk. Influenza, whooping cough and malaria were also early killers and they spread into the human population through the flesh and faeces of pigs and game birds. Until farming groups developed a resistance to these diseases, the effects of outbreaks must have been immediately devastating, and perhaps something of that sort overtook the communities of the great halls.

Plagues

Diseases continue to jump the species barrier between animals and humans. Most recently, AIDS (or Acquired Immune Deficiency Syndrome) has devastated populations in Africa, where it originated in pastoral communities. CJD (or Creutzfeldt-Jakob Disease) infected humans in Britain as a result of contact with meat or animals which had suffered from the sickness known as Mad Cow Disease. Farming is still a dangerous business, and vegetarians have historical as well as ethical arguments to support their choice.

What remains just as mysterious is the apparent disappearance of their very distinctive style of living and building. Later timber halls may exist, as yet undiscovered, but the evidence suggests that the inclination or the skills (or both) to build in that way simply ceased at the end of the 4th millennium BC.

At the same time as Balbridie and Claish were reduced to ashes, farmers were building very different houses on Orkney. Small, stone-built and designed to keep out the incessant wind, they show how differently people lived in what we now think of as the same quarter of Scotland. Archaeology may have scratched only the surface of what has survived from the 4th millennium BC, but it is already clear that great regional diversity existed. No fewer than seven quite distinct types of tomb from the fourth millennium have been found and their distribution follows ancient patterns of movement around Scotland, most of these intelligible as sea, or sea and river, journeys. When attempting to reconstruct some sense of the texture of life in prehistoric Scotland, it is important to be scrupulous with generalizations. Orcadians clearly took a very different approach to the way they treated their dead, or built their houses, from people living in what became Aberdeenshire or the Borders. But that in turn should not lead us to believe that regional groups were inward-looking or insular. As will become obvious, long-range contacts did take place, occasionally down the length of Britain.

The diversity of building styles and food production is often a reaction to geography and geology. The fertile river terraces of the Dee and the Tweed and their handy woodland resources allowed great buildings to grow out of the ground and to thrive, while in Orkney and the Western Isles architecture and farming conformed to the prevailing weather conditions. But the range of lifestyles might also relate to immigration or the lack of it. If the hall builders of the eastern riverbanks did sail from Doggerland or the north-western shores of Europe, it is likely that they brought innovation with them. If no newcomers came ashore in a particular area, it may be that conservatism and a slower pace of change were the norm.

What is clear is that farming was adopted in a different way and at a different pace in different parts of Scotland. Where fertile areas were only lightly populated, early farmers may have gone in for non-intensive methods. There is evidence in the Borders that pioneers were in the habit of burning areas of woodland, planting crops directly into the ashes and cultivating that particular area for only a year or two before moving on to repeat the process with another patch of virgin forest. There were substantial advantages in this. The ground could be – had to be – turned over in small patches with foot-ploughs, hoes or digging sticks. The survival of the roots of mature trees (these are difficult to remove, even with the help of 21st-century technology) made any other approach impossible. The other main advantage was obvious. After only a short period of cultivation, the ground did not become exhausted and did not require to be mucked by beasts or the contents of a domestic midden. Once a fallow area of cleared forest had recovered, and even if five or ten years of natural regeneration had greened over the area, it was much easier to burn and clear it again than to deal with a fresh area of virgin woodland.

And these areas could be managed by small groups with simple tools. The analogy with crofting is once again apposite. Using only a *cas-chrom* or foot-plough, a crofter could till enough ground between the turn of the year and the spring (when he had to have the ground ready for planting) to feed a family of seven or eight. Harvesting such irregular and patchy plots presented few problems if it was to be done by hand with flint or other stone cutting tools. On St Kilda the wind ensured that the barley grew so short that the harvesters simply pulled it up by the roots, else 'we would have nothing were we to cut it'. Cereals were grown at most of the 4th-millennium BC domestic sites discovered so far in Scotland and the methods used by the early farmers to process their crops have survived into the historic period.

Before any sort of corn can be dried, all of the unwanted bits of chaff or straw have to be removed. This used to be done by hand on Highland crofts. Winnowing was the first stage in the processing of harvested corn, and before anything else was done a suitable place had to be identified. Wind was of course essential, but nothing too strong – a steady breeze which held its compass direction was considered to be optimum. For the efficient removal of what in lowland Scotland were called *sheelins*, the husks of the cereal grains, windy places were selected and used every harvest. These places are still remembered in place and proper names (in the Borders 'Shillinglaw' is a fairly common surname). Once the direction and strength of the wind had been assessed, the winnowers (usually working in twos) set down a straw mat to keep their hard-won harvest clean. Then they simply lifted up handfuls of grains and let them trickle slowly through their fingers. Gravity ensured that the heavier grains of corn fell on to the mat, while the breeze carried off the sheelins or chaff. A tail of lighter or smaller grains followed the wind direction and this inferior stuff was used to make *sowens*, a sort of gritty porridge used to fill hungry bellies in a hard winter.

Once the winnowing had been completed, it was important to dry the grains as quickly as possible. In a damp climate such as Scotland's undried corn can easily sprout and be spoiled. On many prehistoric sites much of the cereal to survive had been charred and this is very likely to have been the result of an ancient drying process known as *graddaning*. On Highland crofts and many lowland holdings women did most of the processing of the harvest (although men often posed for such 19th-century photographs as exist) and when grain needed to be dried quickly they lit a fire with the discarded chaff. Very carefully they burnt off the remaining husks and toasted the grains lightly. As soon as the women judged that the corn was clean and dry, they quickly doused the fire. In unskilled hands graddaning could be very wasteful, but the toasting probably improved the flavour of the baked bannocks or griddled oatcakes. On St Kilda the ears of corn were graddaned in a pot or set against heated stones to dry. There was another, very important advantage in using this process. Just as with hazelnuts, charring grains helps to preserve them and protect against the effects of frost or damp.

Wheat-eaters

Broadly, there are three staple cereals consumed by most of the world's population: rice, maize and wheat. After centuries of experiment, wheat turned out to be most suited to a European climate. It is much more nutritious than either rice or maize and its high protein content has made Europeans significantly taller. Wheat also needs less work and is seasonal, while rice-paddies require year-round tending. This allowed early European farmers to diversify and also made it easier for societies to take time off from food production. The only drawback is that wheat is a hungry crop, exhausting the fertility of the soil very quickly. This led to rotation farming and a mixed European diet of cereals, vegetables and meat.

Quernstones were commonly used to grind the dried corn into flour and, because they were made from hard and heavy stone (granite was best), many have survived. The action needed to work trough or saddle querns with a rubbing stone must have resembled scrubbing at a washboard in an old-fashioned laundry. This method of grinding left much grit in the flour and the toll it took on prehistoric teeth is well documented. Many skulls recovered from tombs and elsewhere show mature people with heavy dental wear, their teeth worn down to stumps. Knocking stones were used on remote crofts until well into the 20th century. A large, stable, round stone had a circular depression chipped out of it to receive small quantities of husked barley. Water was added; women sat by the stone and with a wooden mallet knocked the contents into a loose mixture. Barley processed in this way was usually intended for broth or pottage of some kind. Like farm workers all over 19th-century Scotland and long before, the prehistoric peoples probably used pottage as a staple, a thick soup that sat in a large pot by the fire and was added to or diluted as it was consumed.

The harvest was, and remains, the most nervous time of the farming year. Even in the Christian period, the survival of very old pagan practices was tolerated – they might bring luck, and luck with the weather was to be sought by any means. As the first sheaves were cut crofters would winnow out some undried ears of corn, grind them into a rough paste and griddle a small cake. Latterly this was known as the *Moilean Mhoire* or 'the fatling of Mary' (the Virgin Mary). Bits of this were given to reapers to nibble as they set about their work. Clearly Christianized, this little ceremony has ancient origins as a sort of propitiation of the gods. It is impossible to judge how ancient, but the great ceremonial monuments built by the first farmers are ample witness to strong beliefs, and never will their faith, whatever it was, have been so sorely tested as at the harvest. Corn dollies are also ancient, and widespread, made at the harvest from straw to many different designs. Examples survive from the time of the Egyptian pharaohs. The word *dolly* comes from 'idol' and they were usually found pinned above lintels or on the top of haystacks. One of the oldest is the *kern babby* of Northumberland.

Boundaries were also important to farmers. At the beginning of the 4th millennium BC, Scotland might be thought of as an under-populated wildwood where hunter-gatherer-fishers had roamed at will. But the middens on Oronsay and the house at Howick imply territoriality, if not absolute ownership. The square mileage needed by a hunting band was too large to be owned absolutely, but they would have believed that they enjoyed a set of customary rights over it. When farmers (even those descended from hunting bands) began to clear woodland for cultivation, and to build houses for year-round occupation, notions of ownership no doubt hardened. The earliest evidence of this has been found on the Shetland Isles. At Shurton Brae, near Lerwick, a drystone dyke was built some time around 3600 BC. Other, slightly later, but more complete, field systems have survived at Scourd of Brouster and these show interesting attitudes. At roughly 3 ha/6 acres apiece, six fields have been demarcated by dykes built with stones cleared from the fields. Cairns have also been built up within the perimeter of the dykes. In the footings of several runs of walls there are large earthfast stones to be found, and archaeologists believe that these predate the continuous dykes. It seems that the dykes were not at first intended as barriers – some have large gaps in them – but rather as the boundaries of plots: a matter of indicating ownership as well as providing enclosure for animals. The fields at Scourd of Brouster seem not to have been cultivated at first but used as pasture. There are the remains of houses on the site and some of the dykes butt right up against their walls.

On Shetland there is also a system of long dykes which appear to predate the small field boundaries. The latter respect the long dykes and do not cross them. It has been conjectured that the dykes were tribal territory markers, for with a relatively high prehistoric population on Shetland it was important to be unambiguous about who owned what. Many of the old dykes are found under later deposits of peat and their great antiquity is noted in local usage which calls them *pickie dykes* or the 'Picts' dykes'.

Beyond these boundaries lay pastureland proper and in the Norn dialect of the Northern Isles this was called the *hagi* or *hagri*. Much of it was undyked, and checking its more informal boundaries was extremely important, for neighbours were always ready to encroach. This was known as 'the riding of the hagri', and it was an ancient, and brutal, custom. On their tough little ponies the owners or tenants of the hagri rode around to check the bounds immediately after the harvest and always took some young boys with them, usually the sons of tenants. At each boundary stone a young boy 'got a sair treshin sae as he soud mind weel whaur do hagmets stude' ('got a sound thrashing so that he would well remember where the boundaries stood'). Different boys were beaten at each stone, indelible memories imprinted in what was called 'the whipping custom'.

About 300 km/200 miles to the south, not far from Balbridie, early farmers worked a place called Pitglassie. The name translates as 'patch of green land' and might remember a cleared area of woodland. Between

3750 and 3500 BC the farmers lifted the turf, cleared away the stones from a roughly circular area and built a funeral pyre in the middle. They buried the resulting cremations in the same place. This circular area was marked by a ring of 11 or 12 timber posts. A ring cairn was thrown around the site, probably making use of the cleared turf and stones. Pitglassie is significant because it prefigures the wood and stone circles of a later period, and may be the particular forerunner of the recumbent stone circles found in north-eastern Scotland.

A damned good thrashing

In the entry for 23 May 1661, the diarist Samuel Pepys recorded that *beating the bounds* still went on in the seething midst of London, far and away the largest city in Britain. Although converted into little more than an occasion for fun, the remains of a much older ceremony were still clearly evident. The children of the parish of St Bride's, between Fleet Street and the Thames, were led in procession around its boundaries by the constable and the churchwarden. They carried broomsticks and had buckets of water flung at them by fellow parishioners. At various points the children underwent a mock thrashing so that they would not forget the limits of St Bride's, their home parish. Then they were given their reward of bread, cheese and a drink. Even in the late 19th century, *a guid lounderin'* was dished out to boys who accompanied (surely very reluctantly) the men walking and riding around the bounds of the common land belonging to the Border town of Selkirk.

It would be foolhardy to claim that the cremations undertaken in a specially created place at Pitglassie were the earliest religious rituals in Scotland, but this is the earliest record yet found. Much further south, at Cairnpapple Hill near Linlithgow, farmers from the fertile Forth plains climbed up to meet and take part in ceremonies (see plate III). Cairnpapple Hill is singular. Rising out of farmland, it offers a panorama of central Scotland, since earliest times the richest and most heavily populated area. Spectacular vistas open on every side. On clear days Goat

Fell on the island of Arran can be made out in the west, the Highland Line peaks rise to the north, May Island and the Firth of Forth lead the eye out east towards the North Sea and the gentle Moorfoot Hills lie to the south. Almost always, it seems, the early peoples of Scotland chose beautiful and atmospheric places to meet and worship.

Archaeologists date the first traces of activity on Cairnpapple to 3500 BC. At six separate hearths the farmers from the valleys and the coastal plain lit fires on the hill, using only hazel and oak wood. And they deposited axes and pieces of broken pottery in the ground around the hearths. This pattern of ritual is repeated at several other important Scottish sites, such as Balfarg in Fife. Axes and pots were valuable items and it seems that their deposit on the hill denoted some sort of act of sacrifice or propitiation. In the 4th millennium BC the old gods were not necessarily gods of love or even well disposed towards those who prayed to them. They could be malign as well as benign, and to find favour at important times the early peoples left gifts of precious items. This habit lasted a long time. By the 1st millennium BC metalwork had replaced pottery in the scale of value and the Celtic peoples of Scotland used it to propitiate their gods. They came to the shores of watery places such as lochs, lochans, mosses and rivers, and threw swords, shields, daggers, cauldrons and much else into their depths. And like the people who first climbed Cairnpapple Hill and broke their pots so that they could not be reused, they damaged these precious metal objects before committing them to the gods.

Shelties

Shetland ponies or Shelties are often thought to be cute miniature horses with flowing manes and sweet faces. In fact many of them display a bad temper of surprising vehemence, and anyone who becomes over-familiar can receive a nasty nip. No one knows exactly how old the breed is, but it certainly goes back some distance into the prehistoric period. Until the 19th century the ponies roamed the islands in semi-domesticated herds, staying out through the long winter. They were never used as draught animals until June, when it was reckoned that they had recovered their condition. When Walter Scott visited Shetland, he discovered that it was customary to catch one in a halter, ride it to wherever you wanted to go and then simply release the horse to find its own way back to the herd.

Pot-making seems to have been adopted in Scotland at approximately the same time as farming. The old life of hunting, gathering and fishing was more mobile, while pots are heavy, cumbersome and fragile. It was not that the hunters knew nothing of the properties of clay – they used it in hearths and on floors – but they probably chose other materials. Animal-skin containers, woven baskets, bark buckets and wooden cups were lighter, tougher and more practical. But when communities began to settle in one place, pottery appeared in the archaeological record.

The choice of building sites at Balbridie, Claish and Kelso may well have been partly influenced by the presence of workable river clay near at hand. Pots were very useful to early farmers as vermin-proof storage for large quantities of produce. Sometimes they were buried in the ground and securely stoppered, or else positioned handily inside one of the great halls. The use of pottery also changed early cookery. At the edge of a fire, a stout cooking pot sat bubbling with pottage, and sometimes its scalding sides were used to bake flat bread, the dough being slapped on rather in the same way that nan bread is now made in a tandoor in an Indian restaurant. The new emphasis on cereals encouraged new approaches to food preparation, and the softer, more easily chewed texture of hot meals from fireside pots will have pleased all who suffered from broken or worn-down teeth.

Most prehistoric pottery in Scotland was not made on a wheel. Three basic methods were commonly used, although each required skill and experience and the craft of the potter in any community would have been restricted to a few people or perhaps only one. Once a good source of clay had been found, it was puddled to make it pliable. To form a small bowl or cup, the potter first rolled it into a manageable ball. Then, with the thumbs, he or she began to push it outwards, rotating the flattening ball all the time to keep the spread even. When the ball had become a disc, it was worked upwards into the shape of a bowl. This method of *hand-building* was generally used for cups or other smaller receptacles, and their size was limited by the size of the potter's hands.

Coiling allowed the making of much bigger pots, up to 100 cm/40 ins in height and almost as much again in girth. First a flat base was kneaded out and trimmed. Then clay was rolled between the hands to make long thin strings or worms which were simply laid around the base, care being taken to keep all surfaces wet and roughened at the same time. When the pot was finished the joins between coils could be smoothed over with a wooden implement. A variation of coiling was *slabbing*. Like a pastry cook with a rolling pin, the potter flattened long strips of wet clay and built them up on a base in the same way as for coiling.

Once a pot had been formed it was left to dry off in the open air until it was *leather-hard*, that is, hard enough not to lose its shape but still soft enough to be cut. At this point in the process the walls of the pot were shaved down so that firing would be even and thorough, and any decoration was added. Most early pots were unpainted and unglazed, although resin from birch and pine trees was sometimes applied to make the surface less porous.

When enough pots had been made for a firing, the potter placed them in his kiln pit and built a fire over them, hoping that not too many would shatter or crack in the intense heat. Often chemicals in the clay would make pots crack or even explode in the firing.

What persuaded the people who climbed Cairnpapple Hill in 3500 BC to carry pots up with them was not only their value but also their magic. Unlike other prehistoric materials such as wood, stone, plant fibre or bone, pottery was the end result of a magical change wrought in the heat of a fire. Clay was transformed beyond all recognition into something quite other and that metamorphosis made it magical. It is unlikely that empty pots were carried up, and whether food or drink, or both, the contents supplied an additional offering to propitiate the gods. There are plenty of reports of Greek and Roman libations poured out at the altars of their gods and perhaps something like that took place here. Later Scottish pots have yielded traces of a honey-based drink like mead, and also a hallucinogen known as henbane. Perhaps the people drank when the gods drank and both moved closer to each other as a result.

It may also be the case that the pots acknowledged the bounty of the gods, their contents evidence of a good harvest and an offering made in the hope of continued favour. If the pots themselves were finely made and prettily decorated, that could only add to the value of the sacrifice. As in modern Christianity, ritual meals and drinks were almost certainly consumed at prehistoric religious sites, but of course nothing has survived but their containers.

The axes, too, found at Cairnpapple were both practical and symbolic. Razor-sharp flint axes were as much the instruments of the spread of farming as hoes and foot-ploughs. They were used to clear woodland to allow fields to be opened up and cultivated, and they made the timbers of the great halls and lesser buildings. But many of the axes found in Scotland had never been used. Made from igneous rock and polished with abrasives to a dull lustre, some are too small to have been practical. It appears that the axes were symbols, perhaps given as gifts, perhaps for a specific use in religious ceremonies. Some came from an ancient quarry at Creag na Caillich in Perthshire but many, including those at Cairnpapple, were produced in the great axe factory of Langdale in the Lake District. High up near the summit ridge of the Langdale Pikes, in difficult and dangerous places, there are ancient quarries of volcanic stone. Even though more easily accessible and workable deposits lie further down the slopes, the prehistoric miners preferred to climb up and hack the rock out of the highest outcrops they could find. No practical reason for this puzzling choice can be deduced.

Marshill

In 2003 archaeologists came upon a rich burial at Marshill, near Alloa. Some time in the first century BC, a 30-year-old man had been buried with a 60-cm/2-ft-long sword (so far unique for the period), scabbard and sword-belt. Bronze rings were attached to the belt and the warrior had two rings on his toes and a copper pin which had been used to fasten his cloak or tunic at the neck. Perhaps he was a Druid. Even more impressive than this comparatively lavish burial is the continuity of sanctity at Marshill. The remains of burials spanning 2,000 years have been found, and one, dating to around 2000 BC, was uncovered only feet away from where the Druid lay. As the place-name shows, the ancient cemetery on Marshill was an elevated site in the flatlands to the north of the Firth of Forth, and it appears to have been made even more prominent by a huge cairn which has now been totally effaced.

Once the volcanic rock had been won from the high quarries it was cut, fashioned into axeheads and polished. It is clear that the quality of the axes produced in this mysterious process was controlled in some highly organized, semi-industrial manner. For this was no bijou operation with a short lifespan; at Langdale the debris of an astonishing number of discarded axeheads has been found, perhaps more than 75,000. The volume of successful output implied is difficult to calculate but the wide distribution of these distinctive polished axes all over Britain, including sites in the Borders and elsewhere in Scotland, suggests a trade running into six figures at least.

After the period of the mysterious ceremonies on Cairnpapple Hill its use changed, or was reinforced. To mark off the crest of the hill as a sacred place, set apart from the surrounding temporal world, a circular ditch was dug and the upcast used to form a bank on its outside edge. This rose to 1.2 m/4 ft in places, high enough to act as a screen. Inside the ditch 24 timber posts were set in a circle and what became known as a *henge* was created. Recent research contests this sequence of events and it may be that the circle of timber posts predated the bank and ditch. New radiocarbon dates from the henge at New Mains in Perthshire show that the wooden posts were certainly put in place several centuries before the ditching was dug.

However all that may be, Cairnpapple was clearly an extremely potent place, for in the following 3,500 years, a time stretching well into the historic period, it remained a place of great holiness, where important people wanted to be buried. The name itself confirms a continuity of sanctity. Cairnpapple's local pronunciation is *Cairnypapple*, and it betrays Celtic origins. *Carn* is a stone or rock in Gaelic, the locally added *y* stands for 'of' and *papple* is cognate to several place-names in the Western Isles and the Atlantic seaboard. *Bayble* on the Isle of Lewis, the islands of *Pabbay*, *Papa* Westray and *Papa* Stour all relate to the Irish Gaelic word for a monk, *papar* or *papa*, cognate with *father*. Cairnpapple means 'The Priests' Rock'.

Orkney is also an old name, recorded first by the Romans on their reconnaissance of Britain. It means 'The Islands of the Boar Tribe' and stands in a long and local tradition of totem names. On the mainland opposite Orkney is Caithness, called *Katanes* by the Vikings. It means 'The Promontory of the Cats', a name which puzzled prehistorians and toponymists until it was remembered that the lynx or bobcat still hunted the Scottish landscape until the medieval period. And the smaller wildcat still survives today. The totem-memory of the lynx was strong and it was adopted in the 13th century by the confederation of smaller north-eastern Highland clans led by the Mackintoshes. They became known as *Clan Chattan*. Sutherland is called *Cataibh* in Gaelic, another version of the ancient label. And to the south the Romans noted a tribe known as the *Caereni* or Sheep Folk; below them, towards the Beauly Firth, lay the territory of the *Lugi*, the Raven People. Animal totems add more than spots of colour, they say something about how early people saw themselves and each other and what they found heroic and admirable in the natural world.

The beginnings of the association of Orkney with the boar are lost in distant antiquity, but it may be that it was talked of by seasonal hunting parties. The islands appear to have been uninhabited (or at least no traces of earlier peoples have yet been found) before the end of the 5th millennium BC, and boar would have thrived in the absence of regular human predators. The earliest evidence of occupation shows that farming had been adopted in Orkney by 3600 BC and probably several generations before that. In fact, the first sustained colonization of the islands may have been by communities already skilled at cultivation and animal husbandry, and while it was difficult it was not impossible to ferry cattle and sheep across the Pentland Firth in summer in a skin boat. In the 1920s erosion on the coast of Papa Westray nibbled at the edge of what turned out to be a very early settlement at Knap of Howar. Archaeologists found two well-preserved stone houses and ultimately were able to radiocarbon-date them to 3600 BC. The walls of the roughly rectangular building had survived up to door lintel height and its close neighbour was also in a good state of preservation.

Clan Chattan

The prehistoric clan opened itself up to become an umbrella for lesser names. By the 14th century Clan Cat or Chattan had incorporated MacPhersons, Cattanachs, Macbeans, Macphails, Mackintoshes (the largest group), MacGillivrays, Davidsons, Macqueens, Macintyres and several others. This confederacy was led by the Chief of the Clan Mackintosh, also known as the Captain of Clan Chattan. The Macbeans in particular fought bravely at Culloden in 1746. A famous recent descendant never forgot his ancient links with the totem of the cat: in his studio bedroom in Dennistoun in Glasgow, Charles Rennie Mackintosh decorated the walls above the dado rail with a frieze of cats.

Early houses (and late ones) in Orkney are built in stone for the excellent reason that it is plentiful on the island and very easy to work. Coastal deposits of flagstones have the happy knack of breaking into handy rectilinear shapes of varying gauges. This geological accident makes drystone building quick and simple, and many of the prehistoric houses in Orkney have a tidy, squared-off look about them, something not repeated elsewhere in Scotland.

The Knap of Howar settlement is now so close to the open sea that a protective wall had to be built once the excavations were completed.

But evidence from the midden around the site strongly suggests that the coastline has changed radically since 3600 BC. Oyster shells have been discovered, and since they thrive only in sheltered coastal waters it is likely that Papa Westray was once joined to its neighbour, Westray, forming a horn-shaped bay. The houses were built on a patch of land which originally lay a short distance from the sea and the ancient bay, probably behind sand dunes which offered some break against the wind.

Prehistoric sausages

In the long winter months domestic cattle were probably bled for food. In north-western Europe there exists an ancient tradition of making blood puddings, concoctions of flour or meal and herbs cooked with fresh blood. Because it turns black in the process, they are sometimes called black puddings by the more fastidious. The mixture was probably squeezed into the scalded alimentary tubing of sheep or cows and boiled. Haggis could easily have been made by prehistoric cooks. The stomach of a sheep was filled with the chopped (*haggis* is cognate with the verb 'to hack') offal, the items of a slaughtered animal's anatomy which spoil most quickly – the liver, lights, tongue, heart and brains. It would have been a simple matter to add some cereal and stuff the mixture into the stomach container, tie it off with a cord and suspend it in boiling water – just as it is made today.

The midden containing the fragments of oyster shells was not heaped against the walls of the house, as used to be the case on Scottish farmsteads until very recently (and in some cases it is still not far enough away); it appears to have been spread over garden plots to revitalize heavily worked soils. Grains of wheat and barley were found at Knap of Howar and the infield area close to the houses would certainly have been fenced to keep domestic animals off the crops. Cattle and sheep were reared and routinely slaughtered for meat while still young and tender. The evidence for pigs is interesting. They were larger than normal and closer in breed to the wild boars which gave the Orkney islands their name.

Set side by side, the houses at Knap of Howar have of course long since lost their roofs. These were generally made from timber frames (and possibly with whalebones) with living turf laid over them, and a net of boulder-weighted ropes to make sure the wind did not lift the turf. Inside the larger house upright flagstones divided the space into two rooms. The first was reached through a long entrance passage (designed to reduce draughts) and its floor was originally paved. Off to the left another passage led directly into the second house, which was probably used as a workshop. Whispers of rituals were discovered by the archaeologists. In a domestic variant on the ceremonies on Cairnpapple Hill, a tiny pot was buried under a larger sherd in the bigger house. And at some point during its occupation, the workshop was carefully sealed up, almost in the manner of some of the later Orkney tombs. It should always be borne in mind that prehistoric life was constantly informed by religious beliefs – whatever they were. It was not something our ancestors did only on a Sunday.

Fish out of favour

The University of Bradford has recently conducted comparative tests on 167 hunter-gatherer-fisher skeletons and 19 skeletons of early farmers. These show a significant difference in diet between the two groups. The bones of the earlier people indicate a marked preference for seafood, while those of the early farmers reveal meat-eaters. Dr Michael Richards believes that the results are evidence of deliberate changes that took place in the centuries around 3000 BC. 'I think they fundamentally changed their diet, probably immediately, when this new material culture arrived. All this stuff had to be put in a boat to be brought to Britain. It is associated with a package, a whole load of things that appear for the first time in Britain: the first-ever pottery, monumental architecture – Stonehenge is the end result of it – and chambered tombs that you bury everyone in. But you also, for the first time, find cereal grains. I personally think this is all linked with the spread of a new belief system. Even now religions have dietary prescription. Other people have suggested it is much more practical – you don't have to rely on wild foods any more, you can control your food, you can control what you grow. You have a steady supply of food all the time if you have a herd of animals.'

In the 1850s a lost village built on Orkney by early farmers began to emerge from the sand dunes bordering the Bay of Skaill on the western coast of Mainland, the largest island. A violent storm ripped the turf off and blew enough sand away to reveal the edge of the settlement which became known to history as Skara Brae (see plate IV). It offers the most pungent sense yet of how our ancestors lived. Instead of anonymous cropmarks, soil stains or a few boulders strewn in the landscape, here are clearly identifiable houses clustered together in a village. The rooms have well-made stone furniture, a well-designed floor plan, walls still standing up to roof height, and above all an overwhelming sense of use. The people seem to have departed only recently, not 5,000 years ago.

Like Knap of Howar, Skara Brae is on the Orkney coast, facing the mighty Atlantic, and may have suffered from erosion. Eight houses have been identified, but there may have been more on the seaward side. They were built into a huge midden. Not spread over infield garden plots but banked up against the walls of the houses and even up over the roofs, it consisted mainly of marine rubbish, and on a hot summer's day fresh dumps will have been noticeable. And yet the people who inhabited the village appear to have lived and worked for much of the time on top of this large pile of detritus. Many artefacts have been discovered there.

However, it should never be forgotten that, when the weather and the seasons allowed, people from the prehistoric – and historic – periods always preferred to be outside in daylight, especially if they were working. Most of the great illuminated manuscripts of the Dark Ages and later, for instance, were written and painted in the open air. Large windows are a recent architectural innovation, and Skara Brae's houses had no windows at all. Light shone dimly through some of the passages only on the brightest of days, and in the house interiors the fire in the central hearth and perhaps some oil lamps supplied the only illumination. Intricate working of any sort, be it flint-knapping, bone-carving or sewing hides, needed good light to be done properly and efficiently. In the recent past crofters who knitted or used a spinning wheel always sat outside to see clearly what they were doing.

Some of them also sat happily near their middens. Just as at Skara Brae, farm workers in the recent past put their kitchen and other organic refuse into a midden piled up against the house or cottage wall, often buttressed on either side by big stones or some sort of low walling. The midden was a vital means of regenerating heavily worked garden plots and the shelter of a house wall was an immediately useful way of stopping all that precious material from being blown away. The old women who sat by it clacking their knitting needles were used to the smell, if they ever thought about it at all. The delicacy of our modern nostrils is a recent phenomenon. In the long past no one minded natural smells nearly as much as we do now, and the notion of the villagers at Skara Brae sitting on top of their midden would have occasioned no comment at all from a Borders farmhand of the 19th century.

Most of the houses at Skara Brae were laid out according to a specific design. Leading off two long, roofed passageways, the entrances to the houses were also long and low so that draughts were kept to a minimum. But when the large single room of each house was finally reached, there were a number of immediately obvious observations. First, it was possible to stand up straight. As at Knap of Howar, the ceilings were built well above average human height, and in fact it might have been possible to store a good many items in the rafters. Secondly, after the darkness of the passageways, the houses were comparatively well lit and probably warm, if smokey. The square hearth sat in the centre so that its glow illuminated the space evenly. The third effect discernible upon entering a Skara Brae house leads to some intriguing observations.

On the left of the entrance to most of the houses there is an item of built-in stone furniture which forces visitors to turn to the right. Archaeologists believe that the larger stone beds, which always sit on the right, were for men, and that the smaller beds opposite, on the other side of the hearth, were used by women. All of the furniture is stone-built and fixed, and this unchanging arrangement moulded domestic routines and behaviour. If the right-hand side of the house is thought to be the male side and the left the female, then that represents an example of an astonishingly durable cultural habit. On Orkney, farmhouses described as *longhouses*, which were still inhabited in the 19th century, had a right-hand side where there was room to sit and talk. This was known as the *But Hoose*. The left-hand side, where flour and meal were stored, was called the *Ben End*. Single-roomed cottages occupied by farm workers all over Scotland were commonly labelled as *But and Bens*, with the But on the right and the Ben on the left. It was only the increasing availability of moveable box beds that began to alter these ancient divisions. But Scots still welcome visitors with the phrase 'Come away ben the hoose', and usher them in to sit down by the fire and perhaps take a drink.

In a single-roomed house privacy is at a premium. Nineteenth-century mothers and fathers had doors or curtains attached to their box beds and even if not all of the children were asleep, there would at least be nothing to see. The archaeologists at Skara Brae found evidence for canopies and screens of hide around the stone bed-frames which might have afforded some modesty. It is unlikely that nudity offended prehistoric sensibilities, but it may well be that love-making was not something done openly in front of a family audience. However, it is difficult to imagine any of the Skara Brae villagers willingly sleeping alone. Single beds are another modern invention, and before the age of central heating (or any heating except a fire) most Scots slept together for warmth and company. The ancient Orcadians no doubt did the same.

Puffballs

At Skara Brae a number of puffballs were discovered in the midden. They were probably brought back to the village by children sent to hunt fungi. Should an adult have deemed them over-ripe and likely to cause a stomach upset if added to a stew or a savoury porridge, they were discarded. Or perhaps they were never intended as a constituent of a meal but were to be used medicinally. Prehistoric peoples possessed a wide and detailed knowledge of what was edible and when it was edible in the natural world. Fungi are tasty but dangerous. There are 20 poisonous varieties native to Britain, four of them fatally so. But mushrooms and other fungi are easily dried and keep well over the winter. That made them worth rooting out. Mushroom-hunting persists today and one professional gatherer at Tentsmuir Forest in Fife supplies a famous London restaurant with its weekly needs, sending baskets of ceps, chanterelles and other wild mushrooms down on the overnight train from Dundee. A good day's work can earn £400, but for that the hunter has to know exactly what he is looking for, where to find it, and not to over-pick.

Opposite the entrance to each of the Skara Brae houses stood a large shelved dresser. It was not necessarily the most convenient place to keep cooking and eating utensils and other items, but it was certainly the most visible. Perhaps its function included display, rather like those reproduction antique Welsh dressers which are designed to show off china on their narrow upper shelves as well as store it below in cupboard compartments. Equally, there may have been some profound ritualistic function associated with the magical properties of prehistoric pottery which encouraged villagers to put it on show. Between the dresser and the hearth, a large stone seat was positioned facing the entrance, and, it may be imagined, at the head of the table.

The atmosphere of Skara Brae village is vivid, seeming to evoke a powerful sense of life in the 4th/3rd millennium BC as no other place can. In those well-appointed rooms it is possible to imagine a range of family and community occasions: betrothals, celebrations, gift-giving, deaths and births. Much of the dramatic, upstanding evidence of ceremonial for the 4th/3rd millennium BC, the great cairns and stone circles, is often associated with the rituals surrounding death, and the worlds beyond life. But is it not reasonable to believe that birth, too, occasioned a set of formal, and happier, responses? In a prehistoric community with such a powerful sense of itself, a new arrival may have been treated with the same reverence as an elder's departure.

The archaeological record does not of course reflect anything of this balance of attitudes. The evidence is lacking. By its very nature, death leaves a deposit in the ground, but the skeletal remains of the distant past can have much to say about distant lives. Isbister lies on the southern tip of the Orcadian island of South Ronaldsay, and on good days the cliffs of Caithness on the mainland can be made out. Like many locations in the Northern Isles it is a dramatic, beautiful and atmospheric place. The farmer at Isbister in the summer of 1958, Ronald Simison, found one particular part of his land very intriguing. He needed fencing materials and, like many of his contemporaries, he thought of using the local flagstones. There was a promising-looking exposed area near the cliffs at the edge of his land. As he looked around, Simison noticed what he thought was an unnatural rise in the ground. Hard by it was a short run of drystone walling. By this time very curious, the farmer pulled away some of the turf and exposed a bit more. After half an hour's digging at the foot of the wall, he had come across something extraordinary, a collection of prehistoric artefacts, all of them beautifully made. He cleaned the soil off a polished mace-head with a hole ground in it to hold a wooden haft, two lustrous ceremonial axeheads of the sort made at Langdale and Creag na Caillich, a black jet button and an orange-coloured object that might have been a knife. This chance find by an observant farmer began a train of events that led to the excavation of what became known as the Tomb of the Eagles.

The first burials were placed in it around 3150 BC and it was finally sealed 750 years later in 2400 BC, a period almost exactly contemporary with the occupation of Skara Brae. Isbister turned out to be a chambered tomb. Like the houses at Knap of Howar, it was divided by upright slabs of flagstone into a series of compartments sometimes known as stalls, and approached by a long, low passageway. There are 76 chambered tombs in Orkney and each is located near pockets of good farmland. On the island of Rousay, archaeologists found that the number of chambered tombs matched exactly the number of modern farms. It seemed very likely that Ronald Simison had come across the last resting place of his predecessors, the farmers who worked Isbister 4,400 years before he did.

The chambered tombs on Orkney are spaced out, not clustered together in some special sanctified place, and they appear to denote the territories of extended family groups who owned and worked prehistoric farms. At the end of the 4th millennium BC Rousay had a population of between 300 and 650, with around 25 to 50 living on each farm. The village at Skara Brae was probably home to about 50 people. These calculations are obviously approximate, but they supply a reasonable estimate of a contemporary population for Orkney of between 1,600 and 3,200.

Apart from their utilitarian use as an ossuary, the chambered tombs appear to have had an important function as territory markers. What better evidence of customary right to land could there be than a long tradition of interment in it? The establishment of such rights becomes important only in the context of challenge. In the era of the hunter-gatherer-fishers the population sustained by that way of life probably remained at too low a level to create many ownership challenges, or threats of challenge (except perhaps on Oronsay, where burials were inserted into the shell middens at an early date). When farming helped boost population numbers and created more pressure on particular pieces of land, the presence of a tomb full of the bones of ancestors who had worked that land for many generations and enjoyed rights over it supplied solid evidence of the legitimacy of those rights. The eternal presence of the ancestors made it the kindred ground.

Lying amongst the human bones, more corroboration was found. The Isbister tomb is known as the 'Tomb of the Eagles' for the excellent reason that Ronald Simison found exactly that, the bones of at least 15 sea-eagles. These beautiful birds flew off the cliffs at Isbister, fishing and hunting. With brown plumage, white tails and a magnificent wing-span of 1.8 m/6 ft, the sea-eagles usually nest on massive stick constructions, almost always on the faces of sea-cliffs. Like its cousin, the golden eagle, the bird lives a long time, at least 40 or 50 years, much longer than most of the people who lived at Isbister, who would have known individual birds by sight and been aware of their great longevity. It is a powerful image: a community living under the steady gaze of its protector, a great and revered bird flying over the kindred ground, hovering in the updraughts from the cliffs. Swooping into the sea to take fish with its razor talons, the sea-eagle is also content to eat carrion, picking up the carcasses of rotting fish by the seashore. And it would almost certainly have taken the flesh of dead human bodies.

This last offers a telling insight into the prehistoric way of death. In the context of the widespread adoption of totem animals by larger groups of people in later prehistory, it should not be surprising to perceive the presence of the bones of sea-eagles alongside those of people inside the Isbister tomb. They gave it a singular identity, made it a tomb like no other. Amongst the contemporary burials elsewhere on Orkney, there is more evidence of totemism: at Quanterness the bones of songbirds have been found, at Cuween there were dog skulls, and deer antlers at Holm on Papa Westray. Mr Simison believes that with its hornwork walls either side of the body of the tomb, the layout at Isbister mimics the shape of an eagle, wings outstretched, flying westwards towards the setting sun.

But it is the habit of carrion-eating which makes the choice of the sea-eagle as a symbol for the community and identity of the Isbister farmers so very interesting. From close examination of the bones found inside the tomb, it is clear that there were three stages in the journey of death, what happened to a body after life had departed. Many bones shows signs of weathering, of having been left outside in the elements after death but before being placed inside the shelter of the tomb. And some were more weathered than others. What explains the condition of the bones best is the first of the three stages of death – excarnation.

At Balfarg, near Glenrothes in Fife, the outline of what appears to be an excarnation enclosure has been found. Inside a stockaded area there are post-holes suggesting a series of raised platforms on which dead bodies were laid out. Without the protection of the stockade, wolves and other scavenging animals could drag bodies off the plat-forms and into the safe cover of woodland to devour them. And the precious bones would have been lost. In order to achieve a cleaned and defleshed skeleton which could survive entire, it was much better to allow decomposition to begin and have carrion-feeding birds peck at the corpse, ripping off gobbets of tissue up on the platform. Sometimes small finger or toe bones might be lost but the chances were that all the large bones and the skull would be left. Depending on the number of bodies and the hunger of the crows – or the sea-eagles – defleshing could be done quickly. So why leave the bones on the platforms so long that they became weathered?

An explanation which fits that collection of circumstances is that in prehistory death had its seasons. Bodies left to be picked over by the eagles which nested on the cliffs below the Isbister tomb were left outside until it was time for the next stage. Later Orkney society shows its knowledge of and interest in the solstitial or equinoctial turning points of the year and it may be that the second stage, the interment of defleshed bones in the tomb, was not done until the next available such point. That would explain why the bones had undergone varying degrees of weathering. Evidence of ritual meals at Isbister (joints of beef and deposits of broken pottery) add to the impression that regular ceremonies took place. The date of a death might always be a matter of accident but the day the skeleton was buried was not.

The Towers of Silence

Zoroastrians, also known as *Parsis* or Persians in India because they fled there after Moslem persecution in the 7th and 8th centuries, still practise excarnation, the defleshing of dead bodies. On what are called the Towers of Silence Parsi corpses are laid out for the vultures. Dating from the 6th century BC, Zoroastrianism is the oldest of the Indo-European religions to survive into the modern era and is the root of Judaism, Christianity and Islam. Despite their ancient provenance, the Towers of Silence are not popular with other denominations in the

Indian city of Mumbai (Bombay) because the vultures tear off hunks of rotting human flesh and fly over the city. And sometimes they drop bits.

The calendar of death was also influenced by the way in which early society understood it as a process and not only an event. Widespread evidence of the careful disposal of the deceased clearly demonstrates a belief in an afterlife of some sort. Tombs such as Isbister are properly seen as houses for the dead – they resemble those of the living too closely to be interpreted in any other way. And what purpose is there in building such houses if the dead have no use for them in an afterlife? One historian has suggested that the tombs might be seen as prisons, places where the malignity of the departed might be contained and kept out of the world of the living (and others contend that the ditches on the inside of the banks around henge monuments were designed to prevent the escape of the dead). Along with the notion of the afterlife sits the assumption that there was a journey to be made to it. And the living were bound to assist the dead in making that journey, with the proper ceremony, grave goods and suitable accommodation.

These elaborate provisions, much more complex than our habit of putting bodies in a hole in the ground or cremating them, appear to march in step with what prehistoric peoples believed about the soul. It might be interpreted in this way. At the moment of death, of final expiry, it was believed that the *breath-soul* left the body and was by mysterious means returned to a general reservoir of life upon which each new birth drew. After excarnation, the *dream-soul* remained with the body and could be extinguished only when cremation or decomposition took place. A tomb was a chamber of dream-souls, a place where individuals were absorbed into a communal identity, a community of ancestors whose existence constituted the *dream-time* history of an extended family, tribe or people, and which in turn was absorbed into the land upon which all life depended.

This theme of internalism is picked up by the inclusion of the bodies of sea-eagles in the chamber at Isbister, and it tracks a clear sequence. Out of the land comes the food that makes life possible, and at death the corporeal remains of spent life are put back into the land with the bodies of its totems placed beside them. And inside the bodies of the totem birds in the tombs is the flesh of the dream-souls which was nurtured by the fruits of the land.

These ideas of internalism lasted for millennia, well into the historic period, surviving vividly in the Celtic west. One of Gaelic's oldest poems, *Donald mac Iain 'ic Sheumais*, recounts the aftermath of a clan battle fought at Carinish on North Uist in 1601. A MacDonald warrior bleeds to death in the arms of his woman. But as his breath-soul departs, she takes it into herself:

> *Your noble body's blood*
> *lay on the surface of the ground.*
> *Your fragrant body's blood*
> *seeped through the linen.*
> *I sucked it up*
> *till my breath grew husky.*

When the Irish chief Murrough O'Brien was hanged, drawn and quartered in 1580, his foster-mother rushed on to the gallows to pick up his severed head and suck out all of the blood running from it. The old woman, it was reported by the appalled Edmund Spenser, drank the heroic O'Brien's blood 'because the earth was not worthy to drink it'. There is an implication that the blood of an ordinary sort of man might spill on to the soil as it would, without any such drama. These ancient and, to our mind, primitive practices endured very late. Well into the 19th century versions of them were still common in the Celtic parts of Germany, especially Bavaria and Franconia. At public decapitations onlookers were in the habit of rushing forward with cups and other vessels to collect the spurting blood of the victims. When drunk warm, it was believed to be a cure for all sorts of ailments.

The Gaels of the Highlands and Irish west carried over the rest of Scotland other remnants of some of the beliefs of the prehistoric

Orcadians and the tomb builders. Around the time of the battle at Carinish the ancient notion of *duthchas* came increasingly under threat. *Duthchas* applied to the ownership of clan lands, the collective sense in which the lands of, say, the Clan Cameron or Clanranald were held by the whole community who lived on them. Nowhere written down, developed over many generations, it was a general right exercised by families who had lived in the same place since before memory. What threatened was the competing idea of *oigreachd*, or ownership. For many centuries *duthchas* had been qualified, as a customary right, by the exercise of military power. The ability of a clan chief to protect those who lived on the clan lands had been rewarded by the payment of rents in kind and in military service when demanded. This had developed a different sense of ownership. *Oigreachd* means, literally, inheritance, specifically that which is inherited by the successors of the clan chiefs, his sons or his close relatives.

Duthchas began to wither in the modern period, worn down by the centralizing and standardizing tendencies of kingship and the absences of chiefs at court. But *in extremis* its memory could be powerful. Collective ownership depended absolutely on an understanding of genealogy and the continuity of a customary right held by the descendants of those who had always lived on and farmed the land. Awareness of and knowledge of genealogy was central to *duthchas*, and when the clansmen who fought at the battle of Culloden recited their genealogy before charging into battle they were only remembering why they had come to fight. As men chanted their way back through the generations, they asserted an ancient, umbilical attachment to their land, and when they raised their broadswords, they often roared the names of their places: *Loch Moy! Dunmaglass! Gleann Mhor!*

Many of the clansmen who fought at Culloden could recite a genealogy going back 20 or more generations, often with some detail attached to the names. Clan chiefs, kings and other notables frequently went back to what they saw as the dawn of history, often to claim a spurious legitimacy. But the notion that early peoples forgot their genealogy as it receded into the more remote past is an unlikely one. Twenty generations cover 500 years and where the recognition of a clear line of descent and therefore collective title to a piece of land was concerned, memory will have found a way.

The bones of the ancestors at Isbister had great importance for the living and for their own sense of history. However, they do also supply the modern archaeologist with much information about the lives they led. In an important sense the skeletons in the tomb allow the empty rooms at Skara Brae to come to life, since they were the exact contemporaries of the villagers.

An analysis of the bones at Isbister shows a wide spread of age, many children interred along with old people. The age range was, however, restricted in terms of modern life expectancy. The people of the 4th millennium BC tended to die young; only six out of the 400 or so skeletons (or rather, parts of skeletons) found in the tomb lived beyond the age of 40. Because of the dangers of childbirth, women died earlier than men and it appears that only 40 per cent of the sexually mature population was female – a situation which must have made for tensions. The average life expectancy for women was no more than 20 years.

The bones can reconstruct a sense of what the prehistoric population looked like. Men averaged 1.7 m/5 ft 7 ins in height and women 1.61 m/5 ft 3½ ins. Because of the hard work they did the Isbister people were heavily muscled, particularly in the legs, a characteristic that applied to all age groups and both genders. One in six children suffered from osteoarthritis of the spine, and it is clear that as soon as they could walk they were set to work. In the skulls of women an interesting deformity was detected. Across the forehead there was a clear indentation where a brow-band had been worn. In the 19th century Orcadian women still carried creels or baskets in the same way, slung across the back and held by a band passing across the forehead. And within the span of modern recollection fishwives in the port of Newhaven (now a suburb of Edinburgh) still showed the mark made by a *bowtow* or creel-rope. Into the 1970s the last of the fishwives, Esther Linton, sold fish from door to door and carried her creel in that ancient fashion.

Child labour

Farming made large families not just attractive, but possible. The hunter-gatherer-fishers' more mobile way of life had tended to restrict family size, biologically reinforced, as explained earlier, by the long weaning period and its inhibiting effect on female fertility. But when more pairs of hands were needed on a farm, and when animal milk became regularly available, the period of weaning lessened and the possibility of more children increased. Because, in the demanding age of agribusiness, their yield is comparatively low, milking ewes have been somewhat forgotten in Britain. But they were probably the most reliable and easily maintained source of animal milk and the nutritious cheese made from it was no doubt welcome. In the medieval period ewes' milk cheese was known as 'white meats' and a hard variety could keep for a long time, perhaps through a winter. It was often so hard that it had to be soaked and beaten with a mallet before it could be eaten.

There were many cases of degenerative spine disease found in the Orkney tomb; about 47 per cent of the total population had it. This shows that they routinely did heavy work in all weathers. In general the appearance of the people at Isbister did not change for millennia and the medieval population looked very like their prehistoric ancestors, and perhaps not unlike the Newhaven fishwives.

Another curious deformity linked the Isbister people to the 20th century. It appears that the prehistoric peoples of South Ronaldsay were very heavily muscled around the ankles, and some had the beginnings of an articulation for a third bone at the end of the thumbs and big toes. Eight people from the tomb had suffered from osteoarthritis of the big toe. When the lives of the St Kildans are remembered, and the skills and agility needed to claim their harvest of seabirds off the cliffs, it is clear what the Isbister people were doing. Heavy musculature around the ankle comes from repeated flexing, and when inching along the cliff ledges to lift eggs or catch young fulmars, there would have been plenty of that sort of exercise. This is striking evidence of another amazing 5,000-year continuity.

Despite the detailed analytical work done at Isbister and at other tombs, one statistical conundrum remains stubbornly unsolved. Where are all the other bodies? Only a fraction of the prehistoric population of the Orkney islands was interred in the tombs during the long period of their use. What was done with the majority of the bodies? How were they disposed of? There is no evidence of mass graves, or indeed anything else, and only speculation is possible. It may well be that cremation of the sort that went on at Pitglassie provides an answer. Perhaps bones were defleshed and burned to dust, and that dust strewn over the ground that these people farmed. And when it rained their remains went back into the land. This means of burial is undetectable.

Even more mystery swirls around a set of monuments built towards the end of the 4th millennium BC. In Scotland there are 30 so-called *cursus* sites, originally thought to be Roman in origin and used as courses for chariot racing. Almost all of them have been picked up in aerial photography as cropmarks, and they are generally laid out as rectangular areas, defined by excavated banks and ditches or rows of post-holes, or both. One of the Scottish cursus monuments is spectacular and far more substantial than a cropmark. The Cleaven Dyke in Perthshire runs for 2 km/1 mile and has a central bank rising to 3 m/10 ft in places. This is flanked by two parallel ditches dug at a distance of about 50 m/165 ft on either side. It is a remarkable construction, but its function is almost impossible to decode. Apparently the Cleaven Dyke originated with an oval burial mound at its head and first developed as a long tail running behind it. This allows a glimmer of interpretation. If the mile-long earthwork began life as a place for burial, did it continue in that function? Ditches were generally used in this sort of context to demarcate a sacred area, marking it off from the secular world. Was the long run of the Cleaven Dyke a place that carried on being used for burials or at least ceremonies involving the dead? Was it one of the locations where the ashes of the missing generations of Scotland's prehistoric peoples were scattered? Was it a prison for the dead? Archaeology has shown that the Dyke was not all built at once but in 34 short segments. Perhaps as the years wound on and fresh areas for scatter were needed the builders slowly extended the holy ground to accommodate the windblown ashes. But that simply adds one speculation to another, and it is impossible to know what people did when they gathered at the Cleaven Dyke.

Around 3300 BC henges began to appear in Scotland, significantly earlier than anywhere else in Britain. They represent a clear period of change, a time when communal burial monuments such as Isbister gradually gave way to larger, more élitist and certainly more enigmatic forms of religious activity. Henges did not immediately take the form of approximately circular ditches and banks. They may have begun as rings of timber posts or stones when large ditched circles came to be created; they involved a good deal of digging and clearly imply co-operation inside communities – directed either by an individual or an élite. It is difficult to imagine an enterprise on this scale being a matter of communal initiative or control. It may also be the case that the act of henge-building itself was what consolidated power, not the completed henge.

Hengeworld

Henge is a misnomer. Extracted from 'Stonehenge', it was first used in the 1930s to describe a circle of ditching and a bank. But the original sense of it was quite other. The name Stanenge and later Stanchenge was coined in the 12th century and it referred specifically to the great monument itself. 'Henge' is cognate to 'hang' and describes only one bit, albeit the defining bit, of Stonehenge, that is, the lintel stones which were 'hung' on the vertical uprights. The term is unfortunate because for the lay person it conjures up something a great deal more exciting than a barely discernible ditch and bank.

The early purpose of the circles appears to have been twofold. First the ring of posts was set up and perhaps at a later date the ditch was dug for the usual purpose of demarcation, to indicate exactly where the holy of holies lay. There are several instances of sites already thought of as sacred being enclosed by a ditch at this time. It happened at Balfarg in Fife, where the excarnation platforms were raised, and also at Cairn-papple, around the hearths and the deposits of pottery and axes. The second purpose seems to have been exclusivist. The upcast from the ditch was shovelled to the outside edges, and, where measurement has been possible, piled up to a height which would have screened the interior from view. Mystery has long lain at the heart of most religions and the henges seem to inaugurate it in Scotland. Whatever happened behind the screening bank, not everyone was involved and not everyone was allowed to see and understand. We sometimes forget that Christianity built screens inside its greatest churches for very similar reasons.

The majority of stone circles in Scotland are in Orkney and the Isle of Lewis, although many others exist all over Scotland and take differ-ent and intriguing forms. They are large monuments, much greater in scale than the chambered tombs, their construction requiring far more effort and planning. Surviving circles at Brodgar/Stenness on Orkney (see plates v, vi and vii), Calanais on the Isle of Lewis (see plate viii), Kilmartin in Argyll and Balfarg in Fife were also part of ceremonial centres, places that acted as a focus for large communities. Comparing the number of man-hours needed to build Calanais and Brodgar/Stenness with the estimates of prehistoric population levels, it is certain that they were the principal centres of worship on these islands. In turn this allows a political observation. The gradual move (Isbister went on being used until well into the 3rd millennium BC) from the chambered tombs of the kindred ground to the impressive focal monuments strongly suggests a new centralizing force at work: kings of Orkney, princes of Lewis. There must have been a dominating élite of that sort to direct and control the resources required to create Brodgar/Stenness or Calanais – the groups of workers taken away from agricultural work, the transportation of materials, the sustained production of surplus food and the decisions made on the precise layout and location of the henges, the stone circles inside them and the tombs nearby.

That dominance was probably asserted militarily. The production of agricultural surpluses allowed the growth and rise of specialists in society – and one early specialism will have been in warfare. The process by which a warrior class emerged is lost to history but its effects are not. The transfer of control from the kindred grounds to a unified kingdom of Orkney produced the ceremonial centre at Brodgar/Stenness.

The monuments on Orkney were the first manifestation of a new religion, or at least a new version of older beliefs. Whatever they were, the new ideas spread quickly and travelled far. Brodgar/Stenness predates the great henges of the south of England, the famous circles of Wessex at Avebury, Durrington Walls, Knowlton, Marden and Mount Pleasant. These were built around 2500 BC, at least 500 years later, although the first phase at Stonehenge is much closer in date to those in the north. It may be that the adoption of this new belief system owed some of its immediate popularity to politics. If chiefdoms or petty kingships were establishing themselves in Wessex, the centralizing of power symbolized by the henges and the process of their construction might have been an attractive statement to make to doubters, dissenters or conservatives. The ability to create an organization capable of building large monuments was in itself a demonstration of impressive power. And this was something well understood elsewhere. At about the same time as the British monuments were rising, strongly centralized regimes in Egypt caused the great pyramids to be built.

Thom's yard

The achievement of a perfect circle for a henge was not difficult for prehistoric builders. Once a location had been chosen, they knocked a stake into the ground and attached a long rope to it. Keeping it constantly tight, they then moved round and marked the radius on the turf. Alexander Thom analysed many measurements of prehistoric monuments and came to believe that their builders used a standard unit of measurement, which he called the megalithic yard: 2 ft 3½ ins/89 cm. Thom believed that prehistoric society could grasp complicated mathematical principles and designed stone circles according to these. More, he went on to argue that many of the monuments are astrological observatories marking points in the year, times when the sun or moon aligns in a particular way in relation to the stones. While the appearance of the moon or the sun over a stone may have been important to the drama of religious ceremonies, it is unlikely to have been of much use to farmers. In the absence of a diary, they did not need a stone circle to tell them when the seasons changed. In any case this varies every year and people who live their whole lives on the land can feel the year turn – by observing the behaviour of their animals, looking at the soil and sniffing the air.

The location of the ceremonial centre at Brodgar/Stenness, probably chosen by the king of Orkney, made another statement. The henges and their related standing stones are arranged in the middle of Mainland, the largest island in the archipelago, in a place where elemental metaphor abounds. Two lochs sit side by side. To the east is the freshwater loch of Harray and to the west the Loch of Stenness, which may have contained salt water in the prehistoric period and certainly has sea-water spill into it at its southern tip at high tide. The lochs are now linked by a narrow channel running between two peninsulas, but it is likely that in 3000 BC these were joined by an isthmus separating Harray and Stenness. The whole area is fringed by low hills, giving the impression of a wide, natural amphitheatre. At the religious centre of prehistoric Orkney earth, air, sky, water and, as will be seen, fire seemed to come together in a dramatic and elegant synthesis of all the elements.

What was raised by great labour on this site – the circles, standing stones and tombs – is difficult to understand. But at the excavated settlement of Barnhouse which lies on the shores of Loch Harray, close to the Stones of Stenness, there may be a trace of an explanation. A group of houses was discovered which dates from earlier than the monuments. Most of them resemble Skara Brae, although they are not in such a good state of preservation. The walls rise to only a few centimetres. In one quarter of Barnhouse village the excavators found a much larger house with two rooms, both containing central hearths. As at Skara Brae, movement around the space was governed by the placement of stone fixtures and fittings. For example, entrance to the inner room could only be gained by walking around the hearth in the outer. A few feet away from the entrance to the large house the foundations of another, even grander, structure were uncovered. Surrounded by a wall lay a squarish house with a central hearth, and once again those entering it were forced to negotiate their way around or over a small hearth placed disconcertingly just outside the doorway.

In the village around the larger houses examples of a strange artefact were found. Small carved stone balls of intricate, highly detailed design were used at Barnhouse, and they seem to have been symbolic regalia of some sort. Also found at Skara Brae and in Aberdeenshire, these objects were obviously important, for the more intricate took a long time to make – three days, in modern experiments. The great majority discovered so far come from Aberdeenshire and it is likely that they were first made there. Maceheads, like the one discovered at Isbister by Ronald Simison, have also been found at many sites, 76 on Orkney alone. These are the accessories of religious and political ceremony, like the sceptre and orb of medieval and modern kingship, and were probably carried in procession and displayed at important moments.

Henges are not found anywhere else in Europe, and it seems that the new religious beliefs which raised them originated in Orkney. The largest house at Barnhouse offers a sense of where these beliefs began and how they developed. Size matters in architecture and it relates closely to status. The bigger the house, the more important the occupants and the more prestigious its function. At 7.6 by 10.7 m/25 by 35 ft, the largest building at Barnhouse housed those who directed the affairs of the community, both living and dead.

Lot's Wife

Stone circles were often thought to be dread consequences. In Cornwall the Hurlers were the frozen result of Sabbath-breaking by a reckless group of young men who dared to play the Celtic version of hockey on a Sunday. Not far away, the Merry Maidens were also petrified for failing to respect the Lord's Day, perhaps in imitation of Lot's Wife who was turned into a pillar of salt for disobedience. The wedding guests at Stanton Drew in Somerset who forgot themselves entirely and danced on a Sunday must have been an impressive sight before they were frozen in stone. There are no less than three stone circles near the village. These three and others with similar legendary origins are all small-scale circles, and for the gullible it was possible to believe that disrespectful revellers were imprisoned inside their stones. The larger uprights at Stonehenge and elsewhere were, of course, thought to be petrified giants, often spellbound by a witch or the wizard Merlin. The existence of giants living in the distant past was not doubted, since their bones had been dug up in several places. They were in fact mammoth bones, but no one had ever heard of them.

Although the ground plan included a dresser on the far side of the central hearth, the same arrangement as at Skara Brae, Barnhouse hall does not seem to have been lived in. The placement of a hearth at the entrance to the 5-m/16-ft doorway passage was not practical, particularly if, as at Balbridie, many people were thought to occupy such a large interior and went in and out all day. There appear to have been no flagstone room dividers, no bed recesses in the hall and little of the domestic detail found elsewhere. The likelihood has to be that it was a temple, a sacred building modelled on the ordinary houses found on Orkney and related to the nearby Stones of Stenness and the tomb at Maes Howe. The hearth at the entrance is evocative. Those who wished to enter the temple had, symbolically at least, to pass through the fire, to enter another world, the world of the dead. That was what actually happened at cremation. A body which had given up its breath-soul was changed on a pyre and became a dream-soul, part of the community of the dead. It is an old idea, and many rituals which survived into the historic period involved passing through a fire.

On the wrack

Seaweed was very important to prehistoric – and historic – communities. It provided food and fertilizer, and until the 19th century unashamedly pagan ceremonies were conducted in the Hebrides to persuade the old gods to send winter storms to tear the wrack off its holdfasts and blow it up on to the beaches. Libations were poured on the waves and sea-gods such as Shony and Briannuil invoked. Varieties of seaweed such as sea-lettuce, dulse and sugar kelp could be eaten at all seasons of the year and animals were able to survive the winter by browsing the beaches. On the island of North Ronaldsay the sheep still eat seaweed to produce a highly flavoured and much-prized meat. There were also many medicinal uses and filamentous seaweed could be used as thatch, or twisted into ropes, nets or fishing lines. Redware, another variety, burned well on domestic fires. Near the sites at Skara Brae, Links of Noltland and on Westray are runs of low dykes located just above the high-tide mark. They are used to dry seaweed for fertilizer and may well date back to prehistoric times. It was a valuable winter harvest and coastal communities traded it inland in the historic period.

If Barnhouse hall was indeed a temple, who were the gods? Everything points to a pantheon of ancestors, a general congregation of all those who had gone before, or notable individuals picked out for particular reasons, or most likely both, one seen against the general context of the other. Ancestor-gods are worshipped in many communities around the world, and often for the same reason as they were on Orkney. The living owed their lives to them in every vital sense. Successive generations of parents brought the living into the world, and they also represented a life-giving title to land, a livelihood for the living. What moved the expression of that generalized debt from chambered tombs to the construction of henges may have been the need to legitimize the primacy of certain individuals and their particular lineage. The Barnhouse temple, the stone circles and the tomb at Maes Howe may have been raised to the memory and glory of one set of ancestors, the most important of the ancestor-gods, those who might smile and show favour to the living. These were the ancestors of the kings or chiefs and if they were understood to have interceded on behalf of the living, that will have added even greater legitimacy and lustre to the ruling name.

Royal or powerful families have made political use of their genealogy for millennia, often to smooth the transition from one ruler to the next and sometimes to assert greater right over a rival. In 1411, before the Battle of Harlaw, the bard of the Lords of the Isles, Lachlan Mor MacMhuirich, walked out in front of the great crescent-shaped lines of the clans to recite the long genealogy of the Lordship. He took the lineage back into the swirling mists of semi-mythic antiquity, citing Conn of the Hundred Battles, an Irish hero of the 1st millennium BC. At Barnhouse temple similar trails of glory and grandeur may have been chanted.

The long passageway into the temple was oriented towards the sunrise at midsummer. In what would have been a very dark, windowless interior, the effect of a brief flooding with light might have been seen to have magical properties: the moment of a solstitial turn of the year announcing itself in the house of the dead. In related counterpoint, the entrance to the great tomb at Maes Howe is oriented to the midwinter sunset. It is tempting to see the structures themselves as working in a duality, as houses of the dead used in ceremonies at opposite times in the year and at opposite ends of the day; but in the absence of any information about the detail of the ceremonial, little of any substance can be said.

Excavations at the Stones of Stenness carried out in the early 1970s discovered a square hearth in the centre of the circle. Between it and the entrance to the north, there were small stones set in some sort of architectural arrangement and beyond the hearth a series of pits which may have held other features. Only four of the original 12 stones surrounding the circle survive. They are spectacular, one of them 5.8 m/19 ft high, and when all were in place the sense of monumental enclosure would have been awesome. In 3000 BC, when the fire burning in the central hearth caused shadows to flicker on the broad sides of the huge encircling slabs, the inescapable impression would have been of a vast house, a sacred place dedicated to the worship of the ancestors. Perhaps the pits to the side of the fire held the foundations of a large stone dresser, used in some way as an altar or for the display of regalia, maceheads and carved stone balls. Perhaps the smaller stones inside the circle represented other items of furniture. It would have been impossible to attach a roof to the symbolic walls at Stenness, but perhaps that was less important than the fact that the great house of the dead lay open to the canopy of the sky. What mattered to the communities of farmers in prehistoric Orkney more than anything was the weather. It obviously came from the sky, and if it was believed that the ancestors controlled the elements, then it may well have been that they lived in another celestial world above the clouds.

Next to the hearth at Stenness there is a post-hole and this may have been used to fix the pole for the display of the totem animal of the circle. Excavations in the ditch around the stones turned up dog bones and it seems that the dog was particularly revered. By 3000 BC pastoral dogs were already in use by shepherds, but the general identification with man's best friend might not be all that was intended. The rulers of Orkney may have seen themselves as analogous to the sheepdogs, keeping their flock of ordinary Orcadians from harm. In a stock-rearing economy, the symbolism will have been clear enough.

The nearby tomb of Maes Howe is a masterpiece of early architecture, its stones fitted together without bonding of any sort, judged and weighted by consummately skilful craftsmen. It was probably built about 200 years after the Stones of Stenness were raised. The long, low passageway was not designed in that characteristic way to keep out draughts. The dead were not likely to feel the cold. It was made like that in imitation of the secular houses of Orkney, because it was seen as a house for the dead. It may also have been appreciated that the proper, reverential way to enter Maes Howe was in a crouch or a forced bow, after negotiating a 20-m/65-ft passage.

But Maes Howe was originally a henge. Archaeologists have found traces of ditching around the tomb's mound. And inside the chamber the four tall stones which looked as though they helped to hold up the walls turned out not to be structural at all. It seems that the masons built around what were originally four standing stones at the centre of an earlier henge.

Perhaps this adaptation was a logical extension of the power that caused henges to be built in the first place. At Cairnpapple, a later burial in the centre of the circle gives some idea of the ceremony involved. The corpse was wrapped in organic material, perhaps a plaid of woven grasses, and the face had had a burnt wooden mask laid over it. If the body had been excarnated, this may have been a stylized death mask of a sort used in other cultures or a way of showing that the body had passed through fire. A burnt wooden club was laid alongside the body and flowers strewn in the grave. Pots containing food and drink for the journey after death were left and then all was sealed up. Perhaps most significantly, the change in beliefs was demonstrated by the fact that the stone circle was ultimately pulled down and reused as material for the building of a cairn over this single grave.

The idea of sacred ground for burial, and its power after death, continued well into the historic period. Wealthy and powerful people believed that the soil in which their bodies were placed had magic properties, especially if it was in or adjacent to very sacred churches associated with a saint. For many centuries Scottish kings insisted on being buried at Iona because of its links with Columba and because they believed that the ancient sanctity of the soil would literally dissolve their sins and allow safe and speedy passage to heaven. Perhaps burial in the magic soil at Cairnpapple, Calanais or Stenness offered similar guarantees.

Palaeo-meso-neo-lithic

Old, Middle and New Stone Ages have become standard terms in prehistory. The Old or Palaeolithic spans the Ice Age, the Middle or Mesolithic lasted from the retreat of the ice to the adoption of farming, and the New or Neolithic to the period when metals were first used. The Neolithic is generally followed by two more categories, the Bronze Age

and the Iron Age. Nineteenth-century Danish scholars were responsible
for these, the primary purpose of which was to act as tags to help sort
out museum collections of prehistoric objects. They are not very helpful
tags and require so much qualification and explanation that it is better
to use dates where they are available.

Because of the comparative solemnities of post-Reformation Christianity, we tend to think of religious ceremonies as rather static, contem-
plative affairs. In the prehistoric past, there was probably a great deal
of movement when people worshipped. They may have danced and,
although it is impossible to demonstrate or recreate, they probably made
music and sang. The geographical relationship of the much larger Ring
of Brodgar, on the north side of the isthmus separating Lochs Harray
and Stenness, with all of the other monuments and the related standing
stones strongly suggests it as the starting point for a procession. Brodgar
is big, about 100 m/340 ft across, and it was bounded by 60 stones, the
tallest survivor being 4.3 m/14 ft high. Between this circle and the Stones
of Stenness, several standing stones remain and their positioning indicates the line of a ceremonial way across the isthmus. It seems unlikely
that this was walked in silence. A variety of musical instruments were
known to early peoples: drums, rattles, and flutes made from bird bones.
Chanting and singing may also have accompanied the processions. Once
inside the smaller circle and taller stones at Stenness, there may have
been echoic effects to enhance the drama.

Not all stone circles were built to the same design, and all over
Scotland there would have been variations in ritual which called for different religious architecture. In Aberdeenshire, recumbent stone circles
have exactly that, a large recumbent stone laid on its side between the
two tallest stones in the arrangement. It looks like an altar. But what, if
anything, was set on it can only be guessed at. One of the most impressive
recumbent stone circles is to be found at East Aquhorthies in the Don
Valley (see plate IX). Cremations took place inside its perimeter, as they
did in many other circles. It may be that there was a calendar of death

when pyres were lit and skeletons or bodies were burned before being scattered. There is also convincing evidence that the recumbent stones were laid in such a way as to frame the moonset against a distant horizon at particular times of year, almost certainly those with agricultural significance. But perhaps the most significant thing about East Aquhorthies is its name and the long continuity of sanctity it is witness to. In Gaelic it means 'Field of Prayer'.

5

Homely Geometry

Thomas Pennant was thorough. In 1772 he set about organizing a second tour to Scotland by first placing an advertisement in *The Scots Magazine*. He was most anxious to see the Scottish Highlands and Islands for himself, but not to waste time when he was there. So that he could be sure of acquiring useful and accurate information about each of the localities he was proposing to visit, Pennant advised interested and interesting parties of his intentions:

> Permit me to prepare you for my coming, by sending you this notice of my intention of being in your neighbourhood the ensuring [sic] summer, and paying my respects to you. As my stay can be but very short, I am desirous of being at once directed to the objects most worthy the observation of a traveller . . . As my sole objects are my own improvement and the true knowledge of your country, hitherto misrepresented, I have no doubt of your complying with my wishes, which are included in the following queries and requests.

Thomas Pennant was wealthy, as well as impertinent, a Welsh landowner who could afford to satisfy his curiosity about the world by going and seeing it for himself. All that most of his contemporaries knew of the Highlands was alarming. The screaming, headlong-charging armies of savages who had scattered government troops and marched on London in 1745 and 1746 were no doubt a powerful image in the minds of those who thought about the north of Scotland, if they thought about it at all.

Everything about the Highlands spoke of the past, an ancient, mysterious and increasingly romantic past. To the outsider it seemed like another country, and to Pennant a place he simply had to visit.

Since his prime purpose was not sightseeing but to record and, where appropriate, classify what he saw (as a keen naturalist, Pennant had corresponded with the Swedish botanist Linnaeus), the Welshman took along his servant, Moses Griffith, an accomplished artist who could readily produce accurate drawings. And perhaps because of his Welsh background and his sensitivities for language, Pennant determined to travel in the Highlands in the close company of Gaelic-speakers as often as possible. The Reverend John Stuart volunteered and the quality of information gleaned improved accordingly.

The 'other country' explored by the three travellers was indeed different. In 1772 the Highlands and the Hebrides were much as they had been in the Middle Ages, and in many places life had proceeded unchanged for millennia. The agricultural and industrial revolutions lay in the future, and in any case, geography and communications would limit their impact to the marginal. What Pennant and his companions observed was a very old landscape.

Here is the entry made in the journal after landing on the island of Jura:

> Ride along the shore of the sound: take boat at the ferry, and go a mile more by water: see on the Jura side some sheelins or summer huts for goatherds, who keep here a flock of 80 for the sake of the milk and cheese. The last are made without salt, which they receive afterwards from the ashes of sea-tang, and the tang itself which the natives lap it in.
>
> Land on a bank covered with sheelins, the habitants of some peasants who attend the herds of milk cows. These formed a grotesque group; some were oblong, many conic, and so low that entrance is forbidden, without creeping through the little opening, which has no other door than a faggot [bunch] of

birch twigs, placed there occasionally; they are constructed of branches of trees, covered with sods; the furniture a bed of heath, placed on a bank of sod; two blankets and a rug; some dairy vessels, and above, certain pendant shelves made of basket work, to hold the cheese, the produce of the summer. In one of the little conic huts, I spied a little infant asleep, under the protection of a faithful dog.

Cross, on foot, a large plain of ground, seemingly improvable, but covered with a deep heath, and perfectly in a state of nature . . . .

. . . After a walk of four miles, reach the paps [mountains in the centre of Jura]: left the lesser to the south-east, preferring the ascent of the greatest, for there are three: Beinn-a-Chalaois, or 'the mountain of the sound'; Beinn Sheunta, or 'the hallowed mountain'; and Beinn-an-Oir, or 'the mountain of gold'.

After climbing the Paps of Jura and seeing the southern Hebrides 'extended like a map beneath us', Pennant crossed the Sound of Islay to land at Port Askaig. From there he went to:

Visit the mines, carried on under the directions of Mr Freebairn, since the year 1763: the ore of lead, much mixed with copper, which occasions expense and trouble in the separation: the veins rise to the surface, have been worked at intervals for ages, and probably in the time of the Norwegians, a nation of miners. The old adventurers worked by trenching, which is apparent everywhere: the trenches are not above six feet drop; and the veins which opened into them not above five or six inches thick; yet, by means of some instrument, unknown to us at present, they picked or scooped out the ore with good success, following it in that narrow space to the length of four feet.

The veins are of various thickness; the strings numerous, conducting to large bodies, but quickly exhausted. The lead ore is good: the copper yields 33 pounds per hundred; and 40 ounces of silver from a ton of metal . . . .

. . . Not far from these mines are vast strata of that species of iron called bog ore.

These brief extracts from Thomas Pennant's *Tour of Scotland in 1772* are instructive, especially when we attempt to grasp a sense of change in prehistory. As often, it seems that change was more additional than revolutionary. When new ideas entered a community, they did not necessarily drive out old ones, but rather sat alongside what people had always done, sometimes for centuries. In his walks around Jura and Islay, these historical overlaps are more or less what Pennant observed, John Stuart interpreted and Moses Griffiths drew.

The practice of transhumance on Jura in the 18th century was of course to be expected, but the maintenance of the ancient designs for the shielings themselves is remarkable. The conical structures drawn by Griffiths are in essence turf tipis, built by a method that was old when transhumance itself began. John Stuart would have translated the calendar for Pennant. At Beltane the flocks and herds were driven from what the Gaels called *the winter town* up to the higher summer pasture. The herd-laddies (and, as Pennant observed, children often went too) and their beasts spent almost six months at the shielings, what they knew as *the summer towns*. And on Jura they lived in tipis, just as their hunter-gatherer-fisher ancestors had done, altering the original design just enough to suit their changed circumstances. When hide became scarce – even on Jura, the Deer Island – they substituted turf as a covering to keep out the summer squalls off the Atlantic.

The 'large plain of ground' between the shielings and the Paps of Jura was covered in peat. In the 3rd and 2nd millennia BC the weather appears to have become wetter in the north and west of Scotland, increasingly what meteorologists call an Atlantic climate. Peat began to form all over the Hebrides and, as more vegetation grew and died into it, the cover thickened, darkened and blanketed the land. Sometimes modern peat-cutters come across the bare and wizened stumps of ancient trees which flourished before the rain brought the peat to cover them.

The energetic Pennant climbed Beinn an Oir, the highest of the Paps of Jura, but he mentioned its near neighbour, Beinn Shiantaidh. This translates as 'the Enchanted Mountain', or more precisely as 'the Mountain Defended by Enchantment'. No archaeological information exists to confirm or deny its use as such, but the name strongly suggests that the mountain was important in the beliefs of the prehistoric peoples who lived on Jura. As Pennant notes, it is one of three grouped close together, and triplicity was thought to be spiritually powerful in the ancient world. And high places seemed to attract those who felt it was important to be near their sky-gods. There are other magic mountains in Scotland but the group of three on Jura are very reminiscent of the Eildon Hills in the Borders. There are three of these standing close together, and one of them certainly had a huge ceremonial precinct at its summit at the end of the 2nd millennium BC.

Peat

Peat is 90 per cent water. It accumulates when organic matter such as grasses, sedges, rushes and moss pile up on each other faster than they can decompose. Because of the high water content, peat is heavy and as the lower levels of each succeeding autumn's fall of plants are pressed down harder, they partially carbonize, like coal. The texture of peat can vary tremendously depending on local conditions. Sometimes it resembles a dense brown clay and in other places it can be very fibrous. The business of digging and drying peat is very old. The toolkit needed to cut and lift the peats up to the top of the bank, stack, dry and move them is extensive and unique, as is the Gaelic needed to describe what is going on. Some Hebridean peatstacks are monumental at the beginning of the long winter, almost as large as the houses they are intended to heat. And peat-digging is one of the last truly communal agricultural activities left in Britain, a remnant of the sort of co-operation needed to survive in farming society of the 2nd millennium BC.

It is impossible to attach an accurate date to the mines visited by Thomas Pennant when he crossed to Islay. Confronted with something ancient, he usually concluded that it first came into use 'in the time of the Norwegians', or the period of the Norse settlement of the Hebrides in the centuries either side of AD 1000. The likelihood is that the mines were much older. When metalworking arrived in Scotland around 2000 BC, deposits of copper were actively sought so that it could be combined with Cornish tin to make bronze. This could in turn be fashioned into magically shiny, hard and sharp weapons and tools. Nearby, in the Kilmartin Valley in mid-Argyll, there existed a complex, wealthy and sophisticated society which consumed many items of bronze in different ways.

Thomas Pennant's tour through the remnants of Scotland's prehistoric past is more than usually informative. For one thing, in 1772 the past was still visible. And it was still working; the herd-laddies on Jura lived in shielings that would have been immediately recognizable to their ancient ancestors, although the latter would have been perplexed by the peat bog beyond them. But Pennant also saw the beginnings of change in that prehistoric past; on the top of the magic mountain beliefs were changing, and down in the open-cast mines of Islay technology was beginning to change the shape of everyday lives.

The period between approximately 2400 and 700 BC has been labelled the Bronze Age, and although most modern prehistorians use it only as a handy tag rather than as a description of any general reality, it can still be misleading. The expectation is of an age dominated by bronze, a characterization few contemporaries would have recognized. What Thomas Pennant saw in the ground on Islay were the seeds of change. The age after 2400 BC was dominated by eternal preoccupations: how to survive, feed a family, understand the world, how to use beliefs in the gods to ease the bitterness and inevitability of death. And at first the coming of metal mattered little to ordinary people.

As a prelude to the piecemeal introduction of metalworking, prehistoric society in Britain appears to have suffered a recession. Around

2500 BC monumental tomb building declined, chambered tombs were sometimes closed up and blocked, and some settlements were abandoned. More generally, and perhaps more pointedly, there seems to have been a retreat in cultivation. Cleared areas which show the criss-cross marks of the *ard*, the early wooden plough, reverted to woodland. Over extensive tracts of Britain the trees reclaimed the land.

Beliefs were transforming the way in which people understood life and death. In particular, burial practice moved away from the communal to an emphasis on the individual. Chambered tombs, like the one at Isbister, were closed and cist graves began to appear. These were usually rectangular, stone-lined compartments into which a body was fitted and on top of which a capstone or covering of some sort was placed. Many bodies were laid on their sides in the cists with their legs tucked up in a crouching, foetal position. Perhaps they were leaving the world as they had entered it, or perhaps this posture was intended to resemble the eternal sleep of the dead.

Analyses of the soil on the floor of cist burials often show that the grave had been strewn with flowers, some of them identified as meadow-sweet. Its blooms are butter-coloured, and pretty enough, but their chief attraction is their scent. In the Middle Ages meadowsweet was often thrown down amongst the rushes on the floors of halls and houses to refresh the air. The flowers found in cist burials mark the beginning of a long tradition of wreaths and floral tributes at funerals.

Brass and bronze

All alloys of copper used to be known simply as brass, whether they were of zinc or tin. How the latter became known as bronze is interesting, if convoluted. *Aes* is the Latin word for brass and it too was used to encompass both sorts of alloy. The Italian word *bronzo*, from which 'bronze' is derived, came from *aes Brundisium* or 'Brindisi brass', a copper and tin alloy. *Aes Campanium* was a well-known Roman brass used for making bells; it gave the Italian language *campana* for 'bell' and English the more esoteric *campanology* for 'bell-ringing'. But in Britain such niceties remained unknown. Brass was brass and that was that. In the 19th century the British taste for the Italian Renaissance introduced 'bronze' into use, but only when applied to cast sculpture. In the Danish language there was no such distinction, and when Christian Jurgensen Thomsen set out his three-age classification of prehistory he called each 'the Stone Age', 'the Bronze Age' and 'the Iron Age'. This was in 1836, fully 50 years before 'bronze' made it into the Oxford English Dictionary. If a British historian had pre-empted Thomsen, we should probably have been talking of 'the Brass Age'.

The mourners also brought along other things, and at the end of the 3rd millennium BC two of these were new. In many cists pots of a fineness not seen in Britain up to that date were arranged next to the body. Archaeologists have called them *beakers*. Reddish-coloured, decorated with twisted cord pressed into the clay before the firing, shaped initially like inverted bells (and sometimes called *bell-beakers*), these vessels appeared all over Britain at roughly the same time, towards the end of the 3rd millennium BC. It used to be thought that they heralded the arrival of a new culture, a wave of innovative immigrants known as the Beaker People. This interpretation is now largely discredited, but it is nevertheless true that the new pots had a direct stylistic link with earlier European beakers.

But while the appearance of this new pottery is undoubtedly an important development in itself, it is too often forgotten that the beakers were only a slightly different sort of container. In themselves they were not particularly valuable or time-consuming to produce. What they contained was at least as important as the container itself. And since it must have been organic matter, this has mostly disappeared. But crusts of residue have been found on the inside of some beakers and analysis has detected grains of pollen from meadowsweet, along with traces of a honey-based drink. The literal derivation of the name 'meadowsweet' has nothing to do with meadows; it comes from the Anglo-Saxon form of early English. *Mede-sweet* was the original name and it means 'mead-sweetener'. It looks as though at least some burials made a three-way connection with the presence of a sweet alcoholic drink made from fermented honey and water, flavoured and scented by meadowsweet, and poured into a fine drinking vessel. But what was the context of that connection? The remaining items of grave goods characteristic of cist burials might unpack a little more of the mystery.

Squatter, more rounded bowls known simply as food vessels are often found alongside beakers, and the impression of a symbolic, ritual or actual meal on the occasion of a burial is an obvious one. Less clear is the frequent presence of archery equipment. In a cist uncovered at Culduthel, in Inverness, excavators found eight tanged and barbed flint arrowheads and an archer's wristguard made of bone and studded with gold rivets. If the wristguard was made locally this was a very early example of metalworking in Scotland, dating to around 2000 BC. Other Scottish cists contained metal dirks or daggers, decorated armlets and jet buttons (usually imported from Whitby on the Yorkshire coast). Jet was attractive because it polished up to a dark lustre and was electrostatic.

In 2002 the richest beaker burial ever found in Britain was excavated in Wiltshire, near Stonehenge. Dating to 2300 BC, it contained the body of a man who became known as the Amesbury Archer, or, more excitably, the King of Stonehenge. Prior to this, the maximum number of beakers ever found in a cist was two. The Archer had five pots arranged around his crouched body. There were three copper knives, two full sets of archery kit, fifteen flint arrowheads, two gold hair clasps – in all a hundred artefacts. Before this no beaker grave found had more than ten. The most intriguing find was, however, not made of gold or bronze, but was a square piece of greenish stone. It was recognized as a *cushion-stone*, an early version of a last used by metalworkers when fashioning gold, copper or bronze objects. The Archer, it seemed, had a trade and one which awarded him the highest possible status. He was a metalworker, and because of his magical skills, the recipient of the richest Bronze Age funeral yet found in Britain.

Archaeologists were able to make another enormously important discovery. An analysis of the chemical composition of the Archer's teeth showed that he was an immigrant to Britain, a man who probably originated from central Europe, near the northern ranges of the Alps in what is now Switzerland. This discovery has reignited the question of how new technology transmitted itself in prehistoric times. In the case of the Amesbury Archer – admittedly a single case but perhaps others wait to be found – he simply brought it with him, in his skilled hands, in his mind and in the tools in his pack. And he was rewarded in life with a glittering array of precious objects, and unquestionably venerated in death as a great man who deserved a splendid funeral.

In the south midlands of England, near Northampton, another rich burial was found and its circumstances offer some sense of what took place at the funeral. Under a barrow near the village of Irthlingborough a man had been buried with a beaker, some archery kit, a jet button from Whitby, a flint dagger from East Anglia and a chalk object from Wessex. Nothing like as rich as the grave of the Amesbury Archer, it had nevertheless drawn objects, perhaps very deliberately, from a wide area. But even more remarkable was the discovery of the skeletal remains of 184 young bullocks which had been brought to the site of the barrow and slaughtered. These look very much like the funerary gifts of a huge number of mourners from a wide area, maybe an area as wide as that encompassed by the objects in the grave. And it appears that a huge feast was had at a prehistoric wake. Stock-rearing societies measure wealth directly in head of cattle, goats or sheep and the killing of so many was a form of conspicuous consumption only possible for the richest. Excavations further revealed that the body of the deceased had been placed in a small timber structure which may have served as a shrine or a viewing platform for use by mourners. There must have been many hundreds present.

In considering these burials it is important to bear in mind the role of the mourners. Even though tradition and the status of the deceased would have pre-determined much that took place, it was the mourners who put the goods in the grave and created whatever ceremony took place around it. It should also be remembered that the individuals found in beaker burials represented a tiny proportion of the population. They were, all of them, people of high status. The archery equipment may be a reference to hunting or warfare, but in both these cases it was probably symbolic, just as modern honours such as peerages or knighthoods have a symbolic attachment to the monarchy (and horses), but in reality signify no more than that the individual is pre-eminent. The Amesbury 'Archer' was almost certainly no such thing.

Real archers

Ötzi, the ice-man found in an Alpine glacier in 1991 (on a transhumance track leading from winter to summer pasture), was a real archer and not a symbolic one. Dated around 3300 BC, his body, clothes and possessions were well preserved by the ice and with him he carried some archery equipment. Scientists have discovered samples of human blood on his buckskin tunic. They came from six different people and it appears that Ötzi died because he was on the run, caught in a snowstorm, fleeing from a bloody battle. Few prehistoric bows have survived, but one, made out of yew, was discovered in the Borders at a boggy site known as Rotten Bottom. Beautifully made and carbon-dated to 4000 BC, it resembled the sort of longbow used at Crécy and Agincourt by the English archers of the Hundred Years' War, and it would have needed a strong man to pull back the bowstring to its full poundage.

Taking all the evidence together, it looks as though the occasion of such funerals might have been familiar to us in the 21st century. Around the graveside it seems as though the mourners held a ceremony something like a wake. Bringing their own beakers with them, they shared a drink of mead, or another sort of alcohol, with the dead. They ate with them (sometimes mightily as at Irthlingborough) and probably sang, danced and wept. Just as it does now, a big funeral meant a great deal in prehistoric Britain. It was a mark of many things: popularity, respect, regret and status. The bigger the funeral, the greater the man or woman.

At first the impact of beaker culture in Scotland was minimal, burials of the new type being concentrated mainly in the south and east. Despite its vigour in the 4th millennium BC, Orkney has revealed little significant archaeology from this period and the finds thin out in the north and west. And as if to underline how different they were from what had gone before, the new cists were eventually placed well away from the older, more traditional centres of worship. It looks as though small numbers of new people with diverging beliefs had arrived in Scotland, and indeed, after the sensational discovery of the origins of the Amesbury Archer, it is tempting to believe that a limited amount of very influential immigration did take place. However, the assertion that the skulls retrieved from beaker burials indicate a slightly different racial origin has been discredited; it seems that native heads evolved to be more rounded without outside influence and people in general grew taller and became more robust.

However that may be, within a few generations the beaker burials had moved centre-stage. When the old chambered tombs were closed up, sherds of beaker pottery were included in the fill material used. This was no careless accident but a deliberate piece of religious observation – pottery was still as symbolically important as it was in the early days at Cairnpapple Hill. And as the recumbent stone circles of Aberdeenshire and the north-east came to the end of their functioning lives, more beaker pottery was placed inside them. Sherds have been found at Loanhead of Daviot, Old Keig and Berrybrae.

Metalworking came to Scotland at around the same time as the beaker burials and it may be that the same people practised both. But metal entered very slowly into Scottish prehistoric culture. After bronze-making techniques were first used in the south of England, it took seven centuries for them to reach Scotland. There may have been a closed shop in operation, a reluctance among bronze-smiths to pass on knowledge or let it go outside a family group. Next to the grave of the Amesbury Archer lay another rich burial. The young man in it had a pair of gold hair clasps identical to those found in the adjacent grave.

And tests on bone samples show that the young man was closely related to the Archer, although he had been born in Britain. He may have been his son, and was almost certainly another metalworker, the inheritor of magical skills, the mysterious ability to convert dull ore into a shining liquid and then into a lustrous, hard metal object.

Other, more technical reasons inhibited the spread of metalworking. In addition to the metallurgical skills required to mix tin and copper in the correct quantities (these varied, but one part tin to eight parts copper seems to have been the standard) there was the matter of creating a workable forge (with adequate supplies of charcoal and a set of bellows) which could heat the ingredients for the alloy to the very high temperatures needed (1080°C). Mould-making was a craft in itself and a knowledge of potting clays was indispensable. And then there was the business of locating the raw materials, deposits of the metal ores themselves.

In Britain and Ireland tin existed only in Cornwall, but copper was to be found in small quantities in several places, some in Scotland. As observed by Thomas Pennant on Islay, mining began as open-cast and copper was easily recognized in the blue-green veins of malachite or copper carbonate. Bone tools such as antler picks were used to extract it, and at the huge mine at Great Orme, on the North Wales coast, they left white marks on the rock which can still be clearly made out. The process of extraction began with fire. Miners set brushwood fires against promising sites so that the heat would crack and loosen the rock-face. Then it was levered off with antler picks and other implements.

Once the surface veins had been exhausted, miners were forced to tunnel. At Great Orme there may be 50 km/34 miles of galleries worming through the cliffs, and some of them are so small that they can only have been worked by children of five or six. In certain places the miners left caches of a few unused hand-hammers as religious offerings, probably to the gods of the earth: they would have believed that copper grew, like a plant, and that it was important to leave offerings to feed it.

Once the malachite had been hacked out, it was pounded by some of these heavy hand-hammers, some made of granite and weighing more than

14 kg/30 lb. The powdered ore was then smelted and separated from the impurities. This was big business. Mining at Great Orme began in 1860 BC and continued until 500 BC. In that time approximately 2,000 tonnes of copper was won, enough to make 10 million bronze axes. Such was the scale of mining in Britain and Ireland that the supply of bronze artefacts far outran domestic demand, and there must have been an export trade.

One of the side-effects of the increase and spread of metalworking was the creation of long-range, regular trade routes, almost certainly operated predominantly by sea. The Cornish monopoly of tin could hardly have been more inconveniently located for the rest of inland Britain, but the mines did lie close to the sea (as did the mine at Great Orme), the fastest and most reliable medium of travel until the 20th century. The famous seamark of St Michael's Mount on the Channel coast was a traditional port for the tin trade. Boats were beached on the causeway between the Mount and Marazion on the mainland, loaded with tin ingots and refloated by the incoming tide.

Trade routes have always carried more than goods. Ideas travelled in the copper and tin ships and landed all round the coasts of Britain. If some of the bringers of the beaker and bronze culture were originally immigrants, their influence (if not their secret skills) was probably disseminated by sea. Language, and especially the language of innovation, went with that influence and one of the many intriguing questions about the Amesbury Archer is how he made himself understood in Wiltshire. Having come from central Europe, what language did he speak and was it sufficiently similar to the dialects of southern England for there to be little or no need for translation? Was there a close enough relationship amongst the Indo-European family of languages for the Archer to adjust quickly to the speech of his new community, or did he have to learn something completely new to him?

Bronze seems not to have been very important in the Early Bronze Age in Scotland, certainly not to the ordinary people who worked the land. Scarcity no doubt played a part, but initially more weapons than tools emerged from the forges of the smiths. And weapons were the preserve of the leaders of society. Stone axes fell out of the archaeological record fairly quickly, but stone-tipped ploughs and stone querns continued in everyday use for many centuries after the arrival of metalworking. Bronze axes were probably amongst the first widely used tools and because of the fineness and sharpness of the edge they made precise timber working much easier. And with the magical craft of the smith, the more lowly skills of the carpenter began to become important.

Demand for all of these skills, new and not so new, grew apace. The Bronze Age saw a rise in Scotland's population. At such a distance in time, precise calculation is impossible, but educated guesses put it at just below medieval levels. Perhaps 300,000 people lived north of the Tweed in the centuries following 2000 BC, in Britain as a whole maybe two to three million. These figures suggest a high density of settlement, and there is strong evidence of farmers being forced to seek virgin land at higher altitudes. Around 2000 BC the warmer weather permitted cultivation as high as 300 m/950 ft above sea level in some areas of Perthshire and Sutherland, and the total acreage under cultivation in Scotland increased markedly in the 2nd millennium BC. The pressure on low-lying traditional farmland must have been intense and it gave rise to the creation of hill-farms, what are known as platform settlements.

Rushlit

Juncus effusus, or soft rush, grows in watery places all over Britain. Inside its fine green pipes there is a soft and fleshy pith which can be extracted to make rushlights. These are very ancient and very efficient. The pith stalk is dipped into fat (mixed with a little beeswax for a good consistency) until saturated, and can be used immediately. Unlike candles, rushlights need no holder and do not drip scalding wax. They burn with a clear and near-smokeless flame and are bright enough to light most of an average-size room. Prehistoric households will have used rushlights a great deal, especially in seaside locations with access to seal and whale blubber. During the Second World War and its shortages, rushlights were often seen again in the night windows of country places.

The oldest so far discovered is at Lintshie Gutter in Upper Clydesdale. Dated to the centuries around 2000 BC, the settlement stands on a series of shelves of levelled ground dug out of the north face of the hillside on either side of a small burn in the Southern Uplands, near the source of the River Clyde. There are 31 platforms and on each stood a roundhouse. Some were large, at 8–9 m/26–29 ft in diameter. A conical thatched roof was supported by a ring of posts driven into the ground and the walls formed out of wattle and daub, a mesh of small branches and twigs plastered with mud. The people of Lintshie Gutter were stockmen who husbanded cattle and sheep and grew some cereal crops. Their ground was much less suitable for cultivation than the river valleys, but its height above sea level would certainly have allowed a growing season long enough for crops to ripen. Over on the eastern side of the Clyde–Tweed watershed the later platform settlement at Green Knowe contained a number of small inbye fields enclosed by stout stone dykes to keep out grazing animals. The earliest ox-yoke discovered in Scotland dates to between 2000 and 1500 BC, and is obvious evidence that animal traction was used to pull a plough through the ground.

The overall impression from many fragments of evidence, and, of course, the unrepresentative accidents of survival (upland settlements like Lintshie Gutter are detectable and legible because their sites were not ploughed again after the prehistoric period, while many lowland sites have been completely obliterated), is one of an expanding and prosperous community of Bronze Age farmers who were cultivating every possible piece of decent ground. The land became patterned with the homely geometry of small fields, wide pasture and clusters of huts, a panorama that endured for almost 4,000 years and changed little before the agricultural revolution of the 18th century.

But it would be wrong to believe that the habits of the hunter-gatherer-fishers had been consigned to ancient history. One of the most interesting, and common, survivals from this period is known as the 'burnt mound'. Hundreds have been found all over Scotland. Usually their presence is signalled by a grassed-over pile of burnt or cracked stones, and occasionally the remains of a pit. Both are often located near a stream or other source of water. They were field kitchens. In an age before the bronze cauldron became widely available or affordable, the early farmers would build a watertight, stone-lined pit (using clay to seal the edges), and heat up stones in a nearby fire. Having butchered and jointed the meat that they wished to cook – either hunted game or a domesticated animal – they wrapped it in straw or hide to keep it clean. Water was brought from the stream to fill up the pit. The heated stones were picked up with tongs of green wood and placed in it until the water boiled. Then the joint of meat was put in and the temperature of the water maintained by adding more hot stones. It was an efficient, if messy, way of cooking large pieces of meat, and the fact that some of these burnt mounds were found at a distance from any settlement indicates that they were used by hunting parties. Several historians have suggested that they were not in fact kitchens at all but primitive saunas. A hide tent was placed over the pit to create a hot, steamy, sweaty compartment. Native Americans did something very similar with their sweat-lodges, and there is little doubt that prehistoric peoples cared about their appearance. It may be that burnt mounds were put to both uses.

Bottom up

Grass is an enormously successful plant. It has colonized huge tracts of Britain, survives at high altitudes, and thrives on its own destruction. Prehistoric shepherds will have noticed that when both wild and domesticated animals crop it, grass grows even better. There is a unique reason for this. Unlike other plants, which grow from shoots sent out from the top or sides, grass grows from the bottom upwards. And instead of destroying the plant, browsing cows or sheep encourage its growth. Once sheep have grazed a meadow (and are removed before they begin to tear up the roots), the grass thickens into what farmers call a 'mattress'. Prehistoric herds ate meadow-grass, a mixture of all sorts of plants, flowers and herbs. The latter contain strong doses of health-preserving minerals and vitamins. And animals seem instinctively to know what sort of fodder they need to sustain themselves. For example, older members of flocks and herds have been observed eating willow scrub while younger animals ignore it. Willow contains acetylsalicylic acid, the main ingredient of aspirin, and has long been used to suppress the symptoms of arthritis. Most modern pasture is regularly ploughed and resown with new strains of grass developed in the 18th century. This is mainly quick-growing, thick-bladed and good for cropping as winter fodder, but it contains fewer herbs and appears to produce less hardy animals.

Gold also enhanced appearances 4,000 years ago: it always has. And in Scotland the wealthy members of Bronze Age society owned gold objects of great beauty. At Southside, near Peebles and not far from the platform settlement at Green Knowe, two exquisite crescent-shaped collars were found. Known as *lunulae* ('little moons'), they appear early in the Bronze Age archaeological record. The design originated in Ireland, where more than 80 examples have been recognized. Their decoration was applied by hammer and punch and it was particularly rich near the terminal horns of the crescents. *Lunulae* are worn like torcs, without catches of any sort, and put on by gently pulling the horns apart and slipping the collar around the neck. Druids of the 18th and 19th centuries latched on to *lunulae* when they were compiling a suitably ancient wardrobe, but they failed to understand how to wear them. Several illustrations show them as fetching items of headgear, presumably with the terminals gripping the base of the skull somewhere behind the ears.

Them thar hills

Gold is rare. Scientists reckon that its incidence on the earth's surface is no more than 2.5 parts per billion. At 80 parts per billion, silver is comparatively plentiful. The early peoples found gold in nuggets. Most metals react chemically with air and water, but gold is stable and resist-ant to breakdown, what is known as a noble metal. In fact the action of water on seams of gold releases nuggets into rivers and streams. These are called *placer deposits* and are what gave rise to the gold rushes of California and Alaska. The other sort of deposit is a lode and nowhere is there a more productive lode than at Witwatersrand in South Africa. A staggering 40 per cent of all the world's gold has been mined there. In Scotland gold was found in Upper Clydesdale, Sutherland and Perthshire. At Leadhills and Wanlockhead in the Southern Uplands the most famous prospector was Bevis Bulmer. Some of the nuggets he found in 1578 weighed 113–170 gm/4–6 oz. But the largest on record was, allegedly, dug out of Crawford Moor in 1501 and weighed almost a kilogram (2lb 3oz). Gold is still being panned by enthusiasts in the streams around Leadhills and Wanlockhead and a nugget weighing 18 gm/½ oz was found in 2015. Experiments with a wicker frame and a sheepskin in Ireland have suggested how the early prospectors went about their business. Held fast by the frame, the sheepskin is inserted into the gold-bearing stream at a point where the current flows quickly. Gravel is then shovelled on to it, the current pushes it through the sheepskin sieve, and, in theory anyway, the heavy nuggets and grains of gold are trapped. In Greek mythology attractive echoes of this method of prospecting are preserved in the tale of Jason and the Argonauts who sailed to the Black Sea city of Colchis to find a golden fleece hanging from a tree.

Because it can sometimes be found in the form of relatively pure nuggets, often picked up amongst the gravel of a stream or river, gold may have been the first metal to be worked. Bright and eye-catching amongst the grey stones of a river bed, nuggets themselves were probably prized as decorative, rare and therefore valuable items, or simply as attractive possessions, before being altered in any way. In this natural form gold does not require smelting and, once they noticed how relatively soft it was, curious people would have begun to shape and mark it. When heat is applied, however gently, gold becomes readily malleable. Copper and tin both require smelting but are similarly shiny and attractive metals whose early use may also have been decorative.

As yet, no gold objects have been found in the Kilmartin Valley (see plate 1) in mid-Argyll, but it was a rich and busy Bronze Age society nonetheless, and a microcosm of Scotland's prehistory. The valley is on an approximately north–south axis, with the Kilmartin Burn running through it, and it lies between the sea at Loch Crinan and the southern tip of one of Scotland's largest and longest lochs, Loch Awe. Near at hand are the islands of Jura and Islay, and Oronsay with its strange hunter-gatherer-fisher middens. At Oban, a little to the north, a string of caves in the cliff-face above the town has yielded some of the earliest bone and antler tools yet found in Scotland. Barbed harpoon points, pins, awls and bevelled tools witness a busy coastal hunting and fishing ground.

At Kilmartin itself some of the first signs of human activity in the period when farming was adopted are very striking. Around 3000 BC a chambered cairn was constructed at Nether Largie, a henge dug and laid out at Ballymeanoch and, slightly earlier, a stone circle at Temple Wood was in use. These three monuments laid the foundations of what would become one of the most extensive and impressive ceremonial complexes in Britain. Alignments of standing stones were raised in the valley around 2500 BC and three centuries later the first beaker burials took place. There exists also the remains of a major cursus monument and a huge timber circle at one end of the valley. A cist was made next to the tomb at Nether Largie and several others dug elsewhere in the valley. By 1500 BC what archaeologists call the Linear Cemetery had been created.

It was huge, running the whole length of the Kilmartin Valley, perhaps 5 km/3 miles from the remains at Upper Largie to the cists at Rowanfield and Crinan Moss, and the deposit of an extraordinary continuity of sanctity. Reusing and reshaping many earlier monuments, a linear arrangement of at least seven cairns was laid out on the floor of the valley. It is highly likely that the area had been cleared of trees, allowing celebrants to see the whole landscape, its rows of standing stones, its carved rocks, the cairns and the cists and their markers which dotted the sacred valley. Geography has made Kilmartin like a two-sided traverse theatre. People standing on the hillsides to the east and west could see the entire linear cemetery and all the ceremony taking place in it. It is very likely that access into the valley was controlled and formal, perhaps by avenues cut through the woodland covering the hillsides. These ushered down processions of worshippers in some highly ordered, but perhaps not solemn, fashion. The seven or more cairns had been made by piling up stones (occasionally to a height of 5 m/16 ft) over earlier henges, stone circles and tombs, and by 1500 BC all had been made circular.

Under the cairns and in other parts of the cemetery archaeologists have found objects which suggest something of the texture of spiritual life at Kilmartin, at least for the élite who probably officiated. A halberd was most probably carried as an item of regalia by a powerful person, a chief, a priest, or maybe a priest-king. A broad, dagger-like blade inserted into a haft and riveted, it resembled a one-sided pickaxe. Jet buttons and necklaces were retrieved from cists, along with fine beaker pottery and sturdy food vessels. But what most impresses the visitor to Kilmartin is not the collection of – often beautiful – archaeological finds. It is the sheer scale of what went on in this ancient valley of death: not only the immense labour of setting up the stone circles, standing stones and cairns, but the size of the whole monument. It was made on a sufficient scale for thousands of people to worship together, to process, pray, sing, dance and make music at Kilmartin on the days and nights when the priest-kings summoned them to the ceremonies. No doubt the ancient drama of moonlit darkness was used to impart mystery, involve the unseen world of the spirits outside the circles of firelight, see the power of the sky-gods send clouds scudding across the face of the full moon. Torch-lit processions snaked between the cairns and the tall stones, perhaps committing more bodies for burial, certainly venerating those ancestors whose remains lay in the great linear cemetery.

Within 10 km/6 miles of the valley there are more than 100 sites of what has become known as prehistoric rock art. These are mostly patterns of *cup-and-ring* markings cut into exposed outcrops of living rock (see plate x), and they are mysterious. Their motifs are echoed in carvings on the standing stones on the valley floor, and judging from such a density around Kilmartin they must be related to the religious ceremonies that went on there.

The designs appear to be abstract, but they may have had a practical function. Some are cut deep into the rock and are capable of holding liquid or perhaps being filled with colour, or even flowers. In Ireland cup-and-ring markings were still being pecked into rocky outcrops in the 10th century AD, and by that time they were used for receiving libations of milk poured out in a remnant of pagan belief. Aboriginal Australians still carve them and many are to be seen on Uluru (Ayers Rock), one of the most sacred places on the continent.

It may be that, on their journey to Kilmartin, worshippers went via the rocky outcrops showing cup-and-ring marks so that, as they passed, they might offer some milk or mead to the earth gods, or simply touch or kiss the marks. When Christian pilgrims nowadays travel to very holy shrines such as Santiago or Jerusalem, they perform small acts of purification on their journey. They understand that they are moving between two states, two worlds, between the secular and unrepentant and the sacred and penitent, and on the way they wish to improve their spiritual condition. Perhaps the Kilmartin cup-and-ring marks were used in the same way as wayside shrines mark pilgrim routes today, and they acted as places in the landscape which showed the sacred way to another world.

Swords

At first the new metalworking imitated stone and flint models, just as early stone buildings resembled wooden structures. But perhaps the most revolutionary weapon turned out by the smiths was a sword. Nothing like it could have been made in wood, bone or stone. A long, hard, sharp cutting edge must have made the first swords fearsome weapons in skilled hands. And when used on horseback, slashing down at someone fighting on foot, the sword would have ensured an unequal struggle.

Over the rest of Scotland, rock art is often found at higher altitudes, at viewpoints overlooking valleys with good farming land, and where henges and ceremonial complexes were once built. Often what existed on the prehistoric valley floor will have been obliterated by modern agriculture or building work, and the cup-and-ring marks may be all that is left to remember a sacred place lost to history.

On the Hebridean island of South Uist a place-name remembers a remarkable sacred area. The first element of *Cladh Hallan* means a 'burying place', and when archaeologists began to dig there they came upon evidence of cremation and interment, as well as a village of seven conical-roofed roundhouses dating to around 1300 BC. Particularly intriguing was the undoubted fact that the village had been consciously built right on top of a cemetery, the *Cladh*. The way in which the houses were constructed shows that the builders were aware of the prior presence of human remains. In at least one roundhouse the hearth, the heart of the home, was deliberately and carefully placed directly over a cremation burial. Several mummified corpses were found on the site (see pages 78–80), and these added greatly to the mystery swirling around the Cladh.

It seemed to the excavators that the village continued to be used as a cemetery and that the living wished to pass their daily lives in the close company of the dead. Not only do the remarkable Cladh Hallan mummies show this preference very clearly, each of the houses contained recent burials as well. These were often placed in the north-east corner, for reasons now lost. Inside one roundhouse the remains of a woman were discovered, and it appeared that she had been buried holding two of her teeth. At the base of a post-hole the corpse of a baby had been carefully placed on its belly with arms outstretched and its head positioned so that it faced the doorway.

This village of the dead holds dozens of puzzles which will probably remain insoluble to a modern mind, but must have made perfect sense in the context of an entirely forgotten belief system. All that can be said with certainty is that Bronze Age society was very different from ours in the way that it treated the dead, the ancestors. The living wanted to stay close to those who had passed on, and perhaps that hackneyed phrase conveys something of the reason why. Bronze Age people probably did not think of their dead as extinct in the way that a secular society does now. Maybe they lived on in more than memory, passing on to and continuing in a parallel world which needed the constant presence and attention of the living to sustain it. Lost rituals took place which showed how much the dead needed the living, needed to stay in the family, even to be placed inside the houses of villages like Cladh Hallan. And since they understood their own ultimate fate all too well, the living were more than willing to carry on these ancient traditions. Perhaps their own safe transition through the gates of the Otherworld depended on the observation of such pieties.

Burials very often supply the only tangible sense of the lives of pre-historic communities, but they can be unreliable guides. Those graves which have survived undisturbed may well be atypical and are almost certainly unrepresentative of ancient society as a whole, since they tend to contain only members of an élite group. However, they are often all there is to go on and some generalities are possible.

When mourners came to place grave-goods at an interment, gender distinctions were definitely made. Beside the corpses of men lay arrowheads, daggers or dirks, archery equipment, belt fittings, amber buttons, flint or stone axes and tools used to strike sparks to make a fire. This assortment speaks clearly of hunting (real or symbolic) and perhaps warfare, and also of the role of men as providers who ventured away from the home. Burials of women have shale and jet beads, awls, antler picks and hoes. And these are the accoutrements of hard agricultural work, with a touch of prettification thrown in. Again, in the case of aristocratic women, the former may have been little more than symbolism. Flint blades, earrings and pebble hammers have been found in both sorts of graves.

The impression gathered from this brief analysis is a familiar one and it shows a division of labour which lasted for millennia – down to the present day, some would argue. Certainly in an institutional sense it persisted up to the agricultural and industrial revolutions and, in some parts of Scotland, to the early 20th century. Society has forgotten how many women laboured in the fields with hoes, hooks and sickles until comparatively recently in Britain. Men were always able to reserve agricultural work of higher status to themselves, and until farming became mechanized they worked almost exclusively with horses at ploughing and carting while their women toiled in gangs in the fields and the stackyard, bending their backs at weeding, harvesting, muck-spreading and shawing.

Where prehistoric graves have multiple burials over a period of time it seems that, when adult males are buried first, other adults and children can follow them into the same piece of ground. But where an adult female is buried first, it is very unusual to find an adult male interred after her. A clear sense of precedence is detectable, and, along with the evidence gleaned from grave goods, this suggests that Bronze Age society was male-dominated and that lineage was traced through the male line only.

Finds of spindle whorls (for twisting and winding yarn) and loom-weights in the south of England reveal the introduction of the craft of weaving to Britain in the 2nd millennium BC. As the new techniques spread, it may be that the gender distinctions in textile production were first established. A distaff is a stick for holding hanks of wool before it is spun, and on the distaff side spinsters traditionally made the yarn while the men wove it into cloth. In South Uist and Harris, weaving is still mainly an all-male occupation.

Some time in the 12th century BC something dramatic happened. Over several sites in north and west Scotland an abrupt break in cultivation took place. On the upland farm at Tulloch Wood, near Forres, the production of cereals was abandoned and did not resume for more than a thousand years. Similar breakdowns occurred in Sutherland and elsewhere in the north. Overall the cultivation of fields and the growth of crops declined and many farmers moved much more into stock-rearing as a way of supporting life. Upland areas were always likely to be marginal and precarious, but it may very well be that these shifts and decisions were prompted by a spectacular event.

In 1159 BC the Icelandic volcano known as Hekla blew itself apart, throwing an enormous tonnage of dust into the atmosphere. The huge eruption appears to have changed the weather radically and immediately. And, if the volcanic dust screened the sun for several summers in a row, then temperatures would have dropped and the cultivation of crops, particularly at higher altitudes, would have become impossible. Hekla's deadly dust has been found on archaeological sites across the north and west, and evidence as far south as Ireland shows a series of very poor growing seasons. The rings of ancient Irish oak trees which grew after 1159 BC are extremely narrow.

It is difficult to tell how long the after-effects of Hekla persisted, but the eruption may have set in train a downward spiral in Bronze Age society. Some historians believe that the failure of agriculture led to widespread famine and a dramatic drop in population. It may even have halved. And the archaeology of the period has discovered a sharp decline in the production of tools, axes in particular. Weapons were preferred: dirks, spearheads, longswords. It is difficult to avoid the impression of dark times descending over Scotland after 1159 BC, the sufferings of a fearful society, and the rise of fearsomely armed warlords.

6

The Iron Warlords

In the spring of AD 43 an invasion army was massing. Four legions, more than 40,000 battle-hard Roman soldiers, had marched to the port at Boulogne where they were to embark on a transport fleet to carry them across what they called 'the Ocean' to Britannia and on to glory. The eagles of the IInd Augusta, the XIVth Gemina and the XXth Valeria had come from Mainz, Strasbourg and Neuss on the Rhine frontier while the IXth Hispana was led from Pannonia, modern Hungary, by the general commanding the whole army, Aulus Plautius. It was a huge force, no doubt an awesome sight for those who watched the columns tramp across the plains of northern France.

But when the legionaries arrived at the coast they immediately mutinied and refused to board the transports. The Ocean was the limit of the civilized world and beyond it lay the monstrous unknown. It was tempting the gods too far to dare to cross this bleak and cold boundary and no good would come of it, only certain disaster. In any case the Ocean, and in particular the treacherous channel which they were commanded to sail across, was not like the sunlit Mediterranean. High tides and strong-running currents could sweep ships out into the turbulent vastness of the grey unknown, or drive them to the bottom and a watery grave. The army of the great Julius Caesar had almost come to grief when he tempted the gods too far, and Britannia had not been conquered. Nor should it be. It did not belong in the Roman world.

Nothing that Aulus Plautius or any of his officers could say would move the legions off the beaches and into the transport ships. Four years earlier the Emperor Caligula had planned an expedition to bring

Britannia into the Empire, but his invasion force had also mutinied and their refusals had resulted in a humiliating withdrawal. Thereupon, as a symbolic gesture of doubtful power, each soldier had been ordered to fill his helmet with shells from the beach at Boulogne. Perhaps Caligula saw these as trophies. Perhaps he felt that his army had conquered up to the edge of the known world and that a few seashells would somehow represent that hollow achievement.

His uncle Claudius, dragged from behind a curtain by the Praetorian Guard and shoved on to the throne after Caligula's assassination, had decided that he too would risk an expedition across the Ocean. After a difficult two years and the suppression of a serious rebellion in 42, the reluctant emperor badly needed to demonstrate the cardinal imperial virtue, a successful episode of well-publicized military glory. Despite its inhospitable remoteness, Britannia would do, and a carefully stage-managed campaign was planned. If Claudius could achieve something the great Julius Caesar could not do, his power would be confirmed.

The campaign stalled at the first obstacle. Just as happened to Caligula, the superstitious legionaries refused to budge and ignominy loomed out of the sea-mist. Then the eccentric Claudius surprised everyone by despatching one of his ministers, Narcissus, to exhort the troops to support their emperor. As a freed slave, the imperial emissary cut an incongruous figure and many of the mutinous soldiers found the sight of a man from the lowest order of Roman society consorting with aristocratic generals ludicrous. When Narcissus addressed them, they cried *Io Saturnalia!*, by which they meant the annual winter festival when masters and slaves exchanged places. But the daft spectacle appeared to take the heat out of the mutiny, and after Narcissus' exhortations had been heard the legions began at once to embark on the transports.

Aulus Plautius had planned his campaign with care, and the army was divided into three battle groups. A beach-head was quickly established, believed to be at Richborough on the Kentish coast (although it must be pointed out that some scholars now favour a Solent landing, with a later supply base set up at Richborough). After a victory over the British army on the River Medway the Romans marched on to the Thames. While Aulus Plautius consolidated his gains, Claudius hurried north from Rome. Politics demanded good presentation and when triumph was at hand the emperor had to be seen to be leading Rome's conquering armies towards it. They even brought an elephant for Claudius to sit on. Perhaps he did.

Once negotiations had been completed, the army crossed the Thames and advanced on Colchester, the tribal capital of the Trinovantes. There the emperor accepted the submission of 11 British kings, and it happened that one of them had travelled a long way. He was no less than the king of Orkney. Suddenly coming sharply into focus through the mists of millennia, the successor of the man who had commanded the building of the Ring of Brodgar, the Stones of Stenness and Maes Howe was noted as an important player in British, Roman and European politics. So remarkable was the appearance of the Orkney king in Colchester in AD 43 that historians long believed the written source to be a mistake, a scribal error. But it turns out that recent excavations at the impressive broch-village of Gurness on the Orkney mainland show it to have been a royal palace. Sherds from a Roman amphora have been found, and not just any amphora but a type which had become obsolete by AD 60. These particular pottery containers were used for a fancy liqueur consumed by aristocrats, and the nearest example to the Gurness find was uncovered 1,000 km/600 miles to the south, in Essex, near Colchester. The recording of the arrival of northern royalty to bow before the emperor of Rome was no scribe's mistake.

In fact the submission of the king of Orkney in AD 43 was planned and expected, the result of prior negotiation. A sea journey of that distance was not made on spec and it had to be timed to fit in with the imperial itinerary. Claudius stayed only 16 days in Britain before making his way back through Gaul to Rome. The arrival of the northern king was organized because Orkney was important in the creation of Claudius' triumph, and its presentation. Not only was the submission of 11 British kings inscribed on the triumphal arch erected in Rome in 51; the subjection, however nominal, of such a remote place, across 'the Ocean', at the very ends of the earth, showed Claudius' unparalleled power and reach. No other emperor had done as much. When the historian Eutropius was compiling a list of Rome's emperors in the 4th century AD, he took care to highlight – as Claudius' major achievement – that 'he added to the Empire some islands lying in the Ocean beyond Britain, which are called the Orkneys'. Even three centuries after the stage-managed submission of the Orkney king, it was still seen as an impressive extension of imperial power.

From a British point of view the incident shines a sudden bright light on native diplomacy, and much else. Not only was there long-range contact between the courts of British kings; the mechanisms of that contact must have been sophisticated. The trigger for action was the landing at Richborough. Until the legionaries splashed on to the beaches a new political situation which took account of Rome was only ever hypothetical. When the invasion became a reality, at around the end of April in 43, events moved quickly. Perhaps intelligence reports reached the Orkney king at his palace at Gurness, and he and his advisers took a rapid decision on their response. It may be that news of the fighting in Kent was sent north with Trinovantian messengers, who certainly would have travelled by sea, coasting up the eastern shores. Once the Orcadians had come to the view that their interests were best served by joining the other ten British kingdoms in submitting to Claudius, a sea journey would have followed. Between the first landings and the triumphal entry of Claudius into Colchester only a little over three months elapsed, enough time for a journey south from Orkney but no time for indecision or hesitation. And the king himself would need to go, for protocol insisted that a proxy or an embassy would not do. Emperors in search of glory made treaties with kings and not their representatives.

Whatever discussion took place at Gurness, or elsewhere, it must have been well informed and probably much rehearsed for a decision to be so quickly arrived at. Of course the Orcadians were aware of the power and extent of the Roman Empire, of the name and nature of the emperor, and almost certainly had an inkling of his policies and the perennial need for imperial triumph. The king and his advisers must have believed that Rome could, if it desired, stretch north and encompass their fertile archipelago – otherwise why did they so readily submit? More awkward colonies had been absorbed and held in the past. But it is much more likely that the Orkney king wanted to profit from a treaty relationship with the Empire both materially and diplomatically. Perhaps he had territorial ambitions of his own on the mainland and believed that an alliance with the most powerful polity on earth would overawe any local resistance. Given the determination of the Caledonian confederacy to resist Agricola's invasion of the north of Britain 40 years later, it may be assumed that the Romanophile Orcadians and those mainland kingdoms to the south were not on friendly terms.

Whatever their motives and plans and however these turned on local power bases and alliances, the moment when the king of Orkney bowed before the Roman emperor in Colchester shows a degree of sophistication and political nous which jolts and surprises us. But it should not. The historical accident of a written Roman record of the doings of native British kings in AD 43 does not mean that such contact amongst them or such discussion of options and relationships over great distances was new. The Romans arrived and wrote it down, and the record survived, and that is all. It seems highly likely that long-range relationships stretching the length (and breadth) of the British Isles were in fact ancient, possibly even routine.

Around 3000 BC the great stone circles of Orkney rose to encompass a new religion and the concentration of the Stones of Stenness, the Ring of Brodgar, the sacred way between them, and the impressive tomb at Maes Howe strongly suggest the hand of a king-like figure at work, commandeering the substantial resources needed to create an awesome ceremonial centre in the middle of the Orkney mainland. Similarly impressive monuments cluster in another place in Britain – in Wessex, far away to the south. It looks as though the new beliefs were transmitted directly from the circle of the kings of Orkney to the kings of Wessex. If this linkage is secure then the new ideas must have travelled in ships and not through a series of overland contacts, which probably would have produced a string of similar monuments throughout Britain. Maritime technology in 3000 BC was little different from that of AD 43, and good pilotage and good weather would have brought news from the north to the Wessex ports in a matter of weeks. If this conjecture – over three millennia and based on the evidence of only one event – appears impossibly stretched, then the tension can be slackened a little by the knowledge that Pytheas, the traveller from Massalia, almost certainly visited Orkney around 325 BC. He was able to find out about the islands and take a passage northwards up well-travelled sea-lanes. And the archaeological record from the islands shows long-distance trade taking place over those three millennia, at least in stages, if not directly. People from the south of Britain knew how to reach Orkney and the Orcadians were familiar with the long island that lay across the Pentland Firth.

Between the clusters

There is of course an alternative view, that the clusters of monuments in Orkney and Wessex are little more than a matter of accidental survival rather than indicators of cultural exchange between sophisticated élites who ruled there. And it is a powerfully held view. Much has failed to survive (or if it has, it is less impressive than the great stone circles) and recent archaeology in Scotland suggests that the clusters should be seen as less isolated, less singular. At Dunragit, near Stranraer, a ceremonial complex made out of wood (and therefore leaving only faint traces as a cropmark) has been discovered and shown to be much more impressive than the Stones of Stenness or the Ring of Brodgar. There are also the remains of a mound three times bigger than Maes Howe. In both Angus and Dumfriesshire concentrations of cursus monuments have been found – their function is mysterious but may have been of central importance in the unknowable pieties of prehistoric peoples. Early henges also occur in the south of Scotland and it may be that the sort of worship that inspired them spread both north and south from there. What seems certain is that new techniques, discoveries and interpretations will alter the balance of understanding, perhaps radically.

The eruption of the Icelandic volcano Hekla in 1159 BC must have affected the people of Orkney particularly badly. In addition to the screening of the sun by the dust thrown up into the atmosphere, there may also have been a tsunami which engulfed the coastal area. Dramatic effects have been detected by palaeobotanists working in Caithness. Before the eruption pine trees contributed 20 per cent of the ancient pollen recovered in anaerobic cores, but after 1159 BC samples show only 2 per cent, a staggering and sudden decline which can only be attributable to a climatic catastrophe. As we know, the tree rings of Irish oaks growing in the same period show that 18 years of bad weather elapsed before they recovered. Colder and wetter conditions on Orkney encouraged the spread of peat and in some places ancient field boundaries were submerged, and therefore preserved. To the north, on the Shetland Islands, the deterioration of the weather and the encroachment of the peat cover slowly pushed people to abandon upland farms and concentrate on keeping low-lying fields fertile and viable. Increasing reliance was placed on stock-rearing, and flocks of sheep and herds of cattle grazed on the green but damp island landscape. Tending animals was less labour-intensive than arable farming and more suited to the changing conditions, the shorter, cooler summers and the contraction of the growing season. Some prehistorians have gone so far as to posit a general migration inside Scotland from the northern and western Highlands to the southern and eastern lowlands as the weather worsened after the 12th century BC.

Darkening skies, more insistent downpours and an even greater consciousness of the power of the weather may have shifted the emphasis – and the location – of religious belief and practice. Precious objects such as pottery and metalwork had been buried in prehistoric Scotland for millennia. Perhaps people saw this as a way of replenishing the fertility of the earth, renewing its ability to grow clay and metal-bearing ores. It was almost certainly a way of propitiating the gods by offering a sacrifice of valuable items. There was nothing new in that. But the increase in rainfall may have driven the people of the early 1st millennium BC to offer such wealth as they had to the gods in watery places. Hoards of valuable metalwork dating from this period begin to be found preserved in peat bogs, deliberately and carefully placed there with no intention of recovering them. Lochs and rivers also attracted offerings and it may be that these places were seen as the deposit of the elemental will of the sky-gods, where they rained their rain and expressed their anger. That made lochs and bogs, and water in general, the most effective locus for propitiation.

VEI Day

The Volcanic Explosivity Index measures the relative violence of a volcanic eruption. The most important determinant factors are the height of the eruption cloud and the quantity of material thrown out into the atmosphere. The scale runs from zero to eight but is logarithmic, so that each unit of measurement represents a tenfold increase in power. Krakatoa in 1883 gets a six and Tambora in Indonesia, which exploded in 1816, is awarded a seven, the most violent ever. It caused famine all over the world in 'the year without a summer'. The island of Santorini lies in the eastern Mediterranean, north of Crete, and is the rim of a huge, ancient volcano known as Thera. Since the 1930s historians have believed that the eruption of Thera in 1495 BC brought a catastrophic end to the Minoan civilization, the first dynamic, expanding European culture. Minoan Crete developed writing, great maritime expertise and beautiful art and architecture. Danish scientists examining frozen cores from the Greenland ice-cap in 1987 revised the date of Thera's eruption to 150 years earlier, too early to have caused the sudden decline of Minoan civilization. However, the cause and effect linkage has been convincingly restored by a group of American geologists. They have discovered 3-m/10-ft layers of volcanic ash on the island of Anafi, 32 km/20 miles from Thera, and field studies have expanded the distribution of Thera's debris enormously. Samples have been found in the Black Sea and the Nile Delta. This new evidence has occasioned a re-rating of the strength of the eruption to a very rare seven, in the same league of destruction as Tambora. The Americans have described the impact of Thera as 'colossal', with a 15-m/50-ft tsunami hitting Crete only minutes after the explosion. There followed many years of wet, cool summers and the gradual beginning of the end for Minoan civilization. The last palace at Knossos was abandoned in 1380 BC.

In 1780 the new Society of Antiquaries of Scotland recorded a find of 53 Late Bronze Age weapons dredged up from the bed of Duddingston Loch in Edinburgh. All of the swords, spearheads and daggers were found in one place. Later historians have interpreted this as the conse-quence of depositing the objects from a ceremonial jetty built out into the small loch. At Flag Fen in eastern England a very large and elaborate ceremonial complex was created for the express purpose of casting metal and other items into another small lake. Four million timber piles were driven into the marshland to support an avenue leading to an artificial holy island where the offerings were thrown into or placed in the water.

The boggy conditions often turned out to be anaerobic and much metalwork was consequently preserved. This volume of material has allowed some quantitative analysis and prehistorians have predicated a relative collapse in the bronze-making industry after 1200 BC, the production of many fewer axes (which in turn suggests a reduction in agricultural activity) and many more weapons (which suggests a need for them in a more fractious society).

The choice of watery places for elaborate offerings to the gods represents the beginning of what has now become a very ancient habit. Such places, at the cusp of two worlds, have had an enduring attraction for expressions of spirituality; small islands and promontories became the ascetic homes of hermetic Christian monks, natural springs are still revered from Cornwall to Caithness, and the loops of rivers were sanctified by great abbeys and churches. This linkage of sanctity, sacrifice and water has lasted a long time, an outstanding example of the *longue durée*. Glinting at the bottom of wells, in riverbeds where bridges cross and even in artificial fountains, modern offerings of coins can often be seen. After all, these are the most readily available metal objects of value in the 21st century.

When priests or priest-kings walked out on to the jetties at Duddingston Loch and at Flag Fen, their sacrifice would have been witnessed by a large number of people. By projecting into the water, away from the crowded lakeshore, the jetties themselves created a theatrical setting for the principal players. Almost certainly a significant part of the ceremonies would have been conducted expressly on behalf of the watching audience, and it was important for them to be there. If good weather and a safe harvest were prayed for, their lives as farmers would be much easier – interest in this was universal, as everybody needed to eat. But it was important, too, to have witnesses for what would have been seen as conspicuous waste, objects of great value thrown away by someone powerful, indeed, someone who was demonstrating their power by the very act of throwing into the water objects which characterized their élite status – weapons and so on – with no intent to retrieve them.

It is difficult for modern sensibilities to comprehend this. Conspicuous consumption is now mostly self- or family-centred in western society, although the phrase 'if you've got it, flaunt it' does approach the thinking of the prehistoric élite on the lakeside. However, there are much closer near-contemporary parallels for this sort of behaviour which offer a more accurate reading. Amongst the indigenous peoples of the coastline of British Columbia, in south-western Canada, the institution of the *potlatch* lasted until the 20th century and still continues in a nominal form. Potlatches were enormously important gatherings hosted by the chiefs of different tribes and clans within a tribe. Hundreds of people were invited, and part of the lengthy timetable of ceremonies involved gift-giving. Through distributing many gifts, some of dazzling richness, a chief expected to have his status, his customary rights and the legitimacy of his lineage confirmed by the act of his guests' acceptance of his generosity. Behind this simple exchange lay a very profound transaction. If a chief could afford to be so conspicuously generous and a guest acknowledged this by taking his gifts, then a clearly and publicly recognized bond was formed, as much political as social.

When the priests or, more likely, priest-kings threw their swords and spearheads into Duddingston Loch, they were giving gifts to the gods and seeking public confirmation of their status in a similar way. And by making sure that their people and perhaps the cadet branches of clans within their kingdoms or the élites of neighbouring peoples were present to witness such generosity, they made another point. As the weapons splashed into the water, it was abundantly clear to all who was boss.

The depositing of metalwork and other valuable objects in watery places was widespread in Scotland and it appears to have been a major focus of religious activity towards the end of the 2nd and the beginning of the 1st millennium BC. By contrast, the great stone circles and the other ritual centres of the past show little sign of activity at that time and there is relatively sparse evidence for human burial – previously such a rich source of information. And once again the question arises: where are all the bodies? It may be that water was used for burial, perhaps after cremation, or perhaps corpses were placed in rivers or in the sea, where they have left no traces for archaeologists to find.

Instead of raising great monuments or burial mounds, the powerful people of the 1st millennium BC seem to have diverted their resources to the building of houses, or at least habitations of various sorts. Chief amongst these are what archaeologists call *hillforts*. And in Scotland there are many hundreds of them. But they do not look like forts in the usual meaning of the term. If reconstructed many would not resemble the sort of thing built by the US Cavalry. Rather, they are enclosures defined by one or more circuits of ditches, with the upcast being used to create an earth rampart on which a wooden stockade was set. Occasionally the inner rampart was built in drystone; at the gateways (usually two, at opposing ends) there appears to have been more elaborate fortification.

Forts were mostly built on hilltops, thus commanding long views over the surrounding countryside and being easily seen from below. All of these characteristics seem to add up to a defensive structure, but the reality is that many of the first hillforts had far too long a perimeter to be defended against a determined attack. A huge force of soldiers would have been needed to man the walls effectively. In the Borders, the fort of Eildon Hill North has more than a mile of ramparts and five gateways instead of one or two (see plate XI). The ditch and bank enclose 20 ha/50 acres and the remains of no less than 300 hut platforms can be seen. The hill is the north-easternmost of three and from its summit 50-km/30-mile vistas are possible on a clear day. It dominates the lower Tweed Valley and, with its two neighbours, can be seen from almost every approach. The point of building a huge hillfort on the most massive of the three hills could not have been defensive. There is no source of water anywhere on the summit and a force large enough to keep a mile-long rampart intact simply could not be maintained there. The point of Eildon Hill North was political and religious (although the Celtic peoples of Scotland would not have made that distinction). It was built to impress, even overawe all who saw it and made the long climb up from the floor of the river valley. And it was significant that it stood on one of three hills. The Celts were fascinated by triplicity: for example, their gods often took three forms, suffered a triple death or had three characteristics.

More than 90 per cent of Scotland's hillforts are to be found south of the Forth, most of those in the Tweed Basin. Eildon Hill North was first enclosed by its massive rampart some time around 1000 BC. Traprain Law in East Lothian, another impressive hill rising out of fertile flatlands, was also occupied at that time and it too contains hut platforms. Breaking out of the predominantly southern distribution, two large forts existed on the tops of White Caterthun and Brown Caterthun in Angus, near Brechin. Recent investigations have produced a date of around 700 BC for the building of the latter.

The earliest hillforts were also the largest. And at the outset of the 1st millennium BC their creation represents the concerted exertion of considerable power. The digging of a mile-long rampart required detailed planning and the ability to enforce the instructions of the planners. Not only did sufficient labour have to be found, it needed to be fed, organized in work groups and some arrangements for its absence from the quotidian business of farming had to be made. Perhaps there was a rota system over several construction seasons. Whatever the detail, the building of these huge enclosures speaks of great power wielded by a warrior aristocracy and their kings, the same sort of people who made their way down from the hillfort on Arthur's Seat to deposit their swords and spearheads in nearby Duddingston Loch.

There can be little doubt that the hillforts were royal enclosures whose ramparts were intended to mark off the king's, or more probably the priest-king's, sacred space from the mundane world of farming and food production lying at its foot. The making of metalwork was almost certainly monopolized by those who were skilled with weapons and were in the habit of sacrificing them to the gods, and no doubt smiths bellowed their forges to white heat on the windy summits of these hills. A deposit of seven bronze axes was found buried in the flank of Eildon Mid Hill and evidence of metalworking discovered on Traprain Law.

The remains of other activity are hard to discern on the ground, but floating around Eildon Hill North in particular are all sorts of other wisps of circumstantial evidence. To the Celtic peoples of the 1st millennium BC – many historians, some reluctantly, agree that this label can be securely attached at this point in Britain's prehistory – cattle were very important, and they almost certainly supplied a handy index of wealth. At Cnip on the Isle of Lewis archaeologists have come across the bones of a great number of small and scrawny cows. Apparently they were preferred to sheep, even though these animals were far better suited to the available rough grazing and the prevailing weather conditions. This was because of the status conferred on their owners by large numbers of cows, no matter how stunted. Many African tribes of the 21st century, such as the Masai of Kenya, share these attitudes. A faint, surprising Hebridean echo of the exaggerated value of cattle can still be heard in the Gaelic language. On the Isle of Lewis and elsewhere in the west the most effusive term of endearment available is *m'eudail*. Literally it means 'my cattle'.

A more substantial and colourful witness to the importance of cows in Celtic society is the ancient Irish epic poem the *Tain Bo Cuailgne*, or *The Cattle Raid of Cooley*. The date of its composition is unknown (it was finally transcribed in the early medieval period in monastic scriptoria) but much of it appears to reach back into Irish prehistory, perhaps as far back as the second half of the 1st millennium BC. The central role is taken by the boy-hero Cuchulainn, and he is despatched to defend Ulster single-handedly against the armies of Connaught, led by the semi-divine Queen Maeve. The tale turns on cattle and specifically the ownership of the Brown Bull of Cooley. And when, at an early stage, Queen Maeve and her consort discuss which of them is the wealthier, the calculation is reckoned on the basis of the head of cattle belonging to each.

The glacis slope

Ditches and banks have never gone out of military style. In both Iraqi wars of the recent past tank commanders have hidden behind banks of sand. A major problem for prehistoric military architects was erosion. Deeply cut ditches had a tendency to fill in over time and needed regular maintenance. And when a palisade was hammered into the top of a bank of upcast dug from a ditch in front, a few winters of severe weather could cause it to topple. A berm was often introduced, a space between the palisade and the ditch, but this too could prove unstable. By 300 BC fort builders had developed the glacis, a sloping outer face to a rampart which was an extension of the nearer slope of a ditch. This worked well and needed little looking after.

Stock-rearing and the nodal points of the stockman's year inform the plot of the *Tain Bo Cuailgne* and they formed the basis for the ancient agricultural festivals which used to be celebrated throughout Britain. They require exposition and explanation here. The year was thought to begin not in the midst of winter, as it does nowadays, but with the feast of *Samhuinn*. The Gaelic word translates approximately as 'the end of summer', but it is now called Hallowe'en and seen as the start of winter, falling on 31 October. The remnants of old practices can still be recognized. Hallowe'en, and Samhuinn before it, was originally a fire festival and the ceremonies took place around as great a blaze as could be piled up. *Guising* involved taking ash from the fire and daubing it on faces as a symbolic disguise. This was a cue for all sorts of licence. In *The First Statistical Account* of 1796, ministers of the Kirk were busy doing their Christian utmost to suppress what they saw as persistent paganism: 'A sort of secret society of Guisers made itself notorious in several of the neighbouring villages, men dressed as women, women dressed as men, dancing together in a very unseemly way.'

The last smiddy priest

An echo of the ancient pre-eminence of metalworkers could still be heard at Gretna Green until November 2003. Jim Jackson was the last in a long line of smiddy (smithy) priests to marry runaway couples over the anvil. A difference between the marriage laws of Scotland and England which arose in 1754 began a fashion for runaway marriage at Gretna, and also, incidentally, at the eastern end of the border, north of Berwick-upon-Tweed and at Coldstream on the Scots side of the Tweed Bridge. If English couples were under 21 and did not have the consent of their parents, they could not get married, so some eloped to Scotland. And the tradition of a blacksmith as a man of standing found a new expression. When couples were married by the smiddy priest, he clattered his hammer off the anvil and declared them to be man and wife. And if their parents were in hot pursuit, he bundled them into a handy double bed so that they could quickly consummate matters and thereby make the union indissoluble.

The turnip or pumpkin lanterns of Hallowe'en also recall another ancient habit. To the Celtic peoples of the 1st millennium BC the human head acquired great religious significance. It may have been seen as the repository of the soul. The old woman who picked up Murrough O'Brien's severed head at his execution in 1580 and sucked the blood from it certainly believed something of that sort. Roman historians report that the European Celts to the north of them were fond of collecting the heads of their enemies, and isolated human skulls have been found as offerings in several places in Britain. In a cave used as an ossuary at Covesea on the Moray Firth coast, archaeologists have discovered that many of the dead had been beheaded (and some of the heads suspended from the roof of the cave). And, most intriguing, at Stanwix fort in Yorkshire a series of skulls was retrieved from the ditch below the main rampart. It appears that when the Roman legions attacked, some time after AD 70, the priests of Venutius, the native king defending the fort, had set up a row of skulls whose magic would repel the invaders. One writer has memorably called this a 'ghost fence'. And when turnip lanterns have a candle placed inside and are set on a window sill at Hallowe'en, it looks very much as if an ancient belief still flickers in the early dark of the winter.

After Samhuinn, or Hallowe'en, the Celtic communities of the north hunkered down to wait out the winter. At the beginning of February fires blazed again to welcome the festival of *Imbolc*, christianized as the Feast of St Bride. Ewes had begun to lactate in anticipation of lambing and their milk supplied welcome nourishment for hungry human mouths. Imbolc later mutated into Candlemas Eve, the first of the old Scottish quarter days.

On 1 May *Beltane* was seen as another turning point in the stock-rearing year, marking the beginning of the process of transhumance, the annual passage of flocks and herds to upland pasture. This moment used to be celebrated with a particular ritual and its unmistakable pagan nature lasted long enough for the observant Thomas Pennant to notice on his tour of Scotland in 1772. In country districts:

> The herds [herdsmen] of every village hold their Beltane. They cut a square trench in the ground, leaving turf in the middle. On that they make a fire of wood, on which they dress a large caudle [pot] of eggs, oatmeal, butter and milk, and besides these they bring plenty of beer and whisky. Each of the company must

contribute something to the feast. The rites begin by pouring a little of the caudle on to the ground by way of libation. Everyone then takes a cake of oatmeal, on which are raised nine square knobs, each dedicated to some particular being who is supposed to preserve their lands, or to some animal, the destroyer of them. Each person then turns to face the fire, and breaks off a knob, and flinging it over his shoulder, says, 'This I give to thee, O fox, spare my lambs'.

This was a fire festival with a rite of propitiation clearly present and all in the context of a feast, however simple. The final and fourth date in the Celtic calendar, *Lughnasa*, has been superseded by and also rubbed smooth by use in Scotland into *Lammas*. Held on 1 August, this corresponds to the approximate date of many of the traditional cattle and sheep fairs when grass-fattened beasts were sold for slaughter or for breeding. St James' Fair, the oldest recorded in Scotland, did business at this time of the year on the Fairgreen, on the bank of the Tweed opposite the town of Kelso. It died out in the 1930s and was replaced by the Border Union Show, now held a short distance away across the Teviot.

The point of setting out these old quarter dates at length is a simple one. They evolved from the behaviour of domesticated animals, cattle and sheep in particular, and the way in which a stock-rearing society adapted to that behaviour. It is impossible to divine a date for their inception; rather, it is safe to assume their evolution from the time, probably after the 12th century BC, when society in Scotland began to concentrate on animal husbandry as its primary agricultural activity.

This context begins to bring the function of the early hillforts into focus. Their sheer scale does more than suggest them as the power bases of Celtic kings, it insists on it. But they cannot have been large-scale, year-round settlements, a form of prehistoric town. The 300 hut platforms on Eildon Hill North imply a maximum population of between 3,000 and 5,000, more than the modern town of Melrose at its foot. For a permanent community of that size the logistics are impossible. The lack of water supply, the seasonal extremes of weather and the constant need to go up and down for every basic item simply does not allow that interpretation, no matter how attractive the site must have been politically and spiritually. It is much more likely that a priest-king and his court lived for part or even most of the year on the summit of the hill where they could be serviced by retainers or slaves. And it seems also likely that four times a year those who owed loyalty, taxes and had faith in – or fear of – their gods climbed Eildon Hill North and celebrated the festivals where the winds fanned the blazing bonfires. Several old Celtic place-names around southern Scotland support this image. For example, Lanarkshire's Tinto Hill is prominent in the landscape and the derivation of its name is 'Fire-hill'; Tarbolton in Ayrshire comes from 'Hill of Beltane'.

At the western foot of the three Eildon Hills there lies something more than a cultural context. A zigzag of earthworks, banks and ditches following the contours of the ground, terminating at streams or steeply rising banks, appears to have no defensive or domestic function. In fact they resemble stock-pens, secure holding areas for the cattle and sheep brought to Eildon Hill North for the payment of tithes, the portion of a farmer's produce due to the priest-king who lived on the summit, close to the sky-gods, and who presided over the quarterly festivals. In modern renditions of Samhuinn, Imbolc, Beltane and Lughnasa domesticated animals figured centrally. Cattle, no doubt terrified, were driven between bonfires in an act of purification. Horses were washed for the same reason, and milk played an important role in the special foods consumed at those times. Ultimately the four festivals evolved into the Scottish quarter days when agricultural rents were paid and contracts made: that is, Candlemas (2 February), Whitsun (seven weeks after Easter), Lammas (1 August) and Martinmas (7 November).

Kandinsky and the Komi

The Russian painter Wassily Kandinsky (1866–1944) initially wanted to train as an anthropologist and he decided to go on a field trip to study the Komi people in their heartland, an area about 800 km/500 miles north-east of Moscow. To outsiders the Komi appeared to have converted to Orthodox Christianity (forcibly at the bloody hands of St Stephen), but in their private lives they still cleaved to the beliefs and rituals of an ancient paganism. Their shamans presided over secret ceremonies in the forest where the Komi worshipped an animistic pantheon: the sun, the rivers, the trees, often in a series of frenzied dances to the accompaniment of booming drums. A malign forest monster called *Vorsa* haunted the community and required propitiation. The Komi believed that each person had a living soul which shadowed the course of their lives. It was called an *ort* and it expired at the moment when they drew their last breath. Water and fire were prayed to, and the sun seemed to shine at the centre of this old belief system. Later in life Kandinsky drew on his trip as a source of inspiration for his art.

The scale of Scottish hillforts appears to polarize. At the beginning of the 1st millennium BC the very large sites were enclosed, most on prominent hilltops. By 500 BC some of these had been abandoned and many smaller forts came into being, some densely occupied. But the ramparts of these were probably still more symbolic than practically defensive. At Chesters Fort, near Drem in East Lothian, an elaborate circuit of banks and ditches was constructed on a site which was impossible to defend effectively. The fort is overlooked by a higher ridge running close by and it would have been easy for attackers to shower Chesters' defenders with missiles and quickly defeat them. Clearly prestige was far more significant than security to the important man who caused the fort to be built. A cropmark at Dodridge Law, also in East Lothian, shows up a series of defences far greater in area than the small space they enclose. Once again appearances were what mattered, a conspicuous consumption of labour by an élite intent on creating an elaborate setting for the display of undoubted power.

What else went on inside these forts? The huge feast which devoured 184 bullocks at the wake held around the tomb at Irthlingborough in the south of England might prefigure the sort of occasion which is often used to characterize Celtic culture. According to Roman commentators, feasting was beloved by the Celts and it provided another opportunity for conspicuous consumption of a more direct sort. Poseidonius related the tale of Louernius, chief of a Gaulish tribe known as the Arverni:

> [He] made a square enclosure one and a half miles each way, within which he placed vats filled with expensive liquor and prepared so great a quantity of food that for many days all who wished could enter and enjoy the feast prepared, being served without break by the attendants.

The similarities between Celtic feasting and the potlatches of the British Columbian tribes are very instructive. The latter were also organized to last as many as ten days and involved what amounted to the public destruction of large amounts of wealth – by needless and literal consumption. Guests were summoned by a special messenger, and fasted for several days in preparation. Wearing particularly rich clothing and arriving according to rank, they were seated in front of a huge feast. After the elaborate ceremonies of gift-giving and receiving, they then fell upon the food (mainly salmon in British Columbia) and were expected to gorge themselves until they vomited. Meanwhile the host's servants threw candlefish, an oily fish used individually as a lamp, on to the central hearth to make the fire flame brightly. These fish were valuable and their profligate use at a potlatch was expected. Occasionally a chief would step forward to the fire and remove his richly textured potlatch robe. And taking up a knife he would cut it into pieces and distribute them to his followers and guests, literally giving them the shirt off his back. In the course of the longest and most spectacular feasts, the slaves serving the food were sometimes given their freedom.

During the days of feasting a chief would often announce a title which he claimed and would expect it to be affirmed by his guests through their acceptance of his extravagant hospitality. Always the occasion was used for political purposes: the announcement of a marriage contract, an heir presumptive, the mourning of an important death, the welcome of the birth of an heir. Metal objects also had a key role and the gift of the highest status it was possible to give at a potlatch was a burnished copper plaque. And what the host expected in return was an acknowledgment of his role. Many older chiefs wore potlatch hats decorated with rings to show how many they had been able to afford.

When the British Empire arrived on the Pacific coast and pacified the tribes, these occasions were swamped by mass-produced goods such as trade blankets. And by 1884 the Canadian government was forced to ban potlatches because so many had ended in violence, there being no other outlet in the Pax Britannica. They were made legal again only in 1951.

Apart from the Gaulish example of similarly large-scale feasting, the evidence in western Europe comes from objects. Cauldrons able to hold 40–50 litres/9–11 gallons, to boil the butchered carcasses of whole animals, were first made in Ireland around 1000 BC and several have been recovered from watery deposits. Perhaps the most beautiful and informative example is the Gundestrup cauldron from Denmark. And occasionally an elaborately decorated flesh-hook or skewer used for pulling out joints has turned up. At Corrymuckloch in Perthshire a hoard of bronze objects was found in a peat bog: three axeheads, a deliberately broken sword-blade and a large ladle. They were dated to around 800 BC and were almost certainly a votive offering. Like cauldrons and buckets, ladles (these are extremely rare finds and the Corrymuckloch example is unique in Britain) are associated with the habit of holding elaborate feasts.

On Eildon Hill North the priest-kings may have held occasions resembling the British Columbian potlatches on each or some of the Celtic festivals. If they took cattle or sheep from their people as a form of taxation, in return for leadership and perhaps protection, then it may well be that many of the beasts were slaughtered, cooked and eaten on the summit of the hill. Intriguingly, some of the large English hillforts show little evidence of habitation but some evidence of fodder racks for cattle and sheep held for short periods. Whoever he was, the priest-king on Eildon Hill North would not have seen this use of his property as a waste, but rather as a way of confirming his role as a provider, a river to his people.

While the larger and earlier forts sometimes show sparse signs of occupation, the smaller sort were often densely settled. At Hownam Rings, in the Cheviot Hills above Kelso, the fort enclosed ten round-houses at one point, though not all may have been used to house human beings. At Dryburn Bridge in East Lothian a small fort was built around one large roundhouse some time after 750 BC and nearby Chesters Fort seems to have contained several domestic structures.

Excavations have failed to reveal consistent patterns. At different periods, in different parts of Scotland, forts were expanded, contracted, abandoned, the ramparts allowed to decay and some occasionally even deliberately destroyed by the owners. At Finavon in Angus what became known as a *vitrified fort* was excavated. To strengthen its walls they had been timber-laced and, it was believed, burned to fuse both wood and stone together into a hard mass. Or perhaps the fires had been the result of a siege. In fact vitrification has the effect of weakening a timber-laced wall and the intensity of heat needed to melt stone into a fused mass does not allow a military interpretation. Fires set by a besieger could not have developed the very high temperatures needed. It is much more likely that the walls of vitrified forts were deliberately burned with large amounts of fuel continually renewed and stoked to reach the necessary intensity. As an act of conspicuous waste, and perhaps as a signal of a change in leadership and a rejection of the immediate past, it may be that a king caused a vitrified fort to be destroyed in a symbolic fire set by his supporters.

The dense distribution of elaborate forts in Scotland south of the Forth has presented a puzzling phenomenon. How could so many powerful men co-exist in such relatively small areas? Was there a frequent sequence of agricultural surpluses to allow this much building (and maintenance)? If it is remembered that kings and their retinues had to be constantly on the move in the historic period, travelling around their domains so that they could consume the food renders owed to them, then perhaps the picture clears a little. Moving between lowland and upland forts, a royal or aristocratic progress could have compassed a wide area in the 1st millennium BC, and because of the staggered nature of agricultural output in different locations at different times of the year it may have been possible to hold impressive occasions, possibly even potlatch-style feasts, at which rights and obligations were confirmed. And if it is accepted that forts varied in their use as well as in their scale, then a powerful man may have controlled many at one time.

However, there is a difficulty with a purely symbolic interpretation of forts, an archaeological phenomenon which is awkward to fit into that context. Outside the ramparts of several in Scotland, some in Ireland and many in northern Spain and Portugal, there are fields of carefully placed stones embedded in the ground so that they obstruct or slow down charging troops of warriors or cavalry. These are known as *chevaux de frises* and almost certainly existed as wooden stakes (which have vanished) as well as stones. But once again these defences may have come to be seen as a symbolic boundary between the world outside the royal or aristocratic fort and the different, probably sacred, world inside it. In the early stages of their evolution *chevaux de frises* were indeed used to break up assaults on the ramparts, but by the time the stones were planted in the ground outside Burgi Geos fort in Shetland, they were not intended for that purpose. They simply line the path to the site and do not obstruct anything.

All of these pacific interpretations beg an obvious question. Where and how did the Celtic warlords of prehistoric Scotland actually do their fighting? It cannot all have been a matter of show and implied threat.

Warrior aristocracies depend on war for the maintenance of their status, but it is important to be clear about what was being fought over. In contrast to modern thinking, it is unlikely that the Celtic kings of the 1st millennium BC were interested in territory for its own sake, as a desirable piece of geography which they wished to add to the one they already held sway over. What the land produced was much more important, and no doubt they fought hard to control food production. Rather than invading an area and somehow taking it over and holding on to it, they probably moved to assert dominance over whoever was already in authority over farmers and stockmen, another king or another aristocracy. A military contest between members of essentially the same sort of warrior élite had the added advantage of being contained and not prejudicial to the vital work of food production. There is some evidence from the early historical period that battles were fought at agreed times in traditional places, such as fords and road-meetings, easily accessible to those taking part.

A frequent variant on this pattern may have been cattle-raiding or rustling, the sort of thing immortalized in the *Tain Bo Cuailgne*. Ireland long suffered the institution of a warrior cult known as the *Fianna*, meaning 'the soldiers'. These were bands of young, unmarried aristocrats who roamed the countryside on horseback, living by plunder and rustling. The period was seen as one with a rite of passage, but their activities could be very destructive. In the 7th century AD the Fianna were berated by the Church for their lawlessness, but noted because of their hair. The young hooligans followed the ancient Druidic habit of the *ceudgelt*, cutting a tonsure over the crown of the head, from ear to ear, to show a high shaved forehead with long, flowing hair at the back. Such obvious paganism would have been an affront to doctrine, if it had not been copied by Celtic monks who cut their tonsure in exactly the same way.

The Fianna appears to have been a very old institution and the Irish annals of the early historic period show brief glimpses of other aspects of pre-Christian Celtic politics. War was never expressly mentioned in the terse entries because there seemed to be no need. Society was in a constant state of hostility; so many bloody incidents spatter the pages of the annals that it may never have occurred to the monks who copied them that there could be such a thing as a period of peace. Fighting seems to have been the exclusive business of warriors, professional soldiers who were themselves aristocrats and who clustered around aristocratic or royal courts. Lesser folk are never mentioned and kings themselves led from the front, often doing deeds of great savagery. Indeed the *Tain Bo Cuailgne* has only one soldier doing battle on behalf of the whole province of Ulster. Cuchulainn was recognized as the king's champion, and classical sources support this role in Celtic society. The idea of single combat to settle a war lasted well into the Middle Ages, and when Henry de Bohun rode out in front of the English lines at Bannockburn, King Robert de Bruce took an enormous risk in accepting his challenge. The ornamental flesh-hooks found by archaeologists may have had a function at feasts for lifting the champion's portion out of the cauldron. And the emphasis in tale-telling is very often on the powers and deeds of individuals, the cult of heroes. Perhaps military matters were occasionally decided by a contest of champions.

Other tactics related in the Irish annals included more than threats but less than all-out warfare. The rights claimed by a king over another territory were sometimes asserted by a process of *indred*, of harrying the farms and settlements in question. Or *slogad*, which translates as 'hosting', might be used. This involved the mustering of an army of warriors and bringing it to a recognized battle-place. There its leader would demand either submission or a battle. The related Scots Gaelic *sluagh-ghairm* was the precise term for the signal for the Highland clans to muster for war, and in a later lexical development *sluaghiul* came to mean simply 'politics'.

These practices were already very old when the Irish annalists recorded them, though they cannot suggest any more than a hint of what actually took place in Scotland in the 1st millennium BC. But they are at least consistent with some of the harder evidence, and also the tone of that evidence, such as it is.

How warfare was conducted, how men fought (it is very likely that women fought alongside them – St Columba's biographer, St Adomnan, attempted to ban the participation of women in battle) is similarly unclear, but again tradition offers some help. The earliest Roman sources characterize the warriors of southern Scotland as cavalry. In a series of fascinating letters uncovered at the Roman fort of Vindolanda, immediately to the south of Hadrian's Wall, a correspondent observes: 'the Britons are unprotected by armour. There are very many cavalry.' When Tacitus recorded the campaign of Agricola in the north, a short time after the Vindolanda letter, he noted that the native armies still included charioteers.

By 1000 BC horses were in domesticated use in Scotland, both as riding and draught animals. Finds of the metal elements of horse-gear and bridles in particular confirm this. But it is important to grasp immediately that, by modern standards, the animals that wore this tack would have been classified as ponies, emphatically not the great, snorting, black brutes ridden down The Mall by the Household Cavalry, nor the great destriers of medieval knights. Such skeletal remains as have been found show prehistoric riding horses rarely rising over 13 hands. But a cavalry warrior of average height would certainly have been able to ride a pony of that stature without difficulty. They were probably as tough as native breeds are now and able to keep their condition despite hard work. And since stirrups were yet to be invented, legs dangling well below the pony's belly would not have been a problem. In his famous manual of horsemanship of the 4th century BC, the Greek general Xenophon recommended the use of bare legs to grip the sweaty flanks of a cavalry horse so as to have both hands free for fighting or archery. Better purchase could be had if the horse's coat was damp and it was possible to hold and squeeze it around the belly and direct it using only the legs.

By 1300 to 1200 BC Celtic horsemen had developed bitted bridles to gain a faster response from their ponies. On the battlefield a swiftly executed turn or a quick halt could be absolutely critical. And by the 4th century BC the Gauls had invented an H-shaped curb bit which worked by putting downward pressure on the pony's lower jaw – essentially something very like today's snaffle bit.

Parting shot

Archery on horseback called for shorter bows and on the Pontic steppes in central Asia the nomadic warriors who first developed cavalry warfare began to experiment with new materials. Horn from cattle and water buffalo was used in combination with hardwood and it was found that a bow about 100 cm/40 ins long could produce enough poundage to unleash a deadly arrow. Cavalry archers had to be sufficiently at one with their ponies to ride them with only their legs and seat for guidance as they used both hands to fire volleys of arrows. Reports of the Hunnic hordes galloping across Europe marvelled at their ability to turn in the saddle and fire backwards as they sped away from the enemy, as did the Parthians of western Asia – a Parthian shot. But they had the advantage of stirrups, an invention not available to prehistoric cavalry.

There is some evidence that, like modern dragoons, Celtic warriors used their ponies as a means of quick access to the battlefield, where they then dismounted to fight. But even small horses give a considerable height advantage over an opponent on foot and the fearsome Celtic slashing swords appear to have been designed for use by a mounted warrior. Weighted near the tip of the blade, they were at their most devastating in a downward cut. At the mysterious battle at Mons Graupius in AD 83, Tacitus reported how difficult it was for the Caledonians to use their long swords effectively on foot: 'it was awkward for the enemy with their small shields and enormous swords – for the swords of the Britons, having no points, were unsuited for a cut-and-thrust struggle and close-quarters battle.'

Chariots were also used at Mons Graupius when the Roman legions faced the Caledonian confederacy. These were straightforward vehicles with a central pole to which two ponies (perhaps too small to be ridden) were yoked. Driven by one man, they carried another into battle, a warrior who either threw javelins or fired arrows. At Newbridge, on the outskirts of Edinburgh, a chariot burial has recently been discovered which appears to date from around 400 BC. The vehicle had been set into the ground intact and upright, and its use in an implied ritual speaks of a particular importance in the Celtic society of the north. Chariot burials have also been found in Yorkshire, in the territory of the Parisii, a Celtic tribe with origins in northern France. In March 2004, a bulldozer working on the widening of the A1 near Ferrybridge stripped the topsoil off a limestone chamber. In it was a complete chariot burial dating to around 500 BC, almost contemporary with the one found at Newbridge, which was also, incidentally, found very near a motorway. The iron tyres of the chariot do not match and excavators believe that it was assembled specifically for the burial. But the use of chariots almost certainly began even earlier than the dates of Ferrybridge and Newbridge. At Horsehope Crag, in the Manor Valley near Peebles (see plate XII), a shepherd came across a hoard of bronze objects dating to about 750 BC, including fragments of bridles and the constituent parts of a miniature chariot or cart.

Chariots of ire

The greatest chariot battle in history was fought between the Hittites and the armies of the Egyptian pharaoh Ramesses II at Kadesh in 1286 BC. From their power base in central Turkey, the Hittites had developed the two-wheeled chariot, so light that it could be carried by one man. In battle, three were aboard: a driver, an archer or javelin thrower and a shield-bearer to protect them. At Kadesh, in modern Syria, the Hittite kings could put 3,500 chariots in the field, and having chosen flat, unobstructed ground, they moved at tremendous speed to destroy the Egyptian army. It must have been an extraordinary sight. The Hittites understood the relationship between battle-fitness and victory and the chariot corps used the first known horse-training manual. Written by Kikkuli the Mittanian, it prescribes for all aspects of horse management, from the correct feed needed for high performance to the need for exercise for both horse and rider.

By the time Mons Graupius was fought in AD 83, chariots were still in use in Britain, although no longer part of the European Celts' military repertoire. Here is Tacitus again, describing the preliminaries to the battle: 'The charioteers filled the middle of the plain, making a din as they rode back and forth.' But their role seems to have been slight, perhaps even restricted to the show made before battle was joined in earnest, because later Tacitus notes that 'the charioteers had fled . . . . Often too, runaway chariots or terrified, riderless horses with nothing but fear to direct them careered into the ranks from the side or head on.' The riderless horses hint at the presence of Celtic cavalry at the engagement, but there is no direct reference to them actually fighting.

The hoards of metalwork dating from the 1st millennium BC supply a comprehensive sense of the armoury of Celtic warriors in Britain. Swords of several sorts dominated, most of them, as Tacitus observed, designed for slashing and clubbing rather than stabbing. One of the few glints of historicity in the medieval rendering of the tales of King Arthur concerns the name of the most famous Celtic sword. From Old Welsh, *Excalibur* means 'Hard Dunter' or 'Basher', and when Sir Bedivere threw it into the lake after Arthur's death he performed another authentic historical act.

On an onager

Onagers, or wild asses, were used in the prehistoric Middle East as draught animals and also to pull early chariots. They were smaller and quicker than oxen and more readily available than horses. In Sumerian art of the 3rd millennium BC they are shown driven abreast in a yoke not unlike that used for oxen, and they are pulling two- and four-wheeled chariots. Onagers were controlled by long reins attached to rings pierced through their noses or upper lips. Perhaps not surprisingly, the major problem with them was that they were bad-tempered. The Romans nicknamed one of their siege engines 'the onager' because it had a tremendous kick.

Many spearheads were dredged up from Duddingston Loch and they were traditionally hafted on to coppiced ash boughs (in the precise terms of early tree lore, the right length of time for a good spearhaft to grow was reckoned to be ten years), presumably selected for weight and straightness – and also for strength and truth. In the hands of Celtic craftsmen ash was seen as a powerful, reliable wood, exactly what was needed when lives depended on it. Thomas Pennant observed 18th-century Highland midwives take a green ash stick and hold one end in the fire so that its sap oozed on to a spoon held at the other. This was then fed to newborn infants to pass on the virtues of the tree through what was seen as its blood. Shepherds' and cattlemen's crooks were always fashioned from ash wands and it was widely believed that a straying cow whacked with one would never take any real hurt.

In the present age of machine-cut wood, it is easy to forget that ash boughs from the pre-industrial period would have been only approximately straight, and if thrown in battle their flight would be erratic. The strength of the wood was perhaps thought of as a prime virtue because it would not give way and splinter in the close-quarters infantry fighting of the kind practised by the Roman legions.

Tacitus derided the 'small shields' of the Caledonians at Mons Graupius but, like their slashing swords, these appear to have been designed for cavalry warfare. The long and slightly curved wood and leather shields of the legionaries were well suited to the shoving and stabbing of engagement on foot. And in the midst of such scrummages small shields and long swords would amount to nothing less than disaster. It may be that these differences in equipment were crucial at Mons Graupius and the outcome of the battle turned on them.

The Caledonians' shields probably resembled those of their descendants, the Picts, and they looked to have been little more than 30 cm/1 ft square, the sort of things carried by cavalry warriors and used to parry blows rather than absorb their impact. By contrast the large shields of the Romans would have been totally unwieldy on horseback. But long Celtic infantry shields have survived and several beautiful examples have been retrieved from watery deposits in the south of England. The Battersea Shield, pulled out of the Thames in London, is exquisite.

Made from sheet metal, they were too heavy for any practical use and like so much in Celtic society their function was as part of some unknowable ritual.

Three Scottish hoards of bronze shields have been found so far, at Yetholm in Roxburghshire, at Beith in Ayrshire and at Auchmaleddie in Aberdeenshire. Dating from between 800 and 700 BC, the Yetholm examples are beautifully crafted artefacts made in a simple design of concentric circles beaten out from the back of the shield by a smith with a sure and consistent touch, and then further embellished by punch-marks between the circles. In the winter of 2003–4 another shield-like object was discovered close to the 19th-century findspots of the Yetholm shields. However, its design is baffling, quite unlike a shield, for there is no evidence of a boss at its centre and the surface appears smooth and flat. One historian has conjectured that it may be a bronze mirror, another that it may be medieval. At Beith five shields were discovered in a bog, buried in a circular arrangement as though protecting something at the centre.

War-horns, known as *carnyxes*, have also been retrieved from watery places and a Scottish find at Deskford in Banffshire shows the instrument fashioned in the likeness of a boar's head. From its mouthpiece it had a long vertical tube to the boar-shaped bell and the whole length of the carnyx was S-shaped with the head rising 100 cm/40 ins or so above the player. When the Deskford instrument was first found in the 19th century, the wooden clapper or tongue was still in place and when blown it may have made a noise like a football rattle.

The Roman historian Diodorus Siculus noted: 'Their trumpets are of a peculiar kind: they blow into them and produce a harsh sound that suits the tumult of war', and Livy, another Roman, made a general point – one only alluded to by Tacitus at Mons Graupius. He wrote that before battle the Celts were in the habit of making a great deal of intimidatory noise: 'They are given to wild outbursts and they fill the air with hideous songs and varied cries.' And of the eastern Celtic tribes, Livy said, 'Their songs as they go into battle, their yells and leaping, and the dreadful noise of arms as they beat their shields in some ancestral custom – all this is done with one purpose: to terrify their enemies' – and also to encourage any fainthearts in their own ranks.

The composition of Celtic armies is difficult to discover. Late in the 1st millennium BC classical commentators such as Diodorus Siculus and Julius Caesar characterized Celtic society as broadly tripartite. The king and a warrior aristocracy sat at the apex of the pyramid while just below them lay a stratum of professionals: priests, smiths and other specialists. And near the base were the food-producers: farmers and stockmen. Right at the bottom were the unfree, slaves attached to the land or to wealthy households. The cadre of professional warriors nucleated around the king or a ruling family certainly made up the core of any fighting force, but it is impossible to say much more beyond that. At Mons Graupius Tacitus counted more than 30,000 in the Caledonian ranks, a much larger host than could be mustered from the aristocratic élite alone. There must have been a large contingent of farmers on the battlefield that day, armed with whatever they could turn to offensive purpose.

However, it is likely that the confrontation with the Roman legions in AD 83 was highly exceptional, a turning point of such overwhelming importance that it demanded the presence of all able to fight. As they had made their way north Agricola's army must have cut a destructive swathe through the countryside, foraging, looting and worse.

Everyday military encounters on matters of local concern were certainly much more modest in scale. Warbands in the early historic period were small, amounting to a few dozen men, and when the army of the Gododdin of Edinburgh rode south to fight the Angles in North Yorkshire in AD 600, only 300 cavalry warriors made up the host. These were the aristocratic professionals, the immediate retinue of the king, and even though each will have brought more men with him, the scale of the turnout was still far short of that at Mons Graupius. And to underline the relative modesty of military operations in that later period, an early entry in the Anglo-Saxon Chronicle defines an army as more than 30 men.

Craupian Television

The *Grampian* Mountains, *Grampian* Television, *Grampian* Region and *Grampian* anything else are all named after a misprint. Tacitus wrote of a battle fought on the 'Graupian Mountain', but some scholars argue, convincingly, that he mistranscribed the name. The Old Welsh word *crwb*, 'hump', is the derivation, and as a Latin-speaking writer Tacitus got it wrong, substituting a 'g' for a 'c'. The error was compounded in 1475–80 when Francisco dal Pozzo produced the first printed edition of the *Agricola*. In it *Graupius* was rendered as *Grampius*.

Julius Caesar labelled the professional warriors of Celtic society as *equites* or cavalry. It was the usual term used by the Romans for their own aristocracy, but its attachment to the Celts may not be a simple cultural transfer. Just as the ownership of warhorses defined a Roman *knight*, so this marked out the Celtic aristocracy as a different sort of fighter from the foot-soldier, one who could afford a horse to sit on.

The use of horses in warfare appears to be new, something which arrived in the west after the end of the 2nd millennium BC. From its origins in the steppes between the Black Sea and the Caspian, the technique of fighting on horseback seems to have moved westwards gradually, probably with the gift of well-schooled cavalry and chariot ponies. At around the same time tribes from the Caucasus were also in the process of migrating westwards and this may have nudged the transmission of ideas a little more urgently.

In the 7th century BC a new type of slashing sword with a long, narrow, heavy blade was introduced to Britain from Europe. Alongside these, items of horse-gear appear in the archaeological record and there is a palpable sense of this package arriving as an extended series of gifts from one aristocratic set to another. And horse-gear is of little value unless it is accompanied by horses and riders who know how to manoeuvre them in battle and can teach these skills to novices. This point may have marked the beginning of the long tradition of cavalry which stretched to the Celtic horsemen of the Dark Ages, the armoured knights of medieval chivalry and the dashing royalist swordsmen of Prince Rupert's campaigns in the 17th century. With these early gifts of horses, it seems that a knowledge of iron-working arrived in Britain at the same time, perhaps as part of the same cultural and mercantile package.

The change from bronze-working to iron in Britain was gradual. Just as the new technology arrived on the south coast of England, bronze was finally reaching the Shetland Islands. But its effect was revolutionary. Iron ore was far more readily available than copper or tin, and deposits could be found over most parts of the British Isles and Ireland. Bog-iron was also available in the west and the north. Items of iron, much harder than bronze, eventually grew more plentiful and were cheaper to produce.

However, the techniques of smelting and smithing were complicated and hard-learned. Because very high temperatures were needed at most stages of the process of making iron artefacts, charcoal had to be used. To attain a consistent intensity of heat, enclosed, clay-built smelters with flues were developed. But iron could be directly extracted from iron ore and many of the difficulties of working with an alloy were consigned to the past.

In the 7th century BC, smiths began work by *blooming*, extracting a 'bloom' of iron from the ore by smelting and discarding the slag, or impurities, as they went along. Once the bloom was sufficiently refined to be worked, they began to fashion it into artefacts by the process of smithing. After casting the molten metal in a clay mould and turning it out into roughly what was wanted, the smiths heated it to varying degrees and hammered it into shape. At high temperatures they could weld components together by beating them until the joints had fused. Or they could employ heat treatments. When iron is white-hot – at 880–900°C – and is then immediately quenched in cold water, it becomes very hard but slightly brittle. Gentle reheating or tempering releases the stress in the metal and makes it tougher and more durable. This was particularly important in the production of weapons, and with swords a skilled smith could hammer a cutting edge of fearsome sharpness.

The most famous Celtic smith was Culann, and his status was sufficiently high to allow him to invite a king and his court to sup with him. In an early part of the *Tain Bo Cuailgne*, Culann prepared a feast for King Conchobhar of Ulster and went to Emhain Macha (near Armagh) to invite him. On his way the king came across a small boy playing hurling and was so impressed by his prowess that he asked him to join the court at Culann's stronghold. After the boy had killed a fierce guard-dog he offered to replace it with himself, and thereby gained the name *Cuchulainn*, or the 'Hound of Culann'.

Whatever cultural changes rippled through Celtic society in Scotland in the middle of the 1st millennium BC, they would have moved from the top downwards. But the readier availability of iron ore must have spread the artefacts more quickly than in the period of bronze-working. Iron axes were sharper and harder and that fact alone would have made life easier. Evidence of the handiwork of Celtic carpenters can be detected in the landscape of the 1st millennium, for the sites of thousands of houses from that time have been discovered.

Almost all the houses were round, many were large and spacious and all were dark. They were also striking examples of early architecture and the usual description of *hut circles* attached to their archaeological remains scarcely does justice to what were complex and durable buildings. Timber roundhouses were well established in the 2nd millennium BC and their incidence increased in the early centuries of the 1st. In Sutherland alone more than 2,000 have been identified. At Kilphedir, near the east coast north of Brora, hut circles were unearthed which had diameters of 10–11 m/33–36 ft, very spacious rooms by any standard. And the skills and resources needed to build one were substantial. It has been calculated that 650 mature trees were used and that renovations took place over the life of the houses as timbers rotted and were replaced.

The shape of roundhouses was conical. The buildings at Kilphedir had an internal circle of posts which supported a thatched roof, but others were large-scale variations on a basic tipi design and the roof timbers were sometimes planted straight into the ground. Many of those roundhouses with internal posts used them as a means of supporting a first floor reached by a ladder and nestling under the narrowing cone of the thatch. Given the convection of heat, this may have been the most snug part of the house.

An internal ring of posts also had the effect of encouraging a radial arrangement inside the building, like the spokes of a wheel. A hearth lay at the centre and while a family sat by it to eat, keep warm and see more clearly what was going on, they probably retired for the night to sleeping bays around the curved walls of the house. It would have been a simple matter to screen off radial bays with wattle and daub partitions and make a compartment warm with fleeces and straw. Other bays might have supplied handy areas for storage, perhaps space for a family shrine, perhaps a place where animals could be penned, particularly in the depths of winter.

Weapons of choice

Archaeologists are never happier than when they are classifying objects. This is understandable because prehistory depends so heavily on objects and their interpretation. Two sorts of swords were important in early Celtic Britain and Ireland. The Ballintober sword is named after the Irish bog in which the first example was found. It is characterized as having a leaf-shaped blade, although it resembles few leaves found in nature. It looks more like a blade of grass thickened towards the point. This design appeared around 1200 BC and was the earliest weighted slashing sword. The Gundlingen sword was very popular in western Europe after the 7th century BC; it too was weighted in the blade and, when made in iron tempered like steel, could be extremely sharp.

Some roundhouses had high walls. At Kilphedir it appears that the rafters supporting the thatch rested on the wall-heads, as did the flooring for the upper storey. Around the edges of a roundhouse there usually ran a ditch for collecting rainwater run-off and this probably connected with a drain to take it away from the immediate environs of the site. In some locations where water was less easily available from a stream or river, the rainwater may have been collected. At all events these sorts of drainage arrangements were important in places where several houses clustered. If nothing had been done to mitigate the inevitable winter quagmires, it would have been impossible to keep clods of mud and worse out of the houses.

Another problem was light, or rather the lack of it. Roundhouses had no windows and an open door was the only source of daylight available. In the interests of keeping the structure weathertight and as draught-free as possible, all the other gaps will have been plugged. A fire in the central hearth provided illumination and rushlights must have been in continual use. Accidental fire was a constant danger, particularly in summer with a dry thatched roof. The gloom inside roundhouses encouraged their occupants outside whenever the season and the weather permitted. Work such as sewing and mending, requiring good light, was better done in the open air, and when the sun shone many families must have spent as much time as possible outside, going back into the house only to sleep.

The sites of roundhouses have survived more readily in upland areas used mainly for grazing and little cultivated, particularly in the modern period when developments of the swing-plough began to delve a deeper furrow and thereby destroy a great deal of archaeology. A variant known as a *ring-ditch house* became more noticeable after about 700 BC, many of them spotted on the flanks and in the valleys of the Cheviot Hills. The organization of the ground-floor area gave these houses their name. Instead of a hearth or any other traces of domesticity, the centre was a slightly raised, mounded area. Around it lay a circular ditch, often paved, sometimes as deep as 1.8 m/6 ft.

Ring-ditch houses were almost certainly used to overwinter cattle and a better label might be *byre-houses*. The paved ditch was sectioned into a series of stalls where cows could be tethered at night. Having been put out in the fields for the short days if the weather was not too severe, it was important that they were herded inside into a place where they did not have to stand up to their heels in mud. This can cause all sorts of diseases and difficulties for these valuable animals, the most bothersome being the bovine version of mud fever. And as in modern dairies, milkers wanted somewhere clean and reasonably flat to set their stools and buckets. A paved area also helped greatly with the collection of precious manure for the outside midden, even when it was frozen.

Some larger byre-houses had the capacity to overwinter 30 cows and the raised area in the centre could hold as much as 5 tonnes of hay and other fodder. It was important to tether the cows very securely to keep them from getting in amongst the feed store; perhaps that is why some of the ditches in byre-houses were so deep.

Above the cattle stalls the first floor housed the living area for their owners. And as attested by those who lived through the harshness of the winter under the same roof as their cattle until very recently, the heat from the beasts was welcome as it seeped up through the floor. There is indeed an ancient comfort from the company of milking cows as they snort clouds of warm breath into the night air, the wholesome smell of their dung mixing with the sweetness of the milk and their deep, bovine grunts as they move in the stalls, munching their hay, waiting for the morning to come.

Some byre-houses may have been used solely for cattle or the separate storage of precious feed. In the beautiful Bowmont Valley, which winds south into the Cheviot Hills, clusters of these buildings were arranged on either side of a paved street inside a palisaded enclosure. And elsewhere they are found inside the perimeter of early hillforts. At Culhawk Hill in Angus a huge byre-house has been recently excavated. Measuring 20 m/66 ft in diameter and standing 10 m/33 ft high, it was more a hall than a house and its location on an exposed hilltop overlooking the plains of Strathmore implies that it was the home of a powerful man.

Other events in the 1st millennium BC point to the existence and activities of powerful men, and probably powerful women. Around 250 BC the Celtic kings on either side of the Cheviots ordered populations to move, to gather up their belongings and go up-country to create new areas for more intensive farming. Probably as a consequence of population pressure in the Tweed Basin, around the Solway Firth and the valley of the North Tyne and the Hexham Gap, farmers suddenly migrated to areas previously used mainly for grazing and began to cultivate new ground. Pollen cores dating to about 250 BC show a dramatic phase of rapid woodland clearance. Hefting iron axes, the incomers hacked down the wiry trees from the slopes of the watershed valleys and laid out boundaries on their flat floodplains to establish new farms. It soon became apparent that soil erosion was to be a continuing difficulty and rain washed much of the slackened topsoil down to the valley bottoms.

This is very evident in the Bowmont Valley, where the eroded soils have piled up into river terraces. Also evident may be the organization of this sudden invasion. Along the length of the Bowmont Water the ancient royal shire of Yetholm can still be traced. Thirteen farms of great antiquity lie along its banks and some have the remains of cultivation terraces from the 1st millennium BC. Sourhope, Clifton, Shotton and Mindrum are all still farmed and several others have either grown into the village of Yetholm or have been absorbed by other holdings. But the shape of the old royal shire is still clear and in AD 655 it was the personal domain of King Oswy of Northumbria when he gave it to the Bishops of Lindisfarne. Before Oswy came to own it, Yetholmshire had been organized as a *maenor*, an early Celtic version of a shire. It was a royal possession, probably the property of the Gododdin kings who lost the Tweed Basin to the Angles in the 7th century. It may well be that the initiative ordered by a central authority in around 250 BC resulted in the creation of a royal agricultural holding, the ghost of which can still be seen on the landscape. Yetholmshire passed from the hands of the Bishops of Lindisfarne to their successors at Durham before falling into the ownership of the Abbots of Kelso. When the border between England and Scotland hardened in the Middle Ages, only then did the old shire lose its shape.

Aerial photography of cropmarks shows a new density of settlement over wide swathes of lowland Scotland. And in addition to the tell-tale circles of roundhouses, traces of another, somewhat enigmatic set of buildings can often be made out. Souterrains were exactly what the name translates as, underground structures usually attached to the remains of roundhouses. Paved, walled and roofed, these low passageways resemble the long entrances to earlier tombs. But their function appears to be more utilitarian. Essentially souterrains were cellars where food could be safely stored in cool, dry, dark conditions. Grain, meat and especially dairy products could be preserved for a long time if sealed in large pottery containers to keep rodents at bay.

The earliest example of a souterrain was found at Dalladies in Aberdeenshire and it dated from the 3rd century BC. Most occur in the north-east of Scotland, in Angus, Aberdeenshire, Sutherland, Caithness and Orkney. What the appearance of these storage cellars means is something straightforward. There was something to store. So many exist in Angus, for example, that there must have been a surplus of food production which required regular storage in cellars built for that purpose. The roundhouses to which souterrains are attached may be seen as the homes of pre-eminent people, those to whom food renders were given, at least in the first instance, and who ingathered and accounted corn, meat, cheese and other agricultural products from farmers who owed it.

Clearly a substantial political power sent men and women into the Cheviots and elsewhere to create new farms and that power required local organization for it to work, for there to be an exchange of protection by a warrior élite in return for food. Kings sat in authority over aristocracies, who in turn depended on lesser people to superintend the local renders owed to them. It is too much to claim that the souterrains are the tangible remains of a nascent Celtic maenor system in the 3rd century AD or even earlier, but they are the remains of an organization of some sort. And what was stored in them may not necessarily have been surpluses but taxation in kind.

As with every aspect of life, the siting of prehistoric souterrains below ground had a spiritual significance. The peoples of the north had been returning their possessions to the earth for millennia, and perhaps by digging out and walling these cellars they felt they were entrusting the bounty of the land back into it for safe-keeping, and maybe also as a mark of understanding and respect. There should be nothing to surprise us in this, since houses themselves had long enshrined all sorts of rituals. The doorways of most roundhouses were oriented to the east or the south-east, the direction of the rising sun, the morning light and therefore the light of renewal. Deposits of objects and bones in house doorways, in floors and in walls also give a sense of a prehistoric boundary between the domestic and the outside, the security of a family around the flicker of the hearth compared to the dark dangers of what lay beyond the walls.

Perhaps the most enigmatic prehistoric houses of all those found in Scotland are *crannogs*. The name is a Gaelic word and simply means 'a wooden structure'; it makes no reference to why the buildings themselves were remarkable. Crannogs were roundhouses built on artificial islands specifically created for them by the shores of lochs. They are unique to Scotland and Ireland and the remains of hundreds of them survive. When 19th-century drainage schemes lowered the levels of some lochs many were uncovered, and improvements in the techniques of underwater archaeology have identified dozens more.

Reindeer jockeys

Before men domesticated horses, they tamed, trained and rode reindeer. Archaeological evidence from northern Russia indicates that reindeer were pulling sledges around 5000 BC. When the climate warmed after the last Ice Age and the herds began to migrate north, a substantial pocket remained in southern latitudes. The Sayan Mountains of Mongolia rise to over 1,800 m/6,000 ft and over wide areas sustain the sort of grazing of which reindeer are fond. This remote place was also the cradle of the first horse cultures and it looks as though the Mongols learned many of their equestrian skills on the backs of deer. Easily domesticated, able to survive in extreme weather and also substantial, strong animals, reindeer were attractive to stock-rearers. The motivation to ride them came from a need to control the herd. A man on foot would soon become useless, whereas a man on a leading reindeer could make the others follow him and his mount. But when they began to migrate north, and the remaining deer proved too few, the Mongols transferred their technology and skills to horses and began to manage them in herds. When the Russians excavated the prehistoric tombs at Pazyryk high in the Altai Mountains of western Siberia, they came across horse burials. One of the first wore a *chamfron*, an equestrian face-mask, and it was formed like a reindeer head, horns and all. It proved to be a persistent tradition. Horned horses are depicted on the Gundestrup cauldron of 1st-millennium BC Denmark and on a set of fire-dogs from the same period found in Wales; on a chamfron from Torrs in Kirkcudbrightshire two horns were added which would have made the pony look just like a reindeer.

Great labour was involved in the construction of a crannog. Before a house could be raised an island had to be formed near the edge of a loch, presumably where it was not too deep. Piles were driven down into the bed or stones heaped together to make a level foundation on which a house platform could sit. At Milton Loch in Galloway the construction gang opted to set a raft of long logs on top of a bed of thick mud which wobbled when the 20th-century excavators jumped on it. But the decision to build on the mud proved to be sound, since the remains stayed in place for more than two millennia. When the log platform was thought to be secure, a causeway was added and on the other side of the house, facing out into the loch, two small, curved jetties were set so that dugout canoes could be moored at a safe distance from the shore. If anyone wanted to steal them or use them to reach the crannog, they would have had to cross the causeway and pass the house first.

Because of the waterlogged conditions, excavations at crannogs have turned up many wooden objects: bowls, buckets, barrels, boxes, the sort of thing that rarely survives on land-based sites. But what has never been fully explained is the answer to an obvious question: why were such labour-intensive structures built on such difficult sites? Why were they not raised on the shores of the loch? Certainly crannogs set well out from the lochside seem defended by water, but a determined attacker with a boat or bow and arrow could quickly have overcome that obstacle. It has been argued that stock housed in crannogs were better protected from predators, both animal and human, but again a palisaded enclosure worked well elsewhere and was much easier to build than a crannog. Answers may lie in less concrete rather than practical considerations.

There are 20 crannogs so far discovered in Loch Awe and 15 in Loch Tay. Both of these are long lochs and have high mountains on either side. For any powerful person wishing to build their house in a dominant, visible place, the water may have represented the best choice. Lochsides have an amphitheatrical quality and a house placed in the water is singular, dramatic and could have been seen from many vantage points. In addition the sheer difficulty, the conspicuous consumption of labour in creating a new piece of land, raising the island up out of the water to make a crannog, may in itself have been attractive for a leading member of a community. It should also not be forgotten that communication between crannogs must have been easy and quick (and builders of a modern crannog have found it to be completely free of midges). And finally there is the water itself, a liminal, spiritually charged place for a person to be, living in a house at the end of the sort of jetty used for the sacrifice of objects to the gods. If, as seems likely, even small-scale potentates associated themselves with the divine, that positioning will have seemed more than symbolic. Crannogs on the edge of the loch may have been seen as sitting at the edge of the world of men and close to the world of gods.

Many of these remarkable structures proved durable and, from their inception between 1200 and 700 BC, were used well into the historic period. In 1746 fleeing Jacobites were said to have taken refuge in crannogs.

In the Western Isles and in Shetland a stone-built variant on the timber roundhouse came into use in the late 1st millennium BC. Because of their radial groundplan these were known as wheelhouses and many were built into sand-dunes for insulation. From the outside they looked slight, since all that showed above ground was a small conical thatched roof. But inside they were both snug and spacious, the roof height allowing plenty of headroom. As with other types of house, the builders buried offerings of various sorts in the floors and walls as they went along. Sometimes great trouble was taken. In the wheelhouse at Sollas in North Uist, approximately 150 pits had been dug in the floor for the deposit of offerings, and if a ceremony accompanied each one then the business of building must have been an elaborate, very considered process, and not just something done as rapidly as possible to keep the weather out and accommodate the occupants quickly. Everything meant something to these masons. At Cnip on Lewis the body of a 12-year-old boy who suffered from *spina bifida* had been cut into quarters and buried. This may have been a human sacrifice to sanctify a new house, although there is some evidence that the corpse was not fresh when buried.

The names of the individuals who butchered the handicapped boy are of course unknown, but how they described where they lived may be less elusive. Using earlier sources, the Greek geographer Ptolemy compiled a detailed map of Britain and Ireland in the 2nd century AD. While it contains a great deal of very valuable information, shedding a first light on how our ancestors saw where they lived, the map itself is badly distorted. Ptolemy has turned Scotland north of the Tay through 90 degrees so that Britain bends suddenly to the east instead of running broadly north/south. The Greeks believed that in the far north people could not survive in latitudes beyond 63 degrees. If Ptolemy had drawn Britain as it is, then most of Scotland would have exceeded that latitude and extended as far as an impossible 66 degrees north.

That quirk aside, the map of the north supplies the first gazetteer of names, a very early sense of how people identified themselves. Ptolemy notes the names of seventeen tribes, seventeen rivers, sixteen towns or settlements, ten islands, seven capes, three bays and four other places. By no means all of these are intelligible and the map may contain more mistakes than the orientation of the north. Ptolemy had never visited Britain and, like most Mediterranean geographers, he depended on the accounts of others, many of these second-hand, for his information. But the names are almost all Celtic in origin, perhaps altered or badly transcribed but not conferred by outsiders, and certainly the first historical echo of what the early peoples of Scotland said. For these names were surely uttered in common speech.

Aebudae Insulae appears on the map above two islands each labelled with the singular version of the name. They float, out of scale, to the north of Ireland and the double use might refer to one of the pairs of islands in the southern Hebrides such as Coll and Tiree or Islay and Jura. *Aebudae* is the ghost-name of *Hebrides* and the *r* seems to have intruded as a later scribal error. But what it means is shrouded in mist. The great toponymic scholar W.J. Watson believed *Aebudae* to be very ancient, probably pre-Celtic in origin. Other island names are much clearer. *Malaios Insula* is Mull and presumably, as reference to the dominating presence of its mountains, it means 'Lofty Isle'. *Dumna* finds itself far out to sea on Ptolemy's map and is a name with some pedigree, having first been noted by Pliny. It is a Celtic word from a root meaning 'deep', and if translated as 'the Deep-Sea Island', it probably refers to the string of the Outer Hebrides, from the Butt of Lewis down to the Isle of Barra.

Some of the other place-names are descriptive in a similar way but a few offer a sense of the importance of a place and its function. Near modern Stranraer, at the southern end of Loch Ryan, Ptolemy places *Rerigonium*. It means 'very royal place', and that description finds corroboration in an interesting source. The very early poetry known as the Welsh Triads sang of three national thrones of Britain, all of them in the far west and probably pushed in that direction by the success of the Germanic invasions of the 5th and 6th centuries AD. The Triads set these centres of power at Gelliwig in Cornwall, Caerleon in South Wales and Penrhyn Rhionydd somewhere in the north. If Ptolemy's name of *Rerigonium* was to be rendered in Old Welsh, it would be written exactly as *Rhionydd*. The *Penrhyn* element probably refers to the peninsula that makes up the western shore of Loch Ryan. Indeed the name *Ryan* is also cognate to *Rhionydd*. But, more importantly, the palace, the very royal place, lay near at hand.

Not far from Stranraer an archaeological dig at the village of Dunragit turned up Roman coins and artefacts at the remains of an enclosure. *Dunragit* was originally spelled *Dun-Rheged*, the Fort of the Dark Ages kingdom of Rheged which, at its greatest extent, stretched east to the head of the Solway and probably encompassed much of Cumbria and northern Lancashire. In the 6th century AD the most successful Celtic king in Britain was Urien of Rheged, someone well known to the bards who composed the Triads. Urien held several fortresses along the Solway and one of the oldest was at Dunragit. If the modern – and ancient – name of the village contains a remnant of *Rerigonium*, then it shows a continuity which may have reached back into the early part of the 1st millennium BC. And the cropmark of a great wooden henge, together with a burial mound larger than Maes Howe, pushes the antiquity of this site even further back. Powerful, widely-landed kings may have sat at Dunragit and ordered their aristocracy to move some of their farmers off their overcrowded lowland holdings and into the hills to break new ground. Further to the east, the name of one of these early kings may have survived. Ptolemy mistranscribes *Otadini* for the *Votadini*, a people who occupied the Lothians and probably the Tweed Basin. The name means 'the supporters of Fothad', almost certainly the name of a king, perhaps the founder of a dynasty, a personage seen as semi-divine.

Not on Ptolemy's map but listed in a slightly later gazetteer of place-names in Roman Britain is *Medionemeton*. It means 'the Middle Shrine' and was to be found on or near the line of the Antonine Wall. The location and the description both fit Cairnpapple Hill well. Not only does it occupy a panoramic site with long views in all directions across the middle of Scotland, there are also four rock-cut early Christian tombs to the east of the old henge and the later cairns. Again this demonstrates an immense continuity of sanctity stretching over more than three millennia. And the name *Medionemeton* or *Middle Shrine* implies a pre-eminence still understood and accepted in the Roman period.

On Ptolemy's map *Carbantorigum* is plotted somewhere on the western edges of the Tweed/Clyde/Annan watershed, just beyond the

territory of the *Selgovae* or 'Hunters' who controlled the area that ultimately became the Ettrick Forest. The name appears to refer to an
event, for *Carbantorigum* means 'the Slope of the Chariots', probably a
prehistoric battle-site and possibly smoothed out into *Carby Hill* near
Newcastleton in Liddesdale. Given its location on the cusp of the tribal
territories of the Selgovae and the *Novantae* ('the Vigorous People'), it may
commemorate a battle between them some time in the 1st millennium BC.

The map identifies two places, one as *Coria* in the territory of the
tribe known as the *Damnonii*, and the other as *Curia* in the area of
the Votadini. This is not a case of repetition because they both mean
the same thing. *Curia* is a 'hosting-place' where armies mustered and the
Damnonian variant (this name means 'the Deepeners' or more clearly
'the Miners' and it may refer to the extraction of both coal and iron) lies
somewhere in the Clyde Valley. The muster-point of the Votadini is well
north of *Trimontium*, the Roman name for their fortress at the foot of
Eildon Hill North, and all the indications are that it was at Traprain Law
in East Lothian (see plate XIII).

All of Ptolemy's names are interesting, even those whose meanings
are obscure. Almost all the place-names are Celtic and cognate to either
early Welsh or early Irish forms and they confirm something straightforward, that the Romans came upon a culture that spoke a series of
dialects of a common Celtic language for many generations, possibly
as far back as the 2nd millennium BC.

One of the most famous of these Celtic names has endured until the
present day and it certainly dates from approximately 500 years before
Ptolemy's map. When the Massaliot Greek Pytheas sailed around the top
of Britain in 325 BC, he noted what he called *Cape Orcas* or 'Boar Head'.
This is probably equivalent to Dunnet Head, which lies to the south
of what Pytheas knew as the *Orcades*, 'the Islands of the Boar People'.
Totemism appears to have been widespread in the north and when
Ptolemy attaches *Orcas* to Dunnet Head, he also supplies an alternative
name. *Tarvedunum* means 'Bull Fort' and may refer to a coastal fortification now obscure. But the association was persistent. When the Viking

dragon-ships made landfall near Dunnet Head in the 9th century AD, they named their harbour as *Thurso*, which translates as 'Bull's Water'. There is an alternative possibility. Ptolemy's name had passed through several pairs of hands and may have become radically misplaced in the process of transmission. At Burghead, an important Pictish naval base on the southern shore of the Moray Firth, 30 carvings of bulls were found (only six now survive). Perhaps it was *Tarvedunum*, the 'Bull Fort'.

By the close of the 1st millennium BC the Boar People of Orkney, the Shetlanders (one of the earliest names of the islands was *Innse Catt*, the 'Cat Islands') and the southern Cat People of Caithness and Sutherland formed a cultural, and possibly political, unit. Along with some parts of the Hebrides, they began to build the architectural phenomenon known as the *broch*. These tall, tapering towers of drystone are unique to Scotland, and, indeed, outside of the north, only a handful were built elsewhere. Before stone-built castles and towers appeared in the early Middle Ages, brochs must have been the most impressive man-made structures in the landscape.

Raven banner

At the Battle of Clontarf in 1014 two armies faced each other on ground now covered by Dublin's streets. On one side was the Irish host of Brian Boru, on the other a coalition of Viking warbands. And with the latter stood Sigurd the Stout, Earl of Orkney. He had been given a war banner by his mother. The compiler of the Icelandic saga which recounted the story of the battle sang that 'it was a finely made banner, very cleverly embroidered with the figure of a raven, and when the banner fluttered in the breeze, the raven seemed to be flying ahead'. The saga muttered that Sigurd's mother was a sorceress, and when she made the banner she used all of her magical arts. 'My belief is this,' she said, 'that it will bring victory to the man it is carried before, but death to the one who carried it.' And so of course it proved. While Sigurd's standard-bearers fell in battle, he triumphed. But at Clontarf no one would take up the raven banner when its bearer was killed, not surprisingly, and Sigurd himself was forced to do it. To avoid the consequences of the curse, he ripped the pennant off its pole and stuffed it into his jerkin. And then he was killed 'with a spear through him'. The banner was very important, a powerful symbol which needed to be preserved and often defended to the last. Perhaps the power was all the greater because it was ancient. The Viking earls of Orkney controlled parts of Caithness and Sutherland. It may be that they had taken over the totem bird of the Lugi, the Raven People.

Prototypes for the earliest brochs probably originated in Skye but the technology quickly spread north and eastwards. Essentially these remarkable towers can be seen as a development from a traditional roundhouse in an area where timber had long been scarce. At Midhowe on Orkney a modern excavation of a broch has shown the sequence of change. Over an old village and an even older chambered tomb, a roundhouse was built some time around 400 BC. Two centuries later this was dismantled and a second roundhouse constructed. This had stone walls of tremendous thickness and may have itself formed a proto-broch. Some time later this was in turn replaced by a thoroughly recognizable broch tower and surrounded by a small group of stone-built houses connected by alleyways. This was a broch-village and 20 have so far been discovered on Orkney.

On Shetland the near-complete broch at Mousa stands to a height of 13 m/43 ft but may have been untypically tall. Single stone steps known as scarcements can still be seen on the inside of the upper walls of most brochs and these were used to support a first floor of wooden joists and a living area. The ground-floor area was often unlevel – at Dun Carloway there is even a stone outcrop (see plate XIV). Perhaps in the same way as ring-ditch houses, the ground floors of brochs may have been winter housing for beasts. But other examples on Orkney and Shetland show clear signs of permanent human occupation on the ground floor. No roofs have of course survived, but, like those on roundhouses, they may have had a conical shape and been made from thatch. Access to the upper floors was by a stone staircase set into the wall, and, as at Mousa, this was usually constructed between an outer and an inner skin of masonry.

It used to be thought that a series of vertical voids in the walls was a method of relieving the great weight of drystone building and avoiding the danger of collapse over entrances. But it is much more likely that it was part of a system of central heating. Brochs were usually built on exposed locations, many by the seashore, and they had outer and inner walls to ensure that wind-driven rain did not penetrate to the living area. The voids were inserted to draw in warm air generated by the central hearth and circulate it between the outer and inner skins, thereby providing good insulation. In many brochs the area between the walls, often called a gallery, is built in only at first-floor level whereas the wall from ground-level up is solid. This arrangement reinforces the notion that beasts were overwintered on the ground floor and the living quarters were above them.

While their sheer and massive windowless walls give brochs a formidable look, that was probably all that was intended. Like the early hilltop forts and the large roundhouses, they were built to impress and not designed as efficient defensive sanctuaries. Like the Border peel towers they could withstand a foray but not a siege. And it is by no means certain that brochs had a wall-walk at the top, a place where defenders might hurl javelins, fire arrows or slingshots. What seems to have been much more important was handy access to good agricultural land, and on Shetland almost all the brochs are close to pasture.

The general conformity of design and the comparatively short period in which Scotland's brochs were built suggest that their construction was a job done by specialists. It may be that gangs of itinerant masons travelled between the islands and the mainland, consulting with the local grandees on what quickly became a fashionable form of prehistoric architecture. The economic circumstances around this sort of transaction are interesting. Not only does the spread of broch-building imply good and regular communications, it also implies an economy which could pay construction workers rather than dragoon them. Digging out the ditch around a fort could have been the work of those who spent most of their time on agriculture. They already had the tools and the muscles. But the engineering and masonry skills needed to raise a broch speak clearly of specialists. Who were they? How were they paid? Whatever they received, it probably had to be portable. However all that may be, the broch does symbolize something obvious – wealth and the power to spend it. Stock-rearing and farming in the north were clearly lucrative enough to provide an aristocracy with its architecture of choice.

Gurness is impressive, both from the landward and seaward aspects. Standing on the mainland coast of Orkney, overlooking Eynhallow Sound and the island of Rousay, it is surrounded by a broch-village which seems to huddle at the foot of the central tower. Bounded by a ditch on three sides and the sea on the fourth, the site is like a miniature fort, and when a visitor approaches the entrance, a narrow avenue leads directly to the porch attached to the doorway of the broch. Everything at Gurness suggests hierarchy and the power of whoever lived at its centre. The broch dominated the lives of the lesser people who lived in the houses around it. They would have owed obedience, labour and perhaps some sort of religious obeisance to the principal family and its head. Although it is not large, Gurness village is in every sense commanding, and if the finds of Roman amphorae do identify it as the residence of the king who sailed to Colchester to offer submission to the Emperor Claudius in AD 43, then no one should be surprised. The broch-village is not the rude habitation of the ruler of a primitive people subsisting on the edge of the world, but a place with presence and an air of sophistication.

7

Caledonia

In the preface to his bestselling *A History of England*, published in 1911 for schoolchildren, C.R.L. Fletcher offered a concise example of a common historical prejudice: 'It was, however, a misfortune for Britain that Rome never conquered the whole island. The great warrior Agricola did penetrate far into Scotland but he could leave no trace of civilization behind him, and Ireland he never touched at all.' Fletcher went on to mention that with the arrival of the Romans the native tribes at last appeared in written history, but 'I will not even tell you the Latinized forms of their barbarous names.'

We may smile at this, dismiss it as outdated, and even excuse it as a piece of unpleasant ignorance written in the long Edwardian evening of the British Empire. But the uncomfortable truth is that Fletcher's values are still very much alive, and they occasionally surface in respectable modern Scottish historiography. Here is a passage from a pocket guide to the Antonine Wall published in 1979 and written by Professor Anne Robertson of Glasgow University. Referring to the invasion of the north by the army of the governor of Britannia, Lollius Urbicus, some time after AD 139, she notes: 'The troublesome North Britons were forced back into their own mountains, and a penetrative road, guarded by forts, was driven far into Perthshire. The irreconcilable elements in S.W. Scotland were kept in check by a network of roads, forts and fortlets, probably linked with a harbour on the Solway.' And later, when Professor Robertson gets down to details, her identification with the Roman cause seems complete. In describing the sculpture on a distance slab found near the Antonine Wall, she writes: 'On the left side is the figure of a Roman cavalryman riding over four barbarians.'

There are many other, less blatant examples of this sort of thing to be found in the literature dealing with the north in the period from AD 43 to 410, and the cumulative effect is extraordinary. Rarely has an invasion by foreign armies and all its attendant waste and slaughter been so eagerly celebrated by the descendants of the peoples, indeed the 'barbarians', who suffered it. The historical fact is that the Romans were, as usual, utterly ruthless in pursuit of their own interests, occasionally adopting genocide as imperial policy, ordering their soldiers to kill on sight any man, woman or child they came upon while campaigning in the north. In the famous series of letters discovered at the Roman fort of Vindolanda, near Hadrian's Wall, casual mention is made of the *Brittunculi*, meaning 'the nasty little Brits'. It is a short step to *Untermenschen*, and one which many colonizers have made, including the British themselves.

The reality is that the Romans came to what is now Scotland, they saw, they burned, killed, stole and occasionally conquered, and then they left a tremendous mess behind them, clearing away native settlements and covering good farmland with the remains of ditches, banks, roads and other sorts of ancient military debris. Like most imperialists they arrived to make money, to gain political prestige and to exploit the resources of their colonies at virtually any price to the conquered. And, remarkably, in Britain, in Scotland, we continue to admire them for it.

Why? The Romans left us nothing of any enduring cultural value. Their presence in Scotland was brief, intermittent and not influential on the course of our history. Away from the remains of their forts and roads, finds of Roman objects are sparse, particularly to the north of the Forth/Clyde line, and it is really only in the Borders, in the long shadow of Hadrian's Wall, that any great range of archaeology has turned up in the countryside. That is only to be expected. North Britain was always run as a military zone, and while inside the walls of the forts and camps a good deal can be found, there is understandably little evidence of anything approaching a Roman way of life beyond them. To the native peoples the soldiers in their forts remained alien, perhaps more than literally incomprehensible.

By contrast, in what became France and Spain, the experience of the Empire was important. Despite the long period of invasion and turbulence that followed the departure or breakdown of the Roman administration, French and Spanish developed out of the dialects of Latin spoken over 400 years of occupation and many of the civic institutions from that period were adapted by subsequent regimes. But in Britain the Celtic society suppressed by the Romans re-emerged virtually intact after the collapse of the Western Empire at the beginning of the 5th century. Only Christianity may be claimed as something the Romans gave us, but it can scarcely be described as originating with them. The Christian soldiers, administrators and merchants were only the western conduits of the word of God, formulated in a small Roman province.

So why do historians in particular identify with these early invaders and colonial exploiters of Britain and Scotland? One obvious answer is because they wrote things down which have survived. When first Julius Caesar and later the Emperor Claudius took armies across the Channel, it seemed that a sudden, bright Mediterranean light illuminated the pre-historic darkness. Conjecture could at last be replaced by confident assertion based on documentary fact, or at least facts as they were understood in Latin, reported at some distance from the action, and dependent on second-hand partiality and hearsay. Names and identifiable people at last appeared in the British landscape, even if almost all of them were Romans, military and men. The proper stuff of history became available – definite incidents which took place on certain dates in certain locations for certain reasons. Archaeology turned up rectilinear stone foundations which closely resembled other rectilinear stone foundations dug up elsewhere in the Empire, and this allowed clear functions to be ascribed – a bathhouse, a barracks, a temple, a headquarters building. After millennia of blundering about in the primal darkness chasing shadows, clear pictures of our past could be made out after 55 BC and AD 43. And even if they were pictures painted by foreigners and not the natives, at least they allowed our history to acquire some shape, at last. Simple gratitude has a role to play in placing many historians in the ranks of the legions.

So does cultural inclination. The film *Gladiator* opens with a battle scene on the frontiers of the Empire, the Surrey pinewoods doubling as the German forests. Ranks of Roman soldiers wait quietly in formation; the general moves up and down the line dourly exhorting his fellow professionals to do their job. All is organized, in deadly readiness. And then out of the forest explodes a charging, fur-covered rabble of barbarians led by an enormous bearded man with an axe. Roman discipline makes short but cinematically spectacular work of the nameless savages and the audience, normally right behind the underdog, exhales with relief. Like so many historians, they too are for the Romans. For once they want the overdogs to win. Why?

Because the Roman Empire represents Civilization holding the line against Barbarity, Light prevailing over Darkness. When we look at a map of Roman Europe as it was at the end of the 2nd century AD, we see a Mediterranean world of order, trade, wine and sunshine. And to the north lies the long and fragile line on the Rhine/Danube, keeping the darkness at bay. When the western half of the Empire fell in the 5th century, it was followed by the Dark Ages and the chaotic rule of fur-clad men with beards and axes. Despite the undoubted facts of barbarity, corruption and ruthlessness on the southern side of the line, we are all instinctive Romanophiles when it comes to the battles in the deep, dark forest.

We also know much more about them. Until recently our curricula (an apposite Latin borrowing) and examination systems were devised by people whose education had been based on Roman and Greek principles. University entrance insisted on a knowledge of Latin, and up to the 1970s anyone wishing to matriculate at a Scottish university had to acquire a certificate (and pay 10/6d for it) known as the 'Attestation of Fitness'. Unless applicants had gained a pass in O-Grade Latin (and Mathematics), the certificate was withheld. There was no need or obligation to pass, as an outsider might expect, an O-Grade in Gaelic, a living language native to Scotland, but rather in Latin, a dead language spoken by the soldiers and commanders who had ordered the slaughter of 10,000 of our ancestors at the battle at Mons Graupius in AD 83. The scandalous truth is that our education system has supplied us with a great deal more information about the Romans and Greeks than about our own Celtic past. And what is more, older generations can decline *amo*, *amas*, *amat*, and understand that a table is feminine, but they cannot work out how to pronounce the Gaelic names of half of Scotland's geography. It is nothing less than a national disgrace.

C.R.L. Fletcher was writing in 1911 for schoolchildren who routinely studied a globe liberally splashed with patches of red. Even greater than the Roman Empire (the sun did set on that), the British Empire coloured their world picture very vividly. Its existence not only fostered attitudes of condescension, at best, it also installed the British as Roman sympathizers. Like them, our own imperial governors had trouble with 'restless natives', the 'wogs', the 'fuzzy-wuzzies' and the rest. Even if some of the most troublesome to Rome were actually nasty little Brits, it didn't matter. They weren't really like us at all, they existed on the other side of the historical tracks. The chaps we understood were patrolling the ramparts of the Antonine Wall, scanning the northern horizon for signs of unrest. And as far as the irreconcilable elements skulking in the Ochil Hills across the valley were concerned, well, we don't know much about them. And what we do know, the Romans told us.

However, the picture is not entirely distorted and what the Romans did to us and what they wrote about it can be very useful. Some of this written information can be turned through 180 degrees to serve the purposes of native history, surely the most important facet of Scottish history. Often, what the Romans did was a reaction, a counter-measure against rebellion or a response to co-operation. It is possible occasionally to reverse the telescope and use what the Empire reported as a way of understanding something of the politics and culture of the north of Britain in the four centuries between AD 80 and 410.

Flat roofs

British kings in the south were sometimes over-enthusiastic Roman clients. Togidubnus of the Regenses (meaning 'the people ruled by a king') renamed himself Tiberius Claudius Togidubnus and awarded himself the grand title of 'Great King of Britain'. One of his rewards for collaboration may have been the huge palace built at Fishbourne in Sussex. It was a glittering contrast with the dingy and dark roundhouses of the native tradition. Real Roman architecture compared with a mean hut! Light shone everywhere, colourful mosaics decorated the floor and frescoes covered many of the plastered walls. There was a colonnaded garden and large staterooms, and it appears that craftsmen were brought to Britain to do the work. But it turned out not to be comfortable. For a Mediterranean climate the design was fine, but in the winter Fishbourne Palace was freezing. The big, flat-ceilinged rooms were difficult to heat and archaeologists have found scorchmarks where braziers were placed. Some even warped the beautiful, cold mosaic floor. How Togidubnus' servants must have longed for a snug and cosy old roundhouse.

Generals need maps. And when the governor of the province of Britannia, Petilius Cerialis, first led his legions into Scotland some time between AD 71 and 74, he needed to know where he was going. By the simple expedient of asking people who had been there, Roman military intelligence officers would have acquired a rudimentary grasp of the geography of the north, and probably also a good deal of detail about what lay immediately beyond. From Pytheas' *On the Ocean*, copies of which still survived in the 1st century AD, Petilius Cerialis' planners knew that Britain was an island. From the submission of the Orcadian king at Colchester in AD 43, they also knew that smaller islands lay in the Ocean to the north of Britannia, and probably that a scatter of other islands was to be found to the west. The prime question for Cerialis was one of distance. His Emperor, Vespasian, had fought in Britain himself as a military tribune, and it seems that he had instructed both Cerialis and his immediate predecessor, Marcus Vettius Bolanus, to incorporate the whole island into the Empire. But even though the approximate shape of Britain was understood, were Pytheas' measurements accurate? How far did Cerialis need to go to conquer the whole island? How many campaigning seasons would it take? What should be the role of the Roman fleet, the *Classis Britannica*? All of these questions were answered, at least in part, as time went on, but first the Romans had to adopt a strategy, and as they approached Scotland they developed an effective one.

In the north of England the kingdom of the Brigantes was the most powerful and populous in the province. Cerialis adopted the classical strategy of 'divide and conquer', separating the main concentrations of native forces in the Pennines from their allies, the Carvetii in Cumbria and the Eden Valley, and from the Parisii in eastern Yorkshire. Using fortified roads (*limes*, *limitis* in Latin, hence 'limit') he drove wedges between the northern confederacy and subdued each in turn, establishing forts at Carlisle in the west and Corbridge in the east.

Stades

Roman measurement was different from ours and Greek measurement was different again. When Pytheas circumnavigated Britain he kept a record of the distance his ship travelled every day. This must have been very difficult, involving calculations of sailing time, the relative strength of the tides and winds, and his assessment of how far north or south he had moved, working this out by estimating the height of the sun at noon. The Greeks reckoned distance in stades, a unit of 125 paces or 185 m/202 yds in modern measurement (although this seems a bit long). But the stade was not uniform all over Greece. The Attic or Athenian stade was a little shorter (perhaps Athenians were too) and it worked out at 177.6 m/194 yds. Anyway, Pytheas added up all his estimates and wrote in *On the Ocean* that Britain was 40,000 stades in circumference. If he used the standard stade then that comes to 7,400 km, or, with the Attic stade, 7,100 km. Amazingly, Pytheas was not far wrong. The total length of Britain's coastline is 7,580 km/4,710 miles.

Before mounting an advance into Scotland, the governor would have despatched armed patrols to reconnoitre the planned route. And diplomats and translators would have accompanied them where appropriate.

Gifts and assurances were certainly given to the Votadini of the Tweed Basin and East Lothian, because it is clear that they became early Roman clients. Very scant traces of Roman activity have been found in their territory; east of the line of the A68 no forts have yet been discovered in Berwickshire or East Lothian, no roads through the Lammermuir Hills, and the only signs of regular contact are traces of luxury goods. At one of the very few brochs built to the south of the Highland line, at Edin's Hall in Berwickshire, archaeologists have found Roman pottery, glass and metalwork. As a monument to conspicuous – and fashionable – consumption, the lowland brochs were commissioned by the aristocracy, precisely the people whose hearts, minds and stomachs had to be seduced by Roman diplomacy. The only substantial intrusion in the south-east is a Roman road known as the 'Devil's Causeway' leading from the fort at Corbridge to Berwick-upon-Tweed. The remains of the Roman supply port at the mouth of the river are probably irretrievably buried under the modern town.

Where archaeology does exist, it is very instructive about native politics. If the Votadini were friendly to Rome, it was undoubtedly in pursuit of their own regional interests. The pattern of Cerialis' advance, traced by strings of overnight marching camps, shows the execution of a pincer movement around the Selgovae of the central Southern Uplands, rather in the way the Brigantes were isolated. One division of the Roman army marched up the line of the modern A68, making its way over the Cheviots east of Carter Bar, down across Teviotdale, crossing the Tweed near Melrose and taking the ancient road up Lauderdale and over the watershed at Soutra to reach the Forth. The other division took the road north from Carlisle and followed the line of the A74. It is likely that Cerialis led this column because of the dangers on either flank. Not only did this line of advance have the effect of encircling the Selgovae, it also cut them off from the western hillmen in Galloway known as the Novantae. The Roman strategy tells us that the Votadini, the people of the fertile plains, were hostile to the Selgovae, the uplanders and pastoralists. It is an old faultline, one to be found all over Europe and in the farther north of Scotland.

The maps compiled by Cerialis' planners were no doubt added to, updated and corrected as Roman ambition struck deeper into Scotland. First used by Marinus of Tyre between AD 90 and 100, they formed the basis of Ptolemy's map of the mid-2nd century, and the density of information correlates directly with the movement of the army in the north up to AD 87. Aerial photography shows up marching camps strung out along the lowlands below the southern shores of the Moray Firth – the invaders may even have reached as far as Inverness. Beyond there Ptolemy notes only tribal names and coastal features. But south of Inverness and east of the Highland massif there is much more detail. In all 17 tribes are plotted across their territories, and settlements, rivers, and coastal features are indicated. However, the original references for Ptolemy's map were undoubtedly military (as is the case with most maps, including the Ordnance Survey) and any interpretation needs to bear that in mind.

Quick march

Wherever it was operating in the Empire the Roman army marched in a set order. Josephus, a historian contemporary with Agricola, described it. Sent on ahead of the main body was a force of mounted, lightly armed troops who might skirmish with but not necessarily engage with any enemy they encountered, preferring to ride back with intelligence. Then came a group of surveyors and engineers whose job it was to set out the next overnight camp. They were followed by the carriages of the officers and their special guard. Troops of legionary cavalry came next, and behind them the artillery train; then the commanding officers of the auxiliary regiments and the regiments themselves. Marching six men abreast, the legions, one after the other, followed and behind them the slaves led the baggage train. To protect the rear of the column a strong force of infantry and cavalry was positioned, and often more cavalry flanked the advance, especially if it was through hill country.

Tacitus, by contrast, is maddeningly light on information about the peoples of the north, rarely noting names of any sort. In his *Life of Agricola* he adds one more tribe, the *Boresti*, a harbour called *Portus Trucculensis*, a battlefield at Mons Graupius, and the title of the first identifiable Scotsman in our history, *Calgacus*. It means 'the Swordsman'. As C.R.L. Fletcher pointed out, most of the tribal names are Latinized versions of barbarous, or Celtic, names and some are helpfully descriptive. The meaning of *Venicones* is difficult, but the extent of their territory and their relationship with their neighbours is made clear by Roman policy.

When Cerialis advanced north of the Forth, he ordered the construction of another *limes*, this time one which would separate one sort of Scotsman from another. A line of forts and watchtowers was built along a road leading to (and beyond) what is now the Gask Ridge, south-west of Perth. Like much of Scotland's geography, it runs roughly north-east to south-west and formed part of a tribal frontier between the Venicones and the Caledonii. Archaeology is good at sorting objects into cultural types and it confirms the Venicones in Fife, Kinross and Strathtay, while place-name evidence puts the Caledonii in Strathearn and along the foothills and glens of the southern Highlands. For example, Dunkeld means 'Fort of the Caledonians' and nearby Schiehallion means 'the Magic Mountain of the Caledonians'. It must also be significant that the Roman *limes* followed the boundary between the later Pictish provinces of *Fib* (Fife) and *Fortriu* (Strathearn and Menteith), and it is highly likely that this was drawn along a line of ancient provenance.

What Cerialis did on the Gask Ridge was another exercise in 'divide and conquer'. And once again the tactics are instructive. There are no early marching camps to be found in Fife (those at Auchtermuchty and Edenwood, and the coastal supply base at Carpow on the Tay, were built during the invasion of Septimius Severus in AD 209), whereas the territory to the west of the *limes* is studded with forts. The most important are the sequence of so-called glen-blocking forts stretching from Drumquhassle (near Drymen by Loch Lomond) in the south-west up to Inverquharity in the north-east. Situated in the mouths of the glens which delivered arterial Highland routeways to the lowlands, they were forward posts. Each was placed so that its garrison could detect enemy movement and relay intelligence to the *limes* which ran behind them, along the road from Doune up to the Gask Ridge and on to *Bertha*, or Perth.

The location of these forts is obviously the consequence of a Roman judgment but it was based on information gleaned about the system of communications used by the native peoples. While no doubt mostly local in its range, such as tracks leading from winter to summer pasture or from farms to market, this system was part of a wider network which Cerialis' officers took trouble to understand. The fort at Drumquhassle stood at a crossroads, where Strathblane runs north to join the valley of the River Endrick, and both meet the pass at Balmaha which leads west to Loch Lomond. Remembering that the great loch was itself a highway, the fort was placed at a focal point. The garrison at Malling, the next fort up the line, could observe traffic moving westward through the pass at Aberfoyle and also making its way along the northern edge of Flanders Moss towards Stirling. Bochastle sat astride the entrance to the Pass of Leny near Callander, then as now one of the main routes into the heart of the western Highlands, while Dalginross lay at the head of Strathearn and the western approach to Loch Earn. Fendoch guarded Glen Almond and the small garrison at Inverquharity watched movement up and down Glen Clova. What these outposts looked for was anything unusual. Patrols went out each day and if they saw traffic unconnected with the quotidian business of farming or stock-rearing, they reported it. Perhaps they saw a rider who may have been a messenger on diplomatic business, perhaps a string of ponies being led up into the interior, perhaps a distant group of warriors bound for a muster point, perhaps the smoke of more cooking fires than usual.

Mortimer Wheeler

Sir Mortimer Wheeler looked like an archaeologist. With his flamboyant moustache and faintly military wardrobe, he seems to have lived the part. In an early television documentary there is a shot of him being driven in an open-topped Land Rover. The driver is of course seated but Wheeler stands, clutching the top of the windshield, his splendid hair flying in the breeze. All that the sequence required was an appropriate soundtrack, perhaps the Ride of the Valkyries. When Wheeler excavated the beautiful and elaborate hillfort at Maiden Castle, near Dorchester, Dorset, in the 1930s he believed he had found evidence of a battle between the Roman invaders and the native kings around AD 43 or 44. Near the entrance to the fort his team came across a graveyard of male skeletons, many of whom showed signs of a violent death. One had a Roman arrowhead lodged in his spine. Wheeler waxed lyrical: 'That night when the fires of the legion shone out [we may imagine] in orderly lines across the valley, the survivors crept forth from their broken stronghold and, in the darkness, buried their dead as nearly as might be outside their tumbled gates in that place where the ashes of their burned huts lay warm and thick upon the ground. The task was carried out anxiously and hastily and without order, but even so, from few graves were omitted those tributes of food and drink which were the proper and traditional perquisites of the dead. At daylight on the morrow, the legion moved westwards to fresh conquest, doubtless taking with it the usual levy of hostages from the vanquished.' And why not?

When the Romans arrived at the southern edges of the Highland line, they were carrying out imperial policy, occupying, subduing and managing the areas they moved into. Even though history tells us that they spent only a very short time north of the Forth/Clyde line, those who first pitched their leather tents there did not know that. Cerialis' soldiers came with the intention of staying, and one of the clearest pieces of evidence of that is to be found at Fendoch. On the hillside behind the fort are the remains of an aqueduct. Although all that can be seen are the artificial terraces, it is clear that Roman engineers took great trouble to supply the garrison with clean water – because they believed that they had built a fort to last.

The Gask Ridge frontier itself was not a solid barrier like the later walls built at the command of Hadrian and Antoninus Pius. Instead, a road connected a series of forts set up at intervals of a day's march. Along this metalled road engineers raised timber watchtowers, a thousand yards apart, to oversee the landscape (which must have been largely deforested by this period for these to be effective). The system was standard, operating in the same way along the Rhine/Danube frontier, in North Africa and the Middle East. Those who wished to cross the *limes* and enter the Empire could do so only under close supervision. Travellers had to be unarmed, and were compelled to pay a fee and customs dues on any goods they carried. How this worked on the Gask Ridge, in an economy which had not used money up to that point, is an intriguing question. In the course of being supplied with food and goods, it is very likely that the Romans made a fundamental change by paying in cash, some of which was needed when crossing the *limes*. Set times, always during daylight, and set places were fixed as checkpoints, and these were tightly controlled by border troops.

All of this must have hampered the local economy greatly, discouraging the movement of people and goods, and cutting across well-established networks. The first months of the *limes* may have been sparky. But if the Romans had placed the Gask Ridge frontier correctly – for boundaries between different tribal jurisdictions certainly preexisted – then dislocation might have been less severe. Nevertheless the fortified road, the forts and watchtowers which seemed to spring up out of the ground in a matter of days, and the presence of thousands of well-drilled, uniformed soldiers controlling movement across the face of the land, must have struck the native people as extraordinary. Nothing like this level and detail of supervision had been seen or experienced before the legions came. By separating the Caledonians of the north-west from the Venicones of the south-east the Romans changed daily lives dramatically, emphatically announcing their presence, their power and their intention to stay. To those used to the day-in, day-out peace of farming in Strathmore, the intrusion of the Empire must have been bewildering – and to the peoples immediately to the north, alarming.

They were called the *Taexali* or *Taezali* by Ptolemy. It is a strange name whose meaning and linguistic origins are obscure, although it is certainly Celtic. But their territory appears to have been extensive, stretching from the Angus glens up to Buchan and the coast around Fraserburgh. The fishing port stands on Kinnaird's Head, which is marked on the ancient map as 'the Promontory of the Taexali'. But these 18 tribal names may be deceptive. Perhaps Roman intelligence heard of the name of the first tribe their sources came across, and simply applied that to all those in the region. In Russia, the enormous territory of Siberia got its name in exactly that manner. And given the nature of Scotland's geography, it is surprising that classical sources do not name more peoples. Certainly patterns of control will have shifted and changed over time, but the fragmented distribution of good agricultural land and the defined nature of upland boundaries suggests smaller units than Ptolemy indicated.

Dunpelder

Traprain Law literally means 'the hill by the treestead' and therefore the name appears borrowed from a location at its foot, even though it is in Old Welsh. An earlier name was 'Dunpelder', which translates as 'the fort of the palisades'. Archaeologists have found traces of just such a rampart, although given the precipitous nature of the hill it must have been erected as much for show as for defence. In a charter of the 14th century, the two names are twinned in a land grant, 'a chartour of Traprene and Dunpeldare by the Erle of Merche to Adam Hyeburn'. But elsewhere in the document the separate identity was slipping: 'Traprain [is] the same as Dunpeldar Hill'. And by the 15th century the older name had disappeared from use.

The better sort of clan map of Scotland is based on sources from the 17th and 18th centuries, with a substantial number reaching back to the medieval period. And it may offer some help in understanding the general texture of society in the 1st century AD. North of the Forth/Clyde line more than 100 surnames are usually plotted. Closer investigation refines their location to somewhere very specific, a castle or stronghold controlling a territorial lordship which has some geographical logic. The MacLeans of Coll and Tiree are an obvious example, but the case of the Drummonds is perhaps more pertinent. Since the 11th century the name has been associated with the parish of Drymen (which includes the site of the fort at Drumquhassle), and it may derive from the Gaelic *dromainn* meaning 'ridge'. The Drummonds fought with Bruce in 1314 and eventually moved their power-base eastwards when they became Dukes of Perth. Like many of the more powerful Highland clans they acquired clients, usually those who lived around them. The most intriguing example of this sort of arrangement is Clan Chattan (see page 133). Not only is there a clear link with an immensely distant past in the use of the name, it seems also to have long signified a confederacy of small groups of different names who came under the common totem of the cat, or more precisely the lynx, and their origins can still be seen on the map. *Caithness*, as we know, is from *Cat-ness* or *Cat-cape* and the old Gaelic name for Sutherland, *Cataibh*, shows the confederacy moving southwards or perhaps extending its reach. Many old Gaelic place-names support the notion of the territory of the Cat People. *Machair Chat* was the fertile area around Dunrobin Castle, *Braigh Chat* or 'the uplands of the Cats' lie 16 km/10 miles either side of the River Shin, above the Dornoch Firth, and *Dithreabh Chat*, or 'the wilderness of the Cats', was understood to be part of the parish of Kildonan, the bleak country between Helmsdale and Strathbrora. All of these make up the necessary components for a pastoral way of life: summer and winter grazing and a moor for fuel and building materials. Like the territory of the Taexali, this is an extensive area, easily able to accommodate several groups who may have retained sub-identities inside the Confederacy of the Cats.

These half-forgotten map references are not the only trace of ancient politics. Older native speakers of Gaelic might still call a Sutherland person a *Catach*, and the Chief of the Cats, the Duke of Sutherland, is still referred to as *Morair Chat* or *Diuc Chat*.

It is a remarkable survival. The Cats may have fought the Romans at Mons Graupius; they certainly fought at Culloden where one of their captains, Gillies MacBean, charged and reached the government lines even though he was stabbed by bayonet thrusts and had his leg broken by grapeshot. He fought his way through the first rank of redcoats before being cut down by the second.

Tree language

The earliest evidence for native writing in Scotland does not consist of letters and numbers, what you are reading at the moment. There is good evidence that people first wrote on trees. Sometimes these inscriptions were carved in stone; in Ireland the earliest surviving examples date from the 3rd century AD. The likelihood is that even earlier inscriptions have not come down to us, for the excellent reason that the trees have not. Made with a series of straight cuts from a knife or a chisel, the alphabet of this language resembles Nordic runes except that it is usually read from top to bottom. Letters can consist of up to five straight strokes set at different angles and they may have originated as a graphic representation of a five-finger sign language. Perhaps it was similar to the *lingua franca* used by the Plains Indians of North America. The characters carved in stone are arranged around a symbolic tree trunk. More than 30 examples of what is known as 'Ogham' (after its alleged Irish inventor, Ogma) have been found in Scotland, mainly in the north and east. But the most southerly find, in the Borders, is likely to prove the oldest. Ogham inscriptions can be translated and they usually turn out to be names. Their function was probably to act as boundary markers.

Clan Chattan is a vivid example of what might have stood in the shadows behind Ptolemy's tribal names in the north. The *Carnonacae* inhabited Wester Ross and the coastal glens down to Skye, and their name means 'the People of the Cairns', that is, people who built cairns. These may have been seamarks (many such navigational aids still exist on promontories, especially around the island of Harris) or, more prosaically, the results of field clearance. Either way the name is descriptive of something these people did rather than who they were, and it probably acted as an umbrella for the ancestors of the MacKays, MacLeods, MacNicols and MacDonnels who appear on that territory on a clan map of the 18th century. It is of course impossible to be sure of this, but prehistoric personal names in the north were almost certainly related closely to lineage, just as the clan names have been for a millennium at least. The peoples met by the Romans probably took their names from their parentage, and added to them or changed them to avoid confusion.

Below the Carnonacae lay the *Creones*, or 'Borderers' (perhaps an echo of their status is preserved in the description of Moidart as 'the Rough Bounds'), and below them a totem name, the *Epidii*, or 'Horse People'. Ptolemy's tribal names were not coined or conferred at the point when Roman intelligence officers or their sources asked what they were. They had evolved over long periods and they say something, at last, about how the peoples of the north understood themselves.

Some sense of a Mediterranean view of Scotland's geography can be gleaned from the written sources. At Delphi, the place the Greeks called the 'Navel of the World', the historian Plutarch came across an interesting traveller. The year was AD 83 and Demetrius of Tarsus was on his way home from Britain. The emperor had commanded him to sail around the north of the island to make enquiries, observations and, presumably, a map. Demetrius told Plutarch of a gloomy journey amongst uninhabited islands, some of which were named after gods or heroes. He came across one which turned out to be the retreat of holy men who were considered inviolate by the native peoples living nearby. Demetrius did not use the term *Druid* but it may be that he made landfall at Iona. This was a sacred place long before Columba came in the 6th century and its original name suggests the presence of a Druidic grove. Like *Grampian*, *Iona* is a misprint. The correct spelling is *Iova*, and Columba's biographer, Adomnan, always spelt it that way in his life of the saint. *Iova* means 'Yew-island', and these ancient trees had a close association with Druids. In an Irish version of the life of Columba, the writer insists that the saint found a community of Druids on the island when he first arrived. And of course he expelled them. Early Christians often took over places of pagan sanctity and renamed and adapted them for the new faith.

Bridie

Christianity shaded into paganism in its early centuries and these old traditions have much to say about beliefs before the new faith. When Columba determined to build a monastery on Iona, one of his monks, St Odhran, offered 'to go under the earth' as a human sacrifice for the new church. Old deities were readily converted into saints. The fire-goddess Brigantia became St Bride, Brigid or Bridget and she was given an apocryphal, but very Celtic, role in Christ's upbringing. She was his foster-mother. Her feast-day replaced the quarter day of Imbolc and a real St Brigid was said to have flourished in Ireland as an abbess in the 5th century. Perhaps she did.

Five hundred years before Columba made landfall on Iona, it sounds as though Demetrius of Tarsus met a group of holy men who were also Druids, and he was impressed with their powers of divination. When a violent storm raged over the sea, they told him that it was a sign that one of the gods, the 'Mighty Ones', had died. These stories passed quickly into the corpus of what was known about Britain, and when Tacitus came to write the *Agricola*, the account of his father-in-law's campaigns in the north, he included a passage which appears to have come from Demetrius, perhaps via Plutarch. He described the nature of the western ocean:

> Nowhere is the dominance of the sea more extensive. There are many tidal currents, flowing in different directions. They do not merely rise as far as the shoreline and recede again. They flow far inland, wind around, and push themselves among the highlands and mountains, as if in their own realm.

But Tacitus may have seen the sea-lochs for himself. New evidence from an inscription found in Rome suggests that the historian probably served as a military tribune on Agricola's general staff. Found near the barracks of the Praetorian Guard in the north-eastern quarter of the old city, the marble fragment looks as though it was part of Tacitus' funerary inscription, and as such it lists the government appointments he held. And these were prestigious. Tacitus eventually rose to be a senator, but from AD 77 to 79 he may have served in Britain under Agricola. The office of military tribune ranked below legionary consul and legate and there were usually six to a legion. The habit was for each to take command for two months at a time. Promotion to this rank was in the gift of a provincial governor and since there were 24 tribunes stationed in Britain, the preferment of Tacitus was hardly likely to be seen as an example of outrageous nepotism. In any case it was common in the imperial government for a father or father-in-law to advance the interests of his son in this way.

If Tacitus was indeed in Britain from 77 to 79, the balance of the text of the *Agricola* appears to reflect that chronology. There is much more information for the early part of his father-in-law's governorship than for the later – even though the latter is the more dramatic period. And the authority of eye-witness reporting greatly enhances Tacitus' account, setting it apart from the second-hand vagueness of much of what was written about Britain by classical historians. His terse but precise prose also smacks of the observations of a military man.

Politics also informs what was said, and not said, in the *Agricola*. While Domitian was emperor, it would have been dangerous for Tacitus to publish his record of the campaigns in Britain, or at least to publish a history which might over-emphasize his father-in-law's role and talents. But after the assassination of Domitian in AD 96 the atmosphere lightened, and two years later the *Agricola* was read in public by its author and thereafter published as a copied text by booksellers. Nevertheless, it is often coloured by partiality of a different sort as it always strives to place the credit for what was achieved under the supposedly modest Agricola.

Bull's blood

Paganism took a very long time to die out in the remote parts of the Highlands and Islands. In connection with the Celtic festival of Lughnasa, at around the end of August bulls were sacrificed on an island in Loch Maree. This feast had a formal association with St Maelrubha, an early missionary, but his name had clearly been substituted for a pagan deity. In the 17th century the presbytery of Dingwall was outraged at the persistence of this: 'amongst other abhominable and heathenische practices that the people in that place were accustomed to sacrifice bulls at a certaine tyme on the 25th of August, which day is dedicate, as they conceive, to St Mourie as they call him'. In much earlier times Druids supervised the sacrifice of bulls both in pursuit of divination and also for votive purposes, often on behalf of a king. Perhaps the bulls of Loch Maree were sacrificed for the kings of the Caereni, the Sheep Folk.

From various asides in the text, it seems that much of it was based on conversations between Tacitus and his father-in-law, particularly for the later period of his governorship. 'He often used to say' appears occasionally and between AD 84 and 90 there were opportunities for both men to reminisce about what had happened in Britain.

One of the earliest passages in the *Agricola* is particularly informative. Tacitus begins the chapter entitled 'Britain and its Peoples' with a piece of encouraging brusqueness which probably reflects the confidence of the eye-witness observer: 'Hence matters formerly uncertain, which my predecessors embellished in eloquent fashion, will be reported on the evidence of the facts.' He goes on to some observations on geography, before beginning what is the first considered and comparative description of our ancestors, and it is worth quoting at length (translations by Anthony Birley):

As to what human beings initially inhabited Britain, whether native-born or immigrants, little has been established, as is usually the case with barbarians. Be this as it may, their physical appearance is varied, which allows conclusions to be drawn. For example, in the case of the inhabitants of Caledonia, their red-gold hair and massive limbs proclaim German origin. . . .

All the same it is plausible on a general estimate that the Gauls occupied the adjacent island. You can find their rites and religious beliefs. The language is not much different. . . .

Their infantry is their main strength. Some of their peoples also engage in battle with chariots. The nobles are the charioteers, their clients fight for them. In former times the Britons owed obedience to kings. Now they are formed into factional groupings by the leading men. Indeed, there is nothing that helps us more against such very powerful peoples than their lack of unanimity. It is seldom that two or three states unite to repel a common threat. Hence each fights on its own, and all are conquered.

The climate is miserable, with frequent rain and mists. But extreme cold is not found there. The days last longer than in our part of the world, the nights are bright and in the most distant parts of Britain so short that you can hardly distinguish between evening and morning twilight. If clouds do not block the view, they say that the sun's glow can be seen by night. It does not set and rise but passes across the horizon. In fact, the flat extremes of the earth, casting a long shadow, do not project the darkness, and night falls below the level of the sky and the stars.

The soil bears crops, apart from the olive and the vine and other natives of warmer climes, and has an abundance of cattle. The crops ripen slowly but shoot up quickly. The cause is the same in both cases, the abundant moisture of land and sky. Britain contains gold and silver and other metals, the booty of victory. . . .

Agricola knew Britain a great deal better than his son-in-law. Like him he had been a military tribune on the staff of a governor, Suetonius Paulinus, when he arrived in AD 58. Wales was still largely unconquered and the Emperor Nero encouraged the new governor to make inroads. Agricola began a long association with the XXth Legion, and as they marched along the coast road of North Wales the 19-year-old was embarking on his earliest, and perhaps most spectacular, military adventure. What happened next cannot fail to have made an indelible impression.

The name *Agricola* was originally a nickname meaning 'farmer'. The young tribune's full name was much longer: Gnaeus Julius Luci filius Aniensis Agricola Foro Julii. And as the son of Lucius it is likely that he inherited his distinguishing name from his father, who had written a handbook on how to produce healthy vines and grapes. The full name also indicates Agricola's origins and these are intriguing. He came from Forum Julii, now Fréjus on France's Côte d'Azur, and his family were originally aristocrats in the Aniensis tribe. They were not Romans or Italians but Gauls and, significantly, it may well be the case that Agricola could both speak and understand Gaulish. If Tacitus is correct in his assertion that the language of native Britain was 'not much different', then the young tribune might have found the culture of his enemies easier to comprehend. It would have aided diplomacy tremendously if he could have spoken directly to native kings who had not yet learned Latin. Certainly his upbringing in Provence was highly Romanized and both his father and his uncle had entered the imperial élite as senators. But his background was Gaulish and his mother's name, Procilla, was Celtic.

Nothing, however, could have prepared Agricola for what he and the XXth Legion saw when they reached the Menai Straits. On the opposite shore, determined to protect the sacred island of Anglesey, the Ordovices had drawn up their army. Ranks of warriors with spiky, lime-washed hair were beating their weapons against their shields. Black-clad women moved amongst them, screaming curses at the invaders. Like Furies, with their faces and bodies streaked with ash, they carried torches and leaped into the water to hurl challenges and insults. Behind the warriors were

Druids and their ghost fences, rows of skulls facing the legions across the water. Arms aloft, imploring their sky-gods to descend and destroy the Romans, the Druids understood why Suetonius Paulinus had come. It was to be a matter not of conquest but of annihilation. Probably correctly, Roman intelligence officers believed that British resistance was fomented by the Druids and, more, that Anglesey (or *Ynys Mon* as they knew it) was the centre of their power. At the bottom of the little lake of Llyn Cerrig Bach on the island weapons from all over Celtic Britain have been found, suggesting strongly that Anglesey was a focus of pilgrimage.

After some hesitation, Suetonius Paulinus ordered the young Agricola's legion forward and on flat pontoons the infantry crossed while the cavalry swam their ponies through the treacherous tide-race of the Menai. The magic of the ghost fences failed, Roman discipline scattered the warriors of the Ordovices and the soldiers made their purpose clear by spending some weeks on the island cutting down the groves of oak trees sacred to the Druids and hunting down the priests of the old religion.

Messengers hurrying from the south-east caught up with Suetonius' expedition soon after the victory at the straits. It was reported that the province's chief financial officer, Decianus Catus, had committed an extraordinary blunder which showed that he understood very little of Celtic society. When the client-king of the Iceni, Prasutagus, died, Catus had an inventory of all his goods made prior to seizing them and incorporating the semi-independent kingdom into the Empire. No doubt there was an opportunity for personal profit. When Prasutagus' queen, Boudicca, objected, Decianus Catus was astonished. In Roman society women had no more status than children, and he forgot that in Britain they could rule kingdoms. Soldiers were allowed to rape Prasutagus' daughters. Probably at Venta Icenorum, near Norwich, Boudicca herself was dragged out into a public place, stripped, tied to a stake and, in front of her people, whipped by a centurion.

Celtic sensibilities were outraged, and revolt set the south-east on fire. Colchester, London and St Albans were all burned as Suetonius

Paulinus was given the news in North Wales. After a rapid march eastwards, he turned his legions down Watling Street and in AD 60, somewhere in the Midlands, drew his men up to face the rebel queen and her massive army. Tacitus must have been exaggerating when he reckoned that 80,000 of Boudicca's followers were killed and only 400 Romans, but the overall impression is beyond dispute. In defeating the British army, the legionaries were ordered to spare no one, killing as many as could be caught.

As a very young man Agricola witnessed all that happened in AD 60, and he learned lessons he would not forget. In 63 promotion took him away from Britain to serve in Asia, across the other side of the Empire. Through various other postings, Agricola became well schooled in the complexities of the imperial politics of the time. No dour soldier, but an astute observer, he was one of the first in the army to declare his support for Vespasian (also a veteran of campaigns in Britain) in the civil war of 69, known as the Year of the Four Emperors. Rewarded with command of the XXth Legion, Agricola found himself back in Britain, and a year later fighting in the north alongside the new governor, Petilius Cerialis. After the defeat of the Brigantes they would march together over the Cheviots and, with his old comrades in the XXth, the new legate would gather information and experience which would be invaluable some years later.

Even though they expended a great deal of military energy, especially at its mountainous margins, the Romans did not believe that Britain was a profitable province. The geographer Strabo worked out that more money was to be made from customs payments due on trade with Britain than could be raised in direct taxes on the natives. Once the cost of maintaining such a large garrison was deducted, the province itself produced very little cash. And there was even less of an economic reason to venture out of the fertile lowlands to Wales or up to Scotland. In the middle of the 2nd century, as the Emperor Antoninus Pius ordered the building of the wall on the Forth/Clyde line, the historian Aelius Aristides appeared to justify the limit set on conquest by remarking that Rome already occupied all the parts of Britain worth having. And a financial secretary to the imperial treasury, Appian, was even less impressed, claiming: 'the part they have brings in little money'.

So why did successive governors continue to campaign on the margins of Britain? Because it was there, and available, seems to be the blunt answer. Politically, the continuing need for military success was vital to emperors as they established their authority in Rome and, as Claudius realized, success in faraway Britain could be presented as particularly impressive. But there was also an assumption that Rome would roll out its frontiers to encompass the whole of the known world rather in the way that the empires of the 19th century were seen as the prerogative of European nations. Northern Canada is little more than vast expanses of tundra and icefield, but it was coloured red on the map nevertheless.

When Agricola arrived as governor in AD 77, it was midsummer and late in the campaigning season, but the supposedly cautious and modest man immediately acted impetuously. After the Boudicca rebellion of 60, Suetonius Paulinus' conquest of the Ordovices and Anglesey had been abandoned. In 77 Tacitus reported that there was another revolt in North Wales: 'The state of the Ordovices, not long before his arrival, had virtually wiped out a cavalry regiment operating in its territory and this initial stroke had excited the province.' Agricola had seen how nearly Britannia was lost in AD 60, and without proper preparation he marched an army north-west to challenge those whom he regarded as rebels.

> He concentrated the legionary detachments and a modest force
> of auxilia and, as the Ordovices did not venture to come down
> into the plain, led his men up into the hills, himself at the head
> of the column, so as to impart his own courage to the rest by
> sharing the danger. Almost the entire people was cut to pieces.

This was a grisly repetition of a policy of genocide which had been put into effect in the revolt of 60 and something which the ruthless Agricola would do again in the north. After the slaughter of the Ordovices, he got enough of his troops across the Menai Straits (there had been no time to organize boats) to reduce Anglesey again and devastate the heartland of the Druids.

Budget bust

By the 3rd century AD the imperial budget was running at astronomical levels. The administration needed 225 million silver denarii to pay the army, the civil service and the subsidies to buy off barbarians on the frontier. There simply was not enough silver being mined in Europe to mint all these coins and the silver content of the denarius declined sharply. Inflation began to spiral as prices climbed. Finally, in 301, the Emperor Diocletian issued his Edict on Prices. It listed commodities with fixed prices alongside: 8 denarii for a pint of wine or a pound of beef, and so on. Like modern attempts at wage freezes and price controls, it failed immediately. The market took over and coins became 'worth their weight in gold'; precious metal was used as a form of exchange no matter what shape it took – bowls, goblets or cutlery.

Throughout his narrative Tacitus is anxious to ascribe as much of the credit for the conquest of north Britain as possible to his father-in-law and no mention is made of Petilius Cerialis' earlier foray over the Forth. It may be that Julius Frontinus, his successor, withdrew troops after AD 73 so that he could concentrate on subjugating the Silures of South Wales. They had presented severe difficulties and in 52 defeated a legion, probably the XXth. So when Agricola moved his forces northwards into Scotland in 78, Tacitus is vague about geography, even though he was probably with the army himself, but clear that his father-in-law was adding to the empire. And the governor used the well-tried tactic of building encircling forts and roads: 'They were also surrounded by garrisons and forts, with such skill and thoroughness that no new part of Britain ever came over with so little damage.'

It seems that no set-piece battle was offered by the peoples of the south of Scotland, and wisely they relied on guerrilla tactics. Tacitus asserts that on the march Agricola 'chose the sites for pitching camp himself' and in hostile territory this was a matter of the greatest importance. And it helped if you had been there before. Since the Votadini of the south-east offered no threat it is likely that, when Agricola divided his forces to form a pincer around the Selgovae, he took his old comrades of the XXth Legion up the western road, close to the line of the modern A74. At the fort of Crawford in the upper Clyde Valley there is an excellent example of how careful the Romans were in siting their forts. As Agricola's soldiers marched through the hills, their every step was watched and there was a constant threat of ambush. And when the road north from Crawford was built its route shows how wary the Romans were. Rather than follow the flat ground by the banks of the Clyde, the military road makes a laborious climb up the hill immediately to the north of the fort, zigzagging to make the climb easier. The reason why the engineers avoided the obvious route was that it passes through a narrow valley with high ground on either side, the perfect place for an ambush. The Crawford road looks like the result of a hard-learned lesson.

The encirclement of the Selgovae shows up well on a map of Roman remains in southern Scotland. Despite the fact that the archaeology of the 1st millennium BC shows a populous economy in the region, there is no Roman road in upper Tweeddale linking the large forts of Newstead and Castledykes. This was the heartland of the Selgovae and it may simply have been too dangerous a place to send road-building gangs. The choice of alternative routes over the bleak Craik Moor to the south and Clydesdale to the north only underlines the point. In the east, Oakwood fort was built at the mouth of the Ettrick Valley, on a southern slope where the large garrison could observe movement below.

It is further testament to the threat presented by the Selgovae that of only four forts built in Scotland able to accommodate a full cohort, two of them were on the margins of their territory, at Easter Happrew. Perhaps the Romans understood that the hill peoples of northern Britannia could quickly combine, using their upland trails, unobserved by Roman patrols, to muster an army of Brigantes, Novantae and Selgovae which could explode out of the glens without warning.

Roman Romanies

The legacy of the name of Rome itself is fascinating, turning up at unlikely points in European history. One of the earliest variants in the west was 'Ruam', the name the early Irish chroniclers gave to the large monastic towns established at Clonmacnoise and Glendalough. It simply signified a city, since in a completely rural economy Rome or Ruam was the only city known at that time. On the other side of Europe, similar borrowings took place. To Moslems, 'Rum' meant Byzantium, the evolved Eastern Roman Empire, and its citizens, correctly enough, were always termed 'the Romans'. When the Seljuk Turks overran central Turkey in the 11th century, they called themselves the 'Seljuks of Rum' because they had conquered Roman territory. And when Constantinople (the renamed Byzantium) fell to Mehmed II in 1453, he took the title 'Sultan of Rum'. One of the effects of the Moslem takeover was the movement of gypsies across Europe, and the name 'Romany' comes from their association with the Byzantine Empire. The Romany word for a gypsy is 'Rom', a Roman.

The Selgovan kings and their neighbours, the Novantae, would undoubtedly have heard of the slaughter after Boudicca's uprising. They would have known the numerical strength of the opposing forces and well understood the Romans' skill in the sort of close-quarters, disciplined fighting needed for victory in a pitched battle. Tacitus makes no mention of a confrontation and the Selgovans would have resorted to guerrilla warfare, a strategy which would serve them well in their familiar hills. In later campaigns, north of the Tay, the Caledonians adopted a similar approach and the historian Dio Cassius reported that they lured Roman foraging parties into ambush with flocks of sheep and herds of cattle as bait. Perhaps the Selgovans did the same. Whatever the detail of their tactics, they did manage to preserve the integrity of much of their territory and Agricola passed on around them as he moved towards the Midland Valley and the Forth/Clyde line.

The other military void in southern Scotland is Berwickshire, along with East Lothian the land of the Votadini. Aerial photography has found no marching camps there because no army ever had to tramp through its fertile landscape. As a condition of the treaty hammered out between the Votadinian kings and Agricola's diplomats, the ramparts on Traprain Law were permitted to remain intact, and traces of high-status Roman gifts have been discovered on the site. The balance of the negotiations is of course impossible to assess, but logistics and local political advantage must have played a prime part. Then as now, Berwickshire and East Lothian were amongst the most fertile counties in Scotland and the corn harvested from their small fields in the 1st century AD was attractive to Agricola's quartermasters. It was a matter of the greatest importance to ensure that the Votadini became compliant allies. Without their corn, the conquest of Scotland would have been made much more difficult because many of the other arable areas were known to be hostile – Angus and the Mearns, Aberdeenshire and the Moray Firth lowlands. The Venicones of Fife would have been placated for the same reasons. In return the native kings saw their enemies in the hills encircled and even defeated. Like most successful imperialists the Romans only fought as a last resort – successful diplomacy was much cheaper.

The most expensive project undertaken by Agricola and subsequent governors was road-building. There are more than 650 km/400 miles of Roman road in Scotland and its creation absorbed huge resources. Each Roman mile took around 1,000 man-hours to make, but as soon as forts were established the invaders knew that good communications between them were essential. Swift reaction depended on the roads, which had the effect of making a large garrison appear larger. Dere Street (so-called much later because it began at York in the later Celtic kingdom of Deur) was the principal artery and on Soutra Hill in East Lothian surviving stretches are 10 m/30 ft wide. Not only was it vital to move soldiers around occupied Scotland quickly, it was also important to have an all-weather network of roads which could take wheeled vehicles. Carts could transport the volume of supplies needed by the army, whereas ponies with pack-saddles picking their way along muddy tracks presented quartermasters with tremendous logistical difficulties. The early Roman roads are perhaps best looked at in the same way as 19th-century railways. The important thing was to reach a road as early as possible in a journey, because even if it meant a detour or longer mileage it was quicker and easier to travel on a hard, metalled surface, especially in winter. Dere Street remained an important military road for more than a millennium. When Edward I of England invaded Scotland at the end of the 13th century, watchers reported that the army and its baggage train was strung out for 30 km/20 miles as the old straight road traversed the Cheviots. And in 1314 Robert de Bruce waited at Bannockburn for the approach of Edward's son as his forces marched up another Roman road.

The old straight roads

Many Roman roads in Scotland were in reality not straight. Some adapted to the geography and curved round hillsides or zigzagged up them. All of them were designed for carts rather than feet or hooves because Roman quartermasters wanted to move goods around in bulk. Gradients were worked out accordingly. At Inchtuthil, in Perthshire, the quarries for the huge volume of stone required to build the legionary fortress lay at some distance from the site. A road was laid down for the ox-carts going to and fro, and it included a 5-km/3-mile one-way loop which had an easier gradient for those laden with stone than the more direct route used by empty carts. The surface of a Roman road was always cambered in order to facilitate drainage and allow use even in the worst weather.

In order to minimize supply difficulties and maintain an intimidatory presence in the most populous areas, the largest forts in Scotland were built in fertile river valleys. The site at Newstead on the Tweed was well chosen. When Agricola's eastern division climbed up to the Cheviot watershed, they could clearly see the Tweed Valley's major landmark, the three Eildon Hills, and they made straight for them. Near where the Leader Water meets the Tweed, on a height above the southern bank, the

Romans settled on a commanding site with long views to the west, up the Gala Water and into the territory of the Selgovae. Newstead was always intended to be pivotal, a muster-point and a supply depot for campaigning. It sat astride a crossroads. The route from the Cheviots that was to become Dere Street crossed the Tweed below the fort and continued up Lauderdale to Soutra before descending to the Forth shore. There was an east–west road along the southern bank of the Tweed, and up until the medieval period it is very likely that the river itself was navigable down to Berwick and the North Sea. A wooden steering oar for a large boat (with two boathooks) has been found by archaeologists at Newstead, and no other explanation for its presence is plausible. The availability of river transport must have been a boon to the garrison, allowing the bulk import of all sorts of items that might have improved morale.

Newstead was big enough to hold a large garrison, probably a unit or vexillation of legionary infantry and a wing or *ala* of cavalry – perhaps a thousand soldiers in all. The infantry had a daily marching radius of 20 km/13 miles, but for patrols in the hostile western hill-country of the Selgovae, ponies would have been much preferred – if for no other reason than that native forces consisted mainly of light cavalry. A letter found at the fort of Vindolanda, on the other side of the Cheviots, confirms this: 'There are very many cavalry', remarked a correspondent. Elaborate parade masks for cavalry troopers have been found at Newstead and to the west of the fort there was probably a riding school. After AD 86 the walls of the first fort were demolished, the area enlarged to 6 ha/13 acres and the fortifications strengthened to an immense width of 14 m/45 ft. Perhaps the most interesting development at Newstead took place outside the defended perimeter. Communications by signal were important to an occupying army and at the summit of Eildon Hill North, in the centre of the sacred enclosure, the remains of a Roman building have been found. It was a signal station. By the use of fire, or perhaps a reflective metal surface on bright days, messages could be sent and observed. There may have been another signal station on Ruberslaw, 24 km/15 miles to the south, in direct line of sight. Codes were simple but the speed of communication very rapid indeed. But what the tower signified for the native peoples of the Tweed Valley is perhaps a more interesting question.

The scale of the precinct on Eildon Hill North meant that it carried the greatest possible religious significance and the planting of a signal station in its midst was a tremendous desecration – and a deliberate one. Eildon Mid Hill is higher than its neighbour, Eildon Hill North, and it also afforded uninterrupted vistas to the south, north and west. The signal station could have sat there. It is not visible from the fort at Newstead, but the creation of a secondary link could have been managed without much difficulty. If the great precinct had been Votadinian, it is hard to imagine a treaty condoning this sort of blasphemous behaviour by the fort commander. Eildon Hill North was certainly occupied at the time of the Agricolan invasion, and its use was a matter of current importance rather than respect for a sacred past. But if the hill had been Selgovan, perhaps their most holy place, venerated by their priests and kings, and it had been handed over to the Votadini as part of the spoils of war, then the presence of the signal station might be better understood as a clause in an agreement.

Another example of sacrilege took place in lower Annandale, on the western fringes of the territory of the Selgovae. Burnswark Hill is singular, rising out of rolling farmland on all sides. In the 1st millennium BC it was the largest hillfort in south-west Scotland, and like Eildon Hill North it had probably become a fire-hill, used four times a year to mark the Celtic festivals. By the time the legions arrived, its occupation may have been only sporadic, but the association and memories were still strong. As with ruined Christian churches, the hill will have retained the atmosphere of sanctity.

The Romans used it for target practice. From a camp built on its southern slopes they fired missiles from siege engines placed on artificial mounds outside the gates. Some ballista balls have been retrieved from the prime targets, the gates of the hillfort. Archaeologists believe that the original camp at Burnswark was built by the legions of Petilius Cerialis on his foray northwards, and that missiles were first fired in anger at the Selgovae defending the long perimeter.

However all that may be, the native peoples of the Tweed Valley continued to climb Eildon Hill North during the Roman occupation of Newstead fort at its foot and to use its numerous hut platforms. And they were numerous. On feast days and nights perhaps 3,000 to 5,000 people gathered, if all the huts were occupied. The population of Scotland in the 1st century AD is difficult to judge, but places like Eildon Hill North suggest that it was not sparse. And in the *Agricola*, Tacitus offers some more guidance. At the battle at Mons Graupius in AD 83, he reckoned that the Caledonian army was 30,000 strong. It is unlikely that he exaggerated very much for effect, since the Romans almost certainly numbered 20,000, and the scale of the marching camps in the north supports that figure. Even if the opposing forces included non-combatants, as they did when Boudicca was defeated 20 years before, it is still a very large army and it speaks of a substantial population behind it. Medieval historians estimate a population of 500,000 for Scotland in 1100, and since agriculture changed only a little in the intervening period, this may be about right for the 1st century AD. That makes an average density of approximately 40 per square mile in lowland areas and less than half that in upland pasture regions. It was a busy landscape and aerial photography around Traprain Law shows how fertile land was intensively farmed where it drained well.

As governor of Britannia, Agricola had civil as well as military duties. In a remarkable passage, Tacitus records how he set about the process of Romanization:

His intention was, in fact, that people who lived in widely dispersed and primitive settlements and hence were naturally inclined to war should become accustomed to peace and quiet by the provision of amenities. Hence he gave encouragement to individuals and assistance to communities to build temples, market-places and town houses. . . . Further, he educated the

sons of the leading men in the liberal arts and he rated the
natural talents of the Britons above the trained skills of the Gauls.

The result was that those who had just lately been reject-
ing the Roman tongue now conceived a desire for eloquence.
Thus even our style of dress came into favour and the toga was
everywhere to be seen. Gradually, too, they went astray into
the allurements of evil ways, colonnades and warm baths and
elegant banquets. The Britons, who had no experience of this,
called it 'civilization', although it was a part of their enslavement.

Now, this passage must refer largely to the south of England, which
had been part of the Empire for 40 years. The north was still in the process
of being subdued. But it is eloquent about Agricola's policy, and Roman
attitudes, including Tacitus' cynicism, and part of it may have applied
to the client kingdoms of the Votadini and the Venicones. The sons of
their aristocracy may indeed have learned to speak Latin and may even
have accepted some of the dazzling opportunities offered by the imperial system. It was common for the Romans to recruit from the ranks of
conquered armies and there are several examples of British regiments
fighting in Europe on the Rhine/Danube frontier. Policy would have
prevented local levies from serving in their own region, but southern
Britons were evidently considered sufficiently distant and different for
Agricola. According to Tacitus the army invading Scotland had Britons
in its auxiliary regiments. But the army might have been very attractive
to young men. To what had been the relatively closed society of Celtic
Britain, where there was little or no social mobility between the strata
of slaves, farmers, craftsmen, priests and aristocrats, the Empire represented opportunity. Young men were suddenly presented with radical
possibilities: travel and perhaps even advancement.

The fort at Vindolanda, in north Northumberland, in the 70s and
80s offers comparisons. It was commanded by Flavius Cerialis and gar-
risoned by the ninth cohort of Batavians. These originated in the Low
Countries, and as a recently conquered people were allowed to enlist in

the army and retain their own noblemen as officers. This device had the double effect of lifting out a complete military unit from an area requiring pacification and putting it to good use elsewhere in the Empire. British regiments on the Rhine were probably recruited in exactly the same way, and it may be that a Votadinian or Veniconian warband was converted into a cohort and given the job of keeping European barbarians at bay.

In AD 79 the political landscape shifted. Agricola's patron, the Emperor Vespasian, died and was succeeded by his son, Titus. The advance into Scotland continued and the Roman army reached as far as the Tay. And when despatches announcing the new gains arrived at the imperial court, the new emperor was happy to trumpet continuing military success. Wisely, Agricola paused in 80 to consolidate and concentrate on a programme of fort- and road-building. Much has been written about Roman styles of building, and even what variants were adopted by different legions. But as informative a discussion might be had about the native context for these strongholds. Clearly no one welcomed their appearance, and as usual the Romans were ruthless. At Cardean in Angus, a village was simply removed, the roundhouses and inbye field walls levelled and the population scattered so that a fort could be raised. Archaeologists have found Celtic pottery below the Roman stratum. And it is likely that this happened more than once, especially during the period of wall-building in the 2nd century. Good defensive sites were as obvious to a native eye as to a Roman, and when the larger depots were sited in heavily settled areas, considerable hardship must have been inflicted. Large areas of 65 ha/162 acres for some forts removed much good land from the economy; when well-established turf was needed to build ramparts, good pasture land would have been sought.

Dialogue

Roman bureaucracy went into minute detail and provincial governors were in the habit of not only sending regular despatches back to Rome but also requesting all sorts of guidance and permissions from the emperor himself. It was hands-on stuff. Here is an extract of correspondence between Trajan and Pliny the Younger, governor of Bithynia–Pontus in Asia Minor. A longer version is published in Norman Davies' excellent *Europe – A History*.

PLINY: Nicaea has expended 10,000,000 sesterces on a theatre that was tottering and great sums on a gymnasium that was burned . . . . At Claudiopolis they are excavating a bathhouse at the foot of the mountain . . . . What am I to do?

TRAJAN: You are on the spot, decide for yourself. As for the architects, we in Rome send to Greece for them. You should find some where you are.

PLINY: The money due to the towns of the province has been called in, and no borrowers at 12 per cent are to be found. Ought I to reduce the rates of interest . . . or compel the decurions to borrow the money in equal shares?

TRAJAN: Put the interest low enough to attract borrowers, but do not force anyone to borrow . . . . Such a course would be inconsistent with the temper of our century.

PLINY: A great fire has devastated Nicomedia. Would it be in order to establish a society of 150 firemen?

TRAJAN: No. Corporations, whatever they're called, are sure to become political associations . . . .

When Agricola entered Scotland, he had three legions and several regiments of auxiliaries with him. As they tramped through the landscape, screened by cavalry outriders, some prudent watchers would have fled before them, or simply got out of the way. Large bodies of men required large amounts of food and drink and the location of depots such as Newstead, Dalswinton and Castledykes in fertile river valleys was not only sensible from a Roman point of view, it also showed the tremendous confidence of a professional army to commandeer what they needed with impunity. Violent local reaction was futile in the face of such a tremendous show of power, in fact unimaginable except as an irritant.

In 80 Agricola's army spent more time in consolidation. A line of forts was established across the Forth/Clyde isthmus as a frontier. It seems that the emperor, probably on the governor's advice, had decided to bring the advance to a halt. And so in the following year Agricola turned the army westwards to subdue all the territory south of the new frontier. The Romans crossed the Clyde and 'defeated peoples up to that time unknown in a series of successful actions'. The fact that Tacitus did not know the identities of the enemies in the south is understandable. By that time he had almost certainly left his posting in Britain. But the army must have had better intelligence, since the south-west had been close to the frontier since the time of Cerialis' governorship. Having reached the west coast of Galloway, or possibly Kintyre, Agricola looked over to Ireland. He reckoned that conquest would take no more than a legion and some auxiliaries, but if the Emperor Titus had called a halt then there was nothing to be done but consolidate.

On 13 September 81 Titus unexpectedly died after a reign of little more than two years. It was rumoured that his younger brother, Domitian, had had him poisoned. Like all new emperors, he needed a quick triumph and Agricola was handily placed in Britain to achieve it. His governorship was extended by another three years and instructions came from Rome that the whole island was to be conquered.

Accordingly the army moved north again and 'enveloped the states situated beyond the Bodotria [the Forth]. Because there were fears that all the peoples on the further side might rise and the land routes be threatened by an enemy army, Agricola reconnoitred the harbours with the fleet.'

This made every sort of logistical and tactical sense. The British fleet, the *Classis Britannica*, was based at Dover, Richborough and Boulogne and able to join the invasion force quickly. Tacitus noted that the army and the navy were 'often in the same camp' and it is inconceivable that transport ships were not used to bring grain and other supplies to pre-arranged coastal dumps. These ships may have been built in a Celtic style, that is, driven by sail and with a shallow draught and a flat bottom to allow beaching on an ebb tide without damage. A gently sloping, sandy beach would be harbour enough and the war-galley captains were expert at running their ships aground and refloating them. The latter were powered by oars and could be very manoeuvrable in battle, able to increase speed to use their rams effectively, and get close enough to allow their marines to attack enemy ships.

What made life different and more difficult for a general from the Mediterranean such as Agricola was the nature of the seas around Scotland. Tides were much higher and the weather generally less kind. The fleet appears to have coasted up the North Sea during the summer campaigning season without incident, but those who went on to sail around the northern and western coasts may have encountered severe conditions. They sought refuge, reported Tacitus, in a harbour called *Portus Trucculensis*, and the latter translates as 'stormy'.

Poisoned chalices

Historians have described as the golden imperial age of Rome the period stretching from the reign of Augustus to Marcus Aurelius, 200 years of more or less continual territorial expansion and consolidation. And yet the first of these two centuries of glory was presided over by a succession of degenerates, many of whom met violent ends. Tiberius retired early to the island of Capri where he whiled away his time in sexual perversion and cruel games. Caligula made his horse a consul and regularly committed incest with his sisters before an assassin stabbed him in the genitals. Claudius was poisoned by toadstool sauce and Nero had one of his boyfriends turned into a girl by castration and then married him or her. After he took his own life, his successor, Galba, was murdered, as were Otho and Vitellius. Titus was also poisoned and his brother, Domitian, stabbed to death by his wife and her friends. Nine out of Augustus' ten immediate successors were either killed or lived lives of astonishing corruption, or both. Only Vespasian, a tough soldier who had fought in Britain, appeared to be vaguely normal, and, engagingly, his dying words were said to have been, 'Dear me, I must be turning into a god'.

The fleet's secondary purpose was psychological, to make an impression on native morale, and it appears to have succeeded. The Celtic peoples of the north were seafarers and well understood that the fastest and most reliable form of transport was by boat, either on rivers or along the coast. When a large Roman fleet appeared out of the mists of the North Sea, it must have seemed that the reach of the Empire was limitless, and that they found themselves surrounded, with no safe redoubt to flee to. According to Tacitus, it was at that moment that 'the peoples who inhabit Caledonia turned to armed struggle'.

As Ptolemy noted on his map, the area north of the Forth/Clyde line was settled by several peoples; the Taexali, the Vacomagi, the Decantae, the Lugi, the Smertae, the Cornovii and the Caledonii. Tacitus added the Boresti to this list of north-eastern groups, but he referred to the area only as Caledonia, and there is a sense that all were named after the most southerly hostile people. It seems that a confederate army was formed to block Agricola's advance. Roman military intelligence was good, no doubt gleaned from renegades or sympathizers, and the general learned that:

> The enemy were about to attack in several columns. To avoid encirclement by superior forces familiar with the country, he himself divided his army into three divisions and advanced.
>
> When the enemy discovered this, with a rapid change of plan they massed for a night attack on the IXth Legion, as being by far the weakest in numbers. They cut down the sentries and burst into the sleeping camp, creating panic. Fighting was already going on inside the camp itself when Agricola, who had learned of the enemy's route from his scouts and following close on their tracks, ordered the most mobile of his cavalry and infantry to charge the combatants from the rear and then the whole army was to raise the battle-cry. At first light the standards gleamed. The Britons were terrified at being caught between two fires, while the men of the IXth regained their

spirits and now that their lives were safe began to fight for glory. They even ventured on a break-out and a fierce battle followed in the narrow passage of the gates. Finally the enemy were driven back before the rival efforts of two armies. The one wanted to show that it had come to the rescue, the other that it had not needed help. Had not marshes or forests covered the retreating enemy, that victory would have ended the war.

It sounds like a close-run thing. Allowing for Tacitus' partiality, a Roman defeat seems to have been narrowly averted rather than a great victory almost achieved. He mentioned no estimates of casualties on either side. Perhaps the battle at the camp of the IXth Legion is best seen as inconclusive and the following certainly implies that reading:

The Britons, however, reckoned that they had not been defeated by superior courage but by the opportune actions and skill of the general. They lost none of their haughty spirit, in fact they armed their young men, moved their wives and children to places of safety, and ratified the alliance between their states by meetings and sacrifices. Thus spirits on both sides were stirred up as they parted.

The summer following the indecisive attack, Agricola's army was back in the north, seeking an opportunity to bring the Caledonian confederacy to battle. Fighting hand to hand in the confines of the camp of the IXth Legion, blundering between rows of leather tents and their guy-ropes in the darkness, was not the way to confront the enemy. Nor was the attrition of guerrilla warfare in Roman interests. Agricola's best chance lay in pitched battle, in the open, at a place where discipline and professionalism would succeed, even against greater numbers. And late in the summer of 83 his chance came. Intelligence reports told of a huge muster of Caledonian warriors at a place in the far north called *Mons Graupius*, 'the Graupian Mountain'.

Without waiting for his baggage train to assemble, Agricola brigaded his legions together and hurried north to meet the Caledonian host. It was September, and no time should be lost in grasping the opportunity he had been seeking since the army crossed the Tay. Tacitus took up the story and made the battle that followed the central set-piece of the *Agricola*:

> So he came to the Graupian Mountain. It had already been occupied by the enemy.
>
> The Britons were, in fact, in no way broken by the outcome of the previous battle: they were awaiting either revenge or enslavement. They had at last learned the lesson that a common danger could only be warded off by a united front. By means of embassies and alliances they had rallied the forces of all their states. Already more than 30,000 armed men could be observed and still all the young men and famous warriors, whose 'old age was still fresh and green', each man wearing the decorations he had won, were flowing in. No one was more outstanding among their many leaders for his valour and nobility, Calgacus by name, faced the assembled multitude as they clamoured for battle.

Calgacus, 'the Swordsman', appears to have been appointed by the confederacy as their general, someone expert in the arts of war, probably given a title like the Old Welsh *Gwledig*, or 'War-lord'. In the early historic period there are several instances of commands given in this way, to Celtic military leaders who were not kings. Cunedda led an army from southern Scotland in the 5th century to North Wales to expel the invading Irish. His name means simply 'Good Leader' and it survives in the Christian name Kenneth. Vortigern, the native British ruler who allowed the Saxons to establish themselves in Kent, is a similar title, 'Great Lord', and the most famous of all British generals, Arthur, is remembered in the chronicles as *Dux Bellorum*, or 'the Duke of Battles'.

Carry on camping

The difference between a Roman camp and a Roman fort (see plate xv) was to do with permanence. Camps were defended bivouacs thrown up along the line of a march or campaign, and some were occupied for only one night. Forts were intended as permanent garrisons and some were built in stone. The camps must have amazed native observers. Built in an hour or two at the end of a day and mostly removed the morning after, they were masterpieces of military organization. Ahead of the main body of troops, surveyors (called *mensores* or *gromatici*) selected a suitable site. It had to be in a place where attack was unlikely, close to running water but not enclosing too much poorly drained ground, and not too steeply sloping. The mensores first pegged out the lines of the perimeter and allocated space inside it for each unit's tents, the headquarters and the officers' quarters. For a good reason, everything was always in the same place. When the Caledonians mounted their night attack on the IXth Legion in 82, each soldier knew exactly where to run to find his officers, even in the dark. When the main column arrived at a campsite, sentries were posted and most of the men began digging a ditch and using the turf and upcast to create a palisade. The military manuals prescribed a standard size for a piece of turf: 1 ft by 1 ft 6 ins and 6 ins deep (30 by 45 by 15 cm). Twenty-two layers of turf, allowing for sagging, should have achieved a rampart height of 10 ft/3 m. Attached to his pack, each soldier carried two stakes for the palisade and these were set on top. Recent scholarship believes that the stakes were sharpened and tied together to form caltrops. There are more than 200 temporary camps in Scotland.

Before the armies clashed at Mons Graupius, Tacitus put a speech into Calgacus' mouth as he stood forth in front of the ranks of his warriors. It is of course a work of the imagination and, leaving aside the practical difficulties of being heard by 30,000 people, it is more eloquent about Tacitus' own republican instincts than the native politics of North Britain. But here and there bits of information can be gleaned.

First, and most obvious, the confederacy must have felt that their military options had reduced to one. With the appearance of the Roman fleet and the facts of geography permitting less and less room for manoeuvre, they clearly believed that there was no choice but to turn and fight. They had, bluntly, nowhere else to run. Even though the fate of Boudicca was well understood (Tacitus had Calgacus mention her partial success in his speech to the troops) and the battle-hardness and discipline of the Roman army likely to prevail in the open against superior numbers, they chose to gamble everything at Mons Graupius. Desperation must have driven that fateful decision. The movement of Agricola's army through Strathmore and over the Mounth into the Garioch had been like a plague of locusts, stripping the landscape of its harvest, emptying souterrains, slaughtering cattle and sheep by the thousand. The war council which appointed Calgacus knew that their peoples faced starvation if the Romans were not defeated and expelled. And despite Tacitus' claims for the battle at the camp of the IXth Legion, the confederate army had not been conquered. Perhaps at Graupius the gods would smile.

As a last line Tacitus had Calgacus say: 'On then into battle and as you go think both of your ancestors and your descendants.' In this there is a whisper of how a Celtic army behaved immediately before charging at the enemy. When the Roman historian Polybius described the Battle of Telamon, fought against the Cisalpine Gauls and large bands of Celtic mercenaries in the 3rd century BC, he observed that the warriors did not simply mass together. Instead, each tribe took a particular position in the line of battle, possibly as a matter of ancient right and custom. And within these deployments, family or clan groups stood together. In front were the oldest and most experienced warriors and behind them sons, nephews, cousins and perhaps foster-children. Standards were flown, either as pennants or as carved figures mounted on a pole, and very often these were animal totems. Just like the Roman eagles, they were powerful symbols. When Julius Caesar fought in Gaul, he recorded that his Celtic enemies made vows in the shadow of these standards in the moments before battle commenced.

It is very likely that the Caledonian army at Mons Graupius formed up in the same way, in tribes and family groups; perhaps the Lugi carried a raven, or the Cat People had a lynx standard to act as a rallying point in the confusion and mêlée of the fighting. But the traditions of Celtic warfare endured much longer, reaching across 2,000 years from Telamon to 18th-century Scotland. Nearly 100 km/60 miles to the west of Graupius, on Drummossie Moor, near Culloden House, another Celtic army formed up in the same way in 1746. Chased north by a modern, well-equipped and disciplined force, and shadowed by Rear-Admiral Byng's fleet in the Moray Firth, Bonnie Prince Charlie turned his undefeated Highland army and gave the order to prepare for battle. On the moor the clansmen rallied around their chiefs and stood to in family groups. The most experienced and older men were set in front, as they had been at Prestonpans and Falkirk, and with them stood the chief of the name. The Gaels believed that courage flowed down the generations. Facing the jeering redcoats opposite, each man began to do something entirely unique to a Highland army. Before going into battle they remembered who it was they were and why they had come to fight. They recited their genealogy: 'Is mise mac Ruari, mac Iain, mac Domhnaill', 'I am the son of Rory, the son of John, the son of Donald'. Some could go back 20 or 30 generations.

The Battle of Culloden began with an artillery cannonade which ploughed round shot through the Highland lines, but, inexplicably, Prince Charles refused to order the charge. For an hour men in the front rank shouted over their shoulders, begging for the *Claidheamh Mor!* – the order to charge. Finally Clan Chattan could take no more and broke away, racing towards the government lines, screaming their war cries. And when they saw that the *Cataich* were away, Clan Cameron, the Atholl Brigade and the Appin Stewarts broke into the charge. A short time later Gaelic Scotland had been blown to bits by an army which had stood fast and remembered its discipline. And 17 centuries before, something very similar appears to have happened at Mons Graupius.

When Calgacus finished his speech, the Caledonian confederacy cheered 'in barbarian fashion with roaring, singing and inarticulate cries'. Noise was important as an intimidatory prelude (something well understood by bagpipers in Highland armies). Carnyxes were trumpeted and the warriors chanted their battle-oaths and shouted abuse at the Romans who stood opposite, waiting. Some of the warriors in Calgacus' army will have been drunk, more accurately in the translation of a Gaelic phrase 'beside themselves with drink'. It was a transcendence thought to be valuable for battle. Roman commentators often noted a Celtic fondness for strong drink and drunkenness, but for warriors it was used to induce what contemporary Irish sources called *the rage-fit*, a battle frenzy which could produce acts of superhuman courage. Men became what the Vikings later called *berserkers*.

Polybius described the mercenary bands at Telamon as *gaesatae* and this is usually translated as 'spearmen'. But the term is cognate with *geissi*, 'rules of conduct', or 'taboos'. When the Romans saw these mercenary bands strip off all their clothing to fight naked and reveal their tattoos, it may be that they were showing the magical marks of membership of a soldier society, those who lived and died by the *geissi*, warriors bound together by oaths. And their nudity was part of a ritual, a signal to each other and to the gods that the power of the tattoos of the society was power enough. Tacitus does not mention naked warriors at Mons Graupius but it is very likely that there were some.

After Agricola had spoken and exhorted his men that 'it would not be inglorious to die at the very place where the world and nature end', the battle was joined in earnest. The Roman auxiliary regiments were deployed in the centre, the cavalry on the flanks and the legionaries kept back as a reserve, 'stationed in front of the rampart' of the marching camp. The Caledonian army used the slopes of the Graupian Mountain to claim the higher ground but their front ranks extended down to the plain. Between the opposing armies charioteers rode back and forth 'making a din'. As at Culloden the fighting began with one side projecting missiles, and the Caledonian warriors evidently showed great skill at parrying Roman javelins with their swords and small shields. Then the Batavian and Tungrian (also from the Low Countries) cohorts pressed forward to engage in hand-to-hand fighting, the vicious scrummage of pushing and stabbing which characterized Roman battle tactics:

> This was what they had been trained for in their long service, whereas it was awkward for the enemy with their small shields and enormous swords – for the swords of the Britons, having no points, were unsuited for a cut-and-thrust struggle and close-quarters battle.

Tacitus' observation is crucial, for the outcome of the battle turned on this difference in equipment. The long slashing swords and small shields were designed for fighting on horseback, not on foot. In the press of men, with second and third ranks pushing the first forward, it was impossible to draw back a long blade to slash at an opposing infantryman. By contrast the Roman *gladius* was much shorter, and where gaps appeared – and there were many around the Caledonians' smaller shields – the Batavians and Tungrians stabbed and thrust to murderous effect.

Calgacus had positioned many of his warriors on the slopes of the Graupian Mountain, and when the battle was joined they began to descend and moved to outflank the Roman line. But Agricola immediately countered with four regiments of cavalry, and now that the entire Caledonian army appeared to be fighting on the flatter ground, they were outflanked. The Roman cavalry got behind them and the battle began to swing towards Agricola. And then it turned into a rout, and then into a merciless slaughter. So that his soldiers could kill as many of the fleeing Caledonians as possible, Agricola had them form 'a huntsman's cordon' and move through the woods and finish off whomever they had trapped. Tacitus reported 10,000 enemy dead and only 360 Romans. The figures are probably an exaggeration, but it seems that very many were cut down as they fled, yet again a gory illustration of imperial ruthlessness. Agricola remembered the Boudicca revolt and how the great slaughter in AD 60 had effectively pacified the south.

And 17 centuries later the Duke of Cumberland carried on the grisly tradition as his troops pursued and killed Highlanders fleeing from the disaster at Culloden in 1746.

The unlucky IXth

Rosemary Sutcliff's excellent novel *The Eagle of the Ninth* has sold a million copies since its publication in 1954. The alleged disappearance of the IXth Legion somewhere in Scotland has also inspired multiple cinematic projects, including the 2010 British historical-action film *Centurion*. Despite the likelihood that it never happened, the episode is attractive. In the past film producers have lavished fortunes on 'epics' or 'sword and sandal' movies featuring ranks of legionaries in red cloaks and plumed helmets. That there are no facts surrounding the disappearance of the IXth should deter no one. Most successful epics wisely use Rome only as a background to a plot cooked up by a team of writers whose duty is not to teach history but keep the audience interested. *Ben-Hur* and *Gladiator* have entirely spurious but entertaining narratives. Perhaps the film which came closest to documentary reality was *Carry on Cleo*, starring Kenneth Williams as Julius Caesar. The scene just before his assassination at the Senate has him say, 'Infamy, infamy, they've all got it in for me.'

He was right.

The location of the Battle of Mons Graupius has never been certain. But it must have happened somewhere along the line of march traced by the string of temporary camps found in the north-east by aerial photography. At Durno, in the valley of the River Don, north-west of Aberdeen, the outline of a very large marching camp has been found, big enough to accommodate the numbers who fought at Graupius. And near at hand is the singular hill of Bennachie (see plate xvi). *Crwb* in Old Welsh, 'hump', is the root of *Graupius*, a geographical term implying a hump standing by itself, as Bennachie does. Battles also tend to be fought on well-used routeways and near the locations of other battles at different times in history. The Don valley carries the modern A96. Only a few miles from the camp at Durno (when Agricola formed his legions against 'the rampart', it suggests that the camp was very close to the battlefield), the Battle of Harlaw was fought in 1411 between the Lords of the Isles and the Earl of Mar. And a century before, in 1308, Robert de Bruce defeated the Comyn Earl of Buchan at the Battle of Barra, fought in the fields north of Inverurie Castle, not far from the camp at Durno. The surrounding landscape is also rich with prehistoric monuments: the recumbent stone circles at East Aquhorthies and Loanhead of Daviot and several Pictish symbol stones. It is likely that when the Caledonian confederacy chose their battleground, it was in a place familiar to their gods.

The aftermath of Mons Graupius was undoubtedly bloody. Agricola continued his march through the Moray Firth lowlands. The army ate its way across farmland, removing much that would have been needed to survive the winter soon to follow. No doubt many farmers and their families died of starvation in the war-blackened wake of the victorious invaders. And the consequences of the policy of genocide have turned up in the archaeological record. Pollen cores have shown a general breakdown of farming in Aberdeenshire in the 1st century AD, and of a such a scale that centuries would pass before it recovered.

On native sites of the same period, archaeologists have found traces of a curious story. As happened in the south of England at the time of the Claudian invasion 40 years before, hillforts seemed once again to become places of refuge. Many had been abandoned in the centuries before the Romans arrived, but there is evidence of rebuilding and reoccupation, even of new forts, in the north-east. On the higher ground above the glen-blocking fort at Fendoch in Perthshire, there are signs of activity at a place known as *Dun Mor* in Gaelic, 'Great Fort'. Stones had been gathered and piled up in readiness for masons to use in the construction of a rampart. It seems that the site was abandoned before they could begin work. Much further north, in the area of Agricola's final advance in 83, marker trenches were laid out at Little Conval in Banffshire, but again the work went no further. Similar preparations were made in other places, at Dun Hill and Hill O' Christ's Kirk in Banffshire and at Cromar in Aberdeenshire. In the same region aerial photography has made out four Agricolan marching camps at Auchinhove, Muiryfold, Burnfield and Glenmailen. The abandonment of the hillforts and the building of the Roman camps may be related events.

According to Tacitus the triumph of Mons Graupius was altogether too much for the brooding, insecure Emperor Domitian to accept. After his successful campaign Agricola was recalled to Rome with some muttered, unsubstantiated promise of another province to make sure he did return, perhaps the governorship of Syria. But nothing came of it and Agricola made his way back to the imperial court, entering the city at night, and 'was greeted with a perfunctory kiss and then dismissed without a word, into the crowd of courtiers'. And from that time onwards he wisely kept his head down and took no part in the whispers and intrigue swirling around Domitian's palace. But despite Tacitus' spin, there was probably nothing sinister in Agricola's recall. In serving as governor of Britannia for six years he had spent twice as long in the province as any of his predecessors.

The Isle of the Dead

The smaller islands to the west of Britain have long been seen as mystical, perhaps because they lie in the path of the setting sun. *Tir nan Og*, 'the Land of the Ever-Young', lay out in the western ocean and represented a Celtic version of heaven. Iona was seen as sacred before Columba and the Druids may have flourished on Mona, or Anglesey, because it was seen as a holy island. But if the perspective shifts eastwards, Britain itself can be viewed in a similar way. In the 1st century AD, Pomponius Mela related a belief that the Ile de Sein, off the south-west tip of Brittany, was a departure port for the souls of the dead. From there nine priestesses presided over the passage of souls to Britain, which was known as the Isle of the Dead. Perhaps that is why invading Roman soldiers mutinied before they crossed the Channel.

His successor lacked a Tacitus to make him famous, or even known. His name is lost to history. However, the new administration's initial intentions were clear enough. After the victory at Mons Graupius, the territory north of the Tay needed to be brought within the Empire and to do that properly the army had to have a substantial base, a legionary fortress like those at Chester and York.

In a loop of the River Tay near Blairgowrie the army's surveyors came across a very suitable site. A slightly raised gravel plateau called Inchtuthil was large enough at about 80 ha/200 acres and well positioned. Its name implies prior ownership and occupation; it means 'Tuathal's Island'. Nearby was the main arterial track into the Highlands, the heartland of the Caledonians (now the line of the A9), and a large garrison of 6,000 soldiers could expect to draw its provisions from the fertile valleys of Strathtay and Strathmore immediately to the south and east. The fortress at Inchtuthil covered about 21 ha/52 acres and contained several grand buildings. A huge undertaking, it required a vast reservoir of local resources from an already populous landscape. It has been reckoned that a fort of about 2 ha/4 acres needed 620 cu.m/22,000 cu.ft of timber for its internal buildings, towers and gates. Inchtuthil will have wanted around 2,800 cu. m/100,000 cu. ft, or about 7,000 mature trees, to complete it. Forests crashed as Roman work gangs ranged over the Perthshire countryside with axes, saws and carts.

Inside the rampart were 64 barracks blocks, four tribunes' houses, a headquarters building, a hospital, a workshop, a drill hall and many storehouses lining the principal streets. Inchtuthil was in effect a military town and its creation would have both impoverished and amazed the people who lived in the straths around it. On all sides of the fort native settlements were levelled and farmers and their families evicted. What else could a conquered people expect? A legionary precinct of some size was needed, and to the east an ancient and sacred site was used as a boundary. There is some evidence that the central bank of the Cleaven Dyke had been refurbished after 83 and raised in order to provide a clear limit to the precinct. If the memory of sanctity still endured amongst

XI PREVIOUS PAGE The right-hand summit in the Eildon Hills in the Scottish Borders is crowned by a huge hillfort with a mile-long rampart and room for more than 300 hut circles.

XII OPPOSITE, ABOVE The Manor Valley, near Peebles in the Borders.

XIII OPPOSITE, BELOW The crag at Traprain, rising out of the East Lothian farmland, a focus of Votadini power.

XIV ABOVE The broch at Dun Carloway on Lewis in the Western Isles.

xv ABOVE 'Lillia' defence pits near Rough Castle Roman fort, not far from Falkirk.

xvi OPPOSITE, ABOVE Looking from the slopes of Bennachie in Aberdeenshire towards the probable site of the battle of Mons Graupius, AD 83.

xvii OPPOSITE, BELOW Watling Lodge, near Falkirk. The ditching in front of the Antonine Wall has survived in an excellent state of preservation despite its exposed urban location.

XVIII AND XIX ABOVE, LEFT AND RIGHT Details from Pictish stones at Shandwick, Highland.

XX LEFT Pictish stone at Aberlemno in Angus, showing a number of characteristic symbols – a Z-rod, a mirror, a double disc and a serpent.

XXI OPPOSITE This Pictish symbol-stone in Aberlemno kirkyard almost certainly commemorates the great Pictish victory over the Angles at Dunnichen in AD 685.

XXII OVERLEAF Set at the side of a busy modern road (no doubt overlying a busy ancient one), this symbol-stone at Aberlemno obviously dates from the conversion of the Pictish nation to Christianity, but the sculptor was unable to resist adding playful animal carving.

the Caledonians then its reuse as a handy military boundary would have represented another affront.

A magnificent bathhouse was built at Inchtuthil, probably for the use of officers, but even though it was completed no furnace was ever lit to heat its water, and it was never used. In AD 87 Domitian was campaigning on the Danube and, hard-pressed by barbarians, he was forced to recall the IInd Legion, the Adiutrix, from Britain. This led to a significant weakening of the provincial garrison and to the immediate abandonment of Scotland. All Agricola's gains were given up, and Tacitus was scathing: Britain had been conquered totally 'and straight away let go'. Inchtuthil was carefully dismantled, its timber and dressed stone loaded on to carts; under the floor of a workshop a cache of a million nails was buried so that they did not fall into the hands of native smiths who could turn them into weapons.

But much had been learned for future use by an imperial army, and much of that is valuable to a clearer understanding of the native history of Scotland. When the legionaries made their way south from Inchtuthil to Newstead and eventually down to the Stanegate frontier and the Hexham Gap, they left behind a landscape of poverty, waste and debris. But they also left a precious map of North Britain: what Ptolemy was able to piece together from the intelligence gathered during the Agricolan campaigns.

Most intriguing are the 19 'towns' noted on the map. In addition to Rerigonium, Trimontium and Carbantorigum, he plotted *Pinnata Castra* on the Moray Firth coast, *Tuesis* and *Devana* in Aberdeenshire, *Tamia* and *Bannatia* in Perthshire, *Victoria*, *Horrea* and *Alauna* in Fife, another *Alauna* and *Lindum* in the Stirling area, *Vindogara* on the Ayrshire coast, *Corda*, *Coria* and *Colania* in the Borders, and *Lucopibia* and *Uxellum* near the Solway coast. These were not towns, at least not in the sense that we think of now. Archaeology has found no trace of anything urban, unlike in the more Romanized south, for this or any other period in Scotland up to the early Middle Ages.

It is much more likely that Agricola's intelligence officers learned of these places and their names from native people, and that they were meeting-points, hillforts or possibly markets, places where people came together rather than lived together. *Pinnata Castra* means 'Winged Camp', or a camp whose ramparts had places of shelter built into them. It is an odd description, but one almost certainly made by a military man used to building and living in a camp. It implies an exposed site and may refer to the forerunner of the great Pictish naval base at Burghead (rebuilt some time after 300) between Nairn and Lossiemouth. *Tuesis* lay somewhere on the River Spey, while *Tamia* may have been a fort occupied by the Caledonians in one of the more fertile glens of the central Grampian Mountains. The name means something like 'station' or 'base'. *Devana* is simply 'Deetown', but its location appears to be set too far inland for it to be an early name for Aberdeen. Banchory is more likely, apart from the much earlier timber hall at Balbridie, but there is no obvious archaeological feature to suggest a place of ancient importance in that part of the territory of the Taexali. In central Fife there is a much more unambiguous name. Ptolemy plotted *Horrea* which translates as 'corn-store' or 'warehouse', and this was probably an ingathering point for the harvests of the fertile fields of the Venicones, a place of the greatest importance to Roman quartermasters anxious to provision a hungry army. Two more *Horreae* were to be found elsewhere in the Roman Empire, most probably named as such for the same reasons.

Mess

The term 'mess', when applied to the place where servicemen eat together, is, appropriately, derived from the Latin word *missus*, a course served at dinner. Roman soldiers messed together in eight-man platoons, and unlike modern soldiers they had to pay for their food. The daily ration for each man was three pounds of bread, two pounds of meat, two pints of wine (or the equivalent in beer in Britain) and an eighth of a pint of oil (1.4 kg, 0.9 kg, 1.1 l, 7 cl). It was probably issued weekly and the men took it in turns to cook. Cereal, usually wheat, was central to their diet and it was often made into a porridge for breakfast. There was no midday meal and the men had to wait until suppertime for something substantial. An analysis of the contents of a blocked drain at the Antonine Wall fort of Bearsden, near Glasgow, has shown that most soldiers lived on a predominantly vegetarian diet and often flavoured their porridge with wild fruit and nuts which they gathered or bought locally.

Many of the names of the Ptolemy 'towns' are obscure, but the western *Alauna* seems to stand for the Rock at Dumbarton, the spectacular prehistoric fortress of the Damnonii which kept its importance for centuries. *Alauna* means 'the Rock' and the eastern counterpart may be the earliest known name for Edinburgh, or more precisely Edinburgh Castle rock. *Lindon* signified a settlement on a lake and the site of Balloch on Loch Lomond is in the right place, although Ptolemy did not mark the loch itself. *Victoria* is purely a Roman or Latin name and it was probably attached to a place which the soldiers built and had nothing to do with any native settlement. Perhaps after the defeat of the Caledonian confederacy in 83, the builders of Inchtuthil called their military town Victoria.

Rivers often carry the oldest names in the landscape. Many are pre-Celtic, going back to Indo-European roots. *Alt Clut* was another very early name for Dumbarton Rock and it translates as 'the Rock of the Clyde'. Ptolemy called the river *Clota* and this appears to be the name of its god. Clota was feared and revered as the 'Washer' or the 'Cleanser'. *Dee* is also a river-god, while the *Tava* or Tay and the *Bodotria* or Forth both mean approximately 'the Silent One'. And the Tweed was 'the Surger'. In the minds of the peoples who first named Scotland's rivers, they were not only divine but also active in different ways, living and moving through the landscape.

Bog limbo

Preserved by the acidic conditions of peat bogs, more than 100 bodies have been found which date from between 600 BC and AD 400. For obvious reasons, these finds have all been made in Ireland, Britain and

Scandinavia. Many of the bodies show evidence of a ritual, multiple death. For example, Lindow Man (known to his finders as Pete Marsh) from Cheshire appears to have been poisoned, beaten up, hit with an axe, garrotted, had his throat cut and, if he was still alive, drowned in the bog. The archaeologist Timothy Taylor believes that the preservative properties of the peat bogs were well understood and that they were used as a place to put a soul into limbo. And the multiple deaths were designed to confuse the soul, making it uncertain when to leave the body.

Many rivers were also boundaries, and in prehistory the sacred was often celebrated on the margins, in liminal places. The incidence of a particular name for streams and lochs in several widely scattered areas of Scotland is suggestive of this. *Locha* or sometimes *lochy*, or even *lochaidh* in Gaelic, was not a variant on *loch*; instead it means 'black goddess'. And in Fife, Perthshire, Banffshire, Inverness-shire and Morayshire there are 'black goddess' streams, and at the south-western end of the Great Glen there is Loch Lochy and the River Lochy. The former is not a tautology (common enough in place-names deriving from two languages) but means 'the Loch of the Black Goddess'. Some of these lochy places were certainly local boundaries. In the historic period battles have been fought at some of them. And occasionally the name slips into English. The upper reaches of Galloway's River Dee are called 'the Black Water of Dee'.

Old ways of understanding Scotland's internal frontiers have been eclipsed very recently by modern attitudes. We travel easily, quickly and frequently by car, hindered occasionally by the weather and more often by road works than by the facts of geography. We rarely give a second thought to the old boundaries we frequently cross. By contrast, the early peoples did not move overland if they could help it. Water transport, by sea, loch and navigable river, was much more reliable until the railway revolution of the 19th century. And the landward bias of the Roman Empire also occasionally blinds us to the vital role of travel on water. All roads may have led from Rome, and if they were well maintained movement was made much easier. But for millennia before they came and after they left, Scotland communicated with itself by water.

Ancient land boundaries nullified by the railway and then by the car have also slipped out of our way of seeing Scotland. The two distinct cultural areas to the north and south of the Forth were much more meaningful to travellers until Flanders Moss was drained in the 18th and 19th centuries. The extent of the moss, made much worse in winter, underlined the pivotal importance of Stirling. It was the gateway to the north, and the south, unless you had a boat. In the Old Welsh poem composed in Edinburgh in 600, the *Gododdin*, a warrior is described as coming from beyond *Minid Bannauc*. This was the hill country at the head of the River Carron, the Campsie Fells, out of which flows the Bannock Burn. *Beyond Bannawg* may have been an early label attached to someone from the lands immediately north of the Forth. Near Stonehaven the wide and fertile flatlands of Strathmore narrow considerably as the Grampian mountains edge towards the North Sea. This wedge of hills was still known as *the Mounth* in the 19th century and it represented a further barrier to landward travel.

Besides *Victoria*, Ptolemy's other obvious Latin name was *Trimontium*, the fort at the foot of the three Eildon Hills at Newstead. When Domitian withdrew the IInd Legion Adiutrix, it became important again. The imperial military planners drew back the frontier to the fortified road at the Stanegate. This ran through the Hexham Gap along the southern foothills of the Cheviots. Outpost forts were maintained at Glenlochar and Dalswinton in the territory of the Novantae in Galloway, on the western fringes of the Selgovae at Tassieholm, and to the east at Newstead.

Policy was evolving in Rome. As Domitian held the Rhine/Danube line only with great difficulty, he found rebellion breaking out behind him, amongst peoples recently incorporated into the Empire. It slowly became clear that Rome could not continue to expand her northern frontiers indefinitely, and a limit had to be set somewhere. In Britain the Stanegate held and the outpost forts supplied intelligence and some stability in a wide frontier zone to the north and west. From Newstead,

Dalswinton and the others, patrols went out each day to watch for hostile movement in the countryside. Links were maintained with the friendly Votadini, and assurances probably given as traffic continued up and down Dere Street.

In AD 96 Domitian was stabbed to death by his wife (she had help) and replaced by Nerva, an old man who would sit on the imperial throne for only two years. He had adopted the tough and practical soldier Trajan as his heir and under his firm rule the Empire in the West stabilized. Uninterested in expensive triumphs in Britain (and much more disposed to campaigning in the East), he pulled the frontier back to the Stanegate and abandoned some of the outpost forts. In AD 100 Newstead was burned, and while historians have judged that this was done by a retreating garrison and not hostile action, archaeologists have not found the evidence to support them. At Inchtuthil bent nails pulled out of recyclable timber by claw-hammers have been found along with other signs of planned withdrawal. But at Newstead nothing like this has come to light. It may well be that the fort was attacked, perhaps while it was only lightly guarded, by the Selgovan king and his warband and its wood and thatch buildings set aflame. As a hated symbol of the Empire, as the resort of blasphemers and ruthless exploiters, the fortress would have attracted the anger of many who lived in the hills to the west.

The evacuation and sack of Newstead was also an unmistakable signal to the Votadini. No record of any battle or skirmish has come down to us, but the enmity between the Selgovae and their eastern neighbours almost certainly spilled over into something more incendiary when the Romans marched south down Dere Street and left their allies unprotected.

Towards the end of Trajan's reign more trouble was recorded in Britain. Encouraged by the withdrawal from the north and the emperor's strategic emphasis on the east, the Brigantes sent messengers over the hill trails to the Selgovae and the Novantae. The time was right to strike and to strike in combined strength. Between 115 and 120 warbands mustered, rode out of the Pennines and attacked and destroyed the legionary fortress at York. Stationed there was the unlucky IXth Hispana, the depleted legion caught in the night raid on their camp by the Caledonii in 82. Tradition has it that the Brigantian alliance annihilated the IXth and inflicted the greatest dishonour by capturing and removing their eagle standards. More than 40 years after the event, the orator Fronto wrote of heavy losses of legionary troops (as opposed to the more expendable auxiliaries) in Britain at this time, and he compared this disaster with the obliteration of the XXIInd Legion Deiotariana in the Jewish rebellion in Judaea. But the facts are not clear. Certainly the records of the IXth Hispana at York simply cease after 106, but it may be that remnants survived and that they were sent on European postings. What is beyond dispute is the resurgence of native military power. Seventy-five years after the Claudian invasion and two generations after Cerialis' victories and fort-building in the north, the spirit of Brigantian, Selgovan and Novantan independence remained unquenched. In the hill country of Britain Rome was hated, and the reasons for that probably lie in the invaders' policy of indiscriminate genocide.

Since it ran through the territory of the Votadini the eastern end of the Stanegate was peaceful. The situation in the west was very different. There the Romans concentrated large, thousand-strong units known as *milliary cohorts*, and these could be made up of infantry, a mixture of infantry and cavalry or purely cavalry forces. At Stanwix near Carlisle the Ala Petriana, a crack cavalry regiment, was stationed for rapid response, and it may have been needed often. The Eden Valley, the fertile land around the headwaters of the Solway, and the valleys of the Esk and Annan brought together the Brigantes, the Selgovae and the Novantae, and whenever they gathered their warbands the Romans believed that they had sufficient military hitting power on hand to deal with the threat.

By AD 115 to 120, it was clear that changes were necessary. Unable to control movement and prevent the hill warriors from communicating and combining in the west, the commander at Stanwix fort ordered the construction of a turf wall in 119. The initiative for this would have come directly from Rome. Frontier policy was the traditional preserve of the emperor and Trajan's successor, Hadrian, spent most of his reign formulating and supervising it. The forerunner to what became known as Hadrian's Wall was built at first only in the west and it ran from Willowford in the Irthing Valley to Bowness on Solway. Three forward forts were occupied at Birrens, Netherby and Bewcastle and their purpose was to patrol, gather intelligence and deal with the early stages of trouble if they could. It may be that the three forts also had a role in tax-gathering, at least in kind if not cash. If they encompassed a bulge in Brigantian territory that extended beyond the wall (and was therefore seen as an outlying part of the Empire), then such a disposition might make sense. The native name for Birrens offers a little support; it was *Blatobulgium*, which translates as 'the meal sack place', similar to Horrea in Fife. Inside the fort itself, archaeologists came across a dedication to Brigantia, and that points to a close association with the area and perhaps a whisper that Birrens lay on the limit of Brigantian land.

Orders of the day

Inside every Roman fort the day began in the same way across the Empire. At the headquarters building a morning report recorded the number of officers and men present, and listed them by rank and type. A password for the day was issued and the names of the sentries standing watch over the standards were read out. And finally a list of men arriving at the fort and leaving on that day was also compiled. Most garrisons spent 90 per cent of their time not fighting or campaigning and work had to be found for them. Fatigues such as street-cleaning, road-building and maintenance of all sorts were common. If these were to be avoided, a soldier could volunteer to become a clerk. The Roman army needed clerks because it was extremely bureaucratic. Receipts were issued in quadruplicate and each soldier had his own dossier with details of recruitment and service. Files were even kept on army horses.

In 122 Hadrian arrived in Britain, the first emperor to visit since Claudius brought his elephants, and he came with a radical solution for the northern frontier in mind. A stone wall would extend from the estuary of the Tyne to join the turf wall at Willowford. It was a massive enterprise, the wall eventually being built entirely in stone to become a very elaborate military complex, the most emphatic frontier in the empire 'to separate barbarians from Romans'. Milecastles, watchtowers and forts were part of the scheme, and immediately to the south of the wall itself a road was laid down with a ditch and embankments beyond it.

The drain on local resources must have been extraordinary, and it has been estimated that 3.7 million tonnes of stone were used. The logistics were very complex. For every ten men working on building the wall itself, there were 90 finding and bringing forward the raw materials needed. It has been reckoned that over five years 30,000 vehicles and drivers, 5,800 oxen and 14,200 mules were used. While modern volunteers were working on the reconstruction of a fragment of the wall at Vindolanda, it was discovered that ditch-digging was the most arduous task.

As with the Gask Ridge *limes*, the central notion behind Hadrian's Wall was the control of movement, the collection of revenue in the form of customs dues and the gathering and transmission of military intelligence. But Hadrian also intended his wall to impress, to show the Brigantes, Selgovae and Novantae, and the peoples to the north of them, how spectacularly Rome could exercise its power. A cleared zone on both sides of the wall was not only an important aid to security, it also demonstrated how the Empire could change the face of the land as far as the eye could see. And recent archaeology has underlined the great importance of show. To the native peoples of the 2nd century AD Hadrian's Wall did not look as it does now in the better-preserved sections, or even in the reconstruction at Vindolanda, built out of grey stone that seems to blend into the muted colours of the upland landscape. The wall was originally white. Traces of white rendering have been found and it seems that when the masons had completed the stonework they covered it with a lime-based plaster thickened with hemp. It helped make the walls waterproof and kept out the damp, but more than that, it meant that the gleaming ramparts could be seen from many miles away on either side as they snaked along the ridge north of the Stanegate. Rome had divided the island and the barbarians were to be left in no doubt about the magnitude of the power of the Empire.

Hadrian's Wall has never formed the frontier between what became England and Scotland, but it did have an important role in forming attitudes. Beyond the great white wall lay what the Romans called *Britannia Barbarica*, while to the south was the land governed by the soldiers and administrators probably known to the native peoples as *Y Rhufeiniwr* (phonetically, *Roovanoor*), Old Welsh for 'the Romans'. This was of course a heavily loaded distinction; the barbarians were crude and uncultured and the Romans were sophisticated and well educated. While this is also a false distinction, it has been a tenacious one.

After Hadrian's death in 138 there was war in the north of Britain, yet again. Perhaps the hill peoples of southern Scotland took the opportunity of a regime change in Rome to press the garrisons of the wall and the outpost forts. It is inconceivable that the Selgovan and Novantan kings allowed themselves to be uninformed about the vicissitudes of imperial politics. Just as the officers on Hadrian's Wall sent out patrols and gathered information, so the hill peoples to the north would have done the same thing. There was no more important piece of news than the death of an emperor, and it would have travelled like lightning around the Empire.

Self-made eunuchs

Catterick has always had a macho, military image. The north Yorkshire town was home to many retired Roman soldiers, it was the site of a crucial battle between Celts and Angles in AD 600 and was one of the largest modern army camps in Britain. But recent excavation has come up with a different image. The burial of a transvestite priest has been found. He or she was wearing women's clothes, was dripping with jewellery and had an elaborate hair-do. A devotee of the cult of Cybele, which was also popular at Corbridge on Hadrian's Wall, the priest had castrated himself in a gruesome religious ceremony. Using a clamp, similar to one found in the Thames, he had cut off his testicles in imitation of Cybele's lover, Attis, who had made himself a eunuch as a punishment for his infidelity. Mystical eastern religions were popular in the Roman north and temples to Mithras, an eastern god much favoured by soldiers, can be found along the line of the Wall.

At all events, the contemporary written sources are unambiguous about what happened on the accession of the new emperor, Antoninus Pius: '[he] defeated the Britons through the actions of the governor, Lollius Urbicus, and, driving off the barbarians, built another wall of turf'. Although they are not named, the peoples who held territory beyond the Forth appear to have sent an expedition south, most probably in alliance with the Selgovae, the Novantae and the Brigantes. If so, it is the first notice of Caledonian military activity since the Agricolan war nearly 60 years before. His policy of genocide was therefore very effective if it took three generations for the northern peoples to recover. The evidence gleaned from coins, sculpture and inscriptions suggests that this latest battle was a hard fight, one which Roman soldiers were glad and proud to have won.

The immediate consequence of Lollius Urbicus' successful campaign to drive the barbarians back north (where they belonged) was the construction of another wall, what became known as the Antonine Wall (see plate XVII). Historians have argued that Hadrian and his advisers made a strategic blunder in siting the earlier wall through the Hexham Gap, and that the much shorter Antonine Wall (less than half the distance) was at last in the right place. The Romans may not have seen it in the same way. Although the bulk of the garrison of Hadrian's Wall was moved north, the stone wall was not completely abandoned. In any case both structures were not understood as ramparts facing north, but more like military corridors along which men, materials and information might pass. And they also existed as a means of separating and controlling the movement of hostile peoples who might otherwise find it much easier to combine their forces against Rome. Two walls had the effect of chopping northern Britain into militarily manageable segments, a series of buffers against incursions into the increasingly prosperous south. It may also be the case that the Antonine Wall was worth building to incorporate the Votadini into the Empire and protect the Venicones. Hadrian's Wall had certainly left them adrift.

Like Claudius and Domitian before him, Antoninus Pius needed to buttress his succession with a little glory, and military success in Britain once again met that need. No set-piece battles like Mons Graupius are recorded – surely native generals would never again make that fatal mistake – but several reoccupations of Agricolan forts, including those on the Gask Ridge, and the building of some new marching camps show the creation of a wide frontier zone on either side of the new wall.

Three legions marched north to carry out the building work. Beginning at Carriden on the Firth of Forth, the Antonine Wall was built from east to west. Each legion, or part of one, split into two work gangs and began at either end of an allotted section, ultimately meeting in the middle. Both gangs were further divided, with one section working on the ditch and the other cutting turf and raising the rampart. Twenty distance slabs have been found along the Antonine Wall so far, and they record who did what and where. There were 26 forts built into the wall and set much closer together than on Hadrian's Wall. The forts at Balmuildy, Castlecary and (to police the Forth shore) Cramond were made out of stone with their walls rising to a height of 4.5–5 m/15–16 ft, and these must have been especially impressive. The whole effect of the Antonine Wall was very striking, another display of awesome power. When the kings of the southern Caledonians looked south from the ramparts of their hillforts in the Ochils, they would have felt that the Empire had physically moved its frontier north to confront them. The wall stood three times the height of a man; scouts had ridden its length and reported it strangely uniform, with breaks only to allow streams and rivers to pass under bridges. And in the estuaries at either end many Roman ships lay bobbing at anchor, ready to patrol the unguarded shores.

Very unusually, the Antonine Wall left place-names in central Scotland, perhaps as a measure of the impression it made. Kirkintilloch has nothing to do with an early church – its derivation is *Caerpentalloch* or 'the fort at the head of the ridge'; Cramond is a squeezed rendition of *Caer-almond*, 'the fort on the River Almond'. And the medieval name for the wall suggests a realistic appraisal of its nature. It was called *the Grimsdyke*.

Not everyone regarded the Romans with hostility. As we have seen, the Venicones of Fife and the Votadini of the south-east were on friendly terms with the invaders and it may be that the communities living around the eastern end of the wall were compliant, even interested in Romanization. The area around the head of the Firth of Forth was known as *Manau Gododdin* in the 5th century and it may have been the westernmost part of the territory of the Votadini (the names Votadini and Gododdin being closely cognate) in the 2nd. In any event there is a glimmer of native involvement with the garrison at Carriden, in a dedication to the Roman god Jupiter. It was made by the villagers who lived outside the fort. In putting together the cash, and the will to do this small thing, they show themselves as some sort of local unit of organization, if not government, anxious to do something similar to what the invaders were in the habit of doing.

The intensive programme of wall-building encouraged the Brigantes to mount another rebellion. As the Romans' Pennine forts emptied their garrisons in the move north, the Brigantes' warbands rode out of the hills to raid in the south. In so doing they forfeited their right to a *civitas*, a tribal capital at Aldborough near York. The peoples to the north of the Antonine Wall would have been grateful to the Brigantes, for the rebellion was sufficiently serious to force the army southwards until it was contained.

In 161 there was yet more trouble. 'Calpurnius Agricola was sent to deal with the Britons', wrote a near-contemporary, and the general seems to have been active at Corbridge and elsewhere. By the time Marcus Aurelius succeeded Antoninus Pius in 163, the frontier zone in northern Britain must have appeared stretched. Following the imperial dictum that 'what could not be held should be given up', the army was ordered to abandon the Antonine Wall and pull back to Hadrian's.

This must have appeared to the native kings as a victory of sorts. The Empire had advanced into the north, its forces took immense trouble to build a long wall and reoccupy its crumbling outpost forts, and then they were forced to retreat. Around the fires in their roundhouses and brochs, bards will have sung of the prowess of the warbands, the conquerors of Rome; perhaps the Old Welsh phrase 'the Island of the Mighty' came into currency at that time. In 169 the northern frontier was still tense as a Roman historian reported that 'the Britons are on the verge of war'. At Kirksteads, near Carlisle, an altar was dedicated by a legate of the VIth Legion in thanks for 'the successful outcome of action beyond the Wall'. After the abandonment of the Antonine Wall, the Selgovan, Novantan and Brigantian kings may have resumed their alliance. And at the eastern end of Hadrian's Wall, at Corbridge, another dedication was inscribed on an altar after a regimental commander had slaughtered a band of *Corionototae*. The identity of this group is unknown, and recorded nowhere else. A letter found at Vindolanda mentioned the *Anavionenses*, clearly a people local to the area of Hadrian's Wall and also not recorded elsewhere. These two scraps of evidence suggest a much more complex pattern of native settlement than that which has come down to us through the work of Ptolemy and others.

Towards the end of the 2nd century the tide of war had begun to turn. After a century of defeat at the hands of the disciplined ranks of Roman armies, the warbands of the north had learned how to win. The historian Dio Cassius wrote that between 180 and 192, in the reign of the Emperor Commodus:

> ... his greatest war was in Britain. The tribes in the island crossed the Wall which separated them from the Roman legions, did a great deal of damage, and cut down a general and his troops; so Commodus in alarm sent Ulpius Marcellus against them. Marcellus inflicted a major defeat on the barbarians.

It may be that the northern armies penetrated as far as the legionary fortress at York, where they could have found a general, to say nothing of his garrison. No doubt Ulpius Marcellus arrived in Britain with reinforcements and was able to drive the warbands out of the province and thereby restore order. But there was no crushing defeat followed by a surrender and mass killings of the kind carried out after Mons Graupius. Instead, a treaty was negotiated, and one of its terms was that the Caledonian confederacy should not reform. This implies a pre-existing grand coalition in the north and perhaps also in the south of Scotland. The names of the Selgovae and Novantae largely fade out of the historical record at this time, but those Romans and Greeks who wrote about the north were often vague about which barbarians were which.

In 197, when Septimius Severus had finally overcome all rival claimants and established himself as undisputed emperor, Dio Cassius related more bad news from Britain:

The Caledonians instead of honouring their promises had prepared to defend the Maeatae and Severus at that time was concentrating on the Parthian war; so Lupus [governor of Britain] had no choice but to buy peace from the Maeatae for a considerable sum of money, recovering a few captives.

The latter comment suggests more success for the north. If there were captives to recover then hostilities of some kind had taken place and the Romans had been defeated. And it seems that the Caledonians had felt strong enough to revive the confederacy and foray into the south.

This extract from Dio Cassius is also an early mention of a new people. According to place-name evidence, the *Maeatae* or *Miathi* occupied the Ochil Hills and the area immediately to the west. *Dumyat* means 'Fort of the Miathi' and it is one of the more prominent of the Ochils, and *Myot Hill* lies not far away to the south-west. It is made clear by the sources that, like the Caledonians, the Maeatae led a confederate force, drawn from several peoples, presumably those who lived in the shadow of the Antonine Wall.

However large a bribe the allies had squeezed out of the Roman governor's negotiators, it was not enough. In 207 Alfenus Senecio wrote a despatch to Rome which reeked of exasperation: 'There was a rebellion amongst the barbarians and they were laying waste the country, plundering and causing widespread destruction.' Senecio pointed out that he no longer had the resources to control the Maeatae and the Caledonians, and either substantial reinforcements should be sent or the emperor himself should mount an expedition.

Septimius chose the second option, and, unusually, his reasons were clear and have survived. According to Dio Cassius, he wanted to take his sons, Caracalla and Geta, out of the corrupting atmosphere of Rome and knock some discipline into them. A campaign in Britain against the ferocious natives would do just that. He also judged that he needed to find work for an idle army which was 'becoming slack through inactivity', and finally Severus was said to have 'enjoyed winning renown, and after victories and titles he had won in the east and the north, he wanted to raise trophies over the Britons as well'.

For four years York became the centre of the Roman world. In addition to his corruptible sons, Severus brought his unpleasant wife, Julia Domna, the imperial court and the imperial administration to the legionary fortress. He wanted to be sure that there would be no one left in Rome to plot in his absence. And York was almost certainly the muster-point for the huge expeditionary force for the coming war in the north. Severus had summoned the three British-based legions, detachments from other legions based in Europe, the black-uniformed Praetorian Guard and many auxiliary regiments. When this enormous army, the largest ever to invade Scotland, tramped up Dere Street, native scouts must have shaken their heads in disbelief. Marching six men abreast, the infantry stretched for nearly 5 km/3 miles along the road. Behind them the baggage train added a tail of another 3 km/2 miles, and the imperial party must have added a splash of purple at some central, well-guarded point. Protecting the flanks of this prodigious force were cavalry regiments skirting the hills on either side. When the expedition left Newstead, a series of huge marching camps in Lauderdale mark its slow progress. It took four days to cover the 60 km/38 miles to Inveresk on the Firth of Forth, and when the end of the column was leaving one camp, the advance party of surveyors was approaching the next.

In the face of such overwhelming numbers, the Caledonians and the Maeatae quickly offered terms for peace. But they had broken treaties before, and when the emperor left, what was to stop them wreaking havoc again? No, Severus had come to fight, and the emissaries were sent packing.

The *Classis Britannica* had shadowed the advance north and it may have been lying at anchor in the Forth when the marching columns came into view, either at the mouth of the Esk near Musselburgh or at Cramond, where a stone-built fort already existed from the Antonine period. From an analysis of the size of marching camps north of the Forth, it appears that Severus split his huge army and a substantial force was boarded on to the ships in the Forth. As another division marched into the territory of the Maeatae, it may be that the seaborne troops were taken up the Tay and disembarked at Carpow, where the remains of a large legionary base have been found. This manoeuvre was bold and would have landed 20,000 men to the rear of the territory of the Maeatae. They could have moved quickly inland to cut off the Caledonii, or to the south-east into Fife. There is evidence of Severan marching camps in North Fife, at Auchtermuchty and Edenwood, which may have been designed to secure the Venicones and their precious corn.

Whatever the tactical brilliance of the Roman generals and their sea-captains, there was no pitched battle but rather periods of vicious guerrilla warfare as the army advanced. Roman historians reported imperial losses of 50,000, a wild number, greater in fact than the size of the whole expedition. It probably simply signifies heavy losses. Severus appears to have been seeking the old prize of the conquest of the whole island and some historians believe that his huge army reached the Moray Firth littoral, almost as far as Agricola's advance in 83. The devastation was such that it brought the surrender of the Caledonians. There had been no crushing defeat inflicted but the sheer weight of Roman numbers had ground out a victory. There is a tradition that a formal surrender was insisted upon, Severus and Caracalla accepting the submission of the Maeatae and the Caledonian kings with both armies drawn up to face each other. No doubt gratefully, the emperor left his commanders to consolidate their gains and went south to spend the winter at York and attend to other matters.

In 210 the Maeatae rebelled again and drove Severus to ruthless extremes. This time there would be no formalities and no quarter. Dio Cassius was explicit about the genocidal slaughter ordered by the emperor:

> The Britons having broken their agreements and taken up arms, Severus ordered his soldiers to invade their territory and put to the sword all that they met, adding the Homeric quotation that 'they should let nobody escape, not even the children hidden in their mothers' wombs'.

As in the aftermath of Mons Graupius, the archaeological record may hint at the long shadow of such a slaughter. At the beginning of the 3rd century, the density of settlement in the Cheviot Hills thinned out dramatically, with the sort of wholesale abandonment of homesteads seen after the Highland Clearances. And in a type of farmhouse known as *Votadinian*, found in the south-east of Scotland, Roman pottery of the 1st and 2nd centuries has been found. But after the Severan invasion there was no more, suggesting that these settlements had also been deserted in the wake of decades of war.

During his last campaign in Scotland, Septimius Severus became ill and was forced to retire to York. He died there in 211 and his son, the fratricidal Caracalla, assumed command of operations. There was an immediate reversal of policy. In the previous three years Caracalla must have acquiesced in his father's grand ambitions in the north while privately believing them to be a waste of time and resources. According to Dio Cassius, Caracalla 'made treaties with the enemy, evacuated their territory and abandoned the forts'. Scotland was simply not worth all that trouble, and Caracalla hurried back to Rome to consolidate his own position.

The army fell back to Hadrian's Wall and the frontier zone to the north was patrolled by scouts. The fort at Netherby in the Esk Valley became known as *Castra Exploratorum*, 'the Fort of the Scouts'. Altars found in the fabric of the medieval abbey at Jedburgh testify to the habit of patrolling in strength, perhaps even to the extent of sending cohorts into the north. And bribery seems also to have been used. Near Edston, deep in the heart of Selgovan territory, 290 silver denarii have been found at a hillfort, with the latest coin dating to AD 222.

Whatever the detail of Caracalla's new frontier policy, it worked. For nearly a century there was peace – perhaps because of the genocide inflicted in the north, perhaps because the Romans had given assurances in the treaties agreed in 211. Some hints of the mechanics of co-existence can be gleaned from an unlikely source. A Roman road-map of the 3rd or 4th century was incorporated into an atlas known as the Ravenna Cosmography. It mentioned four *loci* in southern Scotland. Similar arrangements elsewhere in the empire defined these as licensed tribal meeting-places, possibly where markets were allowed in the presence of a Roman centurion. Perhaps the scouts from Netherby filled that supervisory role. In any case, the idea was to allow peoples to congregate but not to muster arms for hostile action. It sounds unlikely.

However, the four *loci* shed pinpricks of light on the peace which followed the Severan invasions. *Locus Maponi* survives almost intact as a place-name at Lochmabenstane. It is a huge prehistoric standing stone (now, sadly, fallen) very near the head of the Solway, not far from Gretna. The Lochmabenstane was used as a meeting-place into the historic period, even, later, as a muster-point in the anarchic days of the Border reivers. *Locus Selgovensis* tells who met there but not where. It may have been at the ancient enclosure at Meldon Bridge. The nearby Sheriffmuir continued to be a meeting-place into the 18th century when the Peeblesshire Militia drilled on the flat ground, and it remains a crossroads linking the Tweed, Clyde, Manor and Meldon valleys. *Manavi* is an early use of *Manau*, a 5th-century name for the area at the head of the Firth of Forth. And *Clackmannan* may have been the specific location since it translates as 'the Stone of Manau'. At the centre of the old county town the stone can still be seen, outside the town hall. *Dannoni* was the meeting-place of the Damnonii and it may have been at a very big rock indeed, Dumbarton Rock.

For 80 years, four generations, there are no reports of war in north Britain. From a period of regular, almost incessant conflict, the transition to a truce appears to have been immediate. No doubt it was also welcome. The peoples of the north learned to live with the Roman colonists in the south and, if part of the bargain struck by Caracalla was non-intervention, then that was kept, on both sides. Political change seems to have taken place in the north in the 3rd century, but no details have yet come to light. What is clear is that by AD 296 a new name appeared in the north, perhaps the most mysterious name in British history. In that year the Romans reported that the Picts had broken through Hadrian's Wall and invaded Britannia as far south as Chester.

8

The Last of the British

Scotland was not inevitable. After the fall of the Roman Empire in the West and the collapse of the province of Britannia at the beginning of the 5th century, a political vacuum sucked in several disparate and dynamic elements, and our history could have followed any one of a number of different courses. The ambitions and energies of powerful individuals, a series of accidents and inventions, or good and bad timing could all have combined into different patterns and the Scots might now be living at addresses somewhere in Pictavia, or New Ireland, the Old North, Norseland or even Northumbria. And at different moments all of these historical destinations looked more likely than Scotland.

In the six centuries between 300 and 900 Scotland's native culture was attacked, appropriated, infiltrated and occasionally overwhelmed by outsiders, peoples who sailed across the eastern and western seas. Over that lengthy period the descendants of the first hunter-gatherer-fishers and farmers, the builders of Maes Howe, Balbridie and the sacred enclosure on Eildon Hill North, changed. Gradually they ceased to be British and became Scottish. What follows is the necessarily impressionistic story of how that happened, the last instalment of the story of Scotland before Scotland.

Much of the detail of the process of change is unknowable, lost in the memories of long-dead bards or written in the forgotten chronicles of ancient monasteries. And what has survived to come down to us is often confused, contradictory, partial, lacking clarity of any sort or just plain mistaken. But it is important. The centuries between 300 and 900, what used to be known, not surprisingly, as *The Dark Ages*, are the immense gestation period of what became Scotland, a time when much that goes to make up the modern nation was formed.

~~~

After Caracalla's hasty peace of AD 212 and 80 years without major incident, the garrison patrolling Hadrian's Wall saw what they believed to be a new threat come out of the northern hills. In 296 warbands crossed the wall, or sailed around it, and were recorded raiding far to the south, even attacking the legionary fortress at Chester. They must have been numerous, well-organized and confident. Since 286 Britannia had been under the control of the usurper emperor Carausius, the admiral of the northern imperial fleet. By 296 his successor – and assassin – Allectus had weakened the frontier garrison sufficiently to tempt the warbands south. A year later an anonymous panegyric celebrated the triumph of the legitimate emperor, Constantius Chlorus, over Allectus by comparing it to the expedition to Britain of Julius Caesar. The writer noted a hostile people he called *the Picts* and made the point that they were the enemies of the Britons during Caesar's time, as early as 55 or 54 BC. This meant that the name would have predated *Caledonii* and Ptolemy's other tribal names by some distance, but perhaps the use of the term was an anachronistic slip and the effusiveness of the panegyric writer should not be taken at face value.

Picti, meaning 'the Painted or Tattooed People', was probably a soldiers' nickname, perhaps coined in 296 by those garrisons on Hadrian's Wall who had not seen the northern warbands before. It stands in a tradition of *noms de guerre*: the *Saxons*, called after a short-bladed knife they carried, the *Franks*, whose name means 'the Wreckers', or the *Vikings* who dodged in and out of creeks, or *viks*.

Roman commentators had been interested in the painted people for a long time. Around 235 Herodian offered some detail:

> They are ignorant of the use of clothes . . . they tattoo their
> bodies not only with the likenesses of animals of all kinds, but

with all sorts of drawings. And this is the reason why they do not wear clothes, to avoid hiding the drawings on their bodies.

Three decades after the raid on Chester, Tertullian wrote of the *stigmata Britonnum* and in 400–402 the poet Claudian personified Britannia as a woman with her cheeks tattooed. He went on to praise the Roman army: 'this legion which curbs the savage Scot and studies the iron-wrought designs on the face of the dying Pict'. By 600 Isidore of Seville had gathered some technical information and at last offered an interpretation of what the tattoos signified:

The race of Picts have a name derived from their bodies. These are played upon by a needle working with small pricks and by the squeezed-out sap of a native plant, so that they bear the resultant marks according to the personal rank of the individual, their painted limbs being marked to show their high birth.

The marks also had religious and political significance, because in 787 the church took the trouble to ban them. At the Synod of Calcuth in Northumbria a visiting dignitary, Bishop George of Ostia, brought papal disapproval with him when he railed against those pagans in the north with 'hideous scars' on their bodies, which had suffered 'the injury of staining'.

More than merely the cause of a soldiers' nickname and an observation made by outsiders, the phenomenon of tattooing undoubtedly had great cultural importance. It appears to have outlasted the general British habit of body decoration which prompted Pytheas to coin the name *Pretannike* in the 4th century BC, and became a prime distinguishing feature of a powerful northern people. In sum, their tattoos made the Picts different, and in a literal sense made them the last of the British.

Pictones

France had Picts. Or more precisely, in Gaul Julius Caesar made an alliance with a seafaring people from the coasts of the Bay of Biscay who were known as the Pictones, Pectones or Pictes. Unlike the Picts of the north, they allowed their navy to fight with the Romans against the Veneti of Armorica, or Brittany. *Pit* or *pett* for 'a portion of land' is a word cognate to the Gaulish *petia*, which means the same thing. No references are made to tattoos, but there is a shadow of an alternative meaning for *Picti*. Not only was it a *nom de guerre*, it might also have had a native equivalent which sounded similar but bore a quite different meaning. The Picts may have been known as 'the Portioners'.

In his *Ecclesiastical History of the English People*, the great historian Bede described Britain in the early 8th century in basic and illuminating terms. 'At the present time,' he wrote, 'there are in Britain . . . four nations – English, British, Irish and Picts.' The last named had a separate language and culture, and were much feared in the south as ferocious, rapacious raiders. By the 12th century, when Henry of Huntingdon was writing history, he noted that of all of the peoples listed by Bede 400 years before, only the Picts had disappeared. Since then, they have been gradually transformed into a mystery, a lost civilization, an enigma. Books have appeared with titles such as *The Problem of the Picts*, and many of the hundreds of thousands of web pages devoted to them encourage the notion of a northern Atlantis, an entire culture submerged beneath the sea of history.

Bede was careful to say that Pictish was a different language from British or Irish (Gaelic), or English, and it appears that almost all traces of it have perished. No one now speaks an identifiable descendant of Pictish, and some historians believe that it was in fact very ancient, a pre-Indo-European, prehistoric language – perhaps even an Edenic tongue used by the hunter-gatherer-fishers as they wandered the northern forests. No records written in Pictish have come down to us and such inscriptions as exist seem to be illegible, sequences of gibberish; the lost language of a lost world.

Like most lost civilizations, the Picts have their mysterious monuments. Between about AD 400 and 900, hundreds, perhaps thousands of symbol stones were planted in the landscape of eastern and northern Scotland. The 200 which have survived are likely to be only a fraction of the original number carved and raised. So many have come down to us because the stones were thought to be important, are often impressive, beautifully made and sometimes monumental, set up in places where they could not fail to be noticed, where they were somehow central to the culture that made them. But what do they mean? Many carry abstract designs and a group of symbols whose meaning has been lost. Few historians have been so rash as to risk their reputations on attempts at decoding the collection of Z-rods, fabulous beasts, crescents, double-discs, V-rods and much else. It seems that a reliable key to the cipher is entirely lacking.

What all of this adds up to is the stuff of confusion. But the plain fact is that the Picts did not disappear, they changed. Their language was not gibberish – how could it have been? Those fragments which are still legible or recognizable as transliterations are undoubtedly fragments of a Celtic language. Through patient analysis of personal and place-names and inscriptions, the scholar Katherine Forsyth has convincingly demonstrated that the Pictish language was thoroughly Celtic and not a throwback or a surviving pocket of a pre-Indo-European world. Different from Irish (when St Columba travelled to Skye in the late 6th century, he needed to take along an interpreter) but a first cousin to British, it was P-Celtic rather than Q-Celtic and as such a very distant relative of what has developed into the Welsh language.

This new clarity about Pictish is important because it makes the texture of the culture it described much clearer. A Celtic language was likely to have been used by a Celtic society. And much of what is known from other Pictish sources supports this. According to Tacitus, the Caledonian confederacy at Mons Graupius fought like a Celtic army. Its warriors drove chariots and seemed to rely – too heavily – on the power of a furious charge. Their appearance was Celtic, and the use of body decoration was common across barbarian Europe at that time.

The names of their warriors can be understood by reference to other P-Celtic languages: *Calgacus* meaning 'the Swordsman' and *Argento-coxus* meaning 'Silver-Foot'. And, like other early Celtic cultures, they wrote down nothing and carried all knowledge and understanding of the world in their memories. This made them different only from the Romans, whose habit of keeping written records of all sorts was highly exceptional. The Picts are not a mystery, they are simply not easily or well understood.

Roman sources offer a broadly accurate sense of where they came from, the part of northern Britain which can properly be seen as Pictland or Pictavia. In Tacitus and for three centuries after him, the area north of the Firth of Forth (excluding Fife) was considered to be hostile territory and the homeland of the Caledonian confederacy and its successors. Later sources talked of 'the Maeatae and other Picts' and also of warbands of 'Scots and Picts' raiding over Hadrian's Wall. The placing of the Gask Ridge frontier and a group of later references suggest that the southern focus of Pictish power probably lay in Strathearn, what became known as *Fortriu*. The tribe whose territory it was were described as the *Verturiones*, a cognate name to *Fortriu*. At some point in the post-Roman period the fertile fields of neighbouring Fife came under Pictish control, and at first this takeover was purely political. Judging mainly by the slender means of their name alone, the Venicones were much closer to the Votadini south of the Forth than the Pictish peoples of Fortriu on the other side of the Ochil Hills. The Romans probably bracketed them together as client tribes whose corn was important to the occupying legions. The *Votadini* became the *Gododdin* and left to history the long poem of the same name. Amongst its epic verses there is mention of a place called *Maen Gwyngwn*, or 'the Stone of the Gwyngwn'. This name is closely related to *Venicones* and it means 'the Kindred Hounds'. It sounds very much like a name conferred by allies or close relatives.

In the absence of any surviving records the extent of ancient Pictland has to be deduced from other sorts of sources. With only the occasional stray outlier (like the unmistakably Pictish salmon carved on a stone near Hawick in the Borders), the distribution of symbol stones shows that Pictish culture flourished as far north as Shetland and down to the southern shores of Fife, and generally to the east of the Highland massif. To the west, early symbol stones have been found on Skye and in the Outer Hebrides, but later material is absent. There are remains of characteristic Pictish burial cairns on the northernmost Shetland island of Unst and similar examples all the way down the east coastlands to Leven in Fife. The plotting of *pit* place-names such as Pittodrie, Pitlochry and Pitreavie was long understood to confirm Pictish political geography, but none survives in Orkney or Shetland (because of the 9th-century Viking occupation) and philologists have recently argued convincingly that these coinings postdate the Pictish kingdoms. They appear to have originated as borrowings by incoming Gaelic speakers, who often attached the prefix to their own descriptions of a place they took over. *Pit* means 'a portion of land' and *Pit-lochry* is a compound, with the second Gaelic element meaning 'stepping-stones' (across the River Tummel). If this general reading of *pit*-names is correct then it does not define the borders of Pictland but certainly confirms its heartland along the eastern coasts, from Sutherland to Fife.

Dog Soldiers

The warbands of the North American Plains Indian tribes were organized in soldier societies. They shared secret initiation ceremonies, warpaint and the ethic of brothers in arms. While not at war, which was most of the time, they acted as tribal policemen, overseeing hunting expeditions, camp moves and the arrangement of large encampments. The Cheyenne nation had six soldier societies, most of them named after totem animals: the Fox Soldiers, Elk Soldiers, Red Shields, Bow Strings, Crazy Dogs and the famous Dog Soldiers. When Black Americans fought in the federal army, the native Americans called them 'Buffalo Soldiers' because their curly dark hair reminded them of the mane of the buffalo, and so coined a name for an enemy, based on appearance, which they themselves might have used. The most aristocratic and exclusive society

amongst the Plains Indians was the Kiowa nation's Society of the Ten
Bravest. Their enemies knew and feared them by their warpaint and
each wore a sash. The leader's was long enough to be pinned to the
ground so that he had no option but to fight to the last.

An Irish tradition, sometimes associated with St Columba but probably much later, relates a list of Pictish provinces. Here is W.J. Watson's
translation of the relevant passage:

Seven of Cruithne's children divided Alba into seven divisions,
the portion of Cat, of Ce, of Cirech, children with hundreds of
possessions, the portion of Fib, of Fidaid, of Fotla, and of Fortriu.
And it is the name of each man of them that is on his land.

There is a 12th-century recension of this known as *De Situe Albania*
and it identifies each region in more modern terms. In his *History of
the Celtic Place-Names of Scotland*, Watson combines the two accounts
to produce the following list of Pictish provinces:

Cirech (also written as Circenn)	Angus and the Mearns
Fotla	Atholl and Gowrie
Fortriu	Strathearn and Menteith
Fib	Fife with Fothreue
Ce	Marr and Buchan
Fidaid	Moray and Easter Ross
Cat	Caithness and south-east Sutherland

In *De Situe Albania* the author pointed out that each of the seven
provinces was held by a king, and that under him ruled a petty king or
sub-regulus. The consistent twinning of names and regions implies this
arrangement – the king of Angus and the sub-king of the Mearns and so
on. In contemporary Ireland a similar relationship was more precisely

defined. A *ri* or *ri tuaithe* was the equivalent of a Pictish *sub-regulus*, the king of a tribe or small kingdom. Then there was a *ruiri*, a 'great king' who had power over a number of other kings, but he was outranked by a third category, the *ri ruireach*, the 'king of overkings'. When St Columba visited the court of King Bridei macMaelchon near Inverness in 565, there were important courtiers in attendance. Columba's biographer, St Adomnan, noted that the king of Orkney was there, clearly an important man for he was described not as a *sub-regulus* but as a *regulus*. Perhaps he dominated his neighbours, Shetland and the mainland province of Caithness and south-east Sutherland. An interesting detail confirms a widespread and ancient method of reinforcing the hierarchy of kings. Adomnan was told that King Bridei held Orcadian hostages at his court, probably relatives of their king. This was done to ensure prompt and regular payment of tribute, and the number of hostages held by an overking was an obvious measure of his power and reach. Around 400 an Irish king, Niall of the Nine Hostages (an ancestor of Columba), was famous because he could demand tribute from nine kingdoms, four of them in mainland Britain.

Skating into the empire

Bad weather hastened the fall of the Roman Empire in the West. And in contrast to isolated Britannia, the European provinces suffered immediately, showing how dramatically and rapidly invasion could alter the political landscape. In the winter of 406/7, the Rhine froze solid enough to allow a crossing and a huge host of barbarian tribes scrambled across the ice. The province of Gaul was overrun with at least 200,000 Alans, Suebi and Vandals on the rampage. Several opportunists made attempts on the shaky imperial throne and one, styling himself Constantine III, came from Britannia with an army drawn from the already depleted garrison. The wave of invasion passed through Gaul, over the Pyrenees into Spain and across to North Africa. During this period Andalucia was known as Vandalucia.

A Pictish sculpture from the Brough of Birsay, a tidal island in the Orkneys, supplies an excellent conception of what the overking of Orkney might have looked like. Carved on a symbol stone, a file of three warriors is depicted, and much detail has survived. All of them wear long robes and carry a shield, spear and sword. But there are subtle, and crucial, differences between them. With a more elaborate and curly hair-do and the hint of some sort of crown-like headdress, their leader carries an intricately decorated shield and wears a robe with a fancy fringed hemline. He is clearly a high-status figure, almost certainly a king, and perhaps he leads his sub-kings in procession across the face of the stone. They are dressed in simpler robes and the only decorations on their shields are the four rivets holding the hand-grip in place. And the faces are all different, as if intended as portraits. The king has a pointed beard and a distinctively prominent nose, his immediate follower is also bearded, and the third man appears to be clean-shaven. Sculpture is expensive and it usually depicts only important people. Perhaps the symbol stone at Birsay is a concrete rendition of a set of political relationships in the north of Britain.

Adomnan described Bridei macMaelchon as *rex potentissimus*, but it is unlikely that his great power extended throughout the seven provinces of Pictland as they are set out in the *De Situe Albania*. Most probably he ruled only in the north. Although much communication took place by sea, there is a natural geographical break in the coastlands of eastern Scotland. *The Mounth* is the point at which the Grampian Mountains reach nearest to the North Sea, close to Stonehaven. Above it lay Marr and Buchan, Moray and Easter Ross, and Caithness and south-east Sutherland (Orkney and Shetland having been lost to the Vikings by the time the list was compiled), and below were Angus and the Mearns, Atholl and Gowrie, Strathearn and Menteith, and Fife and Fothreue (Fortriu). Some slight evidence for distinction – and tension – between northern and southern Pictland can be found on old maps. In the 10th century the area around modern Stonehaven was known as *Claideom* or 'the Swordland'. This term was in common use in Ireland for disputed territory between kingdoms.

During the 7th century the focus of Pictish overkingship shifted southwards, settling eventually on the province of Fortriu, or Strathearn and Menteith. Just as Irish overkings were always also kings of Tara, later Pictish overkings were kings of Fortriu. Other, lesser men gradually became *mormaers* rather than kings. Literally the term means 'great steward', from the Old Welsh *maer* which in turn derived from the Latin *maior* and is related to the modern office of *mayor*. The province of Angus and the Mearns points more precisely to what it meant for the Picts. *Mearns* is from *maer* and might be rendered in English as 'the Stewartry', in just the same way as part of Galloway was known until recently. The king of Angus thought of the ruler of the Mearns as his steward, a powerful man who governed what became Kincardineshire as his representative. Certainly a mormaer held land of his own, but he also acted as proxy for the king on his property. In an undatable process provincial kings themselves eventually became mormaers. By 739 there was still a king of Atholl (he was executed by drowning), but his descendants were called mormaers, then earls, and even later dukes of Atholl.

The wide extent of the later Pictish kingdom made personal rule by an overking logistically very difficult. Food renders owed by lesser sorts could be consumed by a peripatetic court, but all of the royal estates could not be visited in the space of a year. The institution of the *thane* evolved in this power vacuum. Originally a royal official, he had responsibility for running the royal estates, and those of mormaers who remained as provincial kings in all but title. Thanes led contingents of warriors from royal estates, dispensed justice in the king's name, ingathered food renders and passed them on after subtracting their share.

This form of territorial organization was old before later names were attached. And it is likely to have been widespread over Celtic Britain. Like the ancient *maenors* in the Tweed Valley, a thanage had several clear constituent elements. Known as a *maer-dref* in the south, the principal settlement housed the thane (and sometimes the king, temporarily) and also had a meeting-place attached to it, and, later, a church. The thanage itself, or *pit* or *pett*, was made up of a series of farms run by people bonded to the land but who were not slaves. In the Welsh sources of the 8th century slaves are mentioned but they appear not to have been numerous.

Atholl army

The Atholl Highlanders are famous as the only private army in Britain. Its members claim descent from the clan host of the earls and dukes of Atholl, and all 50 drill regularly and parade with their artillery detachment to fire salutes on special occasions. They have a first-class pipe band and the present duke is their colonel. Membership is keenly sought and until recently the army boasted a retired major-general in their ranks as a private. The Atholl Highlanders are not, sadly, the heirs of the ancient Pictish host of the kings of Atholl. They were formed for the Eglinton Tournament in 1839 as a ceremonial bodyguard for Lord Glenlyon, the heir to the dukedom. But there is an unexpected connection with the long past. The family name of the dukes of Atholl is Murray, and the noble surname is said to derive from *moireabh*, the Gaelic name for the Pictish kingdom of Moray.

Pictland may be a kingdom of the so-called Dark Ages, but the evidence, both direct and comparative, suggests a highly organized landscape. The produce of some of the most fertile farmland in Britain was counted and controlled by thanes on behalf of mormaers and their kings, and all of them could back their exactions with force if necessary. Most important to a powerful man was his warband – it was the beating heart of royal authority, and much of what he received in food renders was converted into gifts regularly doled out to warriors. Skilled metalworkers made jewellery and elaborately decorated weapons. Horses were prized items and many fine-looking mounts are depicted on Pictish symbol-stones. Cups and other objects associated with feasting have turned up in the archaeological record and there seems to have been a great deal of precious metal in circulation in the north. Perhaps it came from booty plundered in the Roman south, perhaps it was tribute paid by the Roman administration. Archaeologists have come across the remains of precious-metalworking at several Pictish sites. The discovery of moulds shows that circular brooches were popular and these seem to have derived from Roman models, and may have been worn as badges of rank or favour. Praise poems to the 6th-century King Urien of Rheged saw royal generosity as a prime virtue:

Splendid he was, in his many-coloured armour,
Horses he gave to all who asked,
Gathering wealth like a miser
Freely he shared it for his soul's sake.

This attribute of early kingship is directly descended from the ancient generosity of unknown prehistoric kings. At their potlatches, like Urien and the Pictish kings, they too were 'rivers to their people'.

Precise dates for the development of institutions in early Scotland are hard to come by. Maenors certainly existed in the middle of the 7th century when King Oswy of Northumbria gifted what became Yetholmshire to the bishopric of Lindisfarne in thanks for his victory over Penda of Mercia at the Winwaed. But they would have existed as economic units long before. The Manor Valley, near Peebles, is named after the institution of the *maenor* and the dedication of its church to an obscure 4th-century Syrian, St Gorgian, perhaps points to great antiquity. His fame, such as it was, was probably short-lived and may suggest a near-contemporary foundation. However they are termed, as thanages, pits, maenors or shires, these estates are ancient, and for any sort of substantial centralized power to operate effectively, they must have been efficient and their function as reliable food providers well understood.

There is a strong sense of cultural continuity amongst the different peoples of north Britain throughout the long period of Roman occupation of the south. Unlike those who lived above the Rhine/Danube frontier, such as the Franks, Goths and others, the north British did not become Romanized, and after the Empire in the West disintegrated in the 5th century, Celtic political structures re-emerged intact. Despite 400 years of Roman rule and influence, the native aristocracy of the north in particular had retained their status (if not their wealth and military power) and were able to assume leading roles when their opportunity came at last. In contrast to Roman Europe, where French, Spanish, Italian and other languages evolved from Latin, Celtic languages survived in Britain while their continental cousins, Gaulish, Celtiberian and Lepontic, withered. The clear inference is that Britain remained bilingual throughout all strata of native society for the four centuries of imperial rule. Alongside all of these survivals, it is likely that native units of farming, like the *pits* or *petts* and *maenors*, also persisted and developed.

Clock of ages

The neutralizing tide of political correctness has washed over a romantic historical phrase and swept it into the dustbin. No serious person now writes of 'The Dark Ages' and the colourless Early Medieval Period or Early Historic Period have been substituted. No one knows exactly when these and other vague classifications apply but the loss of the equally uncertain 'Dark Ages', with its swirling mist of Arthurianism, is a shame. 'Middle Ages' or *Medium Aevum* was first used by early Christians who wanted to describe the period between the first and second comings of Christ. Renaissance writers redefined it as the interval between the decline of classical antiquity and its revival in Italy in the 15th and 16th centuries. No one now seems to want to have lived in the Middle Ages (as opposed to the Renaissance or the glorious heyday of Rome) and when the adjective 'medieval' is applied to a modern example, it is not intended to be complimentary.

During the 4th century a revitalized Pictish aristocracy led its warbands on raids into Britannia. Frequent references were made to what sound like alliances of *Caledonians* and other Picts and, in 314, to *Scoti*, *Picti* and *Caledonii*. And there is also a notice from Ammianus Marcellinus that the Picts consisted of two tribes, the *Dicalydonae* and the *Verturiones*. These names are closely related to *Caledonia* and the province of *Fortriu* or Strathearn and Menteith. In 305 the Emperor Constantius was in Britain campaigning against the Picts, and seven years later his son, Constantine the Great, was also fighting the northern warbands. It may be that the constant pressure of war forged the Pictish tribes together into a single political entity, a tighter confederacy which may have endured into peacetime. In Europe the tribes along the Rhine/Danube line combined into larger polities in exactly the same way.

In 342 the Emperor Constans hurried across to Britain to forestall rebellion and drive off raiding Pictish warbands which had descended on the outpost forts at High Rochester, Bewcastle and Risingham and burned them. Caracalla's system of patrols in the south of Scotland was still in operation but it seems that Constans' diplomats concluded some sort of new understanding with the Votadini. There is a suggestion that they would be more active in defending the province against Pictish incursion. Whatever was agreed, it had little lasting deterrent effect. By 360 the Scots and Picts had decided to break their treaties with the Roman administration and mount a series of devastating forays into the south. The Emperor Julian sent four regiments under the command of Lupicinus and, while they succeeded in reimposing order, the respite was temporary. Five years later the Picts attacked again, this time in combination with not only the Scots but also the Saxons and a people called the *Atecotti*. This name translates simply as 'the Old Peoples' and they may have originated from the Hebrides. St Jerome believed the Atecotti to be aboriginal savages and claims to have witnessed them practising cannibalism. In any event, the brunt of this raid is likely to have been seaborne. It was the fastest way to move soldiers around, avoided the garrisons on Hadrian's Wall, and even if boats limited the size of a warband they could give warriors the precious element of surprise as they delivered them upriver to cities like Chester and Gloucester. Pictish boats were probably clinker-built, formed around a keel from planks of wood lapped together in what became a North Sea tradition. On the Irish Sea the Scots almost certainly sailed their skin-covered curraghs, some of which could be 12 m/40 ft long and 2.5 m/8 ft wide.

Pictish kilts

The symbol-stones not only offer an early historical glimpse of what our forebears looked like, they also show what they wore. Men sported tunics of varying lengths, sometimes pleated, sometimes with a belt. They might represent an early version of a kilt, which was, after all, no more than a thick woollen robe held together by a belt and folded in pleats for convenience. A fragment of cloth found near Falkirk and dated to AD 235 had been woven in a check pattern. And if a Pictish warrior did want to cast off his clothes before a battle (as Highlanders sometimes did) then all he had to undo was a belt. An Irish source testifies to a 'cowl reaching to the elbow' on some Pictish men, and just such a garment, with a fringe, has been found in Orkney, dating to the pre-Viking period.

The name *Scotti* lends some weight to the notion of seaborne raiding. Like *Pict*, *Saxon*, *Frank* and *Viking*, it appears to have originally been a *nom de guerre* conferred by the Romans, or at least historians who wrote in Latin. The word probably derives from *sgod*, Gaelic for a sail, and its use might have been transferred to signify a boat much in the way that the Saxons talked of theirs as *keels*. To watching sentinels, *Scots* may have become quickly synonymous with 'pirates'. If so, the name must refer to their habit of raiding down the British coasts of the Irish Sea.

The Scots called themselves the *Gaels* and are generally understood to have been Irish in the first half of the 1st millennium AD, only later settling in Argyll. But this may not be accurate. When Bede was describing the desperate political situation facing Roman Britain at the beginning of the 5th century, he clearly believed that the Scots who raided in the south came from Argyll. If he was correct, then the tradition of the migration of peoples from the north of Ireland to Argyll around 500 under the leadership of Fergus Mor macErc is only that, a tradition, an origin myth concocted to comfort and legitimize later kings. Archaeology supplies no evidence to support the migration, and indeed there is a possibility that population movement took place in the opposite direction. It seems likely that people who spoke Gaelic, that is, Q-Celtic as opposed to P-Celtic British, had occupied Argyll since the prehistoric period, perhaps as far back as the early Iron Age. If the region of the south-west coast of Scotland, Ireland and the Irish Sea is understood as an area connected rather than divided by the sea, then such a hypothesis makes sense.

Contact between the military planners of the Scots, Picts, Franks, Atecotti and Saxons was sufficiently regular and sophisticated to allow a detailed strategy to be formulated. In 367 they formed what the Romans called the *conspiratio barbarica*. So that the meagre resources of the defenders of Britannia would be stretched in many directions at once, each group launched simultaneous attacks. Almost certainly coming from the west, north and east, and almost certainly seaborne, the barbarian conspiracy had a devastating impact. After neutralizing the field army of Britannia and capturing its general, the allies launched themselves at the shore forts on the east coast and killed their commander, Nectaridus. Large numbers of soldiers deserted from the garrison and added to the chaos by roaming the countryside. For two years the province was laid waste as warbands plundered and burned.

The Cheyenne confederacy

The Cheyenne Tribal Council had a membership of 44 civil chiefs, as distinct from war chiefs, and it ruled supreme over the whole confederacy. Made up of ten major bands, the Cheyenne nation was spread over a vast area which had been apportioned by custom and practice into band territories. Each person used a combined name to describe his/her identity: an Omissis Cheyenne, a Hevatania Cheyenne and so on. Each band sent four civil chiefs to the tribal council and these men were considered to be the protectors of each and all of the members of that band. Generosity was a particularly prized virtue, and civil chiefs often gave gifts of horses. It is impossible to make detailed comparisons but a non-literate society such as the Pictish confederacy may have carried on a similarly sophisticated form of central government.

Not until the arrival of a tough and experienced soldier, Count Theodosius, in 369 was stability restored. He declared an amnesty for deserters and set about driving the warbands back into their ships and away. Most important was the re-establishment of the northern frontier, and Theodosius moved quickly to shore it up. The border patrols, known as the *areani*, had been complicit in the conspiracy; having been bribed, they failed to warn the authorities on the Wall, and they were disbanded. Instead, Theodosius appears to have begun the process of creating federated buffer kingdoms in the south of Scotland. Two years before, this had been accomplished with some success in containing the Berber tribesmen of North Africa. Surviving king-lists suggest what happened, and the names in them are eloquent. In the years around 369 a man with a Latin name and a Celtic adjective attached to it came to rule the southern Votadini, the people who would be known as the Gododdin. *Paternus Pesrut*, Celticized as *Padarn Pesrut*, means 'Paternus with the red cloak', and the adjective signifies either the conferring of Roman rank on a native king, or perhaps even the imposition of a Roman prefect. Paternus may have governed from the shadowy fortress of *Marchidun*, the old name for Roxburgh Castle near Kelso. *Marchidun* means 'the Cavalry Fort' and on the haughland below it fieldwalkers have come across hundreds of Roman coins, many dating between 369 and 410. Most are bronze radiates, of no intrinsic value like gold or silver coins, and they strongly suggest the operation of some sort of money economy. This in turn tempts the thought that Paternus Pesrut might have been supported by a force of Roman cavalry receiving regular wages. The southern Gododdin king-lists buttress this possibility with more names. Paternus' predecessor, or father, was *Tacit(us)* and his son or successor was *Aetern(us)*. And in the Lothians and the area around Stirling the northern Gododdin were ruled by a man with an unCelticized name, *Catellius Decianus*.

Amongst the other peoples of southern Scotland, more Roman names appeared at that time. In Galloway, in the old territory of the Novantae, *Annwn Donadd* or *Antonius Donatus* reigned. The Damnonii of the Clyde Valley, soon to be known as the kingdom of Strathclyde, listed successive kings as *Cluim* or *Clemens* and *Cinhil* or *Quintilius*. The latter's son was *Coroticus*, a source of profound irritation to St Patrick. When the saint wrote in about 470 to complain about slave raids in Ireland mounted by Strathclyders under Coroticus, he was shocked at their behaviour because he saw them as 'citizens of the Holy Romans' even though three centuries had passed since the Clyde Valley had been part of the Empire. This is an obvious reference to the strong link between Roman-ness and Christianity, and probably to much more recent history – the political consequences of the Barbarian Conspiracy.

Perhaps these names indicate early conversion to Christianity rather than the installation of Roman prefects or the cultivation of client kings, but whatever the detail, the broad political realities are obvious. Theodosius created buffer kingdoms in the south, in the strategically important area between the Roman walls, and in so doing helped accentuate a division hinted at since the days of Petilius Cerialis and Agricola. The peoples south of the Forth/Clyde line were set against the Pictish confederacy of the north.

Another Roman name was intruded into the genealogies at this time. Magnus Maximus, a Spaniard appointed to a senior command in Britannia, was persuaded in 383 to make a bid for the imperial throne. It appears that he campaigned successfully against the Picts in 384 and such was his support for the southern Scottish kingdoms against their enemies in the north that he came to be seen as a founder of the Novantan dynasty in Galloway. And in Wales Magnus was forced to empower native kings to deal with Irish incursions, since it seems likely that he removed the garrison from the legionary fortress at Chester to further his imperial ambitions in Europe. Nevertheless he was rewarded with a place as a founder of several Welsh dynasties. A remarkable poem, *The Dream of Macsen Wledig* or 'Maximus the General', has come down to us, trailing imperial glory as a British army campaigns in Europe. Modern Welsh anthems such as Dafydd Iwan's *We're Still Here*, or *Ri Ni Ma O Hyd*, include *Magnus Maximus a Gymru* as a kind of proto-patriot. It is a surprising, eccentric and persistent hankering after the memory of the Empire.

More raiding took place in the period leading up to the final Roman evacuation from Britannia in 410. In that year the young emperor, Honorius, wrote to the cities of Britannia, presumably in the absence of any other authority, and advised them to look to their own defences. But Roman Britain did not end at that moment. There was no ceremonial handing over of a flag such as happened in Hong Kong in 1997. Instead army pay, no doubt irregular in any case, ceased to arrive and imperial officials ceased to exert central authority. Perhaps the change scarcely mattered because it is likely that many of the towns of the south had sustained their own garrisons for some time before 410, and there are also suggestions that an anti-imperial party was active in Britannia.

There is no doubt that the Picts in particular were a determinant factor in the disintegration of Roman Britain. They often attacked on their own account and seem never to have been absent from any coalition which raided in the province in the 4th century. But they were not intent on conquest, at least not in the Roman style. If they had been, then the Barbarian Conspiracy of 367 must have represented their best chance of taking over Britannia. What attracted the Picts and their allies was plunder rather than a place to be overrun and controlled. After the end of the raiding season, they usually returned home with what was portable and valuable.

It must be significant that the Pictish kings could not extend their power south of the Forth. After 410 the kingdoms of the south of Scotland began to emerge. Strathclyde had its principal fortress on Dumbarton Rock on the Clyde. The sprawling kingdom of Rheged incorporated the Novantae, and under its famous king, Urien, it included *Aeron* or Ayrshire. And the Votadini morphed into the Gododdin, whose kings ruled the Lothians and the Tweed Basin. These polities must have been powerful and well organized because they certainly fought the Picts, and unlike the Romans preserved the integrity of their borders. However, it would be misleading to understand these in the same way as modern frontiers. Fifth-century kings measured their power not in acreage but in the ability to compel tribute. And this in turn was directly related to their personal prestige and the prowess of their warband. At the end of the 6th century Urien controlled much of the south of Scotland and northern England, but when he was assassinated his power passed for a while to his son, Owain, and then quickly evaporated. By the early 7th century Rheged had faded from the map of history. These kingdoms were not states but the personal possessions of charismatic and highly capable men.

~~~

Between 425 and 430 a remarkable episode took place which illustrates how the kings of southern Scotland saw themselves and their part in history. Reckoned in the genealogies to be the grandson of Paternus Pesrut, a Gododdin general known by his reputation rather than a personal name led an expeditionary force of warriors to North Wales to fight and expel Irish invaders. His title was *Cunedda*, meaning simply 'Good Leader' (it survives, as noted on page 279, in the popular Christian name of Kenneth) and the chroniclers located him in Manau-Gododdin, the area around modern Stirling. At least three aspects of this episode make it remarkable. The expedition was successful, the only time when invading barbarians were permanently expelled from the Empire. But why did a warband from the north ride 500 km/300 miles south, to Wales, to fight against peoples who offered no immediate threat to their own native territory? Perhaps a slightly later name supplies the glimmer of an answer. As the Anglo-Saxons gradually fanned out over southern Britannia, Old Welsh speakers began to call themselves the *Cymry*. It is the modern Welsh name for the Welsh and derives from *Combrogi*, a Latin term meaning 'the people with a common frontier' or, better, 'the compatriots'. Maybe Cunedda and the Gododdin aristocracy saw themselves as the heirs of Britannia, the guardians of the Empire with a responsibility to keep it intact. In any event, the permanent removal of a powerful warband from the northern kingdom of Gododdin at least shows confidence that, even in the face of Pictish aggression, men could be spared. And it further underlined the apposition of civilized British against barbarian Pictish and Irish.

This faultline grew wider with the arrival of the word of God. Christianity came to Britain with the Roman legions. Tradition holds the first British martyr to have been St Alban, a Roman officer who sheltered a priest at Verulamium, the town later named after him. His death may have taken place towards the end of the 3rd century and a shrine certainly existed by the time Cunedda rode to battle in North Wales. Archaeology on Roman sites shows how Christian belief spread north with the army, and along the length of Hadrian's Wall soldiers and their families worshipped quietly. In 312 the emperor, Constantine the Great, was converted and elevated Christianity to the status of the official imperial religion. In the north that may have amounted to the official religion of the army, and as such it became quickly and closely associated with Roman rule and prestige.

In Gaul, where Christian churches were more common and better established, the new state religion was concentrated in towns and cities; so much so that the Latin term for country people, *pagani* (cognate with the French *paysan*), became interchangeable with 'pagan' or 'unbeliever'. The same bias was evident in Britain and it is likely that the northwestern focus for Christianity in Britannia became Carlisle, the only substantial town on Hadrian's Wall, a settlement which had grown to become a *civitas*, or tribal capital, by the early 4th century. It was also the place where many veterans retired from service in the Wall garrison. There is solid archaeological evidence for Christian worship in the city at that time, but a sense of its antiquity and organization may be found in a surprising place.

Some time around 430 a party of Irish slave raiders sailed up the Solway Firth. Ranging far inland, away from the Wall and its garrison, they abducted a young man by the name of Succat or Sochet. Carrying him off to the Antrim coast, they sold him to a farmer who worked the boy as a shepherd. After several years Succat escaped and made his way to France where he underwent some form of religious instruction, perhaps even took monastic vows. Around 440, the young man returned home to Carlisle and the valley of the Irthing. His name had been changed to *Patricius* or Patrick. After another period of religious instruction he decided to return to Ireland on a mission of conversion.

Now, the outline of that story comes from St Patrick's own writings, his *Confessio*, and the details of dates and places are supplied by a sensible interpretation of the text. The most likely setting for the saint's early life places him somewhere near the north-west coast of Britannia in the second quarter of the 5th century. In the *Confessio*, Patrick informed the reader that his family had been Christians for three generations. Potitus, his grandfather, had in fact been ordained as a priest and his father, Calpurnius, had been a deacon in the church and a decurion, an elected official in the local government of a Roman city. Carlisle is very likely to have been that city and the focus of an organized and, it seems, flourishing church. Patrick's family also owned a *villula* or small estate which he described as being near a *vicus bannavem taberniae*. This has been convincingly interpreted by Professor Charles Thomas as the village of Greenhead, about 25 km/15 miles inland from Carlisle.

The fat hound

In the early 5th century Christianity in Britain had been infected by heresy, an alternative set of beliefs promulgated by a British theologian called Pelagius. His name is a Latin calque of *Morgan*, meaning 'Son of the Sea', and St Jerome called him 'a fat hound weighed down by Scotch porridge'. Perhaps he came from Argyll, Strathclyde or the Solway. Pelagius' so-called heresy sounds very like modern Presbyterianism. Jerome, Bede and Augustine all condemned him for arguing that men could consciously choose to lead a virtuous life, avoid sin and gain salvation by their own efforts. The orthodox view at the time involved the exercise of God's grace alone.

The city survived the departure of the colonial administration in 410 and continued to be viable for another two centuries. When St Cuthbert was given a tour of Carlisle in 685 by its Northumbrian governor, he was shown the marvel of a working fountain (which implies a working aqueduct and piped water supply) and taken on a circuit of the walls, which appear to have survived largely intact. It was appropriate that the Northumbrian kings gifted a large part of the city to the bishops of Lindisfarne because it is likely that Carlisle was the well-spring of Christian conversion for Scotland as well as Ireland.

Meteors and gerbils

The 530s saw a catastrophic deterioration in the world's weather. It used to be thought that a volcanic eruption spewing masses of tephra into the atmosphere and occluding the sun was the culprit, but now opinion favours a series of large meteoric impacts. Whatever the cause, there is no doubt about the consequences. A terrible plague raged through Europe, ravaging the population. In the middle of the 6th century half a million people lived in Constantinople; a century later, there were only 100,000. The plague began amongst colonies of African gerbils. These sandy-coloured rodents are in fact immune from the disease, and it was their fleas which contracted and spread it. Because gerbils are aggressively territorial, the plague moved fast, transferring to black rats or ship rats. Through the east African ports for the lucrative ivory trade, the rat fleas found their way quickly to Constantinople. The monastic demand for eastern Mediterranean and African pigments to paint the monks' gorgeously illuminated manuscripts may have brought the rats to Scotland and Ireland.

Dated to around 450, the Latinus Stone was found at the ancient church of Whithorn in Galloway. It seems not to be a tombstone but rather the commemoration of the foundation of a shrine or a monastic refuge of some kind. Its erection predates the arrival of St Ninian (probably sent by the bishop at Carlisle around the year 500) and shows that he was almost certainly invited by an existing community of believers. Bede related the first documentary account of Ninian's mission and noted that he was responsible for the conversion of the southern Picts. There is an early tradition of dedications to Ninian in the Stirling area, but the passage in *The Ecclesiastical History of the English People* seems an exaggerated claim – unless it refers to the Novantae and Selgovae of the south rather than the inhabitants of Strathearn and Angus. The church at Whithorn was evidently notable, being built of stone, 'which was unusual amongst the Britons', and known in Latin as *Candida Casa*, or 'the White House'.

More early Christian inscriptions, mostly on tombs, have come to light in Galloway, Liddesdale and upper Tweeddale. It appears that the word of God crept slowly up over the watershed hills on its journey northwards. A large Christian cemetery, dating from 485 onwards, has been uncovered at Edinburgh Airport, and all over the Lothians so-called long-cist burials existed from very early dates. These remains are very important in understanding cultural change, but they are of course mute and sometimes difficult to interpret. Some sense of how Christianity coloured southern Scottish society in the 6th century can be gleaned from poetry. Composed in Old Welsh, written down long after their first recital, these poems are the earliest Scottish literature to survive and the first clear sounds of a native voice. And yet they are obscure, rarely quoted, almost unrecognized as Scottish – probably because their original language was Welsh.

Grumpy Gildas

De Excidio et Conquestu Britanniae or 'On the Ruin and Conquest of Britain' is a title which tells the story. Written around 540 by a native monk, Gildas, it bemoans the fall of Britain to the Anglo-Saxon invaders and blames it on the squabbling, lazy British kings whom he dismisses as 'tyrants'. Several scraps of evidence and inference suggest that Gildas was based somewhere in the north. And his work is structured along classical, rhetorical lines with an introduction, background, outline and detail followed by a summary and then an appeal to the audience to accept the truth of what he has written. Patrick wrote in the same way and the work of these two priests hints strongly at the existence of a school of rhetoric still functioning somewhere in the north. Perhaps it was at Carlisle.

Nine praise poems were composed in honour of Urien, who was powerful in the 580s and 590s, and there also exists a version of an epic work by the bard Aneirin. Known as the *Gododdin*, it relates the tale of a heroic but catastrophic raid into northern England around the year 600. Led by Yrfai, the Lord of Eidyn, or Edinburgh, a cavalry force met the army of the Anglian kingdom of Deira at Catterick and was almost completely destroyed. In the poem, the enemies of the Gododdin were despised as the *Gynt*, an Old Welsh word deriving from *gentiles* and damning the Angles as heathens. By contrast the warriors of Yrfai and the other Christian kingdoms of the north called themselves *Y Bedydd*, or 'the Baptized'. Directly related to the immense and enduring prestige of the Roman Empire, and by extension to the legitimacy of the Gododdin and others as the heirs of Britannia, this was another important distinction between the invading savages and the civilized and godly natives. The Baptized saw the new religion as another version of Rome; it was literate, spoken and written in Latin, led by a bishop in the holy city, and it supplied a trustworthy civil service of clerics who could keep records and bring organization to a society dominated by warriors and kings.

In the beginning Christianity was probably adopted only by the aristocracy, while the old religion retained its hold over the mass of farmers, labourers and slaves who lived out their lives in the countryside. Bound into a version of the *Gododdin* poem, an ancient song was found – with no relationship to tales of warriors and battle – that offers a unique and homely sense of what life was like for the people who worked the land in 6th-century Scotland. Written, like the epic, in Old Welsh, it reads like a timeless piece, something which could have been written in 4000 BC. A woman is singing to her young son what sounds like an elegiac lullaby:

> *Dinogad's speckled petticoat*
> *Was made of skins of speckled stoat:*
> *Whip whip whipalong*
> *Eight times we'll sing the song.*

When your father hunted the land,
Spear on shoulder, club in hand,
Thus his speedy dogs he'd teach,
Giff, Gaff, catch her, catch her, fetch!
In his coracle he'd slay
Fish as a lion does its prey.
When your father went to the moor
He'd bring back heads of stag, fawn, boar,
The speckled grouse's head from the mountain,
Fishes' heads from the falls of Oak Fountain.
Whatever your father struck with his spear,
Wild pig, wild cat, fox from his lair,
Unless it had wings it would never get clear.

This beautiful song is an astonishing flash of light on daily life more than 14 centuries ago. And by itself it ought to dispel any disparaging notions of a primitive people living in a chaotic, somehow formless time dominated by war and warriors.

The main corpus of the *Gododdin* does indeed clang with the din of battle and the boasts of captains and kings. It describes a world of feasting, drinking, fighting, death and glory. And because of the necessary hyperbole of courage, some of it very graphic and beautifully expressed, and because of the licence needed by bards, it seems a world without much human texture, as though inhabited exclusively by confected heroes rather than brave, frightened or charismatic people. The warband of the Gododdin could have fought at Troy or Jericho.

Something of the same sense of unreality is to be found in another very early Scottish text, this time in Latin. St Adomnan's *Life of St Columba* was written (rather than composed) at the end of the 7th century, about a hundred or so years after Columba's death. Its purpose was to impress, help create a cult and create another hero, albeit of a different kind from those of Aneirin. And inevitably much of it has a synthetic quality, purposely elevating its subject from the human to the semi-divine. But unlike the *Gododdin*, it contains a chronology and a clear sequence of events, as well as a good deal of handy incidental detail. Because Adomnan himself was clearly a charismatic and astute man, and also an abbot of Iona who would become sanctified, the life is attractively written, and in effect it assured Columba's fame and pre-eminence. Other Irish missionaries made converts in the Hebrides and along the western coasts of Scotland, but Saints Maelrubha, Donnan, Congall and Moluag had no biographer to immortalize their exemplary lives.

Having founded monasteries in Derry and Durrow, Columba took a band of disciples with him into exile, eventually settling on the tiny island of Iona, off the coast of Mull. Although he was himself an aristocrat from the house of the Ui Neill, originating in the north of Ireland, it seems that Columba did not receive Iona from the Argyll Gaels but from a Pictish king. Adomnan's biography tells of a large and busy monastery much involved in the political life of the times. It may be that in 574 Columba insinuated himself into the inauguration ceremonies of Aedan macGabrain, the new king of Argyll, or it may be that Adomnan invented the occasion as a useful precedent. Whatever the truth of what happened, it probably took place at Dunadd, the ancient centre of power in Argyll. Columba certainly attended the Convention of Druim Cett in 575 with Aedan and perhaps advised him on the question of how his relationship with the High King of Ireland might be reframed. The military services of land forces were conceded but the naval levies reserved to Aedan, a good political outcome. Columba also visited the court of King Bridei macMaelchon near Inverness, and although he seems not to have made much headway in the conversion of the northern Picts, his community of monks was busy with the foundation of a cluster of monasteries across the south-western seaboard of Scotland.

Talking trees

Dendrochronology or tree-ring dating has been of great use to historians working on the early medieval period. It can be pinpoint-accurate, even to a specific year. Oak gives the best results because it lives so long and, when used in building construction, lasts even longer. Marker dates, usually arrived at in conjunction and comparison with other data, are used as a guide. These occur at points of great climatic fluctuations, sometimes caused by volcanic eruption, which affect the width of the rings. Irish oak shows these well and a chronology spanning 7,000 years has been made possible by its toughness and longevity.

Less immediate matters seem to have absorbed Columba a great deal. According to Adomnan, he spent much time in his cell copying and writing manuscripts. In contrast to the old religion of air, darkness, memory and animistic mystery, Christianity was underpinned by the word. In its gospels, psalters, commentaries and tables, the truth was written down and immutable. Holy scripture was venerated for itself, illuminated manuscripts such as the Book of Kells displayed open on the altar like an icon. With several famous mistakes and repetitions, the beautifully painted gospel, almost certainly produced on Iona, was not intended for reading but for reverence, to be looked at in awe and understood as somehow magical in itself. A manuscript reputedly copied by Columba himself was used as a battle standard by the O'Donnells of Donegal. Called the *Cathach* or 'Battler', it was treated as a powerful talisman but rarely opened or read. The gorgeously painted Book of Durrow eventually ended up in the hands of a 19th-century Irish farmer who used to dip it into cattle troughs so that his sick cows, on drinking the water, would be cured. And when the Gaelic-speaking travel writer Martin Martin visited St Kilda in 1697, he brought with him the first book the illiterate islanders had ever seen:

> But above all writing was most astonishing to them: they cannot conceive how it is possible for any mortal to express the conceptions of his mind in such black characters upon white paper. I told them, that within the compass of two years or less, if they pleased, they might easily be taught to read and write, but they were not of the opinion that either of them could be obtained, at least by them, in an age.

When the people of 6th-century Argyll saw the first manuscripts produced on Iona, their reaction would not have been much different.

Almost certainly stimulated by the skills of the Iona monks, the civil
government of Argyll commissioned a census some time in the middle
of the 7th century. Compiled more than 400 years before the Domesday
Book, the document known as the *Senchus Fer nAlban* or 'The History of
the Men of Alba' listed the number of farms in the various territories of
Argyll. By 650 three kindreds had divided the islands and the coastline
between them, and the number of the basic unit of assessment, the *tech*
or house, was attached to each. Here is the list:

Cenel nOengusa
(the Kindred of Angus on Islay)   430 houses
Cenel Loairne
(the Kindred of Lorne in Lorne and Appin)   420 houses
Cenel nGabrain
(the Kindred of Gabran in Kintyre)   560 houses

These houses varied in size ('small are the lands of the houses of the
Cenel nOengusa', wrote the *Senchus* compiler), but the relative strengths of
each of the kindreds are clear enough. The survey was undertaken to assess
military obligations (and enforce them) and, not surprisingly, given the
geography of Argyll, these were primarily naval. Each group of 20 houses
was bound to provide 28 oarsmen, sufficient to row two seven-bench seagoing curraghs. The total levy could combine to launch a powerful fleet
of 70 curraghs, carrying a force of almost 1,000 marines. The statistics of
the *Senchus* are later but they offer some sense of the scale of raiding into
4th-century Britannia. The first recorded naval battle in Britain was fought
in 719 between the fleets of the Cenel nGabrain and the Cenel Loairne. A
separate and less conspicuous passage lists 'the expeditionary strength of
the hostings' and counts the number of foot soldiers from each kindred.

The *Senchus* also estimated the amount of tribute owed by individual
houses and named powerful people who had control over groups of

houses. Presumably these people were local lords and responsible to the kings of each kindred for the ingathering of food renders. This remarkable document was of course backed by a system of accurate and consistent record-keeping over a period of time. Perhaps the monasteries undertook the task. Whatever the mechanics, the *Senchus* shows the operation of a sophisticated political organization able to sustain a well-structured and specialized fighting force which could muster quickly by sea. Nothing like this has survived from anywhere else in north-western Europe for the same period, and its workings are another indication that what appears to us a chaotic, episodic time in our history is only a matter of perception based on the paucity of what has come down to us.

Script

Columba and Adomnan probably wrote their manuscripts out of doors when they could. On bright, calm days the light was better than inside a gloomy monkish cell and few windows had glass. Most medieval scribal work took place in the cloister. When vellum (calfskin) was being used, the pages were first cut to size, then folded and arranged into gatherings. Tiny holes were pricked out to demarcate the writing area and pages ruled with faintly scored lines to keep the script straight. Using ink made from a decoction of oak apples and iron sulphate, and writing with quill pens, the saints set out their texts in majuscule (for big letters) and minuscule (for smaller). They began the habit of leaving spaces between words and used decorated capitals at the start of new sections. The Roman style had been to run words together with virtually no punctuation.

No records like the *Senchus*, or poetry like the *Gododdin* or Dinogad's lullaby, exist for the Picts. Instead the map of northern and eastern Scotland is studded with the sites of 200 symbol-stones (see plates XVIII, XIX and XX), a singular phenomenon with no contemporary parallel in Europe. And there were lots more of them. Considering how useful large pieces of dressed stone would have been to builders, farmers and road-makers, the surviving 200 are likely to be a small fraction of what once stood proud in the landscape. Many were monumental, some intricately, even exquisitely carved, others almost certainly painted, and all of them without doubt objects full of meaning for those who looked on them.

Archaeologists have divided the stones into two sorts. The earliest have been labelled as Class I and they are, in one sense, simpler, with designs cut into large, undressed slabs or boulders. None occur in Argyll, and because of the tenacity of the migration tradition of the Scots under Fergus Mor macErc in 500 (see page 324), the Class I stones have been dated after that. But if, as seems highly likely, Gaels had settled in the south-west long before that, then the origin of the early symbol-stones is pulled further back in time. This adjustment is important because it seems very probable that the animals and symbols carved on them are related to other sorts of evidence from the later prehistoric and early historic periods.

The stones were obviously meant to be read and understood by a non-literate society, and one of the most striking aspects of their lexicon of symbols is how consistent it is. The same or similar designs appear on very many of them. Ten sorts of animals were regularly carved, with some, like the bulls at Burghead, being used on plaques, or the walls of caves or elsewhere, and they are concentrated in particular areas. Remembering the frequent use of totem-names in Ptolemy's list of northern tribes – the Raven People, the Sheep Folk, the Horse People, to say nothing of the Kindred Hounds and the likelihood that many other peoples and their totems remain unnoticed – the use of animals on marker stones in the landscape seems straightforward. Class I stones were generally raised in borderline places, often where good arable or pastoral land meets rising hill country. Where bulls, horses, dogs, deer, boar, snakes, eagles, salmon, wolves and bottle-nosed dolphins (a creature sometimes described, bafflingly, as a 'swimming elephant') are depicted on stones, it seems very likely that they were understood as territory markers. Contemporary Ogham inscriptions in Ireland seem to have been used for the same purpose. And if the totem animals were believed to be magical, then setting their likenesses at the edges of territory might also have supplied an important sense of protection.

The repertoire of symbols is less open to interpretation. Some are immediately recognizable: a mirror and double-sided comb, a snake and a flower. The others are more graphic and seem two-dimensional. But if these symbols are all taken together and related as tokens of the status and religious beliefs of the individuals who caused the stones to be raised, then many of them can begin to be read. The V-rod has been interpreted as a broken arrow, the Z-rod as a broken spear and the so-called 'tuning fork' as a broken sword. Other items, such as the mirror, comb, flower, and a double-disc which might be a stylized version of a chariot, have all been associated with sacrifice and funeral rituals. All over Britain people had been depositing broken or slighted metal weapons in watery places – broken or bent swords, spears and arrows (with only the metal tips surviving). And for millennia funerary practices involved placing expensive grave goods appropriate to the status of the deceased beside their interred corpses. Items such as mirrors, combs, flowers and even entire chariots have often been recovered by archaeologists from prehistoric burials. The crescent so frequently depicted on symbol-stones might represent another item of grave goods or ritual deposit. It looks like a graphic version of that common piece of Celtic decoration, the torc. But it would be foolish to claim that the snake and the notched rectangle are easily understood in this context. Their use and meaning may always elude understanding.

At all events, the prime difference between the old rituals of depositing metal objects in wet places or setting them inside burials as grave goods and what the Picts began to do in the 4th or 5th centuries is straightforward. When the broken spears, arrows and swords were carved on stones instead of being buried out of sight in a bog or a burial, the idea was blindingly obvious – *they were intended to be seen.* By instructing their sculptors to carve this collection of objects, the Pictish aristocracy developed a new and entirely symbolic way of showing their devotion and respect for the gods and for the dead. Instead of actually throwing away metal objects into watery places, they simply set up their representations for all to see. As an upstanding symbol of belief the Christian cross works in much the same way.

Isidore of Seville understood Pictish tattoos as a highly visible way of indicating rank and genealogy, and other writers noted, often disdainfully, the Pictish habit of wearing few clothes so that the markings could be seen – by both gods and men. It seems likely that body decoration (which has of course all perished) found more concrete and enduring expression on the symbol-stones, and like the magical tattoos what was carved needed to be seen to have its power. Perhaps the designs were also cut in wood, like much early Ogham.

Class II stones were carved later and some of them are magnificent artistic achievements. The sculptors and the quarriers shaped these stones into rectangles whose long sides were often cut to a taper, or a narrow top, or a peaked finish. Their dates must be later than the Class I stones (although these continued to be made) because they carry Christian crosses on one side, biblical scenes and sometimes representations of Pictish aristocratic life. As such they are amongst the first pictures of life in Scotland, the first glimpse of what people, animals and objects looked like 12 or 13 centuries ago. The cross-slabs or cross-stones may indeed chart the process of the conversion of Pictland and many of them have been found in dense groups in areas particularly targeted by Christian missions, in Tayside and on the northern shores of the Moray Firth.

Side-saddle

One of the most famous symbol-stones is dominated by an enigmatic and fascinating figure. At Hilton of Cadboll, near Tain on the Dornoch Firth, a hunting scene is depicted on a particularly beautiful cross-slab, and at the top there is a lady on horseback, riding side-saddle. W.D. Oxenham of Edinburgh has noticed that the scene has striking connections with the *Tale of Pwyll and Rhiannon* in the collection of Old Welsh mythology known as *The Mabinogion*. Given that the Welsh and the Picts spoke cousin-languages, the widespread currency of such a story should not be surprising. And if the connection is secure, then it may be that the lady riding side-saddle was intended to be read as Rhiannon, a figure closely related to the pagan female deity Epona. She was a fertility goddess with special links to horses; her name may be the original source of the word 'pony'. The consuming Pictish interest in matters equestrian encourages the notion that they might have had the wit to carve a disguised representation of a pagan deity on the other side of a Christian cross-slab. And if Mr Oxenham is right, the stone may show a rare example of pre-Christian Pictish iconography.

Scenes of life amongst the aristocracy, the people who commissioned the sculptors, are found on the reverse of several cross-slabs (and occasionally fitted in around the cross itself). Horses were clearly very important, and from the wealth of examples, great trouble was taken over breeding, turnout and schooling. These are not the shaggy ponies of later times – like those ridden by the Border reivers – but animals which did much to add to the status of an individual. Some care was taken to depict good conformation and a surprising amount of saddlery detail can be made out. As it was for many centuries afterwards (and probably before), hunting on horseback was a popular and prestigious aristocratic pastime. On stones at Hilton of Cadboll near Tain and Aberlemno in Angus, stag hunts with hounds gallop into life, and elsewhere cavalry warriors sit straight-backed on high-stepping mounts. Judging by the proportions, some horses stood at 15 hands, and given that the introduction of larger breeding stock lay far in the future, these big animals must have been produced from native bloodstock by horsemasters who knew their business.

Animals of all kinds are often beautifully carved on the symbol-stones, executed with a clarity and economy of line reminiscent of the cave painting of the prehistoric period. In fact so much Pictish fauna appears, much of it characterful and playful, that observers have been led to remark that its inclusion shows a genuine love for the natural world and its creatures.

On a cross-slab at Cossans in Angus the only surviving representation of a Pictish boat was carved. Despite weathering of the stone, it looks as if the boat was clinker-built and a stern rudder is clearly visible. At 3 m/10 ft the Cossans stone is tall and, standing on a prominent ridge, very visible from a distance. It was probably a boundary marker erected by people for whom sea travel was an identifying attribute of some kind.

The positioning of cross-slabs in the landscape may have fallen into the same sort of pattern as free-standing crosses elsewhere. Some were used to demarcate a sacred precinct, and the Cossans stone may stand on an early Christian site. Place-names still found on a good map recall the area surrounding the ancient priory at Coldingham in Berwickshire. Applincross, Cairncross and Whitecross hedge the church's immediate environs with powerful symbolism that would have been lost on none who came near. Other crosses were used as prayer-stations on the road to a famous or important church, and stopping at each in turn formed part of the experience of worship. On the approach to the old church at Jedburgh, which predated the abbey, the remains of no less than five crosses have been found. They date between the 8th and 10th centuries. It seems probable that the Pictish cross-slabs were used in similar ways, but the addition of symbols and scenes from secular life adds a great deal of texture and makes the transition from paganism to Christianity somehow more human and local.

After the mid-9th century no more Pictish symbol-stones were made and all knowledge of their meaning was gradually lost. The consistency of the symbol-language might offer a sense of what happened. Over a very wide area, from Shetland to Fife, the same lexicon had been understood by patrons, sculptors and those who looked at the stones. This sort of cultural and religious consistency suggests a degree of political unity amongst the Pictish aristocracy. When the kingdom of Pictland began to fail, the ability of these powerful people to continue their unique tradition failed with it. Political and cultural clout passed to others, people who may have seen the symbols as the language of the past. Native Pictish aristocrats who survived would have had to adapt and demonstrate their allegiance to a new order by abandoning these obvious signs of their own heritage.

The process which led to the fall of the Pictish kingdom in the 9th century was also the process which led ultimately to the beginnings of Scotland. It had deep roots and could have grown in a number of different directions. Three centuries earlier, the most powerful figure in the north was not a Pict or a Scot but one of the Baptized, the *Bedydd*, a native British king called Urien. His praise poems and sporadic notices in chronicles and Easter tables show that he could demand and receive tribute from a huge area. At its greatest extent, his mighty kingdom of Rheged (the name probably meant nothing more than 'the kingdom') stretched from Dunragit or *Dun-Rheged* in the west, near Stranraer, to Carlisle and then south into what is now Lancashire, to Rochdale, whose old name was *Reced-ham*. The bards hailed him as Urien, 'Lord of the Echwydd'. This is Old Welsh for a tide-rip and it refers to the Solway. It meant that Urien was seen by contemporaries as the king of the Solway, and he no doubt often travelled through his realm by sea. *Catraeth* or Catterick, in Swaledale in Yorkshire, was also in his control and some called him 'Defender of Aeron' or Ayrshire.

Urien's name is interesting, and in an age when the multiple repetition of royal names often causes confusion it is unique. *Urien* derives from *Urbgen* meaning 'born in the city'. Carlisle (or York at a stretch) is likely to have been that city and since Urien's extensive area of influence hinged on the axis of the old Roman town it is probable that he was raised there. Urbgen was a name intended to add prestige; it associated the king with the fading glamour and glory of the Empire, it emphasized his Christianity in contrast to the pagans of the countryside, and it spoke of sophistication, of the wider world beyond the Solway where other cities, remnants of Rome, still functioned.

These were not spurious associations. Archaeology at several contemporary sites around the Solway Firth has turned up evidence of trade with Gaul and the Rhineland. And at the same time as Urien strode the

Roman walls of Carlisle, Adomnan's *Life of Columba* relates that Gaulish merchants were in the habit of trading at Dunadd. Wine was a prime import from the south. Not only did the aristocratic feasting culture of Gododdin, Rheged and elsewhere need plenty of strong drink; red wine was necessary for the transubstantiation of the blood of Christ in the celebration of the Christian Mass. Spices, salt and pigment also arrived in continental ships. The pigment was an especially prized cargo, light, small in bulk and very expensive. Iona's painters of illuminated manuscripts used ultramarine from the eastern Mediterranean to colour the Virgin Mary's robes; lapis lazuli from Afghanistan was another rich blue, pink and purple folium came from sunflower seeds, kermes red from North Africa. A moment's reflection on the scale of the resources needed to create a work such as the Book of Kells casts aside the sense that the world shrank markedly after the fall of the Roman Empire. The mechanics of imperial communications, the roads, the cities, the military signal stations – all of these certainly withered. But knowledge was more resilient. The libraries at Iona and at Monkwearmouth were impressive and with their help the known world could be comprehended in a monkish cell. Although he had never visited them, Adomnan felt no inhibition in writing a guide to the Holy Places of Palestine. Using only what he could find in the extensive collection of manuscripts made by generations of monks at Iona, the saint directed pilgrims around Jerusalem, Bethlehem and elsewhere. And the knowledge of sea-travel and all the opportunities for exchange it brought needed no more than the ancient skills and courage which had predated and outlasted Rome's land-based empire.

Wattie the rhymer

Never one to allow reality too much play when it came to finding the right rhyme for his popular epic poems, Walter Scott did an unconscious disservice to a faint echo of the memory of Urien. In a fertile part of the Ettrick Valley, in the Scottish Borders, the Ordnance Survey records four place-names incorporating *Deloraine*. It follows Scott's spelling, but forgets that he changed it to get it to rhyme with 'again' in *The Lay of the Last Minstrel*. Those who live along the Ettrick Water nowadays still use the original pronunciation of *Deloran*, and it means 'the meadow of Urien'.

In the 6th century the old city of Carlisle represented a prize. In contrast to the rights to tribute from the rural economy fought over by native kings, the possession of a city stood for prestige. Inside the crumbling walls of the military fortress (now entirely obscured by the more recent castle) the king of Carlisle could put on the mantle of *romanitas* and legitimacy, while distributing jewellery and other gifts fitting for heroes, and doling out Mediterranean wine to his warbands as they feasted and heard tales in their hall. In 573 the kings of York no doubt enjoyed similar prestige inside the massive walls of the old legionary fort, and it may be that primacy was the issue at stake when their warriors rode north. Did the inheritance of the Empire sit better at York where emperors such as Severus had held court, and others, like Constantine, had been proclaimed? Or did Carlisle, the city of the Wall, deserve greater regard? Whatever the pretext, at *Arderydd* (a name now remembered at Arthuret Church near Longtown) a bloody defeat was inflicted on Gwenddolau, king of Carlisle. The slaughter was so great that, according to a series of very early poems, it drove Gwenddolau's bard insane. Myrddin fled into the 'Forest of Cellydon' to lead a life of mysticism and madness; he fled into myth-history as the Great Enchanter, Merlin.

Kingtime

In early Scotland the date depended on where you lived. Until recently the most common method of reckoning the year was by regnal dates. According to the length of a king's reign, time was worked out from the year he acceded. For example, one source claimed that 'Bridei map Maelchon reigned for 30 years. In the eighth year of his reign, he was baptized by St Columba.' Or not. In Rheged or Gododdin, it was a different year, depending on who was king and how long he lasted.

Across Europe other systems added colour to the mix. The four-year cycles of the Greek Olympiads carried on in the eastern Mediterranean until the 4th century and the Roman Era was based on the number of years since the founding of the city. In Spain and Portugal, the date was calculated from 39 BC, the year of the Roman invasion, and this remained in force until well into the Middle Ages.

After the slaughter at Arthuret, the York kings did not seem to press home any immediate advantage. Instead, Urien, perhaps coming from an aristocratic family or as a relative of the dead king, moved to fill the vacuum and soon after 573 he became Lord of Luguvalium, the Roman name for the city of Carlisle. Although the bards sang that his warband forayed far into the north with their king, returning from Manau with 'herds of cattle surrounding him', it was in the east that Urien found his most dangerous enemies and, eventually, his nemesis.

Since the time of Britannia, Germanic mercenaries had been settling along the North Sea coasts, especially those of Northumberland, Durham and Yorkshire. Many had originally been in the service of Rome. In typically terse terms, Bede recorded a one-line glimpse of a unique fusion between these incomers and the native élites: 'In 547 Ida began his reign'. Ida was the founder of the Northumbrian dynasty and had established himself on the near-impregnable castle rock at Bamburgh. Fragments of a lost North British chronicle can be sifted from the otherwise chaotic compilation known as the *Historia Brittonum*, written some time in the 8th century by the monk Nennius. He added an important gloss to Bede: 'Ida joined Din Guauroy to Berneich'. These are both Old Welsh place-names, the first being the original name of the fort at Bamburgh, the second the Celtic kingdom surrounding it. *Berneich* or *Bernaccia* changed into *Bernicia* and Ida's descendants came to rule over it. In early history names are always important and few more so than this. By adopting the name of the old Celtic kingdom instead of attaching a new Germanic one (as happened elsewhere), by taking over the principal royal centre at Yeavering (*ad Gefrin* in Bede, another Celtic name with the prosaic meaning of 'Goat Hill') and by adopting an aggressive and expansionist policy from the outset, the new kings of Bernicia created the only recognizably Germano-Celtic cultural and political fusion in Britain. In many other areas the early differences were stark.

Numbers probably fostered this phenomenon. In the north-east the Germanic incomers in the mid-6th century were in a very small minority in the midst of the native population, far more so than in the south. There are many fewer archaeological traces of them than elsewhere, since they adopted local burial practices and beliefs, as well as occupying other native centres such as Dunbar in East Lothian, Old Melrose in Roxburghshire and Milfield in north Northumberland. These statistics forced an accommodation. So that they could continue to be understood, old names were retained by the new élite. And so that a continuity of royal authority was apparent, places and institutions important to Celtic Bernaccia were left untouched, at least for a time. Similar circumstances immediately to the south persuaded the Germanic settlers of Deira in north Yorkshire to do something similar and use a version of the old Celtic name of *Deur*.

These niceties mattered little to Urien and his captains. Whoever was in charge in the east had to be removed so that tribute could be rendered to him and his. But the cultural fusion of Bernicia was important; it provided a recurring theme in the early history of the north and substantially diluted a deceptive duality. Armies of Celts did not always confront armies of Anglo-Saxons in the war for Britain. The dynamics of change were much more complicated.

Arthur of the North

One of the few consistent passages in Nennius' *History of the Britons* relates to the campaigns of Arthur, the man he called 'the Duke of Battles'. It is the most frequently cited text in the welter of material about the life and career of this extraordinary man. The Nennius passage lists 13 battles, and since most of them took place at recognizable locations in the north it seems sensible to place Arthur amongst the warbands of the Celtic kingdom of the southern Gododdin. Persuasive evidence has been marshalled to show him as the heir of Paternus Pesrut, with a base at *Marchidun*, the horse fort, otherwise known as Roxburgh Castle, near Kelso.

At first Urien was successful against Bernicia. Some time in the 580s he and his son, Owain, destroyed the forces of *Fflamddwyn*, 'the Firebrand', at a place called *Argoed Llwyfein* at the west end of Hadrian's Wall. *Fflamddwyn* was a nickname given to King Aethelric of Bernicia, probably by his Celtic Bernaccian warriors. At any rate he failed to live up to it, and the bards of Urien were scathing:

When Owain slew Fflamddwyn,
It was no more than sleeping.
Sleeps now the wide host of England
With the light upon their eyes.

Encouraged by success and possibly anxious to buttress his eastern possessions at Catraeth, Urien sent out messengers to negotiate a coalition with other Celtic kings. Perhaps he was in a position to demand it. A grand army massed for the descent into Bernicia, a fatal incursion which would drive Ida's dynasty into the sea. Rhyderch Hen, king of Strathclyde, joined with Morgant of the southern Gododdin, and Guallauc came from Lennox, the area to the north of the Clyde Basin. Aedan macGabrain from Argyll was persuaded, as was his neighbour across the North Channel, King Fiachna of Ulster. Their combined host swept through what is now north Northumberland, and the Irish warriors stormed Bamburgh, driving the remnants of the Bernician garrison on to Medcaut, the Island of Tides. This was Lindisfarne, only a little way up the coast. Urien chased them but rather than risk more casualties in battle, he ordered his army to lay a siege. Unfolding their leather tents, they encamped at the mouth of the River Lowe and waited for the Bernicians and their Celtic allies to begin to starve.

But the siege and the expected triumph turned into a disaster. 'Through jealousy,' wrote the chronicler, 'and on the initiative of Morgant, Urien was assassinated.'

Grubenhäuser

The remains of these 'sunken buildings' were for a long time the only reliable indication of Anglo-Saxon settlement. Dug into the ground to a depth of about 50 cm/20 ins and 6 by 4 m/20 by 13 ft in area, they used to be thought of as the architecture of a primitive people. But after the discovery of the great timber halls at Yeavering, the sort of thing immortalized in *Beowulf*, perceptions changed. At the village of Sprouston in the Scottish Borders, cropmarks show a Northumbrian township with traces of *Grubenhäuser*. They are now interpreted not as damp and unsophisticated houses but as storerooms and workshops.

Medcaut was one of the last times Celtic kings threatened to overwhelm Germanic-led armies in the north. After 590, there was little but defeat. And in 600 near-total disaster engulfed the army of the Gododdin at Catraeth. Like Urien's, the forces led by Yrfai, Lord of Eidyn, were also an alliance. Warriors had come north from Elmet, a native kingdom based around modern Leeds. Men from Aeron, Pictish warriors from 'beyond Bannauc' and 'the Sea of Iudeu', men from the north Welsh kingdom of Gwynedd (probably named after its saviour, Cunedda) joined them. But it was the background of the leader of the allies, of Yrfai himself, that was most startling. In the *Gododdin* poem he was described as 'Yrfai son of Golistan', showing that his father was *Wulfstan*, clearly a Germanic name, possibly a warrior from Bernicia or Deira. Was there an élite at the Gododdin court in Edinburgh, a group of warriors imported as mercenaries by the kings who sat on the castle rock? It seems likely. A line from the poem suggests that Yrfai might have gained authority of his own as a second-generation Gododdin warrior: 'It was usual for Wolstan's son – though his father was no sovereign lord – that what he said was heeded.'

At Degsastan in 603 Aedan macGabrain was again in battle against the armies of Bernicia. It seems that the men of Argyll and their allies had been raiding in the south and that the king of Bernicia, Aethelfrith, chased, caught and defeated them at Addinston, a place in the Leader Valley where it climbs up to the watershed at Soutra. Aethelfrith's warriors also used a Celtic nickname for their Germanic king. For soldiers, it ranks as complimentary; it was *Am Fleisaur*, meaning 'the Artful Dodger', another small instance of the cross-culturalism veined through aristocratic politics in the north.

Old King Cole

He may indeed have been a merry old soul, and also a real person. For the 5th century the king-lists often note a powerful ruler in the Pennines and award him a founding role for several dynasties, including Rheged. He was known as *Coel Hen* and was certainly seen as a king. *Hen* is Welsh for 'old' and yields the nursery rhyme title. His area of influence coincided with the late Roman province of Britannia Secunda and Cole may have been a Roman appointment, perhaps the last of the generals known as 'the Duke of the Britains'.

By 631 Yrfai's lordship of Eidyn had fallen into the hands of the Bernicians, and ten years later they took the *Urbs Guidi*, the fortress on Stirling Castle rock which dominated Manau. The realm of Gododdin was effaced and the gradual infusion of Germanic culture and language into the Celtic society of the south-east of Scotland began.

Aethelfrith, the Artful Dodger, had manoeuvred himself into a position where he could succeed Aelle as King of Deira, and add it to his realm of Bernicia. Northumbrian kings were usually kings of both, but despite this a separate identity always seems to have been insisted upon. In 616 Edwin of Deira became ruler of Bernicia and Aethelfrith's three sons, Oswy, Eanfrith and Oswald, were forced to seek sanctuary at Fortriu, in the court of the kings of Pictland. As Edwin's warbands reached further north and began to exercise more permanent control over the Tweed Valley, the new king sought to add the veneer of legitimacy to his undoubted military power. Where the Gododdin, the Baptized, were forced to give up more and more tribute rights, Edwin and his counsellors realized that they were becoming masters of an area which was, at least nominally, Christian. And no doubt they thought it politic to convert. Fragments of a lost North British chronicle offer a fascinating alternative to Bede's assertion that in 627 St Paulinus came up from the south on a mission to make Christians. The fragments say that it was not Paulinus but Rhun, bishop of Carlisle, brother of Owain and son of Urien, who first baptized King Edwin of Northumbria. Because he usually interpreted events from a southern perspective and wished to award the credit for the conversion of the northern English to Rome and the church founded by St Augustine in Kent, it seems that Bede suppressed the proselytizing role of Rhun and the early church of Rheged.

Prophecy

When Wales play the England rugby team at the Millennium Stadium in Cardiff, the scoreboard shows *Cymru vs Lloegr*. The Welsh name for England is interesting, for the literal meaning is 'The Lost Lands'. The Welsh never forget that their culture and language once ruled the whole island of Britain and, over an immense period, until the 16th century, they never ceased to hope that Welsh-speaking kings would rule again in London. They also hoped for a Redeemer, a Son of Prophecy, to lead that triumphant return. Eight names from the mists of myth and history are consistently listed: they are Hiriell, Cynan, Cadwaladr, Arthur, Owain ap Urien, Owain Lawgoch, Owain Glyn Dwr and Henry Tudor.

In 631 Edwin was defeated and killed in battle at Hatfield Chase by the combined forces of Penda of Mercia and Cadwallon, king of Gwynedd. This was a signal for the return of Aethelfrith's sons from the Pictish court. First, and briefly, Eanfrith ruled in Bernicia, then Oswald took over both kingdoms before giving way to Oswy in Bernicia in 642 and then in Deira in 655. Once again dynastic politics waxed complex.

A fragment of the *North British Chronicle* noted that Oswy had cemented an alliance with Rheged by contracting a diplomatic marriage to a princess of Urien's house. His bride had the beautiful name of *Rieinmellt* – it means 'Queen of Lightning'. But the alliance was short-lived: it seems that Rieinmellt died tragically young. To preserve her memory, it may be that Oswy endowed the ancient church of Hoddom in Dumfriesshire. Dedicated to the Strathclyde saint Kentigern (another title often mistaken for a name – it means 'Great Lord'), the site was excavated recently and, appropriately for a holy place in the land of the *Bedydd*, the remains of a baptistry were uncovered.

What is significant about the brief marriage of Rieinmellt and Oswy was the willingness of the expanding and ambitious kingdom of Northumbria to make meaningful links with native kingdoms. On either side of the Celtic/English divide, whatever served interests best was done, and despite later rewritings of history that often meant a much greater native involvement in the emerging Anglo-Saxon kingdoms than is generally allowed. If the young queen had lived and borne children, the new Germanic dynasty might have taken on even more of a Celtic accent than it did.

Pit, cill, wic and dalr

In addition to *pit* names, several other prefixes and suffixes to place-names emerged in the early historic period. And, like *pit*, they were all introduced by incomers. *Cill* is from the Latin *cella* and was used by settlers from Argyll to denote a place with a church such as *Killin*, *Kilmacolm* or *Kildonan*. *Wic* or *wick* came north with the Northumbrians and meant 'a farm' dependent on a centre, rather like *pit*; it is found in *Berwick* (barley-farm), *Darnick* (hidden farm) and *Hawick* (hedge farm). *Dalr* was Norse for 'valley' and appears on the map as the tautological *Glendale*, as well as *Helmsdale* and *Laxdale*.

Meanwhile, no less complex a picture emerged in Pictland. After 631 it seems that a sequence of kings of Strathclyde descent began to rule.

They were followed by successors who had the support of Northumbria. The turns and twists of dynastic politics in the north were labyrinthine as aristocracies who were related and who must often have known each other jockeyed for positions of power. Individual details are uncertain and sometimes confusing, but it is the general direction of change which was significant. More everyday matters of food and shelter concerned the vast hinterland of farmers whose hard work supported these élites. But they cannot have been unaffected by changes in the control of the land. When a Northumbrian *arriviste* replaced a Celtic lord, a new master would inevitably have exercised power differently. Perhaps some sharp initial lessons would have been necessary to assert a new authority. And if the rights to receive food renders passed to the church, their stewardship might have forced the pace of conversion in the countryside.

Language slowly changed. Many of the Northumbrian warriors spoke English and, as they moved northwards and settled, it became the language of power, no doubt demanding understanding at the point of a spear on occasion. Bilingualism will nevertheless have been the norm for many generations, as it continues to be in the Gaelic-speaking heartlands of Scotland. To Gaels, English is the medium of government, the official and commercial language, while Gaelic is for the hearthside and family, and the working of the land. A distinction of that sort is likely to have begun to form in south-eastern Scotland in the 7th century.

Christianity was an important part of the mechanics of power brokerage at that time. The role of Bishop Rhun in the conversion of Edwin may have been ignored by Bede, but he could not gloss over the fact that Edwin's successor, Oswald, did not send to Rome or to the south of England for help in creating the organization of the new Northumbrian church, but to Columba's monastery on Iona. In response, Aidan arrived to become bishop of Lindisfarne and founder of monasteries at Old Melrose and Coldingham.

Despite the defeat at Hatfield Chase, the reach and influence of Northumbrian kings continued to stretch in all directions in the 7th century. They claimed recognition as *Bretwaldas*, or 'Britain-rulers', and it may be that to underscore this title with substance Oswald's successor, Oswy, moved to find a new wife not, like Rieinmellt, from a native royal house, but from the south. He married a Kentish princess. Eanfled was evidently devout, having been raised in the church founded at Canterbury by St Augustine. Her arrival at Bamburgh produced a domestic conflict which may have supplied the spark to ignite an important political conflagration. The pivotal date in the Christian calendar was and remains Easter, the time of Christ's Passion and the holiest week of the year. In order to avoid a clash with the Jewish feast of the Passover, a convoluted formula had been worked out involving the first full moon on or after 21 March. The Book of Common Prayer still contains the precise calculations needed. When she arrived at the Northumbrian court Eanfled found that, for various historical reasons, her church reckoned the dates differently from the Celtic church of Aidan and his successors at Lindisfarne. On Easter Day, King Oswy found himself feasting alone because, according to his wife, it was Palm Sunday. Clearly something had to be done.

Now, the differing dates for Easter might appear little more than a pretext for the ensuing contest between Columba's Iona and Augustine's church of Canterbury, but it was in fact an important matter for an expanding Christian kingdom. The date of Easter determined the whole liturgical year and a different way of reckoning it made the dates of all the major festivals fall on different days. And more, early Christians believed that the holiest festival of the year was the occasion for a spiritual battle. At Easter God fought Satan for control of the world, and it was vital that believers all prayed hard for victory at the same time. A difference of dates split the Christian army in two and gave Satan a chance of winning.

To resolve the matter of the date, and other issues, Oswy called a conference. At the Synod of Whitby in 664, he listened patiently to the arguments and then ruled in favour of the Kentish church and his bishop, Wilfred. It was of course primarily a question of jurisdiction and, crucially, Iona's defeat helped to turn Northumbria into a more thoroughly English kingdom. After 664 Wilfred enthusiastically expelled native clergy from their churches and was himself rewarded with the bishopric of Northumbria. If Oswy had been swayed in Iona's favour then, once again, the cultural cast of the north might have been markedly different. But it turned out that, in addition to Latin, God spoke English and not Gaelic.

Their takeover and consolidation of Gododdin and Manau encouraged the Northumbrian kings to push even further north. A policy of preferring puppet rulers on the Pictish throne advanced their ambitions sufficiently, and by 669 Wilfred was claiming to be bishop of Pictland as well as Northumbria. But when Oswy died in 670/71, the Pictish aristocracy took the opportunity to remove his placeman, King Drest. With the support of the mormaers and their warbands, Bridei map Bili took up the Pictish crown, even though he was the son of the king of Strathclyde. But despite support from Dumbarton for Bridei, the response from the new king of Northumbria, Ecgfrith, was emphatic and determinant. In 672, somewhere between the rivers Carron and Avon, the Pictish army was not just defeated, it was massacred.

This one-sided battle was not, however, between two competing outsiders who coveted the crown of Pictland. Because of generations of diplomatic exchange and intermarriage, Bridei had a genuine hereditary claim to the throne. Through his grandfather, Neithon, he asserted his right to rule in southern Pictland. Whatever its intricacies, contemporaries clearly thought his claim worthy of support, and in the decade after 672 Bridei was able to rally the Pictish warbands and re-establish sufficient independence to force Ecgfrith to march north again.

In 685, near Forfar, Bridei turned to face the Northumbrians, this time with a very different outcome. Few battles are truly pivotal, but what happened at Dunnichen does seem to have turned the tide of history. Several chroniclers noted the day, some with great precision. Around 'three o'clock in the afternoon of Saturday 20 May 685, there was fought Gueith Linn Garan, the Battle of the Heron's Pool', wrote the compiler of the *North British Chronicle*. The Northumbrians called the place *Nechtansmere*, or 'Nechtan's Lake', and others knew it as Dunnichen. Bede gave no name, but he could not avoid recounting that Ecgfrith had only himself to blame, for he acted against the advice of St Cuthbert.

What happened was very different from the rout of 672. The Northumbrians were massacred, Ecgfrith and all of his royal bodyguard slaughtered, and the Picts and Strathclyders regained control of their kingdoms. The apparently unstoppable advance of the descendants of Ida was halted and rolled back to the shores of the Forth. And to celebrate and mark their signal victory, the Picts raised a symbol-stone which has survived and which shows what took place on 20 May 685 at Dunnichen.

Standing in the churchyard at Aberlemno, in Angus, only 10 km/6 miles from the battlefield, the monument to Bridei's triumph is a fascinating document, eloquent and beautifully made (see plates XXI and XXII). On the reverse side from the cross is the only clear battle-narrative ever found on a symbol-stone. It reads like a comic strip in a newspaper, with four scenes arranged in sequence from top to bottom. In the first a mounted figure who may represent Bridei chases another mounted warrior. In his haste to escape, the latter has thrown away his shield and sword. This man may be Ecgfrith. Bede's description of the battle talked of the Northumbrian king being 'lured into narrow mountain passes' by an enemy who 'pretended to retreat'. Perhaps this first scene shows Ecgfrith turning and fleeing at the moment when he realized that an ambush had been sprung. What identifies the escaping warrior as a Northumbrian is his helmet. During excavations at the Coppergate in York a very similar design, rounded with a long nose-guard, was discovered. It dates not to 685, the year of the battle at Dunnichen, but to about a century later, when the Aberlemno Stone was carved.

The scrum

When opposing ranks of infantry locked together on the battlefield, the side that pushed harder often won. Shields with prominent metal bosses could be used as an offensive weapon, and with accurate stabbing and thrusting an enemy line could be broken, turned and attacked from behind. When ranks of spearmen were equally matched, a curious effect was produced. Because most men are right-handed, they held their shields with the left and depended for cover on the man fighting on their right. The cumulative effect of left-handed pushing tended to make an infantry battle wheel in a clockwise direction until a breakthrough was made. This ancient tradition has given rise to the phrase for a trusted lieutenant as 'a right-hand man'.

The second scene shows Ecgfrith, or a mounted Northumbrian warrior wearing the same sort of helmet, attacking a group of Pictish infantrymen. The sculptor clearly understood a good deal about military tactics because he has been careful to arrange the men into a proper battle formation of three ranks. At the front stands a warrior with a sword and a round, curved shield with a very prominent boss. When the opposing cavalry charged, he had to withstand the shock of impact. But to support him, another man stood just behind holding a long spear which projected well beyond the warrior in the front rank. Along an extended battle-line an array of bristling spear-points might have inhibited or even deterred a charge, forcing cavalry ponies to wheel away. And behind the two warriors shown immediately engaging the enemy stood a third man holding a spear, acting as a reserve.

In a third scene, carved at the foot of the stone, the Bridei and Ecgfrith figures face each other on horseback. Ecgfrith appears to be on the point of throwing his spear while Bridei readies himself to parry it. And in a final act, tucked into the bottom right-hand corner, the Ecgfrith figure lies dead on the battlefield and a raven, a carrion-feeder often associated with defeat, pecks at his neck.

The Aberlemno Stone is a nationalist symbol. Carved a century after the great victory, its message was both simple and powerful: Pictland was different, and in 685 that singular identity had been preserved by force of arms. And perhaps it also suggested that its independence would always be vigorously defended.

At about the same time as the battle for independence at Dunnichen, the warbands of Rheged were losing theirs. Before undertaking his fatal expedition to the north, Ecgfrith had been pushing Northumbrian influence westwards. No battles are recorded but a consequence of Ecgfrith's success was reported in the *Annals of Ulster*. From the year 682, exiled British warbands had been fighting down the eastern coasts of Ireland, either as mercenaries in the service of Irish kings or on their own account. In 684 the Northumbrians mounted an expedition to raid along the eastern Irish seaboard. It may well be that the British warbands were the last remnant of the host of Rheged, which had recently been defeated by Ecgfrith's men, and the Northumbrian expedition was an attempt to finish them off before they could regroup or recruit Irish allies. Whatever the outcome, the name of Rheged was not heard after that time and the famous house of Urien passed into memory.

Following the death of Ecgfrith, a series of Northumbrian kings steadily advanced their interests in the west. Around 700 two beautiful Anglian crosses were set up at Bewcastle (inside the old Roman frontier fort) and at Ruthwell in Dumfriesshire, and by 731 the ancient church at Whithorn had become the centre of a Northumbrian bishopric. Pehthelm was the first incumbent and his name appears to reflect how he and his masters saw his role. *Pehthelm* means 'Leader of the Picts'. Since he was much too far south for the name to refer to his Galloway flock, it must have signified an aspiration rather than a reality. After Ecgfrith had defeated the Picts in 672, he established a bishopric at Abercorn whose mission was the conversion and eventual spiritual leadership of the north. The ambitious Wilfred no doubt encouraged the foundation, even though it lay on the edges of Northumbrian influence. Perhaps Pehthelm's see at Whithorn was a successor of sorts. It was a persistent ambition for the next bishop was Pehtwine, which means 'Friend of the Picts'. By 750 King Eadberht had pushed up into Carrick and Ayrshire, close to the borders of the native kingdom of Strathclyde.

Despite these encroachments (and a serious defeat for the Picts in 711 in Manau), there was no repetition of the threat posed by Ecgfrith.

In 758, Eadberht's son was assassinated and his kingdom gradually descended into a long period of internal turmoil and factionalism. Pictland, Strathclyde and Argyll appeared to exchange kings and influence, and to live in periods of comparative harmony punctuated by short interludes of dynastic squabbling. Several rulers enjoyed long and stable reigns. Nechtan, son of Derile, lasted from 706 to 724, and he has often been credited with the wholesale adoption of Christianity north of the Forth. According to Bede, this Pictish king wrote to Ceolfrith, the abbot of Monkwearmouth and Jarrow, asking for advice on how to set up a church (and how to fix the correct date of Easter) after the Northumbrian model. This passage is unlikely to have been a propagandist's invention, since the event took place within Bede's adult lifetime and the letter was addressed to his own monastery and its abbot. To fabricate or exaggerate something which all of his readers would have known to be untrue, no matter how sympathetic they might have been, does not sit easily with the careful, painstaking approach to research that informed the rest of Bede's work.

However, it seems highly unlikely that Pictland remained pagan as late as 710. Christian kings from Strathclyde, such as Bridei map Bili, would have found the transition to a pagan kingdom awkward, and in addition there is plenty of evidence for earlier attempts at conversion, all of which are unlikely to have failed totally. Bede himself wrote that Ninian had led a mission to the southern Picts and Adomnan reported that Columba had gone to Bridei macMaelchon's court near Inverness in order to bring him and his people into the church. Perhaps the overall picture was patchy, Christian conversion only piecemeal or confined at first to the aristocracy, and the Celtic nature of what did exist was not to Nechtan's taste. In 717 he had the Columban monks expelled from Pictland. However, it is true to say that the majority of the most impressive cross-slabs were carved during and after the reign of Nechtan, and it may be that the Pictish church simply became organized and assertive – and Pictish – at the outset of the 8th century.

Holy rood

The Ruthwell Cross is a beautiful example of the sculptor's art, but it also has a role in the early history of English literature. Written in Northumbrian runes cut on the lower, narrow sides of the cross-shaft are two extracts from one of the earliest surviving poems composed in English, *The Dream of the Rood*. It forms part of a highly sophisticated scheme, in both poetry and sculpture, for reading the whole cross, and it is based on the idea that the cross upon which Christ was crucified had a personality. Here is the second stanza:

I [lifted up] a powerful king –
The Lord of Heaven I dared not tilt.
Men insulted both of us together;
I was drenched with blood poured from the man's side.

In 724 Nechtan's interest in religion became more intimate. Forced to abdicate, he retired to a monastery. Three related contenders then engaged in a long struggle to succeed him. After at least nine major engagements, Oengus eventually defeated or killed his rivals and placed himself on the throne. One of the last battles in the wars of the succession was fought against Nechtan, who had come out of monastic retirement to reassert his rights. When he was defeated by Oengus in 729, it was reported that Nechtan's tribute-collectors, his *exactatores*, were killed in the fight. This is significant because these men were usually in the service of the king of overkings, known in Ireland as the High King. It looks as though Nechtan had reclaimed his old office and that the wars were fought between the kings of Pictish provinces: almost certainly Fortriu, probably Angus, Atholl and Fife.

Oengus I also reigned for a long time, from 729 to 761, and with his new foundation at St Andrews he supplied a focus for the national church. By importing the relics of a major biblical saint and building a church to house them as far east as it was possible to be, he distanced himself and his people from Columba and Iona. Despite this, Oengus is an Argyll name and he almost certainly had aristocratic Argyll blood somewhere in his ancestry. By 789 Constantine I was king of Pictland and, as the son of Fergus, undoubtedly of Argyll royal lineage, from the Cenel nGabrain. After 811 he was also listed as king of Argyll, probably the first to rule both kingdoms, and towards the end of his reign, he founded a monastery at Dunkeld in the Pictish province of Atholl (or possibly refounded an earlier Columban church on the site). Perhaps the adoption of the name Constantine and its association with a Christian emperor was intended to reflect his northern Christian imperium. There is also a connection with St Andrew. It was said that the saint's relics were taken to Constantinople during the Emperor Constantine's reign in the early 4th century.

This early Argyll king of the Picts was, it seems, not an isolated case. In addition to Columban monks, other Gaelic speakers may have migrated across Drumalban to settle in the east. By the time the list of Pictish provinces was made in the 8th century, two of them had Gaelic names. Atholl is from *Athfotla* meaning 'New Ireland'. And its dependant, Gowrie, on the northern shores of the Firth of Tay, is cognate with the name of the kindred of King Constantine, the Cenel nGabrain. Perhaps the foundation of Dunkeld, in the heart of Atholl, was no accident. Increasing Argyll influence in the east may have lain behind Nechtan's expulsion of the Iona monks in 717 and his attempt to forge supporting links with Northumbria.

Since the wars of the succession won by Oengus I, there were more and more hints of developing Argyll influence in the east. By the end of the 8th century, this gradual infiltration was jolted into seismic political movement by a series of shocking events which came, as it were, out of the blue. For the year 793 the *Anglo-Saxon Chronicle* recorded:

Terrible portents appeared in Northumbria, and miserably inflicted the inhabitants; these were exceptional flashes of lightning and fiery dragons were seen flying in the air, and soon after in the same year the harrying of the heathen miserably destroyed God's church in Lindisfarne by rapine and slaughter.

The Vikings had sailed into history. In 794 the Northern Isles and the Hebrides were attacked and two years later landings were made on the Irish mainland. Even at a distance of 12 centuries the shock of the first Viking raids is still palpable. Iona was repeatedly pillaged and, in 806, 68 monks were slaughtered. The kingdom of Argyll was quickly becoming untenable. Some of Columba's precious relics went to Ireland for safe-keeping, well inland, and others were eventually carried over Drumalban to the new church at Dunkeld, also far from the dangerous sea.

By the time Constantine's brother, Oengus II, had begun to rule, the focus of the joint kingdoms of Argyll and Pictland had shifted decisively to the east. Based on Fortriu, perhaps at the royal palace at Forteviot, the royal administration continued to function despite the increasing scale and severity of the Viking attacks. But in 839 the hammer blow finally fell. At a battle somewhere in Fortriu the Pictish king, his noblemen and his host were slaughtered by a Viking army. Oengus' sons, Eoganan (who had succeeded his father) and Bran, were killed along with many of their relatives. But no invasion or occupation followed. Vikings had begun to settle in Orkney and Shetland, but for the most part they were still intent on raiding and plunder. After the catastrophic battle in Fortriu an opportunity beckoned for the man from whom all subsequent Scottish kings would be counted. In 840 Kenneth macAlpin first asserted his rights as king of Argyll and, soon after, he moved to establish himself in Pictland and Fortriu.

The valley of the dead

Stretching south-west into the Southern Uplands from near Selkirk, the Yarrow Valley can be a windy, lonely place. But its bleak geography hints at a curious prehistory. One of Britain's most intriguing post-Roman inscribed stones stands at Whitehope Farm. It appears to commemorate a battle and the death of two native princes some time in the 6th century. They were Nudus and Dumnogenus, perhaps remnants of the Selgovan aristocracy. All around them are the echoes of an ancient burial ground. Near the farm lies the 'Dead Pool' and the tradition of a mass grave of slain warriors. Two other nearby standing stones align with the memorial stone (itself probably a standing stone before the letters were chiselled on it) and the strange name *Annan Street* is adjacent, for a patch of boggy ground to the north. The historian Walter Elliot has come across the possibility of several large and very early cemeteries at Whitehope, all dug on the same platform of high ground as the standing stone sits on. Perhaps it was a burial place for the Selgovan kings.

MacAlpin was not the first king of Picts and Scots but he did begin to assert the primacy of Gaelic culture in the east. Perhaps the weakness of the decimated Pictish aristocracy left the way open for newcomers from the west to impose themselves. Within a five-year period, Kenneth I had disposed of such Pictish resistance as remained, and by 845 was in undisputed control.

In the spring of 870 lookouts on the ancient fortress of Dumbarton saw something which astonished and terrified them. Two hundred Viking longships were sailing up the Clyde to lay siege to the principal stronghold of the kings of Strathclyde. After four months it fell, and the Vikings dragged its defenders and many native aristocrats off to the slave markets of Dublin. It was a crushing blow to the old kingdom of the Damnonii, directly comparable to the battle in Fortriu 30 years earlier. Surprisingly, King Artgal evaded capture, but had the great misfortune to fall into the hands of Constantine, son of Kenneth macAlpin. Far from sheltering Artgal from a common enemy, he had him put to death. Strathclyde fell under the influence of the kings of Argyll and Pictland, and by 890 the native aristocracy was taking ship for North Wales. The Welsh *Chronicle of the Princes* noted: 'The men of Strathclyde that refused to unite with the English had to depart from their country, and go to Gwynedd.'

It was a sad and abrupt end for an ancient British kingdom, but at least the emigration to Wales helped to preserve its history, the traditions, poetry and king-lists of southern Scotland for the early historic period.

As the English pressed on the borders of Wales, eventually invading and colonizing, the last of the British remembered their glorious past, and sometimes the past of the other *Cymry*, the peoples they called the *Gwyr y Gogledd*, or the 'Men of the North'.

In Pictland, the Gaelic kings of Argyll were establishing the primacy of western ways. After 878 Giric 'was the first to give liberty to the Scottish church, which was in servitude up to that time after the custom and fashion of the Picts'. And when Constantine II succeeded, he and his bishop of St Andrews, Cellach, made this public declaration in 906: '[They] pledged themselves upon the hill of Faith near the royal city of Scone, that the laws and disciplines of the Faith, and the rights in churches and gospels, should be kept in conformity with [the customs of] the Scots.'

These are only the best-known examples of the official suppression of Pictishness, and other, more local processes of change will have gone unnoted. The old native culture seemed to wither quickly. After the middle of the 9th century no more symbol-stones were made and the language of the men who carved them began to slip into desuetude and eventually extinction. Gaelic became the language of the future. By the reign of Constantine II a new name had come into general currency. Instead of *Pictavia* or *Fortriu* the kingdom became known as *Alba*, still the Gaelic name for Scotland.

With the fall of Strathclyde, the passing of Rheged and Gododdin, and the takeover of Pictland, the last native British kingdoms were effaced. And their peoples began to experience gradual cultural change. Gaelic and English had replaced the dialects of Old Welsh as the languages that described what became Scotland, and by 900 a long continuity with the prehistoric past had been broken. And with the passing of the last of the British, the Painted People, the story of Scotland begins.

Further Reading

This is in no way an exhaustive bibliography but rather an alphabetical list (by author) of books which might be enjoyed by anyone who wishes to pursue a pleasant course of study. I recommend all of them.

Aitchison, Nick, *The Picts and the Scots at War*, Stroud 2003

Allen, Stephen, *Celtic Warrior 300 BC–AD 100*, Oxford 2001

Armit, Ian, *Celtic Scotland*, London 1997

Ashmore, P.J., *Neolithic and Bronze Age Scotland*, London 1996

Barclay, Gordon, *Farmers, Temples and Tombs: Scotland in the Neolithic and Early Bronze Age*, Edinburgh 1998

Barclay, Gordon, *Cairnpapple Hill*, Edinburgh 1998

Birley, A.R., *Tacitus: Agricola*, Oxford 1999

Breeze, David, *Roman Scotland*, London 1996

Breeze, David, and Dobson, Brian, *Hadrian's Wall*, London 1976

Burl, Aubrey, *Great Stone Circles: Fables, Fiction, Fact*, London and New Haven 1999

Calder, Jenni, ed., *The Wealth of a Nation*, Edinburgh 1989

Campbell, Ewan, *Saints and Sea Kings: The First Kingdom of the Scots*, Edinburgh 1999

Carver, Martin, *Surviving in Symbols*, Edinburgh 1999

Coles, B.J., 'Doggerland. A Speculative Survey', *Proceedings of the Prehistoric Society* vol. 64, 45–81, 1998

Cruickshank, Graeme, *The Battle of Dunnichen*, Balgavies, Angus, 1999

Cummins, W.A., *The Age of the Picts*, Stroud 1995

Cunliffe, Barry, *Facing the Ocean*, Oxford and New York 2001

Cunliffe, Barry, *The Extraordinary Voyage of Pytheas the Greek*, London and New York 2001

Cunliffe, Barry, ed., *The Penguin Atlas of British and Irish History*, London 2001

Darvill, Timothy, *Prehistoric Britain*, London and New Haven 1987

Davies, Norman, *Europe: A History*, Oxford and New York 1996

Davies, Norman, *The Isles*, London and New York 1999

Edwards, K., and Ralston, I., ed., *Scotland After the Ice*, Edinburgh 2003 (originally published as *Scotland: Environment and Archaeology, 8000 BC–AD 1000*, Chichester 1997)

Fenton, Alexander, *The Northern Isles: Orkney and Shetland*, East Linton 1997

Fields, Nic, *Hadrian's Wall, AD 122–410*, Oxford 2003

Finlayson, Bill, *Wild Harvesters: The First People in Scotland*, Edinburgh 1998

Forsyth, Katherine, *Language in Pictland: The Case Against Non-Indo-European Pictish*, Utrecht 1997

Foster, Sally M., *Picts, Gaels and Scots: Early Historic Scotland*, London 1996

Fraser, James E., *The Battle of Dunnichen 685*, Stroud 2002

Frere, Sheppard, *Britannia*, London and Cambridge, Mass. 1967

Gosden, Chris, *Prehistory: A Very Short Introduction*, Oxford and New York 2003

Hancock, Paul, and Skinner, Brian, eds, *The Oxford Companion to the Earth*, Oxford 2000

Hanson, W.S., *Agricola and the Conquest of the North*, London and New York 1987

Hedges, John, *The Tomb of the Eagles: A Window on Stone Age Tribal Britain*, London 1984

Hingley, Richard, *Settlement and Sacrifice*, Edinburgh 1998

Houston, R., and Knox, W., eds, *The New Penguin History of Scotland from the*

Earliest Times to the Present Day, London 2001

Hunter, James, *The Last of the Free. A Millennial History of the Highlands and Islands of Scotland*, Edinburgh 1999

Hunter, John, and Ralston, Ian, eds, *The Archaeology of Britain*, London 1999

Keppie, Lawrence, *Scotland's Roman Remains*, Edinburgh 1986

Lowe, Chris, *Angels, Fools and Tyrants: Britons and Anglo-Saxons in Southern Scotland AD 450–758*, Edinburgh 1999

McCulloch, Andrew, *Galloway: A Land Apart*, Edinburgh 2000

Macdonald, Donald, *Lewis. A History of the Island*, Edinburgh 1978

Maxwell, Gordon, *The Romans in Scotland*, Edinburgh 1989

Maxwell, Gordon, *A Gathering of Eagles: Scenes from Roman Scotland*, Edinburgh 1998

Mithen, Steven, *After the Ice. A Global Human History 20,000 BC–5000 BC*, London 2003

Oram, Richard, *Scottish Prehistory*, Edinburgh 1993

Pollard, Justin, *The Seven Ages of Britain*, London 2003

Ritchie, Anna, *Picts: an Introduction to the Life of the Picts . . .*, London 1989

Ritchie, Anna, *Prehistoric Orkney*, London 1995

Ritchie, Anna, and Ritchie, Graham, *Scotland, Archaeology and Early History*, London and New York 1991

Robertson, Anne S., *The Antonine Wall: A Handbook to the Roman Wall between Forth and Clyde and a Guide to its Surviving Remains*, Glasgow 1960, repr. 1968, 1973, 1979

Ross, A., and Cyprien, M., *A Traveller's Guide to Celtic Britain*, London and Boston 1985

Ross, Stewart, *Ancient Scotland*, Moffat 1991

Schama, Simon, *A History of Britain 3000 BC–AD 1603*, vol. I, *At the Edge of the World?* London 2000

Smyth, A.P., *Warlords and Holy Men. Scotland AD 80–1000*, London 1984

Steel, Tom, *St Kilda*, London 1975, repr. 1981, 1988

Sykes, Bryan, *The Seven Daughters of Eve*, London and New York 2001

Turner, Val, *Ancient Shetland*, London 1998

Wagner, Paul, *Pictish Warrior AD 297–841*, Oxford 2002

Wainwright, Frederick Threlfall, *The Problem of the Picts*, Edinburgh 1955

Watson, W.J., ed., *The History of the Celtic Place-Names of Scotland*, Edinburgh and London 1926

Wickham Jones, C.R., *Scotland's First Settlers*, London 1994

Wilcox, Peter, *Rome's Enemies, 2, Gallic and British Celts*, London 1985

Acknowledgments

Everybody needs encouragement. No matter how grand, accomplished or dourly self-sufficient, every writer needs even more encouragement. It is a solitary, insecure business, what I once described to my friend George Rosie as miserable, scribbling drudgery. That must have been a worse day than usual. But despite my bleats and groans, I was the happy recipient of a great deal of encouragement in writing this book. I hope all that help shows and I want, at the outset, to acknowledge an unstinting amount of kindness and generosity of spirit.

Barry Cunliffe is a great historian, and, like most people at the pinnacle of their powers, he has a generous spirit. Barry took much precious time to read the manuscript and his comments and involvement proved to be absolutely crucial. I owe him a great debt of kindness. George Rosie, Walter Elliot and Katherine Bell also waded through the manuscript and each supplied both encouragement and important advice. Gordon Barclay took great and very welcome trouble to offer highly informed and perceptive criticisms. Liz Hanson and David Lyons contributed excellent photographs. Thanks to all.

Elisabeth Ingles edited the book with tremendous tact, persistence, intelligence and great good humour. And thanks, Elisabeth, for one priceless piece of information which went straight in. Thanks also to Colin Ridler for the faith to publish *Before Scotland* and to my agent, the redoubtable David Godwin, as ever, for his special brand of encouragement and for his good cheer.

I have dedicated the book to John Goodall. He taught me Latin and Greek all those years ago. It was a tremendously important experience for me, even if I didn't realize it at the time. I do now.

Alistair Moffat
Selkirk,
August 2004

Sources of Illustrations

Index

Scotland's Forgotten Past

'Illuminating 36 neglected or misunderstood
episodes in Scotland's history, this book
deserves a place on the school curriculum'
Alex Massie, *The Scotsman*

'Subtle and engaging'
The Field

'Engaging ... beautifully written
believe-it-or-not episodes from Scottish history'
The Wee Review

While Scotland's history cannot be separated from its kings and queens, saints and warriors, there is a rich story to tell about the country's lesser-known places, people and events. This colourful history of Scotland tells those other tales, half-forgotten or misunderstood, that have been submerged by the wash of history. Bringing these stories to light and to life, *Scotland's Forgotten Past* reveals the richness and complexity of this nation on the northwest edge of Europe.

Alistair Moffat guides us from the geological formation of the land that makes up Scotland to the first evidence of human habitation right up to modern times. In the process, we learn about the cave of headless children, the origins of the Scottish kings and the real heroes of Scottish independence, the invention of tartan and the romance of the Highlands, Scotland's answer to Shakespeare, and the many US presidents with Scottish heritage, among many other fascinating tales brought to life by Joe McLaren's attractive woodcut-style illustrations. Even the most knowledgeable Scot will experience a sense of newfound knowledge and appreciation for this unique country, its history and its people.

With 37 illustrations